Calendar

OF

PLEA AND MEMORANDA ROLLS

Calendar

OF

PLEA AND MEMORANDA ROLLS

Preserved among the ARCHIVES of the CORPORATION of the CITY OF LONDON at the GUILDHALL

A.D. 1413–1437

Edited by

A. H. THOMAS, M.A., LL.D.

OF ST CATHARINE'S COLLEGE, CAMBRIDGE
DEPUTY-KEEPER OF THE CITY RECORDS

PRINTED BY ORDER OF THE
CORPORATION UNDER THE DIRECTION
OF THE LIBRARY COMMITTEE

CAMBRIDGE: AT THE
UNIVERSITY PRESS
MCMXLIII

CAMBRIDGE
UNIVERSITY PRESS

University Printing House, Cambridge CB2 8BS, United Kingdom

Cambridge University Press is part of the University of Cambridge.

It furthers the University's mission by disseminating knowledge in the pursuit of education, learning and research at the highest international levels of excellence.

www.cambridge.org
Information on this title: www.cambridge.org/9781107464025

First published 1943
First paperback edition 2014

A catalogue record for this publication is available from the British Library

ISBN 978-1-107-46402-5 Paperback

CONTENTS

CORRIGENDA

p. 3, n. 5, *for* Calais *read* Wales.
p. 19, l. 30, *for* John *read* Robert.
p. 59, l. 21, *for* executors *read* testator.
p. 146, l. 5, *for* James *read* Jacobus.

INTRODUCTION

THE PLEA AND MEMORANDA ROLLS calendared in this volume cover the period 1413 to 1437, each roll being the record of a single mayoralty. Two rolls, those of Richard Merlawe (1417–18) and John Perneys or Perveys (1432–3), which are missing, had gone astray before the early years of the 19th century, when the present enumeration was adopted. As the City records are now so fully known and listed, the only chance of their survival would appear to lie outside the walls of Guildhall.

During the twenty-two years included in the present Calendar, the matters considered worthy of enrolment by the City clerks are of the same general character as in previous rolls. They give further information or supply illustrative detail on a number of topics, apprenticeship, orphanage, the law merchant, foreign merchants and trade, City custom, household goods, textiles, metalwares, furs, jewellery, the everyday life of the citizens and social conditions in general. Among other matters, mention may be made of an action (p. 174) against a surgeon for an alleged error of treatment—a case which reveals the part played by astrology in the medical theory of the middle ages. Another new feature of interest is the lengthy record of prosecutions for usury in 1421 (pp. 95–109) and 1435 (pp. 285–7). It is no easy task to discover exactly where medieval men, under the guidance of the Church, drew the line between legitimate enterprise and immoral gain accruing from the use of capital. The several prosecutions give specific instances of actions which offended the conscience of the City authorities. We learn also that the latter had been accustomed from time immemorial to punish "bargains of horrible usury and false chevisance", irrespective of any sanction from the national authorities.

THE LANGUAGE OF THE RECORDS

The increasing use of English

A noticeable difference between the present Calendar and its predecessor lies in the increased number of enrolments in English. Before 1413 no more than three documents or groups of documents in English were entered in the Plea and Memoranda Rolls.

In 1406 a certain John Osbarne, son of the Constable of Dunster Castle, and Walter Gregory, vicar of a parish unnamed, made sworn statements as to a feoffment and re-enfeoffment whereby John, the last Lord Mohun, then expecting to go abroad on military service, had settled the castle and other manors upon himself and his wife Joan and their issue, thus bringing his daughters into inheritance[1]. A few years later, doubtless in connection with the purchase of the Leadenhall and its market by the Corporation in 1409, a certain Robert Rykedon brought in three English documents for enrolment. These consisted of two letters of credence written by Sir John Hawkwood, the famous leader of the White Company, at Florence in 1392 and 1393 and an indenture having the effect of a nuncupative will[2]. Though legal or semi-legal in character, they must be classed as private documents. The same description applies to a threatening placard placed by unknown persons in 1412 on a garden door close by a mud wall which they had demolished[3]. The only official English documents copied into the City records up to this date are four proclamations issued by the mayor and aldermen in 1383, 1387 and 1411[4]. Hitherto proclamations had been invariably written in French, and several instances of the use of French[5] in this class of documents are still found, but from this time forward the majority are couched in English[6].

Among the English enrolments in the present Calendar are five awards in arbitration. During the preceding century disputes were from time to time submitted to arbitrators, usually four in number, two being chosen by either side, with an umpire to make the award if the four failed to agree. The awards were usually presented to the court in French. In the early 15th century the mayor and aldermen, probably as a natural development of the equitable jurisdiction of their court, began to assume the function of arbitra-

[1] *Cal. of Plea and Memoranda Rolls*, 1381–1412, pp. 279–82.

[2] *Ibid.* pp. 308–10; cf. pp. 257–8; said by C. L. Kingsford to be the earliest private letters in English, *Prejudice and Promise*, pp. 22–3. See also *London Topographical Record*, XIII, p. 10.

[3] *Cal. of P. and M. Rolls*, 1381–1412, p. 313.

[4] Letter Book H, fos. 172, 223; I, fo. 111; the texts are set out in H. T. Riley, *Memorials of London and London Life in the XIIIth, XIVth and XVth Centuries*, pp. 480, 481, 500, 580.

[5] Letter Book I, fos. 112, 147v., 178, 212v.

[6] Texts are set out in H. T. Riley, *Memorials*, pp. 628–9, 635, 645, 664–5, 668–9, 670–3.

tors, acting either as a whole or as a committee of the mayor and twelve aldermen or delegating the duty to one, two or four aldermen. Their awards are recorded in Latin. In 1430, however, Alderman Robert Large brought his award into court in English, and his example was followed by three other bodies of aldermanic arbitrators[1]. The earliest award in English, interesting as being addressed to the "Lord Mair", was delivered by two non-official citizens in 1414[2].

Three further enrolments in English are also of some interest. In 1425 two servants of John Holland, earl of Huntingdon, who had been captured at Baugé in 1421 and was now a prisoner in Anjou, brought into court a letter (pp. 182–7) from their master asking that a writ and a deed relating to his ransom might be enrolled. Five months later the earl appeared in person before the mayor and aldermen to acknowledge the deed, together with a declaratory document setting forth the terms. The story they tell illustrates the mercenary character of medieval wars, where a leading incentive was the hope of capturing important prisoners, from whom heavy ransoms might be exacted[3]. In this case a complicated family arrangement secured the earl's release. His mother, Elizabeth, sister of Henry IV, had married as her second husband Sir John Cornwall. To the latter had been assigned by the king in 1417 the count of Vendôme, taken prisoner at Agincourt, whose ransom had been fixed at 46,665 gold crowns valued at 11,665 English marks (£7776. 13*s*. 4*d*.). By the fortune of war the earl had fallen into the count's possession either because he had been captured by adherents of the count or had been acquired by his friends in some other way. Vendôme, in his captivity in England, naturally stipulated that his own freedom should be the price of Huntingdon's, thus leaving the problem to be solved between the son and the stepfather. Out of his "grete godenesse and kyndenesse" Cornwall consented to abate Vendôme's ransom by 2665 marks, to take in part exchange two other prisoners, the seigneurs de Gaucourt and Estouteville, with a sum of money contributed by the king, valued together at 5000 marks, and to receive other

[1] Below, pp. 237, 253–5, 256–7, 283. [2] pp. 17–18.

[3] Cf. the negotiations for the ransom of Thomas de Voudenay, taken prisoner at Poictiers in 1356, Letter Book G, fo. 58; H. T. Riley, *Memorials*, pp. 290–1; and Richard Whityngton's speculative purchase of a prisoner taken at Agincourt, below, pp. 91–3.

miscellaneous sums of money and bonds of Huntingdon's friends to make up the balance. On these terms Vendôme had been released and Huntingdon in turn had received his freedom.

Another English enrolment of 1431 concerns a dispute (pp. 256–8) between a widow, chief legatee of her husband, and two others as to their respective rights to any ransom which might accrue from the capture of Alfonso, count of Denia. This would appear to be that count of Denia who was taken prisoner at the battle of Najara some sixty-four years before, and with regard to whom blood had already been shed[1].

In the remaining English enrolments there are several points of legal interest. Reynold Barentyn, a nephew of Alderman Drew Barentyn, and his son Drew[2] agree by an English indenture (pp. 195–6) of 1425 to deliver muniments and evidences relating to properties in the parish of St John Zakary which had been in dispute between themselves and Alderman Henry Barton. The action, as usual, was recorded in Latin (pp. 191–3) and mention is made therein of the City customs that a deed on enrolment in the Husting had the same force and effect as a fine at common law outside the City, and that citizens could devise lands and tenements to their wives for life and to other persons in fee simple, fee tail, for life or otherwise. Livery of seisin of tenements by placing the ring of the door in the hands of the recipients is mentioned in another English document (pp. 265–6) of 1432. This is a declaratory deed from Ralph Barton notifying that William Myldenhale, whose will is recited, had mortgaged a tenement in the parish of St Mary Aldermary and had afterwards devised it to his daughters Jonet and Eleyne, to whom the said Ralph had delivered seisin on payment of the sum of money due to him. Another English will (pp. 277–80), that of William Caldewell, saddler, devises the remainder of certain tenements to the Craft of Saddlers, in accordance with the City's custom of devise in mortmain. Two further English documents (pp. 291, 298–9) are certificates, relating that Alderman Robert Tatersall had acquired the manor of Wanstead by a fine, and afterwards, moved by remorse in his conscience at having purchased a property which he knew to be entailed, he had instructed his co-feoffees to restore it to the next heirs in tail.

[1] C. L. Kingsford, *Chronicles of London*, p. 14 (Julius B II, fo. 15).

[2] On this important Oxfordshire family see *Notes and Queries*, CLXXXI, pp. 156, 206; CLXXXIII, pp. 190, 350.

His son now enrols the documents in fulfilment of his father's wish. The last English deed (p. 300) is a covenant of the sale by Philip Caxton of the manor of Wratting to John Cristemasse, draper—no doubt an enrolment of the original formerly in the possession of Earl Winterton[1].

The greatest number of English enrolments in the period covered by the rolls consist of certain returns of the inquest juries of the wards, known as the Wardmote Presentments[2]. At the winter wardmotes, held in the latter part of December, and from the 15th century on St Thomas's Day, juries of householders were impanelled to whom the Articles of the Wardmote Inquest were read. They were then given a day to bring in their verdicts or presentments of defaults, which in due course were brought before the mayor and aldermen at a "General Court" (afterwards known as the Grand Court of Wardmote) on the Monday after the Epiphany. In practice the procedure seems to have been more elaborate than in the above description from the City's Liber Albus[3]. Some wards sent in a return for the whole ward. Others presented separate returns from the parishes within their boundaries, and in these cases it would appear that the real work of presenting defaults had been carried out by parish juries[4]. The language of the verdicts varied from ward to ward, apparently at the choice of the ward clerk. As interesting as the increasing use of English is the survival of French at this date. Of the returns (pp. 115–41) made on 11 Jan. 1422, four only are in Latin, fourteen in French and eight in English. Aldersgate Ward (p. 127) uses Latin for the opening sentence and English for the verdict. The ward of Farringdon Without (pp. 124–6) presents its return in English and includes a return from the parish of St Sepulchre in the same language, followed by that of St Andrew, Holborn, in Latin, from which we may perhaps infer a legal training of the parish clerk. At the next presentment in 1423, Bishopsgate Ward (p. 153) changed from Latin to French and the return deals with the ward as a whole and not separately by the six parishes as in the

[1] See *The Times*, 18 Dec. 1942.

[2] The returns are set out in abstract in the present Calendar. The texts are printed, with critical notes, in *A Book of London English*, 1384–1425 (Clarendon Press, 1931), by Prof. R. W. Chambers and Miss Marjorie Daunt.

[3] *Munimenta Gildhallae Londoniensis* (Rolls Series 12), I, pp. 36–9.

[4] Below, pp. 121–4, 125–6, 127–9, 131, 136–7.

preceding year. The wards of Cordwainer Street (p. 152), Farringdon Within (p. 153), Broad Street (p. 156), and the Within portion of Cripplegate (p. 158) abandon French in favour of English, though curiously enough three of the wards which again return in English now adopt French preambles. Not all the ward presentments of 1423 have survived, but the result of the above changes is two returns in Latin, eight in French and twelve in English, showing a marked movement in favour of the native speech.

In the City's Letter Books, which are concerned more with the administrative than the legal courts, there is a similar increase in the number of English enrolments. At the end of Letter Book I the City clerk has recorded in English[1] those statutes and ordinances relating to purveyance which were recited in the Parliament of 2 Henry VI after being ordered in the previous year to be proclaimed and observed[2]. The translation from the French of the Statutes into English clearly emanated from the Chancery. Of a more civic character is an inquisition taken at the Guildhall as to an alleged forgery of a conveyance, followed by a confession or self-exculpation written by a certain John Canesby, clerk, otherwise called "Sir John the Morowemasse prest" of St Bride's, Fleet Street[3]. Since proceedings in court, though recorded in Latin, were from 1362 supposed to be conducted in English in place of French[4], the choice of giving a précis of a confession in Latin or of recording the actual words in English would depend upon the clerk's estimate of its importance. This no doubt was responsible for the preservation of a document connected with the suppression of Lollardry. John Russell, a woolpacker, was charged in 1416 with having slandered Thomas Fauconer, late mayor, who had been active against the Lollards[5], by alleging that he had suppressed a charter of pardon in favour of Richard Gurmyn, baker, and had caused the latter to be burnt at Smithfield, together with the pardon. The pleadings are recorded in Latin; Russell's confession, written in English, is reproduced in full[6].

1 R. R. Sharpe, *Cal. of Letter Book I*, pp. 288–98.

2 *Statutes of the Realm*, II, p. 213.

3 Letter Book K, fo. 11v.; *Cal. of K*, pp. 17, 21–2.

4 Miss M. Dominica Legge, "Anglo-Norman and the Historian" (*History*, Dec. 1941, p. 167), thinks that the statute was not obeyed.

5 H. T. Riley, *Memorials*, pp. 576, n. 3, 617–18; Letter Book I, fo. 155.

6 *Ibid.* fos. 194v.–195v.; *Memorials*, pp. 630–4.

The remaining English passages in the Letter Books of this period are in the nature of innovations, gradually becoming settled custom. They consist mainly of petitions, ordinances, proclamations and letters. These classes of documents had hitherto been written in French or less frequently in Latin, and they continued to be written in French from time to time until that language had fallen out of fashion. It survived only in the City law-courts, where bills of complaint initiating actions by customary and common law, and petitions, which led to proceedings in equity, still followed the ancient fashion. As late as the 18th century apprentices, who sought remedies in court for non-enrolment, lack of instruction and certain other grievances, were supplied with printed forms of petitions in French, with blanks for names and dates—a striking instance of conservatism. But ordinary petitions to the administrative courts ceased to be written in French between 1430 and 1440.

Closely connected with petitions were ordinances. The Courts of Aldermen and Common Council rarely legislated unless stimulated to do so by some body which desired the amelioration of its own or general conditions. Even where no petition is recorded, the wording of ordinances often reveals that the suggestion had come from without. Not infrequently a petitioning body would set out its desires in the form of an ordinance, which was adopted word for word, and either prefaced by a statement that the court had so ordained, or ended by a note in Latin to the effect that the above articles had been approved. The fact that French remained the traditional language of petitions long after it had ceased to be understood by the common people, involved as a consequence that throughout the 14th century until as late as 1432 the ordinances of a large number of misteries, some representing very humble crafts[1], were drawn up in a language which must have been unintelligible to many of their members.

Already, however, during the stormy period 1384–6, when a struggle was waged between the victualling and non-victualling guilds, a petition in English had been forwarded to the Chancellor by the Mercers[2]. The lead in preferring petitions to the City

[1] E.g. Cordwainers and cobblers, 1395; Hurers, 1398; Fletchers, 1403, 1432; Forcermakers, 1406; Joiners, 1427, and Bakers, 1428. See H. T. Riley, *Memorials* and *Cals. of Letter Books, passim.*

[2] R. W. Chambers and M. Daunt, *London English*, pp. 20, 33–7.

authorities in that language was taken in 1423 by the physicians and surgeons of the City[1], who were then desirous of being combined in one craft. Each paragraph of their petition begins with the words "Also please it you to ordeyne" and the document concludes with a sentence stating that the mayor and aldermen had granted that the articles should be "putte in execucion". In the same years a dispute between the Shearmen and the two or three persons who enjoyed a monopoly of shear-grinding led to an ordinance[2] fixing prices for satisfactory workmanship and providing for assistance in turning the grindstones. In 1430 an ordinance fixing the seasonal price of butter was couched in the native speech[3], obviously in order to obtain wide publicity. The Common Council was the next to follow the new fashion by presenting a bill in 1433 to the mayor, aldermen and sheriffs praying that all persons obtaining the privileges of the freedom should continuously dwell within the City and take their share of its burdens. It was followed by an Act of mayor, aldermen and commons dealing with the whole question of the freedom, the methods of acquiring it, and the duties attaching to it[4]. The Skinners in the same year petitioned against alien merchants, who seem to have been Italians, coming in galleys into the port of London and bringing furs of budge and lambskin "wroght untrewely[5]". The Turners in 1435 made a like complaint against divers "foreins" who had been importing measures, bushels, half bushels and pecks, turned out of green timber, with the result that these measures, when dry, became deficient in content. Authority was given to their wardens to exercise oversight over all such imports. To the same period belongs an undated petition of the Girdlers[6] praying for certain modifications of their ordinances issued in 1344, with a further petition of 10 Nov. 1435 desiring a limitation in the number of apprentices and more stringent rules for securing better quality in materials and workmanship[7]. It must be remembered that up till 1432 there had been an even larger number of petitions and ordinances in French. Henceforward English became the usual vehicle of non-legal petitions and English or Latin the languages in which the resulting ordinances were granted.

[1] R. W. Chambers and M. Daunt, *London English*, pp. 108–15, from Letter Book K, fos. 6v.–7v.
[2] R. R. Sharpe, *Cal. of Letter Book K*, pp. 22–4.
[3] Letter Book K, fo. 68v.
[4] *Cal. of K*, pp. 161–6.
[5] *Ibid.* pp. 170–1.
[6] *Ibid.* p. 193.
[7] *Ibid.* pp. 197–201.

Proclamations of this period fall into two classes, those dealing with national or civic affairs of importance, and the announcements, either read publicly or affixed to the pillory, when citizens underwent that penalty for their misdoings. Of those already mentioned above (p. viii) the warning issued in 1387 against speaking, moving or publishing anything in despite of the king, queen and those about his person, obviously owed its inspiration to the king's council, and this is true of most of the proclamations made between 1416 and 1418 in connection with the war in France. No doubt they were translated into English so as to attract the notice of the mariners and soldiers to whom they were addressed. But it is a curious fact that one-third of the number of proclamations issued at that time were couched in French. As they were addressed to the lords, knights, esquires, captains and leaders of men taking part in the expeditions a more courtly and traditional form of address may have been thought necessary[1]. This consideration would of course not apply to the second class of proclamations[2]—those connected with the pillory. In this case the warning was intended for the populace and especially for the less educated portion of it.

It has been said that "the letters which Henry V wrote to the City of London and the City's replies form the oldest connected series of English letters which has been preserved". Henry V, as Mr C. L. Kingsford pointed out, "could and did write well in English as is shown by his note on a State paper"—'for the secreness of this Matere I have writen this Instruction wyth myn owne Hande and seled hit with my Signet of th' Egle[3].' All Henry's English letters to the City were in fact sealed with his signet and it is not impossible that they were also written with his own hand. A solitary letter under the signet in French[4] is headed "on the king's behalf"—a distinction which does not appear in the English letters. But though the king wrote in English, the civic authorities were more conservative. To his letter announcing the surrender of the castle of Touques, the mayor replied in French[5]. The king's brother,

[1] H. T. Riley, *Memorials*, p. 627; Letter Book I, fos. 178, 212v.

[2] *Cal. of I*, pp. 196–7; *Memorials*, pp. 668, 670, 672, 673; *Cal. of K*, pp. 16–17.

[3] C. L. Kingsford, *Prejudice and Promise*, p. 23; *Foedera*, IX, 427–30.

[4] 22 Sept. 1415, announcing the capture of Harfleur, *Memorials*, pp. 619–20, from Letter Book I, fo. 143. Privy Seal letters, emanating from the Council rather than the king, continued to be written in French for some time. *Ibid.* p. 654.

[5] *Ibid.* and n. 8.

the duke of Clarence, also preferred the older fashion. The same year, when the king wrote in English to announce the capture of Caen, the duke sent a letter in French[1], and the same was the case next year when the two brothers wrote to tell of the fall of Louviers[2]. However, in 1419 the king and his brother both announced the capture of Pontoise in English and the City's answers, written under the mayoralty seal, were also in English[3]. From this time onward letters from the king, the duke of Bedford, Henry VI and Cardinal Beaufort, with the City's replies, were all in the native tongue[4]. French ceased to be used in correspondence except with French-speaking towns abroad.

The spheres of Latin and French

Before leaving the subject of languages, a few words should be said as to the respective spheres of Latin and French in the City records. Litigation in the courts was recorded in Latin until the Commonwealth. The actual pleadings, written or oral, were probably in French until the statute of 1362 ordered that as the French tongue was but little understood, all pleas should be pleaded, shown, defended, answered, debated and judged in the English tongue[5]. In 1302 an action of debt in the Sheriffs' Court between two foreigners was reversed on appeal by the Mayor's Court. Sewn to the roll is a *cedula* containing a reasoned judgment in French apparently delivered by the mayor or recorder, annulling the process and proof because, *inter alia*, the witnesses differed as to the source of the indebtedness, whereas according to the Law Merchant they ought to agree, and because there was a difference between the sum mentioned in the writ and that in the proof[6]. But while the attorneys and the recorder doubtless spoke French in court, there is reason to believe that witnesses gave their oral testimony in English. In an action in 1300 where the plaintiff sued for detinue of a goshawk (*ostorius*)[7], one witness said the defendant had acknow-

[1] H. T. Riley, *Memorials*, p. 657; *Cal. of I*, p. 185.

[2] Letter Book I, fo. 215. Text set out in J. Delpit, *Collection générale des documents Français qui se trouvent en Angleterre*, pp. 221–4.

[3] Letter Book I, fo. 236–236v.; texts set out in R. R. Sharpe, *London and the Kingdom*, III, pp. 362–5; Delpit, *op. cit.* pp. 227–9.

[4] Sharpe, *op. cit.* III, Appendix A, *passim*.

[5] See above, p. xii, n. 4.

[6] A. H. Thomas, *Cal. of Early Mayor's Court Rolls*, pp. 181–4.

[7] *Ibid.* pp. 127–8.

ledged receipt of "*Anglica lingua unum Goshauek*", while the other described the bird as "*Anglica lingua simpliciter unum hauek*". It seems clear that the clerk is reporting the actual words used. On the other hand, in the same year a collector rebuked a fellow-collector for attempting to demand double payment for the return of a pledge, to which the dishonest taxgatherer is recorded as replying "*Jeo ay chie a vous & au Ray ausi*". No doubt this was the attorney's rendering of the defendant's abusive remark into the French of the bill of complaint, for it is difficult to believe that a citizen with the very English name of "Ralph the mason" had used French in the heat of argument[1].

As regards legal instruments, the conveyances recorded in the Husting Rolls are almost without exception written in Latin, and Latin continued to be the favourite language for such deeds until the early 16th century. But during the period ending with the present Calendar, lesser legal instruments, leases, quitclaims, letters of attorney, bonds and indentures of agreements and covenants were frequently drawn up in French. As mentioned above, bills and petitions initiating actions at law or equity were by custom written in French and to these must be added the numerous applications for leave to sue at common law outside the City[2], either because the cause of action was extraneous or because the City was unable to compel the attendance of defendants or witnesses. Awards in arbitration were often presented in French[3] until about 1430, when Latin or English became the normal usage[4].

The actual deliberations of the administrative courts, the decisions at which they arrived and the orders issued on the miscellaneous matters engaging their attention were recorded in Latin. But as shown above, when ordinances and regulations were the direct result of or embodied in petitions couched in the traditional French, they too were written in French. For no apparent reason beyond custom documents issued under the mayoralty seal were almost invariably couched in French. These included both testimonial and ordinary business letters, though those written to ecclesiastics at home and abroad were generally in the language of the Church. Precepts to aldermen to summon their wardmotes, to assess and levy contributions, to set the watch at midsummer and

[1] *Ibid.* p. 58.
[2] Below, pp. 7–8; see Index under "Common Law".
[3] Below, pp. 25, 62–3, 67, 166.
[4] Below, pp. 237, 253–5, 256–7, 283.

Christmas, to send in returns of men-at-arms, to prevent sales of articles at more than the regulated prices, and generally to carry out in their wards the policy of the central body, all of which were issued by the mayor, were also in French. As we have seen, important proclamations, national and civic, were issued in the same language until in the reign of Henry V a change-over to English was made. Among other documents recorded in French are the oaths of the several City officials, ranging from the recorder to the humble aleconner[1], and the returns of the sworn masons and carpenters, who in 1428 were still reporting in French on building-disputes between neighbours[2]. No explanation beyond custom can be given for the last two examples.

The character of London French

The French written and spoken in England during the 13th, 14th and early 15th centuries is usually described as Anglo-Norman, though it contained other elements. Miss Legge points out that the wool-trade with Northern France and Flanders exposed the language used by travelling merchants to the influence of the Picard and Walloon dialects and that the wine-trade brought a similar contact with the Gascon dialect[3]. It has also been remarked that the vocabulary contained words of Romance and Teutonic origin and that Middle English and Latin affected the syntax[4]. In spite of Higden's insistence on the uniformity of the "language of Normandy" in England, as contrasted with the varieties of dialects both in France and England, it is probably true to say that London French may be classed among the "better non-literary Anglo-Norman writings" and that it was closer than the rest to the general run of continental French. A knowledge of French, good enough to be understood in the several districts of France, was essential to the large numbers of London merchants, factors, apprentices, shipmasters and professional clerks engaged

[1] *Liber Albus* (R.S. 12), I, 306–19; *Cal. of Plea and Mem. Rolls*, 1364–1381, p. 256; 1381–1412, p. 92.

[2] *Ibid.* 1364–1381, p. 150; 1381–1412, p. 178; below, pp. 218–19; cf. sworn information in French of the fishermen of the lower Thames, 1381–1412, pp. 116–17.

[3] M. D. Legge, "Anglo-Norman and the Historian," *History*, Dec. 1941, pp. 174–5.

[4] G. F. Chapple, "The Correspondence of the City of London, 1298–1370," June 1938, Univ. Lond. Ph.D. Thesis, pp. 45, 132, 181, 200, 208–9.

in continuous trading abroad or in business correspondence. London was a busy centre of foreign commerce, and the long-continued use of French in its records was probably due to the fact that it formed a necessary part of the young clerk's and merchant's training.

GIFTS OF GOODS AND CHATTELS

Another feature which distinguishes the present Calendar from its predecessors is the number of deeds described as "gifts of goods and chattels". From this time forward they occupy an ever larger space not only in our London rolls but also in the rolls of Chancery. In this Calendar it has not been thought necessary to do more than preserve the names, with the dates on which the deeds were brought in for enrolment. The form of the instrument varies very little. It conveys all goods and chattels, live and dead, of whatsoever kind or wheresoever they might be, to have, hold and dispose thereof, without any reclamation or condition whatsoever. No consideration is mentioned. That these deeds, so large in number, were not as a rule the outcome of generous impulses or evidence of a general desire among medieval men to divest themselves of their possessions must be obvious. But in the great majority of these disappointing documents, which occupy so much space, no reason appears for the gift. The very few instances where a clue is given suggest that the deed might serve various purposes, and that the gist of the matter usually lay in an unrecorded and unwritten agreement between the parties.

It should be noted first that the goods and chattels are specified in only rare instances. In 1435 a dyer gives to a tailor the vats, cisterns and other vessels in his house belonging to his occupation, but no other goods or chattels[1]. This has the appearance of a pledge rather than an outright gift. In 1404 a vintner gives four pieces of silver with silver covercles and all other his goods, jewels and chattels. Here the silverware was probably a token of delivery of seisin, the goods still remaining in the hands of the donor[2]. This was clearly the meaning of a deed of 1397, when a Canterbury man puts the donee in possession of the goods and chattels by delivering to him "in better evidence" thereof a dagger *stipatum*

[1] Below, p. 277.

[2] *Cal. of P. and M. Rolls*, 1381–1412, p. 267.

(probably hafted) with silver[1]. Sometimes silver spoons and other articles served the same purpose. Whether the rest of the goods followed there is nothing to show. One suspects that in many cases the token sufficed as a symbol of legal ownership.

A few instances in the previous century supply reasons for these gifts. A Flemish innkeeper, who had stood surety for two English purchasers of cloth in the Hall at Ghent, complained in 1345, through his own city authorities, to the mayor and aldermen of London that one of the merchants, in order to defraud the sellers, had given away all his goods and chattels to his son-in-law and another man, thus leaving the complainant liable as surety[2]. In the upshot the donees agreed to relieve the innkeeper of his liability. A gift of goods and chattels to a group of friends by the ill-fated Sir Nicholas Brembre, when dangers were thickening round him, was obviously designed to prevent their forfeiture as "felon's chattels". A month later he was appealed of high treason and ultimately brought to trial by the Merciless Parliament on 20 Feb. 1388, suffering the fate of a traitor. An equally provident conveyance of his lands and tenements, on the day before the appeal, was designed to save his real property[3]. That these deeds sometimes served evasive or dishonest purposes is shown by the formula that the gift was made "without fraud or guile". One form of this fraud is indicated in the statute 3 Henry VII, c. 5, where the Commons complained that such gifts "be made to thentent to defraude ther creditours of their duties". The debtor, having made over his goods and chattels to friends for his use, "goth to seyntwarie or other places privyleged" and there lived leaving his creditors unpaid[4]. It was enacted that all "dedes of gyfte of goodes and catalles made or to be made of trust to thuse of that persone or persones that made the same dede of gyfte be voide and of non effecte". It is probable that this act remained largely a dead letter, because unwritten agreements and trusts could not easily be proved and the gift, on the face of it, was absolute. Moreover, most of such gifts and agreements were doubtless made for quite honourable reasons. The form of the deed is given in the 18th-century editions of Jacob's *Law Dic-*

[1] *Cal. of P. and M. Rolls*, 1381–1412, p. 259.
[2] *Cal. of P. and M. Rolls*, 1323–1364, pp. 214–15.
[3] *Cal. of P. and M. Rolls*, 1381–1412, p. 134 and n. 1.
[4] *Statutes of the Realm*, II, p. 513.

tionary; it was evidently still in use for various purposes, among which we are probably correct in assuming that trusteeship was one.

A clear instance of a fiduciary gift occurs in 1381. John atte Wode, salter, made a gift of all his goods and chattels, including apprentices, to his daughter and son-in-law and four other persons on condition that they provided him with necessaries and took charge of him (*ad gubernandum*) for life. The donees promised to dispose of his goods after his death according to his wishes, if he were, before that event, of sound mind to frame such wishes. On the death of his son-in-law, the donor, then being *compos mentis*, made a new gift to his daughter, who agreed to provide him competently, according to his rank, with food, clothing, bed, shoes and other necessaries including 14*d*. a week to spend as he liked[1]. Many other gifts to relatives are recorded, in which a trust of some kind though not stated may be surmised. In addition to the wife, son or brother there are generally several other donees, who are often persons of official importance, among whom John Carpenter, town clerk and official trustee for the City, is frequently found[2]. These gifts may have been made before a merchant went abroad on business, or in order to facilitate the administration of property after death, in the same way as lands and tenements were vested in feoffees for the purposes of a will[3]. It is not unlikely that this latter was the reason why Robert Brendwode, salter, on 22 March 1428 made a gift of all his goods and chattels to Alice his wife, Master William Lynwode, official of the Court of Canterbury at St Mary le Bow (the probate officer), Henry Barton, alderman, and Thomas Rolf, sergeant-at-law[4]. Such gifts also would serve to evade the City customs of orphanage and of the division of personal estates into the wife's, children's, and "dead man's" portions[5]. Perhaps travel abroad or sickness may have been the reason why Robert Coventre, grocer, in 1434 gave all his goods and chattels to Alice his wife, Thomas Canynges, grocer, and Benedict Harlewyn, draper, who on 12 March 1436 brought in a deed restoring to him such goods as he had previously given to them. On the same day Coventre again gave his goods and chattels to Richard Hill and Richard Bartfeld,

[1] *Cal. of P. and M. Rolls*, 1364–1381, p. 294.
[2] Below, pp. 250, 256, 260, 283, 290.
[3] Possibly the reason for Alderman Hugh Fastolf's gift, *Cal. of P. and M. Rolls*, 1381–1412, p. 176.
[4] Below, p. 220.
[5] R. R. Sharpe, *Cal. of Wills*, I, p. xxiii; *Remembrancia*, p. 312.

with a power of attorney[1]. He died six years later, having survived his wife. Similar reasons may have led John Michell, stockfishmonger (p. 283) on 11 April 1435 to make a gift of all his goods and chattels to Alderman Henry Barton, Thomas Morestede, esquire, the famous surgeon, John Carpenter and four other citizens. Michell had been an alderman for many years and had served the office of mayor in 1424–5. If he was then under Morestede's care, he recovered his health sufficiently to take a further term of office next year, 1436–7, continuing as an alderman until his death in 1445[2].

It is a remarkable fact that many of these gifts of goods and chattels were made by men of the aldermanic class and by commercial magnates engaged in the import and export trades, who carried on business dealings for many subsequent years and died possessed of large estates. In these cases dishonest motives can be ruled out, and some form of trust or attorneyship was probably the object of the deeds. In other cases no guess can be made and there is no clue to explain why Thomas Richere, painter (p. 267), in 1432 gave his goods and chattels to such notable personages, connected with the royal family, as Henry Bourchier, "earl" of Ewe, and John Cornwall, Lord Fanhope, or why two Milanese ladies and an esquire of Verona (p. 171) were given the goods and chattels of Lucia Visconti, of the ducal house of Milan, widow of that Edmund Holland, earl of Kent, who died in 1408 of wounds received in Brittany. It is equally mysterious to find William Cantelowe, mercer (p. 250), who afterwards was sheriff, alderman, master of the Mercers' Company, member of Parliament and knight of the Bath in 1461, giving all his goods and chattels in 1430 to twelve persons, including four aldermen, the City recorder and the town clerk.

A few instances indicate another purpose for which the gifts of goods and chattels might be used, namely either in satisfaction of a debt or as pledge for payment. Where a debtor had no prospect of being able to raise the amount due, an actual transfer may have taken place. This is suggested by a gift from Bernard Barbo of Venice (p. 290) in 1436 to Master Thomas Frank, Doctor in Medicine, and William Toby, clerk, of all his goods and chattels with the exception of his wearing apparel. But in most cases the goods and chattels probably never left the donor's possession, the

[1] Below, pp. 271, 289. [2] A. B. Beaven, *Aldermen of the City of London*, II, p. 4.

deed of gift being equivalent to a mortgage of lands and tenements where only legal instruments passed, the mortgagor remaining in occupation of the property. Normally debts were secured either by recognizances under the Statute of Merchants enrolled in Guildhall or by civic recognizances entered in the City chamberlain's books, by bonds or other obligations[1]. In the recognizance the debtor acknowledged that in default of payment the amount should be levied from his lands, rents and goods. But though a recognizance was regarded as a judgment in itself, execution was by no means automatic. Proof of non-payment might be necessary, and execution might require the intervention of the court's officials in levying the debt. With a gift of goods and chattels no such difficulties arose, for the creditor was already legally if not actually in possession either of the whole or part of the repayment. In 1377 a Lucchese merchant, Torellus Gascoyn, makes a gift of all his goods and chattels in part satisfaction of a debt of £30. There is reason to believe that he retained his stock in trade and that the debt was duly paid, for he was still engaged in trading three years later[2]. Another foreign merchant from Zeeland, described as a chapman, appears to have used his merchandise as a pledge for his current expenses of board and lodging. In 1375[3] he makes a gift, followed by a quitclaim of all his goods and chattels in the house in which he was living in Candlewick Street and elsewhere in London to a certain John Peterson. In 1381[4] he executes a recognizance of a debt of £120 for victuals supplied to him by Peter Blower, dyer, and again makes a gift of all his goods and chattels as an immediate security. It is evident that though arrangements of this kind might turn seriously to the disadvantage of the donors, donees were content to observe the spirit rather than the letter of the gift. A certain William Bartelot, mercer, on 10 Sept. 1392 enters into a recognizance of a debt of £1000 payable at Christmas, and a month later makes a gift of all his goods and chattels to the creditors. A marginal note records that three years later the latter acknowledged satisfaction and the above "obligations" were cancelled[5].

[1] On these instruments see *Cal. of P. and M. Rolls*, 1381–1412, pp. xxxiii–xxxiv.

[2] *Cal. of P. and M. Rolls*, 1364–1381, pp. 234, 264.

[3] *Ibid.* p. 209.

[4] *Ibid.* p. 284.

[5] *Cal. of P. and M. Rolls*, 1381–1412, p. 197.

THE WARD PRESENTMENTS OF 1422 AND 1423

In discussing the use of English in the City records, mention was made above that the largest single section of English enrolments in the Calendar was concerned with the Ward Presentments of 1422 and 1423[1]. These presentments are of considerable interest as illustrating both the development of municipal services and the social conditions of London in the 15th century. Unfortunately, except for these years, it was not considered necessary to copy the returns into the rolls and books, and it is probable that such original files as were preserved finally disappeared in the Fire of London, the only exceptions being 15 membranes of the presentments of Portsoken Ward for the years 5–22 Edward IV and 23 Henry VII. A few records of proceedings against individuals, with excerpts from the presentments of their wards occur here and there in earlier rolls. On 23 Dec. 1298, for instance, a number of persons were brought before the Mayor's Court for riotous conduct and for keeping disorderly houses. They had been reported before Adam de Hallingberi, alderman of Aldgate Ward, at his winter wardmote, and their names had been forwarded in the ward presentment. Similar offenders were dealt with in 1300 and 1304[2]. In 1338 the return of the ward of Farringdon Without is preserved with the mayoral precept summoning the wardmotes for Sunday after Lady Day[3]. The midsummer wardmote of this ward next year brought a further batch of evildoers into the Mayor's Court, the offenders being of the same character as before—bullies, nightwalkers, protectors of women of ill-fame and keepers of disorderly houses[4]. In 1373 we have presentments of the wards of Langbourn, Portsoken, Aldgate, Queenhithe and Castle Baynard, but as they deal almost entirely with unlawful enclosures, obstructions of the streets and insanitary conditions, it is probable that they represent only portions of the returns[5]. Two other prosecutions, one of a Billingsgate man[6], who was a common dicer and nightwalker and said to be a corrupter of the wives, daughters and maidservants of his fellow-citizens, and the other of the

[1] Below, pp. 115–41, 150–9.
[2] *Cal. of Early Mayor's Court Rolls*, 1298–1307, pp. 23, 74, 155–6.
[3] *Cal. of P. and M. Rolls*, 1323–1364, pp. 187–8.
[4] *Ibid.* p. 109.
[5] *Cal. of P. and M. Rolls*, 1364–1381, pp. 156–7.
[6] *Ibid.* p. 139.

rakyer of Cheap Ward, who was bound over not to remove the dung and ordure of his own ward into the neighbouring ward of Coleman Street, followed on the ward presentments of 1371 and 1384[1]. For the 16th century the only surviving copies of ward presentments belong to Tower Ward and are found in a book of precedents to which the compiler, possibly the ward clerk, was still adding in 1610. They cover some sixty years. From 1668 until the present day the series of original ward presentments is almost complete. Though not so full of information as in earlier centuries, they throw much light on conditions in London immediately after the Fire. As time passed other remedies than prosecutions in the Mayor's Court were found for the grievances which the ward juries had ventilated in their presentments, and the returns tended to contain little more than the appointments of ward officers. Finally in 1856 a recommendation of the Corporation Inquiry Committee that those parts of the mayoral precepts for summoning wardmotes, which related to the impanelling of inquestmen, should be omitted, was agreed to by the Common Council[2] and the Court of Aldermen[3].

According to that portion of the Liber Horn which is dated 1311 it was provided (fo. 232) by ancient ordinances that there should be four principal wardmotes in the year attended by all inhabitants of the ward except knights, clerks and women, at which everyone over the age of fifteen years must be put in frankpledge and take an oath of fealty and loyalty to the king. At the wardmotes held about Michaelmas, Christmas and Easter the civic ordinances must be read and the *Eschaweyours* and watchmen chosen, while at the Whitsuntide meeting special measures must also be taken against the danger of fire during the coming dry season. Though there is evidence of wardmotes held about Easter and midsummer, the meetings, to judge from the precepts recorded, seem to have been narrowed down during the 14th century to that held on or about the Feast of St Thomas. John Carpenter, the City's "common clerk", writing in 1419, tells us that wardmotes must be held at least once in the year, but they might also be held twice or several times by virtue of warrants issued by the mayor[4].

A number of these warrants or "precepts", as they were more

[1] *Cal. of P. and M. Rolls*, 1381–1412, p. 71.

[2] *Minutes*, 30 Oct. 1856.

[3] *Minutes*, 29 Nov. 1856.

[4] Liber Albus in *Munimenta Gildhallae Londoniensis* (R.S. 12), I, p. 36.

commonly called, have been recorded. They vary somewhat in content. That of 19 Dec. 1343 enjoins each alderman to make careful inquiry of all the Articles of the Wardmote and then draws attention to matters contained in those articles relating to lodging-house keepers, suspicious characters, the carrying of arms and the cleansing of the streets. It concludes by asking for a report as to whether the proposed enclosing of St Paul's would be to the prejudice of any in the City, and requiring that the names of all persons indicted of felony or other trespass be certified under the seals of the twelve ward-jurors[1]. Sometimes the aldermen are ordered to see to the setting of the Christmas watch, to prevent overcharges for bread and ale, to ensure the quality of these provisions, to provide for the collection of money granted by Parliament, to fine absentees from the wardmote the customary 4*d.*, to take care that street-lanterns are lighted over Christmas, and to certify to the mayor's General Court any matter presented in the wardmote, which they may be incapable of redressing, in order that due redress and correction may be made according to the good usages and customs of the city[2]. In 1410 the precepts direct the aldermen to ensure that their wards return the prescribed number of common councilmen. This was repeated in 1411 and again in 1423[3], probably as a reminder to the ward clerks, who may have been remiss. All the above precepts were issued in French. The first English precept appeared in 1437[4]. It calls, *inter alia*, for the election of constables, scavengers and beadle, and a rakyer to keep clean the streets and lanes of the ward, the constables being empowered to distrain, if necessary, for the salaries of the beadle and rakyer.

For the guidance of the inquest jurymen, as well as for the benefit of the ward inhabitants at large, certain ordinances were read in the wardmote. The earliest text of these standing regulations is preserved in the Liber Horn (A.D. 1311) under the title "*Ceo sount les chapitres des les assises & establisements Des aldermans que sount a moustrer en pleyn Wardemote*[5]". Either the whole or

[1] *Cal. of P. and M. Rolls*, 1323–1364, p. 156.

[2] *Cal. of Letter Book H*, pp. 276, 293, 337, 348, 361, 418; *Cal. of I*, pp. 53–4, 61–2.

[3] *Ibid.* pp. 89, 98; *Cal. of K*, p. 19.

[4] *Ibid.* p. 215.

[5] Liber Horn, fo. 232. A later version is given in *Lib. Alb.* (R.S. 12), I, pp. 257, 332–6.

a part of the regulations was also brought to the notice of citizens in the annual proclamations or "cryes" issued by the mayors soon after taking office[1], to which several references are made by the jurors in their presentments. The claim to ancient usage, both in the articles read in the wardmotes and in the proclamations was well-founded. Many of the paragraphs were borrowed almost word for word from the regulations ordained by the king in 1285[2] when he took the City into his hand and from their later issue *c.* 1294[3], while others obviously derive from the "Assizes read by the mayor and reputable men" in 1276 and 1277[4]. They were in fact a summary of civic legislation for many years past, some portions of which, relating to the structure of houses and precautions against fire, can be identified as having originally formed part of the Assize of Buildings of 1212[5].

The actual articles submitted to the ward juries are set out in the Liber Albus[6]. They order the jurors to present all affrays against the peace, inhabitants of ill-fame or not under frankpledge, women of evil life, defective ovens and furnaces, sales by taverners and others by measures which had not been sealed by the aldermen, offences against the assizes of bread and ale, gamesters and riotous persons received in inns, outlaws, hucksters, houses roofed with reed or straw, the fouling of the streets with rubbish and ordure, the keeping of pigs and cows, lepers, usurious bargains, purprestures, nightwalkers, extortions by City officers, persons guilty of maintenance and champerty, overpayment of artisans and labourers and projecting tavern signs. As will be seen in their verdicts below the jurors felt themselves free to complain of many more inconveniences and defects than mentioned in the articles. It is clear that the aldermen had done their duty in making the dwellers in their wards acquainted with the general body of civic regulations.

[1] Liber Horn, fos. 237v.–249v.: "*les Articles des auncienes usages qe deivent estre cries par mi la dite Cite.*" Cf. Liber Custumarum, fos. 201–205v.; *Lib. Alb.* (R.S. 12), I, pp. 260–80.

[2] *Cal. of P. and M. Rolls*, 1323–1364, pp. xx, n. 3; xxi, n. 1; Liber Ordinacionum, fos. 197–202v.; Liber Horn, fos. 211v.–18.

[3] Letter Book C, fos. 15v. *seqq.*

[4] *Cal. of A*, pp. 215–19; Liber Horn, fos. 265–7.

[5] B.M. MS. 14,252, fo. 133v.; *Lib. Cust.* (R.S. 12), II, pp. 86–8; *Eng. Hist. Rev.* XVII, pp. 729–30.

[6] *Lib. Alb.* (R.S. 12), I, pp. 337–8: "*Inquisitiones Wardemotarum.*"

How far these presentments achieved their object it is difficult to say: The fact that many of the complaints made in 1422 are repeated in 1423 shows that the jurors were not satisfied; they say of certain grievances that they had been many times presented and nothing done. The same complaints of negligence appear in the presentments of Portsoken and Tower Wards in the next two centuries. In the precepts the aldermen were ordered to present such defaults as they were not of themselves able to correct, but there is no evidence that correction took place in the wardmotes or that offenders were tried and penalties inflicted there[1]. As a rule the aldermen appear to have left the general maintenance of public order to their beadles and constables, only intervening themselves when they happened to be in the neighbourhood of a brawl. The beadles, for their part, seem to have relied on the authority of their office, backed by the Mayor's Court. In 1299 the beadle of Walbrook Ward, patrolling with the watch, intercepted three persons carrying arms and without a light, who refused to surrender to the peace and wounded some of the watch. The beadle identified one of the offenders and charged him in the Mayor's Court[2]. The same procedure was followed in the case of two riotous persons who forcibly broke into a house on the pretext that they wanted a room in which to practise buckler-play and then assaulted the beadle when he came up, carrying his staff of office, to maintain the peace[3]. If necessary the beadle could raise the hue and cry by horn and voice to summon the men of neighbouring wards to help. This happened in 1302 when the beadle and watch of Walbrook were assaulted by a number of young workmen. The offenders were put in the Tun, the prison on Cornhill, and appeared in the Mayor's Court two days later, where evidence was given that on the night before the offence these persons and others had filled an empty cask with stones and set it rolling down Gracechurch Street to London Bridge to the great terror of the neighbours[4]. One of the principal duties of the beadle was to safeguard public morality and in so doing they exercised an oversight on the

[1] In 1374 three *scawagers* "indicted" in the ward of Billingsgate for extortion were sentenced in the Mayor's Court to imprisonment for disobedience to their alderman and for refusing to "plead" before him. *Cal. of P. and M. Rolls*, 1364–1381, pp. 180–1. This probably means no more than that they were sent for to explain their conduct.

[2] *Cal. of Early Mayor's Court Rolls*, p. 57.

[3] *Ibid.* p. 86.

[4] *Ibid.* pp. 124–5.

chaplains of the City chantries, who were offenders far too often[1] It appears that on complaint made in the wardmote against disorderly houses, the beadle after warning given was entitled, with the help of the neighbours, to remove the doors and windows as a sequestration[2].

As in the case of the beadles most of the evidence of the aldermen's own activities comes from the prosecutions of those who assaulted or insulted them. Alderman John Causton, who took to task a dyer for throwing stinking trade refuse into the street was called certain opprobrious names which the clerk Latinizes as "*shredulum falsumque*[3]", and another alderman who arrested a woman for a similar offence was dubbed "*falsum latronem et rusticum veterem & defractum*[4]". None of these offenders were punished in the wardmote. It was the Mayor's Court which bound them over in tuns of wine or sentenced them to imprisonment or the pillory, while the aldermen in many cases interceded for a mitigation of the penalties.

One or two cases, however, seem to take us back to a sterner time when the alderman in his wardmote may have wielded a greater authority. In 1387 a certain William Hughlot, a servant of the king, forced his way into a man's house and attacked him with a dagger and afterwards drew his sword upon an alderman who was passing at the time and intervened. In the affray a constable of Fleet Street was wounded. The Mayor's Court gave judgment that the offender's hand be cut off—the ancient penalty for striking an alderman. An axe was brought in and the prisoner's hand laid on the block. But on the prayer of the alderman and others this penalty was remitted and imprisonment and the pillory substituted, which in turn were reduced to a penitential journey, with a lighted candle weighing 3 lbs., through the streets from Guildhall to St Dunstan's in the East[5]. A similar offender had been sentenced in 1298 to walk from the place of his crime to Guildhall, with bare head and feet and clothed only in his tunic, carrying in his hand an axe to expiate his offence against the alderman as a justice and guardian of the "vill"—a word which probably denotes the ward[6].

[1] *Ibid.* p. 70; *Cal. of I*, pp. 273–87.
[2] *Cal. of E.M.C. Rolls*, pp. 218–19.
[3] *Cal. of P. and M. Rolls*, 1323–1364, p. 162.
[4] *Ibid.* 1364–1381, p. 15.
[5] Letter Book H, fo. 210; H. T. Riley, *Memorials*, pp. 490–4.
[6] *Cal. of E.M.C. Rolls*, p. 6: "*tamquam justicie & Custodi ville.*"

The London commentator on the laws of Edward the Confessor, writing about 1210, tells us that aldermen had the same dignity and power as the reeves of hundreds and wapentakes in their bailiwicks under the king's sheriffs throughout the kingdom[1]. This would imply presiding over a court with a wide jurisdiction in pleas of trespass and where thieves, taken with the mainour of stolen goods, might be condemned to death. It has been said of London a century earlier under Henry I: "it seems certain that each ward had its court, the wardmoot of later records, which corresponded in function to the court of a rural hundred[2]." Unfortunately no evidence has survived to decide for us whether in the 12th or earlier centuries the wardmotes possessed a jurisdiction which seems to have been exercised by at least one soke-court and to have been claimed by others[3].

THE EARLY HISTORY OF THE WARDS

The wârd-returns, together with John Carpenter's treatise in the Liber Albus and much information in the City's Letter Books show that in the 15th century the wards were developed units of local administration. To some extent their functions had been enlarged as the authority both of the civic and the national governments increased and demanded more from them. But the main lines of their activities appear almost as soon as the first references to them in the 12th century. While there is no need to accept Dr Stubbs' description of London under its port-reeve and bishop at the time of the Norman Conquest as being "only a bundle of communities, townships, parishes and lordships of which each has its own constitutions", it is probably true that most of the business of local government was carried out in the separate wards and that the activities of the central City court, the Husting, were mainly legal.

For the period before the Norman Conquest evidence is scanty and inconclusive. A curious record of civic organization is found in the *Judicia Civitatis Lundonie*[4]—a body of rules drawn up between 930 and 940 by the bishops and reeves belonging to London for mutual protection and the apprehension and punishment of

[1] Liebermann, *Gesetze der Angelsachsen*, I, p. 655.
[2] F. M. Stenton, *Norman London* (Hist. Assoc.), p. 10.
[3] *Liber de Antiquis Legibus* (Camd. Soc. O.S. 34), pp. 243–4; *Placita de Quo Warranto* (Rec. Comm.), p. 456, but note *ibid.* pp. 460–1, 464, 470, 471, 473.
[4] Liebermann, *Gesetze*, I, pp. 173–83.

thieves. Apparently there already existed a frith-gild composed of inhabitants of superior rank (*eorlisce*) and humbler persons (*ceorlisce*). For this association new regulations were drawn up in accordance with Æthelstan's laws recently promulgated at Greatley, Exeter and Thundersfield. The framework consisted of groups of ten men, of whom one was leader, under the supervision of *hynden* men or hundred men, and monthly meetings with feasting and ale-drinking (*bytfylling*) were held when report was made as to the fulfilment of the rules. There was a common fund for compensation to those whose property was stolen and payments for energy in catching thieves. Those who were remiss were fined. They had the right of executing summary justice on thieves taken with the evidence of guilt upon them, and the gild was entitled to one half of the thieves' goods.

A theory has recently been advanced[1] "that the hundreds were first formed as private associations or frith-gilds and were part of the response of the countryside to the edict of Greatley, with its sequels at Exeter, Faversham and Thundersfield". The character of the frith-gild, we are told, may be seen in the *Judicia*. We have here the name of the hundred and tithing, which though personal was quasi-territorial from the first. The hundred is adopted and made obligatory on the whole country by Eadmund[2] but it is Eadgar's fuller code which shows the adoption of the private organization, now given a formal court of judgment by folkright, into the machinery of government[3].

This attractive theory has been subjected to searching criticism, mainly in its treatment of the question of jurisdiction, and as regards the transition from a personal association to a geographical district[4]. It is also difficult to believe that in the pre-Conquest period, with its lack of communications, a complex division of the country into territorial units for administrative, jurisdictional and police purposes could have been effected by royal decree, and that within some thirty years. If the monthly meetings of Eadgar's hundred can be linked with the monthly *bytfylling* of Æthelstan's London frith-gild, they can with as much probability be connected with Eadweard's earlier injunction that every reeve hold his gemot

[1] J. E. A. Jolliffe, *Const. Hist. of Medieval England*, pp. 116–20.

[2] III Eadmund, 2 (940–6), Liebermann, *Gesetze*, I, p. 190.

[3] *Ibid.* I, pp. 192–4, dated by Liebermann 946–*c.* 961.

[4] H. M. Cam in *Eng. Hist. Rev.* LIV, p. 485.

every four weeks[1]. The hundred has an air of antiquity about it and probably had its roots far back in the past. Liebermann was inclined to think that the *boldgetæl* of Ælfred's laws[2] was the unit which afterwards came to be known as the hundred. Others would trace a connection with the 6th-century ordinances of Childebert and Clothaire, in which again there are suggestive parallels[3].

If thus the evidence is too shadowy to support the theory that Eadgar's hundred owed its origin to the frith-gild as seen in the *Judicia*, can we trace any connection between the latter and the London wards, which from the 13th century onwards were regarded as the civic version of the rural hundreds? It is tempting to discern in the hundred-man the forerunner of the later alderman with his police duties. The groups of ten men may be regarded as analogous to those groups upon which after the Conquest the system of frankpledge was superimposed. The summary justice on hand-having thieves continues under the name of *infangthef* and *outfangthef*. In the *Judicia* when a suspect is apprehended whose guilt is not immediately apparent there appears to be some kind of inquiry, no doubt in the City courts. Three centuries later the ward juries present suspected criminals for trial. Moreover, as London apparently never possessed a gild-merchant, it is tempting to connect the *bytfylling*, the monthly convivial meeting of the *frithgegildas*, with the ancient Guildhall, which Giraldus Cambrensis tells us was an *aula publica quae a potorum conventu nomen accepit*[4]. All these parallels are suggestive. If they are not sufficiently strong to establish a connection, the alternative seems to be that the arrangements set forth in the *Judicia* had no permanence and left no trace behind them.

On the other hand, there are several features of the later wards, fully as important as the protection of property, of which no forecast appears in the *Judicia*. In the 13th century such public services as existed were mainly performed by the wards, the municipal government merely exercising a supervisory function. Nor is there

[1] II Eadweard, 8; Liebermann, *Gesetze*, I, p. 145, dates this law 924–5.

[2] Ælfred XXXIV (*c.* 871–901), Liebermann, *Gesetze*, I, p. 70; II, p. 26. See H. W. C. Davis in Stubbs, *Select Charters*, 1942 ed., p. 78, n. 1.

[3] *Ibid.* pp. 79–80.

[4] *Rolls Series*, 21, iv, p. 436; on gild-ale drinkings see W. R. Lethaby, *London before the Conquest*, p. 177. He suggests tentatively (p. 136) that the wards were "identical with the Peace gilds of Athelstane's enactment".

any mention of military organization, well developed in the early 13th century, which was equally necessary in the 10th, and which obviously then existed, as shown by the spirited resistance to the Danes. It appears unlikely that one need alone should bring about territorial subdivisions.

It is difficult also to reconcile the ancient boundaries of the wards with the clear-cut arithmetical system of the *Judicia*. The dividing lines of certain wards follow the streams descending to the Thames from the flooded area north of the wall, a fact which suggests either defensive or property units. The wards vary greatly in size and from 1252 onwards, when there is evidence as to population, it does not appear that the smaller wards were more densely inhabited than the larger; their contributions to civic or national purposes were, generally speaking, in ratio to their size. The curious shape of several of the wards adds another element of mystery. Though the majority are almost bisected by principal streets[1], which suggests an aggregation of trades or handicrafts, one or two run athwart a number of less important lanes. Langbourn Ward, enclosing Lombard Street and Fenchurch Street, is shaped like a dumb-bell. So too are the northern portion of Bridge Ward and the southern of Bishopsgate. The neck of the latter consists today of the roadway alone. Farringdon Within Ward has the appearance of a heraldic manche and an isolated portion is completely enclosed by Cripplegate and Aldersgate Wards. Some wards have portions either jutting or extending like long arms into or between other wards, as for instance Lime Street, Bishopsgate and Castle Baynard Wards. There is little evidence of any alteration of intra-mural ward boundaries after the Conquest, and these irregularities must either be original or due to ancient modifications, the reasons for which can only be guessed. Property metes and bounds were probably one of the reasons. Then there is the strange fact that though parish and ward boundaries coincide for stretches here and there[2], many of the parishes lie astride one or more ward boundaries, thus opening up the question of priority of date. It is clear that any inquiry into the origin of the wards must proceed

[1] W. R. Lethaby, *London before the Conquest*, pp. 131–5; H. A. Harben, *Dict. of London*, pp. 610–11.

[2] Harben, *op. cit.* notes that this is the case with all the ward boundaries running up from the river for some distance. In his view the division into wards came before that into parishes.

from a study of their physical contours and the parishes cannot be left out of account.

With these and other considerations in mind Dr Page suggested several origins for the wards. His argument is not free from ambiguity, for after stating that they were originally devised for military purposes, he identified some ten of them with ancient sokes of the City, with which they were probably coterminous[1]. Yet other wards were formed from streets or centres of trade, such as Bread Street, Cordwainer Street, Vintry, Cheap, Coleman Street, Broad Street, Candlewick Street, Bridge, Billingsgate and Lime Street Wards. If we understand Dr Page aright, the sokes of landowners and trade localities formed ready-made natural units upon which the duty of supplying men for defence, watch and ward was imposed by the king or his portreeve. It is a theory which is not inconsistent with the topography of the wards and it finds support in the earliest names *warda* (1111) and *custodia* (*c.* 1210), by which they were described[2]. That defence was an essential element in their constitution is probable. Professor Maitland suggested that we have in the alderman of the ward the military captain of the burgmen[3] and Dr Round regarded the 12th-century London wards as "units for defence and ward, each under its own alderman, with the sheriff at the head of the whole system[4]". But it would be over-simplification to consider that the ward came into existence for purely defence purposes. Like the hundred it has an air of antiquity about it. We may suspect that it had its origins even before the Danish invasions as a primitive organ of local government and that turbulence from within and danger from without led to arrangements for watch and defence, even as other needs led to equally important functions.

The earliest mention of an alderman comes from the middle of the 10th century. In two cartularies[5] of Prior Eastry's time (1285–1331) is recorded an agreement between a certain Brihtmer of London, on the one hand, Stigant the archbishop, Godrich the

[1] *London, its origin and early development*, pp. 173–6, but see F. M. Stenton, *Norman London*, p. 15, for a contrary opinion.

[2] *9th Rept. Hist. MSS. Comm.* p. 67b: "Tursten, alderman of the ward"; MS. 14,252, fo. 106v.; *Eng. Hist. Rev.* XVII, p. 505; J. H. Round, *Commune of London*, p. 255.

[3] *Township and Borough*, p. 50.

[4] J. H. Round, *op. cit.* p. 255.

[5] Christ Church, Canterbury, Registers B, fo. 263, and E (formerly C 5), fo. 11 v.

thane and the convent of Christ Church, Canterbury on the other, whereby Brihtmer gave to the latter his house, garden and outbuildings, and a church dedicated to All Saints, to come into effect after the deaths of his wife and two sons[1]. The heading of one copy in Register E, perhaps copied from the dorse of the original, gives the date 1053. A document of 1098–1108 preserved in B.M. Cotton Faustina B VI, fo. 100, containing a list of London churches belonging to the priory, describes Brihtmer as "*senator*[2]", which we may translate as "alderman", and mentions that his surviving son Aegelwin paid two shillings annually. Though here wrongly described as the church of St Peter, there can be no doubt that the church in question was that of All Hallows, Lombard Street, which is recorded as paying the above amount in 1200 and 1292.

It is possible that the place-name Aldermanbury, first mentioned (Aldresmanesberi) about 1128 in the survey of St Paul's lands[3], may even then have been an ancient name. In spite of its genitive singular form Dr Stenton[4] suspects a derivation from ealdormen in the plural, which would give the meaning of a "fortified enclosure" of the aldermen. Taking into account its proximity to the earlier Guildhall, he suggests that we may have in the name of the latter "a trace of an association of aldermen formed in Old English times and obsolete already in the early Norman period". Mr C. L. Kingsford[5] also identified the street with the aldermen of the City, and agreeing with Stow's view of the meaning of "bury", considered that his "explanation of Aldermanbury, as the bury or Court-hall of the aldermen, now called the Guildhall" seemed a sound one. This leaves the origin of the name "Guildhall", which appears in the same document of 1128, still unsolved, as it must

[1] See B. W. Kissan, *Lond. and Middx. Arch. Trans.* vol. VIII, Pt I, New Series, pp. 57–65; *Privy Council, Mayor etc. of London* v. *Eccl. Comm. Cases for appellants*, pp. 102–3; J. Tait, *Medieval English Borough*, p. 266, n. 1.

[2] See letter of Archbishop Hugh of Rouen to the "illustrious senators" etc. of London, cited by J. H. Round, *Geoffrey de Mandeville*, p. 116; F. M. Stenton, *Norman London*, pp. 18–19; Fitz Stephen's description of London, *Lib. Cust.* (R.S. 12), II, p. 9, "*habet Senatoriam dignitatem*"; *Lib. Alb.* (R.S. 12), I, p. 32, "*quod apud Romanos Consul vel Senator dicebatur apud nos dicitur Aldermannus.*"

[3] *9th Rept. Hist. MSS. Comm.* p. 66 (from Liber L, fos. 47–50v.); facsimile in J. E. Price, *Guildhall*, pp. 16–20; cf. H. W. C. Davis in *Essays presented to T. F. Tout*, pp. 55–9. For date see J. H. Round, *Geoffrey de Mandeville*, p. 436.

[4] *Norman London*, pp. 15–16.

[5] *Stow's Survey*, ed. C. L. Kingsford, I, p. 292; II, p. 337.

remain, but both writers are probably on firm ground in believing that the street is evidence of a pre-Conquest alderman or aldermen[1].

It is a noteworthy fact that from the first mention of an alderman by name in 1111 all references to them, scanty though they are, show them exercising functions which were part of their normal work in later centuries. Many of the deeds enrolled in the Husting from 1252 onwards were witnessed by aldermen, and in the margin is the note "two shillings paid (*ii s. pac'*)". We are told in the statement of London laws drawn up between 1206 and 1216 that where land is bought or sold in a ward, even though it be sokeland, it is the alderman who receives a fee of a gold besant or two shillings, while the sokereeve is entitled only to lesser dues[2]. The above-mentioned deed of 19 July 1111 is a grant of land from the dean and chapter of St Paul's and is witnessed by Tursten, alderman of the ward, which was probably that afterwards known as Castle Baynard[3]. In 1115 Osbert the alderman witnesses a conveyance of land at Cornhill[4]. Azo the alderman witnesses a similar grant in 1142, and in an agreement concerning lands of about the same date, to which he was witness, he receives his fee of two shillings, Salidus the beadle of the ward being given fourpence[5]. Later deeds show Hugh Tabur and William Fitz Alice, aldermen, and the beadles, Rodland and Roger as witnesses[6].

Another early mention has reference to the ward's duty of supplying information by inquest of office. A writ of Henry I issued between 1110 and 1133 orders an inquiry *per probos homines de warda* as to whether a hithe on the Fleet River, used by the ships of St Paul's to unload stone, was the property of the church or of a certain Henry *arborarius*, and whether the ships were by usage quit of toll and custom[7]. Later in the century when Henry II issued the Assize of Novel Disseisin (1166)[8], inquiry was made as to the already existing custom of *freshforce*. Report

[1] Dr Page, *London*, p. 140, suggested that Aldermanbury took its name from "the alderman of the Frith Gild of the City". He believed (pp. 128–9) that there was a royal residence between Aldermanbury and Wood Street. No one appears to have advanced the theory that the street may have taken its name from the ealdorman Æthelred, son-in-law of King Ælfred, to whom the latter entrusted the keeping of London, *A.-S. Chron.* II, 71.

[2] B.M. MS. 14,252; *Eng. Hist. Rev.* XVII, p. 494.

[3] A. B. Beaven, *Aldermen of London*, I, 363.

[4] *9th Rept. Hist. MSS. Comm.* pp. 61–2.

[5] *Ibid.* pp. 67b, 62a.

[6] *Early Charters of St Paul's* (Camd. Soc. 3rd Ser. 58), pp. 89, 105.

[7] *Ibid.* pp. 26–7.

[8] Pollock and Maitland, *Hist. Eng. Law*, I, p. 145.

was made to the king and his justices that where it was alleged that a man had been disseised without judgment, as of fee, an inquiry was made by the oaths of the alderman and neighbours as to whether such disseisin had taken place[1]. Doubtless there were many other inquiries of which no record has come down. Thus the wards had had long training in the duty of returning verdicts, when in common with the juries of the hundreds they were called upon to supply answers to the articles submitted to them in the great Inquests of 1274–5, whereby Edward sought information as to royal rights and liberties and the behaviour of officials, royal and civic[2]. There is plentiful evidence of their work as inquest men and jurymen, carrying out the same duties as the hundreds in the sessions of the Itinerant Justices[3], presenting suspects before the justices of Gaol Delivery at Newgate, giving evidence in response to writs, and making returns to the Articles of the Wardmote Inquests.

The watch and defence systems of the wards had evidently reached a considerable stage of development in the early years of the 13th century, when they are first mentioned. Two passages in B.M. MS. 14,252 deal with the seasonal watches. Of the three chief folkmoots of the year, to which citizens were summoned by their ward beadles, that held on the Feast of St John the Baptist dealt with precautions against fire. The Christmas meeting was held for the setting of the watch[4]. This apparently lasted from Christmas Eve to the Epiphany, during which the hours of duty extended from compline in the evening until the *daibelle* from the chapels had sounded matins. At this time, which may have been some twenty years before the compilation of the MS., the arrangements were under the direction, not of the mayor but of the sheriff or sheriffs. The watchmen from the large, medium and small wards, originally twelve, eight and six men respectively, had been reduced by the sheriffs to eight, six and four. It was their task to guard the quarter or street (*vicum*) peacefully during the night. *Escavingores* were to be chosen to inspect the night-watchmen and their

[1] B.M. MS. 14,252; *Eng. Hist. Rev.* XVII, p. 708; Lib. Alb. (R.S. 12), I, p. 114.

[2] *Rotuli Hundredorum* (Rec. Comm.), I, pp. 403–33. For sworn inquests in 1262, see *Lib. de Ant. Leg.* (Camd. Soc. 34), p. 51.

[3] B.M. Add. Ch. 5153; P.R.O. Assize Roll 547; *Lib. Cust.* (R.S. 12), II, pp. 347–62.

[4] *Eng. Hist. Rev.* XVII, p. 502; *Lib. Alb.* (R.S. 12), I, pp. 118–19; Stubbs, *Select Charters*, 9th ed. pp. 312–13.

arms and to report any defaults to the sheriffs at the next Husting[1]. There are frequent references to these seasonal watches throughout the middle ages and from time to time different arrangements were made for apportioning the task between the wards[2]. In the Tudor period the Midsummer Watch, as described by Stow[3], still survived as a pageant and the culminating spectacle of an annual holiday.

Meanwhile, no doubt, the everyday duty of maintaining order was carried out by the ward officials with the aid either of persons deputed for the purpose or of the neighbours in accordance with the Assize of Arms of 1181, the ordinances of 1233 and 1252 providing for the nightly watch and the appointment of constables, and the consolidating statute of Winchester[4]. In certain arrangements for a special watch in 1294[5], the ordinary watch by the wards is mentioned as a matter of custom, and the first series of Mayor's Court Rolls beginning in 1298 shows the system fully established and working with the same efficiency as in succeeding centuries.

As regards armed defence and military operations there is more and earlier information. An account, probably written about 1215, describes the measures taken "in the time of King John at his request and with his assent". The aldermen must hold their wardmotes of all men over the age of fifteen years. Each is to swear to make a contribution on the sum of his chattels and rents, the amounts being higher for non-citizens, and four men of each ward were to be chosen to deliver the money to Guildhall. Every alderman in his ward must inspect each man's arms, and as many men as possible must be mounted. Each parish was to have a pennon, and the parishioners under their pennons must, when summoned, follow the alderman's banner to the place assigned to them for the defence of the City[6]. With this description may be read the statement of the services and rights of Sir Robert Fitz-Walter, Castellan of London, the well-known baronial leader of John's reign, as claimed by his grandson in 1303[7]. As lord of

[1] *E.H.R.* XVII, p. 505; J. H. Round, *Commune of London*, p. 255, gives the text, printed also in Stubbs, *Select Charters*, 9th ed. p. 312.

[2] *Lib. de Ant. Leg.* (Camd. Soc. 34), p. 55; *Cal. of A*, p. 227; H. T. Riley, *Memorials*, pp. 35, 142; *Cal. of C*, pp. 20, 153.

[3] *Stow's Survey*, ed. C. L. Kingsford, I, pp. 101–4.

[4] Pollock and Maitland, *Hist. of Eng. Law*, I, p. 565.

[5] *Cal. of C*, p. 21.

[6] B.M. MS. 14,252, fo. 124; *Eng. Hist. Rev.* XVII, pp. 726–8.

[7] *Lib. Cust.* (R.S. 12), II, pp. 149–51; *Stow's Survey*, I, pp. 62–5.

Baynard's Castle he held the office of Chief Banneret of London. In time of war, it was his duty with nineteen mounted officers to ride to St Paul's there to receive from the mayor, sheriffs and aldermen the banner bearing the representation of St Paul and a horse of the value of twenty pounds. A marshal was appointed, the great bell of the City was rung, the assembled citizens in arms followed the leaders to Aldgate, where counsel was taken as to the defence of the City, and a standard-bearer chosen to lead the forces if service was required outside the walls. No member of the FitzWalter family is mentioned as being present when the citizens in 1264, disappointed by the Mise of Amiens, appointed a constable and marshal and sallied forth to burn the earl of Cornwall's manor at Isleworth[1]. The contingent which was so disastrously routed at Lewes in the same year was probably the last composed of citizens as distinguished from mercenaries. Henceforward the task of finding and equipping soldiers for service outside the City was apportioned among the wards and took the form of a monetary levy[2].

The duty of internal defence, on the other hand, still remained the responsibility of the individual citizen. During the troubles of 1263 a general watch for the city at large was abandoned in favour of a watch by the several wards, each inhabitant being required to have his arms ready[3]. In succeeding years, and especially during the wars of Edward III, many schemes were drawn up for the defence of the gates, walls and river, either on the initiative of the citizens or in obedience to royal command. The effectiveness of the system was seen in the suppression of Wat Tyler's insurrection and the successful defence of the City against the Bastard of Fauconberg.

A final word may be said as to the number and nomenclature of the wards. In the list of properties belonging to St Paul's, *c.* 1128, twenty wards are mentioned[4]. Of these, three can be identified with certainty—Cheap (*warda fori*), Aldgate (*warda Alegate*) and Walbrook (*warda brocesgange*). One is called *warda episcopi* and the remainder are described by the names of their aldermen. Various attempts have been made at local identification

[1] *Lib. de Ant. Leg.* (Camd. Soc. 34), p. 61.
[2] *Cal. of P. and M. Rolls*, 1323–1364, pp. 132–3.
[3] *Lib. de Ant. Leg.* p. 55.
[4] *9th Rept. Hist. MSS. Comm.* p. 66; see above p. xxxv, n. 3.

and for some of the suggestions there appears to be fair probability[1]. As the survey only relates to those wards in which St Paul's held property, there is no reason to suppose that the list is complete. It is probable that the City was already divided into twenty-four wards, including Portsoken, which in 1125 had been given to the prior of Holy Trinity by a body of burgesses representing the ancient Cnichtengild. That is the number we find in the Great Rolls of the Exchequer of 12 and 14 Henry III (1227–8 and 1229–30), where the assessments of the several wards to tallage are set forth. In these lists twenty-one are described by the names of their aldermen, Cheap has both its local name and the name of its aldermen, and Portsoken and Bassishaw (Bassushag) are named as such[2]. In a 12th-century deed there is mention of Geoffrey the alderman of "Langebord", a name having reference to the Lombards and Lombard Street, but afterwards corrupted to its present form of Langbourn[3]. Dr James Tait has noted two curious instances of wards with parish names. In 1200 three pledges are described as being *in wardis Sancti Martini et Sancti Andree de Estchepe*. The second of these is clearly Billingsgate Ward and Dr Tait suggests that the first may be St Martin Orgar and the ward that of Candlewick Street[4]. The Hundred Rolls in 1274–5 add Coleman Street and Dowgate[5]. In a list which may be dated 1185–7 the whole of the then existing wards appear for the first time under local names[6]. Farringdon Ward is there called "Lodgate and Neugate". Later it was known as "Flete" Ward and "Fletestrete" Ward, first appearing as "Farndone" in 1311[7]. It was divided by statute of 1394 (17 Richard II, c. 13) into the present wards of Farringdon Within and Farringdon Without. The ward of Lodingeberi (*i.e.* Lothbury) is represented by the modern Broad Street, the latter name being first mentioned in 1293—*Warda de Lotheberi modo vocatur Bradestrete*[8]. Finally, in 1550, when Edward VI conveyed to the City his liberties and franchises

[1] A. B. Beaven, *Aldermen*, I, pp. 363–4; W. S. Loftie, *London* (Hist. Towns Ser.), p. 96; W. Page, *London*, p. 176; H. A. Harben, *Dict. of London*, pp. 610–12.

[2] A. B. Beaven, *op. cit.* I, p. 366.

[3] *P.R.O. Ancient Deeds*, A 5853; *Stow's Survey*, ed. C. L. Kingsford, II, p. 307.

[4] *Lond. Topog. Rec.* XV, pp. 1–3.

[5] *Rot. Hund.* I, p. 431; but not Cornhill as stated by Loftie, *op. cit.* p. 74. Cf. A. B. Beaven, *Aldermen*, I, p. 370.

[6] *Cal. of A*, p. 209; *Stow's Survey*, II, 286.

[7] *Cal. of C*, p. 190; *D*, pp. 140, 236.

[8] *Cal. of C*, p. 12.

ERRATUM

page xl, line 23 *for* 1185–7 *read* 1285–7

in Southwark the ward of Bridge Without was created[1]. As the inhabitants could not be forced to take up the freedom, they have never taken any part in the election of an alderman. By an Act of Common Council of 1711 it was directed that on a vacancy occurring the ward was to be offered in order of seniority to those aldermen who had served the office of mayor[2]. With this creation, the present number of twenty-six wards and aldermen was completed.

[1] City's Repertory, fos. 231 v., 234.
[2] R. R. Sharpe, *London and the Kingdom*, I, pp. 442–4.

CALENDAR OF PLEA & MEMORANDA ROLLS *of the* CITY OF LONDON

ROLL A 43

Rolls of memoranda of the time of William Crowmere, mayor, in the end of the first and the beginning of the second year of King Henry V Membr. 1

Writ of protection in favour of "our beloved clerk," Master Philip Morgan, who was then about to cross to Holland on an embassy (*ambassiata*) concerning the king and the realm. Dated at Westminster 18 June 1414. *18 June 1414*

Bond of Richard Burgate, brewer, to Henry Whitby, cutler, in £60 to save the latter harmless against any claims arising from his executorship of the will of John Lye, pouchmaker, deceased. *20 June 1414*

In a dispute between Thomas Pyke, draper, and Peter Gran of Gascony and Bertram Walcote, chandler, as to payment for goods supplied to the latter, the mayor and twelve aldermen awarded that the said Bertram pay 40 marks and the said Peter £26 6s 8d, by equal portions at Michaelmas and Christmas. *19 May 1414*

Theodoric van Wettyr, citizen and goldsmith, and Bertram Clayherst, merchant of Almaine, came before the mayor and agreed to submit their differences to the arbitration of John Brikles, draper, and Robert Holand, acting for the said Bertram, and Richard Balman and John Rous for the said Theodoric. *17 Sept. 1414*

Recognisance by John Knyvynton *alias* John de Aula of Litchurch, clerk, of a debt of £40 due to Thomas Pyke, draper, and William Multon. Membr. 1 *b* *17 Aug. 1414*

Whereas James le Botiller, draper, by his will enrolled in the Husting A° 11 Edw. II[1] devised certain lands and tenements *Aug. 1414*

[1] R. R. Sharpe, *Cal. of Wills enrolled in the Court of Husting*, 1, p. 276.

in the parishes of St Mary Bothaw and St John Walbrook to the prior and convent of the new hospital of St Mary without Bishopsgate to provide two secular chaplains to celebrate for the souls of the donor and others for ever in the church of St Mary Bothaw, in Aug. 1414 came William Robert, rector of the said church, and Richard Elton, Robert Tatersall, Peter Wymondham, John Reyner, John Umfrey and Hamo Elyot, parishioners, complaining that the prior, Robert Pynchebek, and the convent were remiss as to providing chaplains, and praying the mayor and aldermen to discuss the matter with the prior and convent. The parties were summoned and agreed to accept the arbitration of the mayor and John Preston, the recorder, who, after inspecting the will and hearing both parties, awarded that the prior should pay to the rector and parishioners the sum of 17½ marks per annum, for providing two fit and honest chaplains, and that in case the payment were in arrears, it should be lawful to the rector and parishioners to enter into the tenements and take distresses until they were paid their arrears, and further that both parties should enter into recognisances of £40 to carry out the award.

30 Aug. 1414 Bond of Walter Shirley of Salisbury, grocer, to Walter Gawtron, draper, in £16, to accept the award of the mayor and six aldermen on disputes between them as to the freighting of certain of Walter Shirley's wines in a ship belonging to the said Walter Gawtron and Edmund de Dertmouth, and also to save the said Walter harmless against any claims of John Clerc of Salisbury for wines similarly freighted.

Membr. 2 A list of the goods, chattels and moneys belonging to John Olyver, draper, at the time of his death on 17 Aug. 1406, when they came into the hands of William Weston, draper, and William Wanstall, scrivener, as executors of his will.

First, 5 cloths of *ray*[1], the field being *piersblewe*[2], and 5 with the field azure, at 5 marks each; 2 of *ray* with the field green *gaude*[3], 3 of *ray* with the field *bukhorn grene*, 4½ of *ray* with the field red, 3½ of *ray* with the field *sangweyn*, 5½ of *ray* with

[1] Striped material.

[2] *Sc.* perseblue, a shade of blue. Derivation uncertain.

[3] *Sc.* gaudy-green, a yellowish green colour produced by the plant weld, Fr. *gaude*, the *reseda luteola*.

the field white, at 40s each; 2 of *ray* with the field black and 3½ of *ray* with the field *plonket*[1], at 33s 4d each; 3 of *ray* with the field russet, 5 cloths of motley green, 5 of motley russet, 6 of *smal ray* green, 4 of *smal ray* russet, 8 of motley *blewe* and 2 of motley red of Salisbury at 2 marks each; 10½ of green *medle* of Winchester, 9½ of brown *medle* of Winchester, 13 of red *medle* and 10 of *plonket medle*, at 36s each; 30 of Gildeford blanket at 20s each; 8 of *blewe medle* of Winchester at 33s 4d each; 8 of *persblew* of Essex at £5 each; 18 of *blewe medle* of Colchester at 5 marks each; 34 of blanket of Redyng at 36s each; 2 of *gaude grene* of London make at £5 each; 2 of green of *lyre*[2], 5 *doseins* of *persblewe*, 3 *doseins* of *asure blewe*, 4 cloths of better blanket of London make at £7 each; 1½ cloths of better scarlet at £18 the cloth; 2 of *sangweyn engreine*[3] and 2½ of *violet engreine* at £10 the cloth; 4 of *mustervilers*[4], 2 of black of *lyre* and 2½ of black *fyn* at £6 each; 1½ of *frostymede* and one of *soppys in Wyn* at £7 the cloth; 4 rolls of green *fryse*, 5 rolls of blue *fryse*, and 3 rolls of black *fryse* of *lyre* of London make at 33s 4d the roll; 6 rolls of russet *fryse* and 4 rolls of white *fryse* of *Galys*[5] make at 20s the roll; one *pyle* of *remenauntz* to the value of £10; and 9 dozens of *chaux*[6] of divers colours at 13s 4d the dozen.

Item, one *sale*[7] of red and black *tapicerye*, 2 *bankers* and 12 *quysshons* of the same set (*suyte*) to the value of 40s; one *sale steyned*, 40s; 2 tables with 2 pairs of *trestelx*, one *countour*[8], one *cuppebord* and one long *chaer*, 8 *stoles joyned* with one good *chaier*, 40s; one pair of *aunderns*[9] of iron weighing 300 lbs. at ¾d the lb.; one hanging *lavour*[10], 6s 8d; 9 *basyns* with 8 *lavours* weighing 100 lbs. at 4d the lb.

[1] A grey or light-blue colour.

[2] Originally cloth of Lire or Lierre in Brabant, usually in the phrases, "black of lyre," "green of lyre." Later it became a trade description. See below "black fryse of lyre of London."

[3] Originally dyed with "grain," the insect kermes, but later dyed in any fast colour. See *N.E.D.* sub "engrain."

[4] *Sc.* musterdevillers, originally cloth woven at Montivilliers in Normandy.

[5] Calais.

[6] Hose.

[7] Appears to be a set of hangings for a *sale* or hall.

[8] A counting-board.

[9] Andirons, fire-dogs.

[10] *Sc.* laver, a washhandstand.

Item, one *almerye*[1], 4 shelves, 10s; 6 *bordclothes*[2] with 6 *towailx* of Paris work, 40s; 8 other *bordclothes*, 100 pieces of napery, 4 marks; 200 pieces of *peautre* weighing 400 lbs. at 2½d the lb.; 3 silver *salers*[3], 5 dozen spoons, 6 *bikers*, 12 *plein cuppes*, 2 *basyns*, 2 ewers, 2 *potelpottes*, 12 silver *gobolettes* weighing 632 oz. troy at 2s 4d the oz.; 16 large masers well bound with silver and gilded[4], £32; 4 knives well harnessed with silver and gilded, 10s.

Item, 16 *pottes*, 8 *pannes* and one *chauffour* of brass weighing 342 lbs. at 3d the lb.; 6 *spittes*, 3 *trevettes*, 2 *fryingpannes* with 2 *droppyng pannes* of iron, weighing 407 lbs. at ¾d the lb.; 20 quarters of charcoal (*charbones*) at 8d the qr.; 6 *flicches* of *bachoun*, 4 *sydes* of *boef*, 30s; 2 qrs. of salt at 5s 4d the qr.; one large *bathingfat*[5], 1000 of *talughshyde*[6] for *fuayll*, £4 6s 8d; one *alegist*, 2s; 4 barrels, 3s 4d; 2 qrs. of *furment*[7] at 6s 8d the qr.; 2 axes, 2 *hacchetz*, one saw with 2 iron *wegges*, 2s 6d; 4 pairs of *potellbotells*[8] and 2 pairs of *quartbotells*, 4 tubs with one *knedyngtrough*, 4s 4d.

Item, 2 beds with 2 testers of *tapicerye* of large *assise*, at 10 marks each; 4 beds of worsted hangings with all their furnishings (*apparailles*) well embroidered at 40s each; 12 beds of Winchester work with 12 testers at 13s 4d each; 10 pairs of blankets, 8 mattrasses, 5 marks; 29 pairs of sheets, one good *fetherbedde* with 2 bolsters and 12 *pilwes*, £10; 4 *chestes joyned*, one chest of spruce well bound with iron, 20s; 7 *furres* of *cristigrey*[9] for *hopelondes*[10], 10 marks; 4 *furrez* of *fycheus*[11] for *hopelondes*, 10 marks; 2 furs of *bever*, £5; one *jakke* of black

[1] *Sc.* ambry, a cupboard or locker.

[2] Table-cloths.

[3] Receptacles for salt.

[4] *Bien liez ove argent & endorrez*, i.e. silvergilt.

[5] *Sc.* bathing-vat, bath-tub.

[6] *Sc.* talshide, lengths of wood for making faggots. The sizes of talshide were prescribed by 43 Eliz. c. 4.

[7] *Sc.* frumenty, a kind of wheat or spelt. An early use of the word in this sense.

[8] Two-quart or half-gallon bottles.

[9] A variety of grey or *gris* fur, which according to the Liber Horn, fo. 249 b, was the back of the squirrel in winter. "*Memorandum qe Gris et bis est le dos en yver desquirel.*" It has been suggested that it means Christmas grey, or cresty grey, i.e. tufty, full-coated, the fur then being at its best. J. Hodgkin considered the word to be a repetition, *gris de grey*.

[10] *Sc.* houpland, a long tunic.

[11] The fur of the foul-martin, fitchew or polecat.

velwet and harness of armour (*hernyse darmure*) for four men, 40 marks; £50 in a pouch; £50 in a chest; £700 in a bag in money counted out; one gold ring with a seal, 120 gold rings, 15 gold *ouches*, weighing 60 oz. at 20s the oz.; 4 oz. of *calperell'*[1] at 2 marks the oz.; one *cercle* of gold and *perell'*, £20; one *hanap* of gold weighing 19 oz. at 20s the oz.; one gold ring with an *emerawde*, 6s 8d; 20 *hanaps*[2] of silvergilt and 20 *hanaps* with covers of silver (*coverez d'argent*), 10 *potellpottes* of silver, 6 pottle pots of silvergilt, 3 silver basins with 2 silver ewers, weighing 80 lbs. troy weight, which were put in pledge to John Olyver by John Pretelwell, esquire, of Essex for the sum of 100 marks, and in default of payment at the time of John Olyver's death they came into the hands of the said executors; *item*, 3 dozen *vessell' granisshe*[3] of silver, 20 *plein hanapes* of silver, 12 *gobolettes* of silver, weighing 150 lbs. troy weight, which were put in pledge to the said John Olyver by my lady Straunge for the sum of 200 marks and in default of payment they came into the hands of the said executors. [*French*]

Roger Olyver, son of John Olyver, received so much stock, live and dead, and grain of diverse kinds and other goods at Fulbourne as belonged to his father, in satisfaction for his marriage portion, to the value of £103 6s 8d.

Item, for clothing of the said Roger, his wife and others, for his marriage, £10.

Item, the said John paid a certain Whitehobbe of Cambridge, for a debt of the said Roger, £26 13s 4d.

Item, the said John paid a certain man of Walden for a debt of the said Roger, £24.

Return to a writ by William Crowmere, mayor, late one of the justices of Oyer and Terminer for London and Middlesex, that on 9 Jan. 1414 Thomas Cornvyle surrendered himself to prison on an information for treason and felony brought against him by a servant, whose name the mayor did not know, claiming to be a servant of Thomas, then earl of Arundel, and that the said Thomas Cornvyle remained in Membr. 2 *b*

[1] Possibly seed-pearls used for a woman's caul, or ornamented net-cap.
[2] Cups. [3] Garnish, a set of vessels.

prison until 27 Jan., when the mayor and sheriffs sent him before the king[1] at Westminster with the cause of his taking and detaining, as required by the king's writ.

Membr. 3
8 June 1414

Memorandum that on 8 June 1414 Roger Olyver, son of John Olyver, late citizen and draper, brought a bill of complaint against William Weston, draper, and William Wanstall, scrivener, executors of his father's will, that whereas it was immemorial custom of the city that the children born in matrimony of free men of the city, if they had not been advanced in their father's lifetime, should on his death have a third part of their father's goods, chattels and money after the payment of his debts, and that when one of the children had so been advanced, the other children or child should have the third part, and whereas the said John Olyver died on 17 Aug. 1406, leaving a son, the plaintiff, by his first wife Isabella, the said son not having been advanced, a daughter Joan by his second wife Elianore, who had been suitably advanced, and a widow, his third wife Alice, surviving him, and whereas the deceased left goods and chattels of the value of £1198 11s 6¼d, and in money £800, and debts due to him £213 14s 4d, as appears in two schedules annexed, which debts had been collected before 20 March 1411——the executors had not paid the plaintiff his third part, but had detained it to his damage £2000. [*French*]

After three defaults the defendants appeared on 22 June and demanded a copy of the bill and a day to imparl according to the custom of the city. Afterwards on 8 July they said, by way of protestation[2], that on the day of the presentment of the bill they had none of the goods of the testator except £17 8s 9d, that the custom of the city was not as stated in the bill, and that the goods and chattels alleged to have come into their hands were not of the value named, and by way of plea,

Membr. 3 *b*

they said that none of the goods, chattels and debts mentioned by the plaintiff had come into their hands except certain goods,

[1] Into King's Bench.

[2] In pleading this was a formal protest against certain statements, which the defendant could not directly deny without duplicating his plea, and which he could not pass over without mention lest he should be held to have tacitly admitted them.

chattels and debts contained in a schedule which they exhibited to the court, which they were prepared to verify. They prayed judgment. And as regards the goods, chattels and moneys contained in their (the defendants') schedule, they said that the plaintiff ought not to have any action against them, because they had paid divers creditors of the testator the sum of £94, as appeared by their schedule; and whereas the testator, with John Payn, John Wederisfeld, Robert Essex and the plaintiff jointly held to them and their heirs 2 messuages and 190 acres with appurtenances in Fulbourne, co. Cambs, with £10 per annum beyond reprises, of the feoffment of William Hanyngfeld to the use of the testator, the testator before his death had by deed of release and confirmation made an estate in fee simple in the messuages and lands to the plaintiff, who was then of full age, and had delivered to him divers goods and chattels then at Fulbourne, viz. sheep, oxen, horses, carts, hay, corn, barley and other grain to the value of £103 6s 8d, and woollen cloth to the value of £10, and had further, on behalf of the plaintiff, paid to divers persons named in the defendants' schedule the sum of £50 13s 4d, being debts owed by the plaintiff, which they were ready to verify, which being so, the plaintiff had been competently advanced in his father's life time, wherefore they demanded judgment whether the plaintiff had any action against them.

And the plaintiff in his proper person could not deny the matters pleaded and alleged by the defendants.

Therefore it was considered that the plaintiff take nothing by his bill and be in mercy and that the defendants go quit thereof.

Roger Olyver came into court and acknowledged as his deed a general release to William Weston, draper, and William Wanstall, scrivener, of all actions, suits and demands against them. *21 Sept. 1414*

Memorandum that John Thorley, esquire, senior, gave notice to the mayor in Guildhall, by John Murydon, chaplain, Thomas Mitford and Robert Keleby that he wished to take his writs of right against John Lincoln, clerk, Richard Walgrave, knight, John Hynkebey, Robert Clerk, clerk, William *3 Nov. 1414*

Hanyngfeld, Thomas Lopham, Thomas Hokkele, clerk, James Hogge and Robert Velaunce, tenants of two parts of the manor of Fakenham Aspys with appurtenances co. Suffolk, and against Rose Cavendyssh, tenant of the third part, returnable before the king's justices of his Common Bench on the octave of St Martin, according to the form and effect of indentures between himself and others on the one part and John Hynkele and William Cavendyssh and others on the other part.

[*French*]

29 July 1414 Memorandum that John Guy, master of the ship "*le Trinite*" of Plymouth and Menauton *alias* Menaldus de Lartiga of Bordeaux, merchant, came to an agreement as regards a claim for £40 freight for wines laden in the said John's ship, on terms that William Reynold, vintner, whom the said John had appointed as his attorney, should have the key of a cellar in which 16 casks of red Gascony wine belonging to the said Menauton were stored, and that he should receive the sum of £40 from the first money accruing from the sale of the wine, with liberty to sue for that amount if the wines were not sold within seven weeks.

Membr. 4 *5 July 1413* Bond of William Poteman, son of Guy Poteman, draper, deceased, to John Profyt, chamberlain, in 20s, not to fish in the Thames without permission.

10 July 1413 Thomas, son of Thomas Peverell, brings a plaint of intrusion against Philip Burton, Giles Burton, Nicholas Kymbell, John Bryan, tailor, and Richard Walsshe, fruiterer, touching his free tenements in the parishes of St Dunstan in the East, St John Walbrook and the Blessed Mary of Fanchirche.

10 July 1413 Robert Weston, prior of the house and church of St Mary Overe, brings a plaint of intrusion against Nicholas Mokkyns, warden of the chapel of Corpus Christi or college of St Laurence Pulteneye, London[1], touching his free tenement in the parishes of St Mary Abbechirche and St Laurence Pulteney.

[1] The chapel of Corpus Christi and college of St Laurence Pountney was erected by John de Pulteney about 1334. *Cal. Pat. Rolls*, 1334–8, p. 60.

The king sent a letter close dated 14 April 1413 containing a copy of the enrolment of a deed in the rolls of Chancery, whereby William Roo, skinner, made a gift of all his goods and chattels to John Payne, John House, John Lemman and Peter Penne, skinners, the deed being witnessed by William Combe, John More, John Trethewy and others on 4 Nov. 1408, in order that the mayor and sheriffs might proceed with the prosecution of the said donees, John, John, John and Peter. *1 July 1413*

Quitclaim from John Lardener, esquire, to William Kedyngton of Clare co. Suffolk, late his apprentice. *4 July 1413*

Quitclaim from Emma, widow of John Hert, haberdasher, to John Shadworth, mercer, John Micholl, vintner, Nicholas Aghton and Adam Broun, stockfishmongers, executors of her husband's will, who in turn acknowledged a quitclaim to the said Emma. Membr. 5 *28 Aug. 1413*

Bond of John Dowble, fishmonger, John Stachesden, fishmonger, Hugh Neal, brewer, John Byle, cutler, Richard Cobald, armourer, and Walter Walssh, *friser*[1], in 100 marks to John Whitby, rector of St Peter's on Cornhill, for the good behaviour of the said John Dowble towards him. *30 Aug. 1413*

Memorandum that Robert Banburgh and Robert Bever, wardens of the mistery of Drapers, John Prentout, John Somer, Thomas Mountgomery and John Claveryng, drapers, who were chosen arbitrators between John Inhewe of Bokkyng, plaintiff, and Geoffrey Glemesford, defendant, brought in an award concerning an action for a debt of £28 due on the sale of woollen cloth. *19 Sept. 1413*

William, prior of Holy Trinity within Aldgate, brings a plaint of intrusion against Henry Pountfreyt, John Cokeyn, John Prophete, Robert Skrace, Thomas Neweport and Thomas Porter touching his free tenement in the parish of All Hallows Graschirchstrete. Membr. 6 *20 Nov. 1413*

[1] An unusual word in the city. Probably for friezer, one who creates a nap on cloth.

16 Dec. 1413 Writ of *certiorari* demanding that the tenor of the record and process of an action of debt before the mayor and aldermen between Agnes Brightwell, plaintiff, and William Rody, defendant, be sent to Chancery. Dated at Westminster, 16 Dec. 1413.

Return of William Crowmer, mayor, and the aldermen that on 6 Nov. 1413 Agnes Brightwell came into court before the mayor and aldermen in the Chamber of the Guildhall and brought a bill of debt against William Rody, mercer, for £60, in which bill she alleged that her son-in-law William Gritford, being her attorney and merchant overseas, lent that sum to the defendant in the parish of St Margaret Moysy on 22 July 1406, to be repaid by him to the plaintiff, which he refused to do. Process being continued, the parties appeared on 22 Nov. 1413 before the mayor and aldermen in the Inner Chamber of the Guildhall, when the plaintiff prayed the court to examine the parties, because the matter in her bill partly concerned the law merchant. Thereupon the parties submitted themselves precisely and peremptorily to the examination, discretion, award, decree and sentence of the mayor and aldermen, who ordered them to bring into court all evidences, written and unwritten, on 24 Nov. On that day, as it appeared from the evidences and the reasons put in by both parties that the defendant had sealed letters of payment to the plaintiff for £60, and that the plaintiff had received 16 pipes of salt and other goods to the value of £7 8s 4d, they awarded that the defendant pay the plaintiff the balance due, viz. £52 11s 8d.

1 Dec. 1413 In the presence of William Crowmer, mayor, and Richard Whityngton, Thomas Knolles, Richard Merlawe, Robert Chichele, Thomas Fauconer, William Louthe, Henry Barton, Stephen Speleman, Nicholas Wotton, William Norton, John Penne, John Lane, Thomas Pyke and William Sevenok, aldermen, in the Inner Chamber of the Guildhall came John Bally, who being sworn on the Gospels said that Thomas Dyster, late citizen and mercer, owing to the confidence which he had in him, caused certain persons to be bound in the sum of 800 marks payable to the deponent, and that after Thomas Dyster's death he delivered to Robert Domenyk, one of the executors, by the hands of John Hertwelle, the sum of £250 to build a chantry and a further sum of £182 for the use of Ellen, the testator's daughter, in part payment of £400 due to her both by legacy and owing to the deaths of her brothers, Thomas and John; and that an agreement existed between himself, John Hertwell and Robert Domenyk that John Abbot, mercer, should know nothing of these payments.

Jacques Jonghe Jans of Erlem[1] in Holland, one of the attorneys of John de Basseveld, Jacques Huguesone, Jordan Claisson, Roger Sawyn and Paulkyn Caengard brought certain letters of attorney sealed with the court seal (*sigillo ad causas*) of the town of Dam[2], which were enrolled as follows:— Membr. 6 *b* *26 Dec. 1413*

The *Burchmaistres*, *Echevins* and *Counseil* of the town of Dam certify that John de Bassevelde and Jacques Huguesone, with Joordan Claisson, Rogier Sawyn and Paulkyn Caengard, burgesses of the town, appeared before them and appointed Jacques Jonghe Jans of Erlem and Girard Werner of Bruges their joint attorneys to represent them before the king of England and his council and all others his justices and officers for the recovery of 53 tuns, 1 pipe and 1 cartel[3] of Poitau wine, lately freighted at La Rochelle in three German ships by their factors and servants for discharge at Lescluys[4] in Flanders, which were captured by men-at-arms of the king of England at Beauisle-sur-Mier[5] and taken to England, as appears more fully in the certificate granted to the attorneys, who were empowered to make agreements, give letters of acquittance, plead, make and receive demands, contest cases, plead exceptions, challenge judges, make replications, duplications, triplications and quadruplications, verify essoins on oath, answer to interrogatories, accept judgments, interlocutories and definitive sentences, enter appeals, demand adjournments for counsel and generally to do such things as their principals might do. [*French*]

Reciprocal bonds of John Lane, mercer, and Nicholas Carrewe, esquire, of co. Surrey in 1000 marks to abide by the Membr. 7 *17 Nov. 1413*

[1] Haarlem. [2] Damme. [3] *Sc.* quartel, a quarter-cask.
[4] Sluys. [5] Belle Isle.

award of William Askham, William Sevenok, William Waldern and Nicholas Wotton in disputes between them.

20 March 1414 Agnes Wawton, daughter of Thomas Wawton, esquire, brought a bill before the mayor and aldermen in the Chamber of the Guildhall against Alice Virly, her mistress. The latter made four defaults, and Thomas Donyngton, serjeant of the Chamber, reported that she had withdrawn from the city and had left no one to provide for and teach her apprentice, nor had she assigned the apprentice to any other person of the same mistery. Accordingly on 27 March it was considered that the said Agnes be exonerated from her apprenticeship.

26 March 1414 John, prior of Christ Church, Canterbury, brings a plaint of intrusion against Henry Pountfreyt, saddler, John Cokayn and John Profyte, fishmonger, touching his free tenement in the parish of All Hallows Graschyrch and S[t] Benedict Graschirch.

28 April 1414 Memorandum that John Aleyn, mercer, came into the Chamber before the mayor and aldermen and after informing them that Robert Domenyk, mercer, was indebted to him in £128 8s 3d, prayed leave to prosecute him at the common law at Westminster or elsewhere, which request the mayor and aldermen granted.

Membr. 7 *b*
31 May 1414 Bond of Tidmann Hasard and Tidmann Harry, goldsmiths, of Trajecceum[1], to Richard Ikelington, fishmonger, in £80 to appear before the mayor and aldermen whenever required until the end of an action brought against them by the said Richard and to fulfil the judgment and final determination of the mayor and aldermen.

Memorandum that the abovementioned Richard and Tidmann Hasard agreed to abide by testimonial letters under the seal of the town of Middelburgh in Zeeland concerning certain conditions, which Tidmann alleged with regard to certain letters, a copy of which was placed in the file of the mayoralty of William Crowmer. On 13 July 1414 it was found by the letters from Middelburgh that the business had been initiated

[1] There were several towns with the Latin name Trajectum. Trajectum ad Mosam, Maestricht; Trajectum ad Oderam, Frankfurt-on-the-Oder Trajectum ad Rhenum, Utrecht, sometimes in the form Ultrajectum.

on the conditions alleged by Tidmann. Accordingly the mayor and aldermen gave judgment that Tidmann should be quit of all claims for £72 arising from two letters of payment directed to John Malteby, which the said Richard had obtained from William Marcheford, merchant. At the same time Tidmann promised not to sue the said Richard in England or overseas for delays and trouble caused to him in the matter.

James Reymes, bladesmith, and Stephen Mychell, *laborer*, having submitted their differences to the mayor and aldermen, it was found that the said James had unjustly troubled the said Stephen by suing him in the Sheriffs' Court. He was ordered to withdraw his action, and not to sue him again about that matter in any court, spiritual or temporal, on penalty of losing the freedom. *12 July 1414*

Nicholas Wotton, on behalf of Henry Wertesburgh *alias* Stuce, citizen and goldsmith, and Bertholomew Bettini, on behalf of John Pontadour, merchant of Lucca, came to an agreement as regards a sum of £110, claimed on letters of exchange, the terms being that Gerard Danidze, merchant of Florence, enter into a recognisance to pay £50, and Alan Everard £60 to the said Henry, but that these recognisances should be cancelled if it could be proved by authentic letters that Henry had recovered the sum of £110 overseas. If not, the recognisances should stand and Henry should return to John Pountadour the letters of exchange or an acquittance for the above sum. *1 June 1414*

Afterwards, authentic letters under the seal of Bruges were produced showing that the moneys had not been paid, whereupon Gerard Danidze paid the sum of £50 due from him and a first and second letters of exchange were returned to John Pountadour. *12 July 1414*

In a dispute between Margaret, wife of John Bokyngham, esquire, and Cristina Aylmer the mayor and aldermen, inasmuch as the said Margaret swore that she had no evidence whereby the said Cristina was bound to her or her husband, awarded that Cristina pay her 18s 4d for all previous claims, and that the said Margaret deliver to the said Cristina all *8 July 1414* necessaries belonging to her, after which the parties made satisfaction to each other.

Membr. 8
10 Dec. 1413 Roger Notyngham, son of John Notyngham of London, who had been apprenticed for a term of nine years to John Drewe, *pyebaker*, prayed to be transferred to another master as the said John was unable to instruct him, being now out of his mind (*est ore distract de memoire*), and the facts being vouched by many persons of credit, he was exonerated from his apprenticeship to the said John and committed to John Halsale, *pasteler*, to serve the remainder of his term.

[*Latin and French*]

12 June 1413 William, abbot of St Peter Westminster, brings a plaint of intrusion against William Middelton, Guy Laurens, grocer, John Beamond, Richard Osbarn and William Banastre, taverner, touching his free tenement in the parish of St Margaret Bridge Street.

25 Jan. 1414 Writ of *habeas corpus*, demanding that Thomas Cornevile of London, carpenter, be brought before the king[1] at Westminster with the cause of his taking and detaining. Witness W. Hankeford at Westminster, 25 Jan. 1414.

Return of the mayor and sheriffs that on 9 Jan. 1414 a servant of Sir Thomas, earl of Arundell, had laid an information before the mayor against Thomas Cornevile for treason and felony touching the king's person, and that the said Thomas had voluntarily surrendered, declaring that the information was unjust, upon which the mayor had committed him to prison to await the order of the king and his council. Nevertheless he would be brought *coram Rege* as required.

3 Feb. 1414 Writ of *corpus cum causa* demanding that Tidmann Hasard be brought into Chancery with the cause of his taking and detaining. Dated at Westminster, 3 Feb. 1414.

Return that the said Tidmann had been taken at the suit of Richard Ikelyngton by virtue of a bill levied before the late mayor and aldermen according to the law merchant and the custom of the city and that he remained in prison for lack of

[1] Into King's Bench.

mainprise. Nevertheless he would be brought before the king in Chancery as required.

Writ of *certiorari* demanding the production in Chancery of the record and process of an action for debt of £100 levied in the court of Ralph Lobenham, sheriff, and removed into the Chamber of Guildhall before William Walderne, late mayor, between John Walden, plaintiff, brother of the archbishop of Canterbury, and John Twyford, esquire, defendant. Dated at Westminster 1 March 1414. Membr. 8 *b* *1 March 1414*

Record and process as demanded above. The plaint, being levied on 19 Oct. 1412 in the sheriff's compter in Milk Street, was removed into the Chamber before the mayor and aldermen on 21 Oct. 1412. On 4 Nov. the plaintiff in his declaration alleged that the sum of £100 was due on a bond to himself and his late brother. The defendant obtained leave to imparl and on 20 Nov. he pleaded that the said John Walden ought not to maintain his action against him, because he, the defendant, at the time of making the bond, was forcibly taken by the said John and his covin to the church of St Vedast and there assaulted with knives and daggers and threatened with death if he did not make and seal a bond to the plaintiff, and thereupon in fear of his life he made the bond to the plaintiff, all of which he was ready to verify, wherefore he prayed judgment that the plaintiff be precluded from his action. The plaintiff pleaded that the defendant entered into the bond of his own free will and prayed that it be inquired of by the country, and the defendant did likewise. On 4 Feb. 1413 a jury of the venue of St Vedast said on oath that John Twyford of his own free will made the bond and delivered it to the said John Walden.

Memorandum that on 8 July 1411 John Weston, the common counter[1] of the city, came before the mayor and aldermen Membr. 9 *8 July 1411*

[1] *Communis narrator*. He is also described as common serjeant, the titles being interchangeable at this time. Thomas Marwe, appointed in 1491, was the last to be so described. His successor Thomas Grene, who was appointed common serjeant *c.* 1495 held that office until 1521. In 1518 it is mentioned that Roger Cholmeley was appointed in *unum Communium Narratorum* of the city, a distinction between the two offices having apparently been created. City's Journal 9, fo. 275 b; Repertory 3, p. 20; Journal 10, fo. 50 b.

in the Inner Chamber of the Guildhall and, *ex parte* the liberty of the city, showed that John Abbot, mercer, one of the executors of Thomas Dyster, late mercer, had in his hands divers goods and chattels of the testator and moneys levied from debts, which belonged by legacy to the testator's orphan children, Thomas, John and Ellen, and prayed that the said John Abbot might be summoned to render account on 21 July before two aldermen and two commoners as auditors according to the custom of the city. The said John, being summoned by Thomas Donyngton, one of the serjeants of the Chamber, appeared and together with John Middleton, Simon Bartelot, John Cosham and John Stratton, mercers, entered into a bond of £400 to John Proffyt, chamberlain, that he would accept the award of the court of mayor and aldermen. Thereupon William Waldern and John Lane, aldermen, and Alan Everard and John Whatele, commoners, were chosen as auditors to hear the account and to make a written report in order that the mayor and aldermen might be informed how the sum of £400 devised by the testator to his orphans might be levied.

Afterwards on 14 Dec. 1413 the auditors appeared before the mayor and aldermen and reported that John Abbot had presented to them a roll of accounts, whereby after diligent examination it appeared that he had carried out his duties as executor well and faithfully, that he had in his hands only the sum of £5 3s 4d unpaid, and that a sum of £638 16s 4d still remained to be recovered from debtors of the testator. The mayor and aldermen affirmed the account as just and consonant with reason and on 2 Jan. 1414, the chamberlain showing no reason to the contrary, the bond was cancelled.

22 Feb. 1414 Recognisance of John Tredewe, skinner, to John Wodehous, esquire, of a debt of £80 payable at Lady Day.

27 July 1414 Recognisance of John Tredewe, skinner, and Thomas Philip, mercer, to William Waldern, mercer, of a debt of 43 marks payable at Michaelmas.

"To oure Worshipfull Lord Mair[1] of the Citee of london. Membr. 9 *b*
Like un to youre soverain discrecioun to have consideracioun how Robert Pellikan & Stephene Barry now late were chosen and ordeyned arbitrours bitwene John Sadeler, vinter, of London of that o part and Thomas Bradley of that othir part For to make a finall accorde and determinacioun of all manere matieres, acciouns and causes beyng bitwene the forsayde John and Thomas, Uppon whiche ordenaunce we the forsayde Robert and Stephene arbitrours seyng evidences of either partie by good deliberacioun and avisement makyng relacioun to yow of oure awarde and accord in that partie.

First as touchyng tenementz, shoppes and here appurtenauntz with ledes, necessaries, hostilmentz and other appurtenauntz whyche the forsaide John and Thomas boughten joyntly to gidre of Anneys Kent of London in the parisshe of alle halwen the mechille[2] in Thamisestrete atte london, we bene acorded and awarden that the forsayde John shall delivere fully & cleerly to the forsaide Thomas atte the chois of the same John all his righte state and terme comyng in alle the

[1] The earliest instance of the phrase "Lord Mayor" in English. A great deal of controversy has taken place as to the origin of this courtesy title. It used to be said that it dated back to 1354, when a charter granted that the mayor's serjeants might carry gilded or silver maces, but the charter does not call the mayor "lord mayor," nor is there any evidence that it was considered at the time to confer any title. However, the importance of the mayor is shown by the fact that in connection with the poll-tax of 1379, the mayor of London was assessed on the same scale as an earl and the aldermen as barons. *Rot. Parl.* III, pp. 57–8, *Item le Meir de Londres paie come un Conte iiii li, Item les Aldermen' de Londres chescun come un Baron xls.* The usher of the duke of Gloucester, possibly compiling his material before the latter's death in 1447, puts on the same level of social rank, viscounts, legates, barons, suffragans, mitred abbots, the three chief justices, and the mayor of London. *Early English Meals and Manners* (E.E.T.S.), pp. lxxiv, 70. Meanwhile in the 15th century there are a number of passages in which the mayor was described or addressed as "Lord Mayor"; 1440, Letter Book K, fo. 190; 1467, Journal 7, fos. 144 b, 146 b; 1469, *ibid.* fos. 199 b, 201 b; 1471, *ibid.* fo. 236 b; etc. In 1525 Henry VIII addresses a letter to "my lord Mayr," Repertory 7, fo. 8 b. As time passes the clerks who write the records omit the prefix "Lord" more rarely, until from 1535 onwards the mayor is invariably described as "Lord Mayor." It must be remembered that men who received a special summons to parliament and would now be described as members of the House of Lords were frequently described in the 14th and 15th centuries merely as "knight" or "chivaler." The practice of calling them "Lord" is fairly contemporary with the usage of "Lord Mayor."

[2] The Great.

forsayde tenementz, shoppes and here appurtenauntz with ledes necessaries and hostilmentz paying the forsayde Thomas to the same John atte the state makyng xii li sterlings.

Also in the same manere we awarden in caas that state resonable be made to the forsayde John by the same Thomas thoroughe here both consent than shall John paie to Thomas atte the state makyng xii li sterlings.

Also we have hadde avisement and in sighte of a bill of the forsaide John Sadeler in whiche he asked of the forsaide Thomas xli li x s ii d and as touchyng that bille we have founde by evidence and recorde credible that the forsaide John is paiet and content there of xxiii li xvi s i d q[a].

Also as touchyng a certein covenaunt made & consented bitwene the forsaide John and Thomas in this fourme, that the forsaide John sholde fynde oille & asshen to the forsaide Thomas suffisiauntly for his sopehous atte as good pris as ony othir man couthe yt bye, payng the same Thomas therfore and more overe every woke in encrece to the same John ix s vii d ob. Of wyche encrece every woke the forsaide John hath received paiement for lxxvi wokes, and for as moche as we have knowing by relacioun credible that the forsaide John fonde oille and asshen but only xvi wokys we awarde in feith and conscience by oure arbitracioun that the same John shall rewarde and restore a yeyne to the forsaide Thomas for every woke ix s vii d ob. as longe tyme as he fond neither oille ne asshen that is for lx wokes whiche amounteth in monoie xxviii li xvii s vi d.

And so alle thinges a forsaide accompted we fynde the forsaide John endetted to the forsaide Thomas cleerly xi li iii s v d q[a]."

Membr. 10 *12 March 1414* Memorandum that John Weston, common counter of the city, brought into the Inner Chamber of the Guildhall a bill in which, as common serjeant-at-law of the city and in pursuance of his duty to protect the interests of orphans, he prayed that John Bally, one of the executors of Thomas Dyster, late citizen and mercer, be compelled to bring in to the Chamber the sum of £400, the testator having caused divers debtors of his own to be bound to the said John Bally in £500 and more, which the latter had since received from them. [*French*]

The said John appeared on summons and said that the testator had caused divers persons to be bound to him in 800 marks for the purposes of his will and had named him as one of the executors, but that he had refused administration. In his will the testator devised £100 to each of his three children and £100 to a posthumous child by his wife Joan, if one should be born, but if not, this amount was to be divided equally between the other three children. In case the children died and no posthumous child were born, half the legacy was to go to the widow Joan and the other half to be expended for the good of the testator's soul. By the same will Robert Domenyk, Henry Somer, Dennis Lopham, Laurence Hampton, Thomas Barwe, John Abbot and the defendant were appointed as executors, of whom only Robert Domenyk and John Abbot accepted administration. The widow Joan proved to be not pregnant, and the other children died except Ellen, who was under age and who had married John Hertwelle, mercer[1]. Subsequently he himself had been several times sued by John Hertwelle and John Abbot to pay the £400 legacy, and he now prayed that they be summoned to court, to show cause why he should not be exonerated therefrom.

The parties having appeared on summons, John Bally took the oath to speak the truth on all matters contained in the bill. He said that some time, during the first year of the present king, John Hertwelle, on behalf of his wife, sued John Abbot before the mayor and aldermen for the £400 abovementioned, to which John Abbot pleaded that he had rendered account before auditors appointed by John Chichele, mayor, and had paid everything due from him, saying further that John Bally had the sum of £400 and more, which he prayed might be Membr. 10 *b*
brought into court. Thereupon the present defendant had admitted receiving over £500 recovered from debts, of which he had paid £250 to Robert Domenyk to be used for a chantry for the souls of William Strete and the late king Edward III.

[1] Hertwelle, who was guardian of the children, appears to have married his ward Ellen when she was about twelve years of age. See *Cal. of Letter Book I*, p. 111.

He had been put to great expense and labour in collecting the debts and had suffered in health by the prosecution directed against him. But if allowances were made for his costs and security were given that the chantry would be built he was willing to pay the balance though he was not legally bound to do so. Thereupon William Waldern, the mayor, had ordered him, together with John Hertwelle and Robert Domenyk, to come to an agreement. This they had done on 29 July 1413, when he paid John Hertwelle the sum of £400, by assignment of the executor, Robert Domenyk, which sum John Hertwelle accepted in full satisfaction of the legacy. At the same time John Hertwelle had begged him not to tell or reveal to John Abbot that they had come to an agreement, and he had promised to keep the secret so long as he could honestly do so.

The plaintiff, John Hertewell, could not deny the facts alleged by the defendant, and added that he would never have believed that John Bally would reveal the payment of the money aforesaid for a thousand pounds.

Afterwards on 22 Nov. 1415 the parties appeared before Nicholas Wotton, mayor, and the aldermen to hear their award and judgment, when, after full consideration of all evidences touching the matter, it was adjudged that the said John Hertwelle, being satisfied of the £400 legacy, do not in future trouble or implead John Bally in any of the aforementioned matters.

Membr. 11
23 Feb 1412

Be it remembered that John Hertwelle, guardian of the orphan children of Thomas Dyster, deceased, came before the mayor and aldermen in the Chamber of the Guildhall and claimed from John Abbot, one of the executors of the will, the sum of 100 marks, which the latter had received on the sale of certain lands and tenements, rents and services in the counties of Oxford and Northampton for the purposes of the will.

The said John Abbot appeared on 26 Feb. and said that the testator had enfeoffed Thomas Denton and Robert Domenyk, who were still living, and others now deceased with these lands for the benefit of his son John, his children Thomas and Ellen being already provided for, with remainder to the heir of the testator's sister Denise. One property in Bannebury and Bodycote co. Oxon was let on a fourteen years' lease, and a certain William Ryver, esquire, of Salisbury had subsequently been enfeoffed with it, and as it was burdened with military service to Thomas Wykeham, knight, William Ryver had enfeoffed Henry Somer and Laurence Hampton with it, and they had sold it, at his (John Abbot's) request, receiving for it the sum of £12 10s, which was handed over to him. Another property in Plumpton, co. Northampton, had been encumbered against William Haredon by an action of *novel disseisin* and a further messuage in Northaston co. Oxford, which was demised for 23s 4d per annum, was encumbered towards William Somerton, because the testator had sold it to him. Accordingly Thomas Denton and Robert Domenyk had made an agreement with William Haredon and William Somerton, whereby they quitclaimed the properties to the latter for the sum of £55, the money being handed over to John Abbot—making a total of £67 10s less expenses.

The mayor and aldermen having made an allowance for expenses, the said John Abbot paid into court the sum of £64 8s 4d and was adjudged by the court to be exonerated.

Afterwards on 24 Nov. 1413, a certain Thomas Gylle, as son and heir of the abovementioned Denise, claimed this sum on the death of Thomas Dyster's son John, his claim being opposed by John Hertwelle. Thereupon, at the request of Thomas Gylle, the court examined on oath the executors, Henry Somer, Dennis Lopham, Thomas Barwe, Laurence Hampton and John Abbot as to the intentions of the deceased. On this testimony and on John Hertwelle failing to show cause Membr. 11 *b*
to the contrary, the court on 13 Aug. 1416 adjudged the abovementioned sum to Thomas Gylle.

Membr. 12
18 Nov. 1411

Account rendered on 18 Nov. 1411 by John Abbot, one of the executors of Thomas Dyster, by the advice and consent of Robert Domenyk, his co-executor, before William Walderne and John Lane, aldermen, and Aleyn Everard and John Whatele, commoners, auditors appointed by the mayor and aldermen to discover how the sum of £400 could be raised for the orphans from the goods, chattels and debts in the inventory of Thomas Dyster's goods, which amount to £4336 9s 3d.

From which must be deducted £1746 13s due to certain creditors—	£1746 13s 11d
Of which Domenyk had paid £1503 19s 1d, leaving £242 14s 10d due Thus there remained to the testator and the executor Domenyk	£2589 15s 4d
Less for costs and pleas divisible between them	36 5s 5d
Thus there remained to the testator and executor Domenyk, who were partners...	£2553 9s 11d
From which must be deducted Domenyk's share as a one third partner—£851 3s 3½d, and a third of the residue due to the widow Joan, who married Domenyk £567 8s 10¼d	£1418 12s 1¾d
Of which sum thus due to him Robert Domenyk had received £1237 2s 9d Thus there remained for the purposes of the will	£1134 17s 9¼d
Of which Domenyk had paid £48 19s for the funeral and for the soul of the deceased and £187 1s 10d for legacies and Abbot had paid in legacies £145 14s 10d	£381 15s 8d
Thus leaving for the good of the testator's soul	£753 2s 1¼d
Memorandum that Robert Domenyk had received of the sum mentioned in the inventory........................£2955 6s 11d And John Abbot........... 203 16s	£3159 2s 11d

which had been used as above stated.

Memorandum, in debtors of Norfolk who were bound to John Bally in the sum of... £533 6s 8d Item, in debtors and tallies delivered to John Abbot £643 19s 8d	£1177 6s 4d
Out of which money still due, there ought to be paid to creditors........................	£242 14s 10d
Item, still payable to Robert Domenyk and his wife	£181 9s $4\frac{3}{4}$d
Item, still due to the testator..............	753 2s $1\frac{1}{4}$d
Sum to be paid..................................	£1177 6s 4d
Memorandum that the debtors and tallies for £643 19s 8d delivered to John Abbot could not be recovered by him, since some were not due and others had been pardoned. Of this sum Robert Domenyk as a partner ought to bear $\frac{1}{3}$ part, i.e. £214 13s $2\frac{3}{4}$d and also a third part[1] as having married the widow Joan, i.e. £143 2s $1\frac{1}{2}$d	£357 15s 4d
Certificate of the auditors that the said John Abbot had paid everything due from him except £5 3s 4d which he had just received, i.e. 30s from the executors of Richard Forster, and £3 13s 4d from Julian Walden. Thus there remained to be levied of the debts owed to the testator, as appeared by a schedule annexed, the sum of £638 16s 4d, which schedule was deposited in court on 14 Dec. 1413 to remain of record.	£638 16s (4d)

A list of persons owing money to the late Thomas Dyster. Membr. 13

Thomas Kemp of Wy, 12s; Richard Bradwell 13s 4d; John Skot, 10s; John Cornwalez, £6; Turry Drippston, 26s 8d; Thomas Semble, 54s 4d; Agnes Lewesham, 13s 6d; Richard Clyfford for the Wardrobe of King Richard, £10;

[1] I.e. of the residue, after deduction of $\frac{1}{3}$ part.

Sir John Smard, priest, 11s 4d; Thomas Missenden, 11s 4d; Thomas Gudlac, £3; Alice Belgrave, 7s; Arnald Gylham, 33s 4d; money of King Richard borrowed at the Guildhall, £10; Thomas Purdauns, £18 19s; William Marchford, £4 7s; Piers Belgrave, £8; Thomas Denton, £57; Master Henry Harborow, £40; Thomas Burton, £33; Steward Corsour, £7 4s 8d; Esmond Wyseman, 33s 8d; John Hawez, 10s; Roger Hoy, 10s; Richard Edward, 5s 8d; John Philippot, £52 11s 3d; Maistre Denys, 40s; Julyan Waldene, 5s; Roger Caudray, 46s 8d; Thomas Cley, £4; Cok William, 25s 9d; John More, £6 16s 10d; Markez le Fayre owes for his wife 11s 6d; Robert Napton, £10; John Sekelbris, 13s 4d; William Burton, £3 17s; John Loveney, *Garderober*, £22; Marke Marcate, £5; William Parker, 30s; Alexander Poyntell, 13s 4d; Thomas Brenaunt, £12 6s; Nicholas Brynchesley, 13s 4d; Hugh Clerk, £5; Nicholas Banastre, 20s; Margery Semble, £3 6s 8d; the bishop of Lincoln, £3 8s 4d; Hogkyn Clerk, 53s 4d; John Payn, *botiller*, £8; Robert Speke, mercer, £12 10s 10d; William Parker, 43s; Thomas Gay, 27s; Richard Gegge, 40s 3d; Nicholas Huberd, 41s 8d; Thomas Frend, 6s 8d; John Hanwell, 6s; William Talbot, tailor, 13s 4d; John Cok of Kerdeff, £7 17s; Thomas Cosyngton, £10 16s; Gilbert de Lambaleyn, 20s; Griffith de Webourley 56s; Richard Hatton, £3 6s 10d; John Mariot, 24s 11d; John Hampton, 16s 8d; Laurence Andrewe, £6 2s 2d; John Gymmyng, £20; Robert Barmby, 14s; Geffrey Odyham, £3 3s 2d; Gerard Clokkemaker, 6s 8d; Roger Bas, £4 2s 8d; William Wilcotes, 35s 9d; Thomas Mayneld, 41s 8d; John Emond, 26s 8d; Hugh Clerk, £3; In 2 tallies the sum of £45 16s 11d.

A parcel of a house in Banbury and 6 acres of land, £8; the rent of John Langhorn, £6; the debts of John Dyster, £7 13s 4d; William Rosse, 35s; Piers Belgrave, £4 5s; John Baxster, £8; John White, 24s; Esmond Man, £4 11s; Foucher, £3 13s 4d; Crouche, £16 19s 4d; Robert Caudray, £7 5s; John Topp, £12; Mark Markate, 13s 2d; one parcel belonging to Dyster, £48 19s; one parcel which is not due from Caudray, 51s 8d; one parcel of John More, £5; the debt of Walter Newnton, 20s; the debt of John Wetewell, 25s 6d.

Sum total:—£638 16s 4d. [*French*]

ROLL A 44

Rolls of memoranda of the time of Thomas Fauconer, mayor, for part of the second and third years of King Henry V Membr. 1

A dispute having arisen between Richard Barlewey, chandler (who had the lease of a tenement from the prior and convent of S[t] Mary without Bishopsgate, in succession to Richard Hoke, brewer,) and Joan, widow of William Kyngescote, with regard to a vacant plot of ground belonging to the tenement, which abutted on the south side of the "*Herteshed*" then in the tenure of the said Joan, the mayor and aldermen, who were asked to arbitrate, gave as their award that the said Joan should hold the plot of ground during the lease for 2s annual rent, on condition that the water falling from Richard's premises should be allowed to descend on her ground and that the said Richard should provide a grate and a covered-in gutter.

Writ to the mayor and aldermen forbidding them to proceed with actions sued by Thomas Foster, fishmonger, and Richard Tyndell, brewer, against Geoffrey Empyngham, chaplain, servant of Thomas, earl of Arundel, the king's treasurer, since it was an ancient custom that persons sitting in the Court of Exchequer should not be impleaded elsewhere while the court was in session, wherefore the said Thomas and Richard were to be warned to prosecute their action before the barons of the Exchequer on 10 Dec. if they so wished. Witness W. Lasyngby at Westminster, 4 Dec. 1414. *4 Dec. 1414*

Return to the same that the plaintiffs had been warned to sue in the Exchequer.

Award of John Caston, John Swan, William Carter and John Bright in a dispute between William Stone, *whitawier*, and William Audre, clerk, to the effect that the latter make to the former a general acquittance and pay him the sum of £31 11s 8d. [*French*] *21 Jan. 1415*

Membr. 1 *b*
8 Nov. 1414

Writ to the mayor demanding information about a deed of 8 Jan. 1381, said to have been enrolled in the Husting[1] and to have thereby the force of a fine at common law, whereby William Spencer and Joan his wife, daughter and heiress of John Jordan, late citizen, conveyed by feoffment to Geoffrey Manfeld, John Chilley and Sir John Witeney, chaplain, all their lands and tenements with a quay at Billingsgate, the reversion of a messuage and the third part of the quay after the death of Idonea, wife of John Stokyngbury and widow of John Jordan, a tenement with two cellars in Fyncheslane called "Puddyng lane" in the parish of St Margaret Briggestret, two shops in Bridge Street and the reversion of another shop in the occupation of the said John Stockyngbury and Idonea his wife——this deed having been cited by John Reche on a *scire facias* before the king in his court, against Agnes Crosby, Thomas Bradwas, John Crosseby and Philip Clerk, to show cause why nine messuages and a quay should not be restored to him and certain letters patent of the king's father should not be revoked to him, the said letters patent being as follows:

(1) Issued to the said Agnes Crosby and Thomas Bradwas with regard to the property, value £16 per annum, belonging to Joan, daughter of John Jordan, which Joan was an idiot, and her property in the king's hands.

(2) Issued to John Crosseby with regard to the wardship of the said Joan, and her property to the value of 20 marks per annum.

(3) Issued to Philip Clerk with regard to the wardship of certain lands and tenements to the value of £10 per annum.

Witness W. Hankeford at Westminster, 8 Nov. 1414.

19 Dec. 1414

Robert Thornley, esquire, senior, gave notice that he wished to take out a writ on behalf of John Murydon, Thomas John and John Warkeworth against Richard Waldegrave, knight,

[1] See Husting Roll 110 (35). A year later, in 1382, the feoffees reconveyed the property to Joan, then a widow, and in 1384 she and her third husband, Thomas Lyncoln, fishmonger, once more conveyed the properties to feoffees. *Ibid.* 111 (33), 113 (5). She had previously been married to Richard Ponte, mercer, see below, p. 29 and Husting Roll 107 (32–6).

Robert Clerc, clerk, Thomas Loppeham, John Lincoln, clerk, James Hog, Robert Valaunce and Thomas Hokley, clerk, for two parts of the manor of Fakenhamaspes co. Suff., and also a writ in the names of the said tenants against Rose Cavendyssh, for the third part of the manor, both writs being returnable on the octave of St Hilary before the justices of the Common Bench, in accordance with agreements between the said Robert Thorley and others on the one part, and John Hynley and William Cavendyssh on the other. [*French*]

William Hore was attached by Baldwin Tettesbury, one of the mayor's serjeants, to answer John Estmond, vintner, in a plea of trespass wherein the latter complained that the said William on 10 May 1411 entered the plaintiff's house in the parish of St Mary le Bow with force and arms and carried away 10 pieces of *motle worstede*, value 10 marks, 14 pieces of plain *worstede*, value £8 15s, and 20 lbs. of Paris silk, value £16, against the peace and to his damage 100 marks. Membr. 2 *11 May 1415*

The defendant, at the instance and request of the plaintiff according to the custom of the city, was examined and charged (*allocutus*). He did not deny but confessed the trespass, whereupon the plaintiff prayed judgment and damages on his confession. Therefore it was considered that the plaintiff recover the damages specified in his bill and that the defendant be in mercy.

Writ of protection in favour of John Riggele, *alias* Power, archer, then about to cross the sea in the company of John Fastolf, esquire. Dated at Westminster, 27 June 1415. *27 June 1415*

Similar writ in favour of Thomas Kynot, citizen and grocer, then about to cross the sea in the company of Sir John Cornewall. *28 June 1415*

Gift of goods and chattels from Laurence Andrew, mercer, to Richard Aylmere, William Foucher, mercer, and Thomas Panter, scrivener; witnesses, John Brampton, barber, Henry Newman, brewer, William Randolf, armourer, Thomas Horwod, capper, John Basill, currier, Walter Bradmere, purser, Reginald John, tawyer. Dated at London 1 Jan. 1415. *23 Aug. 1415*

Membr. 2 b
4 May 1415 Memorandum that whereas on 27 Jan. 1415 Thomas Moore, dean, and the chapter of St Paul's Cathedral, on the one part, and Robert Widington, grocer, on the other, entered into bonds of £100 that the dean and chapter, on the one part, and Robert Widyngton and Katherine his wife, John Sayer, William Chestreford, John Maskall, Thomas Badby, Robert Whappelode and John Baldok, feoffees of divers tenements of the said Robert Widyngton in the parish of St Margaret Briggestrete, on the other, would accept the award of William Walderne and William Crowmere, aldermen, concerning a certain quitrent of 8s 10d claimed by the dean and chapter, without prejudice to an assize concerning the said rent[1] then pending between the parties—the arbitrators on 4 May 1415 awarded that the whole ground of the tenement of which the said Robert and the others were feoffees, together with ground of a tenement adjacent, of which Thomas Lovell and Lucy Morys were feoffees, lying in Crokedlane between a house late of Edmund le Treyre and now of the said Lucy, widow of Thomas Morys, on the south, a house late of Austin Baker now of Richard Rochewell, fishmonger, on the west, the king's highway leading through Crokedlane on the north and Briggestrete on the east, should henceforth be charged with the quitrent, and that the said Robert pay 6s 8d damages. It was considered further that the assize be proceeded with, this award notwithstanding.

1 July 1415 Thomas Grey, grocer, and Maud his wife bring a plaint of intrusion against Robert Fitz Robert, senior, Robert Fitz Robert, junior, and Margaret his wife, touching his free tenement in the parish of St Pancras.

12 July 1415 William Marchall, son of Richard Marchall, late of the parish of Wygan co. Lancs, came before Thomas Fauconer, mayor, and the aldermen, complaining that, being under fourteen years of age, he was brought to the city on 3 July by a certain William Bradshawe, esquire, and put in charge of a certain John Chestreford, leatherseller, in the parish of All Hallows Honilane, to await the return of the said William

[1] *Novel disseisin* or *freshforce* could be brought for recovery not only of tenements but also of rents.

Bradshawe, who was about to cross the sea in the company of the king[1], and that after the said William's departure, the said John had bound him as an apprentice for eight years against his will. On being summoned John Chestreford appeared in court with one part of the indentures, and as he was unable to deny the allegations, and the boy was clearly under age, it was considered that the said William Marchall should be exonerated from his apprenticeship.

Writ to the mayor that whereas William, son of William Brynkele, had sued Agnes Crosseby, Thomas Bradwas, John Crosseby and Philip Clerk on a writ of *scire facias* before the king in his court to show cause why certain letters patent relating to the wardship and tenements of Joan, being an idiot, daughter and heiress of John Jordan, should not be revoked, the king desires information as to a deed mentioned in the *scire facias* as having been enrolled in the court of Husting[2] on 18 Oct. 1378, whereby Richard Ponte and the said Joan, then being his wife and *compos mentis*, granted the reversion of a brewery called "*le Sterre*" with certain shops on the corner of St Michael's Lane towards Candilwykstret in the parish of St Michael Crokedlane to Roger, late parson of the said church, Robert Sprotburgh, late parson of St Margaret in Briggestrete, and Richard de Waymington, chaplain. Witness William Hankeford at Westminster, 1 Feb. 1415. Membr. 3 *1 Feb. 1415*

Return of the mayor that the deed was enrolled as alleged and that it was then recorded that Richard Ponte and Joan his wife were separately examined as to the deed, which they acknowledged to be their own, and prayed that it might be enrolled, whereupon at the request of themselves and the other parties it was enrolled.

Indentures between John Wodecok, son and heir of John Wodecok, mercer, on the one part and John Shadworth, mercer, on the other, witnessing that the former on 20 March 1413 had entrusted to the latter the sum of 520 marks to make *19 Feb. 1415*

[1] This case and the two protections above were connected with the English expedition to Normandy, which led to the battle of Agincourt on 25 Oct. the same year.

[2] Husting Roll 107 (32–6). See above, p. 26, as to her later marriages.

certain payments therewith and to return the balance, in accordance with which the following payments had been made by consent of John Wodecok, who by this document acknowledges himself content and acquits and discharges the said John Shadworth.

15 March 1414 to John Credy, squire of the mayor of London, for lands and tenements in Orpington, 100 marks.

5 April 1414 to the said John Wodecok, £20.

10 Oct. 1414 at Abyngdon co. Cambridge to the same, 40s.

29 Nov. 1414 to John Martyn and Thomas Colred, apprentices-at-law, for legal advice, 13s 4d; for two dinners for the same, 6s 8d.

15 Feb. 1415 to Henry Halton and William Turnell for lands and tenements in London, late of John Creke, tailor, £200.

Balance of £56 18s 4d repaid to John Wodecok. [*French*]

Membr. 3 *b*
14 Feb. 1415

John Strecche, chandler, was attached to answer Ralph Gresvale, ironmonger, in a plea of trespass by virtue of a plaint levied in the compter of Thomas Aleyn, sheriff, in the parish of S[t] Mildred in the Poultry. Both parties having appeared in Guildhall the plaintiff declared in his count that on 8 March 1413 the defendant had forcibly carried away a ship and gear belonging to the plaintiff of the value of £40 in the parish of St Dunstan in the East within the liberty of the city to his damage £100. In answer, the defendant pleaded that the ship belonged to himself and one Richard Martyn, and the plaintiff had arrested it in a suit he had against a certain John Ryver, who was then one of the crew, as being John Ryver's ship, and that the plaintiff had the ship valued and then carried it off to Sandwich, where he, the defendant seized it, without that[1], that he was guilty of seizing the ship within the liberty of the city. He prayed judgment that the plaintiff be precluded from his action. The plaintiff pleaded that the seizure took place

[1] *Absque hoc quod culpabilis est etc.* According to Jacob, *Law Dictionary*, these are "words of exception made use of in a traverse"; as the defendant pleads that such a thing was done at B etc., *absque hoc*, that it was done at etc. The French equivalent is *sans ceo.* It is a direct denial of a statement of fact made in a declaration or pleading, and it might be taken as an issue for the trial of an action. In later days *et non* could be used instead of *absque hoc.* See Tidd's *Practise* (1821 ed.), II, p. 714.

within the liberty and prayed that it be inquired of by the country; and the defendant did likewise. Wherefore the sheriff's serjeant, John Jolyff, was ordered to summon a jury.

Afterwards the mayor and aldermen ordered the action to come before them in the court of the Chamber of Guildhall and the parties appeared on 5 March 1415. The defendant being charged asked peremptorily that the issue of the plea should be tried peremptorily by the oath of the plaintiff according to the custom of the city and that the jury should be discharged. Thereupon the plaintiff was sworn on the Gospels according to the custom and maintained that the seizure took place on the Thames within the liberty as declared in his bill. A jury was summoned for 21 March to inquire as to the damages sustained by the plaintiff by reason of the trespass, which damages they taxed at £38. It was considered that the plaintiff recover this amount and that the defendant be in mercy.

Gifts of goods and chattels: 28 Feb. 1415, Hugh Kinder, tailor, to John Norton, esquire, William Lilye, pewterer, John Tropenell and Alexander Farnell, tailors; witnesses, Ralph Walsham, Thomas Stone, William Austyn, John Boston, John King; 6 March 1415, William Multon to Thomas Pyke, draper, William Wenard, esquire, of co. Devon, Andrew Bondeby, clerk, and William Kent, skinner; witnesses, Robert Whityngham, Henry Anketill, William Grantham, John Combe, John Mowbray. Membr. 4

Writ reciting the king's prerogative of being satisfied from a debtor's goods before other creditors, and demanding that Thomas Leycestre, deputy of Thomas Morstede[1], the king's *Scrutator*[2] in the port of London, and William Sawce, controller[3] of the said *Scrutator*, who were said to be in prison in the city, whereby they were prevented from attending to their duties and rendering account for the issues of their scrutiny, *1 March 1415*

[1] This was probably the famous surgeon of Henry IV, Henry V and Henry VI. See below, p. 174 n. 1.

[2] "Searcher" seems to be the contemporary English word. *Rot. Parl.* IV, p. 176 a.

[3] *Contrarotulator*, one who keeps a counter-roll to check a treasurer or keeper of accounts.

be brought before the barons of the Exchequer at Westminster with the cause of their taking and detaining and the tenor of any inquisitions concerning them, and that proceedings against them in the city be stayed until further orders. Witness R. Westwode at Westminster, 1 March 1415. By the Red Book of the Exchequer and by the barons.

Return of the mayor and aldermen that Thomas Leycestre and William Sawce, under the name of "*subscrutatores*" in the port of London, had been brought into the Chamber of Guildhall to answer charges of extortion, whereof they had been indicted by an inquisition, and that they were unable to bring them before the barons of the Exchequer, because they had been allowed to go at large, having found sufficient mainprise.

15 Nov. 1414 Memorandum that whereas disputes had arisen between Robert Denny, knight, and Thomas Beaumond, chandler, the former claiming from the latter an annual payment of a pottle of oil called "*metoyle*" and one bushel of green peas so long as he dwelt in Robert's tenement in Bredstret, the parties appeared before the mayor and aldermen on 15 Nov. 1414. The said Thomas pleaded that he had acquired the unexpired portion of a lease of the tenement from Robert Austyn, but that he was not responsible for any contract between Robert Denny and Robert Austyn, because he had not promised to pay him anything. Robert Denny replied that it had been agreed between Robert Austyn and Thomas Beaumond that the latter, in addition to the rent, should make the above payments.

As Robert Austyn was in court, the parties agreed to abide by his testimony. Thereupon, as it was found by examination of Robert Austyn that Thomas Beaumond was equitably (*de racionis equitate*) bound to make the above payment, it was considered by the mayor and aldermen that he do so in future.

Membr. 4 *b*
11 Dec. 1414 Richard Clifford, clerk, who had been sued for a debt of £100 by Thomas Wandesford, woolmonger, and William Norton, draper, and had been attached by divers goods in the hands of the plaintiffs by way of foreign attachment, made four defaults, whereupon the plaintiffs prayed that the goods be

valued and delivered to them under sufficient security according to the custom of the city. The goods were valued by oath of Thomas Halle, mercer, and Nicholas Chinall, *setter*[1], as follows: One mantle (*capa*) with the arms of England worked on it, 20 marks; 2 mantles of blue velvet, 10 marks and 20 marks; and one entire vestment (*vestimentum*), 26s 8d. They were delivered to the plaintiffs under mainprise of John Stratton and John Abbot, mercers, to be restored to the defendant if he appeared within a year and a day and was able to annul the action.

Writ to the mayor as one of the justices of Gaol Delivery of Newgate demanding that the indictment for felony before the sheriffs and coroner against John Spencer of Thoryngton co. Devon, butcher, then a prisoner in the Marshalsea, which indictment was brought before the justices at the last Gaol Delivery, together with the process thereon, be sent before the king on Wednesday next, in order that the indictment might be tried there. Witness W. Hankeford at Westminster, 4 May 1415. *4 May 1415*

Return that John Spencer of Little Toryngton co. Devon, *travelyngham*[2], was indicted before the sheriffs and coroner, and an indictment was sent by them to the justices, but as the justices desired further advice as to the sufficiency in law of the indictment, there was no further process to report; nevertheless the indictment would be returned as directed.

Plaints of intrusion: Agnes, widow of Thomas Duke, skinner, and William Aston, against John Brooke, waxchandler, and Margery his wife, touching their free tenement in the parish of St Bride Fleet Street; William, abbot of St Peter, Westminster, against Sir Robert Newton, master or warden of the hospital of St Bartholomew in West Smithfield, John Sourby and Thomas Halle, touching his free tenement *3 June 1415*

[1] Said by Riley, *Memorials*, p. 60, to be an arrowsmith. On the other hand Walter Coketon, setter, *Cal. of Wills*, II, pp. 467, 468, 470, is described in Husting Roll 159 (39) as a *vestyment maker*, which would explain why Nicholas Chinall, setter, was called in as a valuer of mantles and vestments. *N.E.D.* has a reference A.D. 1515 to "setters" as persons engaged in woollen manufacture.

[2] *Travelyngman*, a wayfarer.

in the parish of S[t] Alphege within Cripplegate; Thomas More, dean, and the chapter of S[t] Paul's against John Michell, John Wyssyngsete, Walter Bew, Alan Brett, John Cressewell, John Santon and Katherine his wife, touching their free tenement in the parish of S[t] Botolph without Aldredesgate, *alias* Alderychesgate; John, abbot of S[t] Mary of Glastonbury, against John Twiford touching his free tenement in the parish of S[t] Benet Shorhogge.

4 June 1415 Writ to the mayor and sheriffs that, whereas by writ of the Exchequer of 20 April they had been ordered to seize into the king's hands the goods of John Eton of London, mercer, to which return had been made that it was impossible, owing to the shortness of time, to specify the goods thus seized and their value, they are now commanded to have the goods valued by oath at the best possible price and to send information thereof not later than 7 June, meanwhile keeping the goods in safe custody until further orders. Witness W. Lasyngby at Westminster, 4 June 1415.

Membr. 5
17 April 1415 Memorandum that whereas disputes had arisen between Bartholomew Pelegryn of Bologna (*Bononia Crassa*), merchant, and James Bernardyn of Lucca, merchant, concerning the sum of £500 claimed from the latter, the parties came before the mayor and aldermen on 28 Jan. 1415, when the said James, in addition to certain pledges delivered to Benedict, attorney of the said Bartholomew, entered into a bond of £450 that he would render an account within eight days to the said Bartholomew in the presence of Peter Gile and Geo Bovy, merchants of Lucca, arbitrators, and would find sufficient security to pay any debt due from him and to fulfil the terms of the award, which bond was entrusted to Nicholas Sandey of Lucca, merchant, for return to the said James if he fulfilled the conditions, or for delivery to the said Bartholomew, if he failed to do so.

And whereas the said James did not render account, the said Bartholomew on 9 April brought a bill demanding that Nicholas Sandey deliver the bond to him. The latter pleaded that he did not know whether the conditions had been fulfilled or not and prayed that the said James be summoned.

Thereupon the mayor, having learnt from Nicholas Bernardyn, brother of James, Peter Gile and Paul Miliany, merchants of Lucca, that the said James would be able to appear on 17 April, ordered John Charlton, serjeant of the Chamber, to summon him for that day. As he did not appear, it was considered that the said Bartholomew have delivery of the bond.

9 April 1415

Bartholomew Pelegrino of Bologna, merchant, having brought a bill against James Bernardyn of Lucca, merchant, to render account of goods to the value of £400, and the defendant having failed to appear on 9 April 1415 and having subsequently made three defaults, the plaintiff prayed that certain goods of the defendant in the hands of the plaintiff and Gerard Danidze, attached as a foreign attachment, might be valued and delivered to him. The goods were valued by oath of William Caundissh and Laurence Hampton, mercers, as follows: one *cilour*[1], one *testour*[2] and one *coverlit* of arras worked with gold, £21 11s 8d; 5 *costers*[3] of arras without gold, £15 15s; 3 *fethirbedds* with the bolsters, 10 marks; one *pouche* and one girdle harnessed with silver, 26s 8d; one image (*signum*) of gold called "*le swan*", with a diamond on the breast, 2 sapphires, one garnet and 38 pearls, £7; and 8⅛ oz. of pearls, £8 2s 6d. They were delivered to the plaintiff under pledge of Gerard Danidze and Annericus[4] Burghis to restore them to the defendant if he were able to annul the action of the plaintiff within a year and a day.

Membr. 5 *b*
15 April 1415

Brother Walter Grendon, prior of the hospital of St John of Jerusalem in England, prays an assize of nuisance against Richard Burne and Juliana his wife, John Gamboun and William Merlyn touching his free tenement in the parish of St Michael Queenhithe.

22 April 1415

The master of the order of Burton St Lazarus in England, warden of the hospital of St Giles without London, brings a

[1] *Sc.* celure, the canopy over a bed.
[2] When appearing with the word celure, this word usually means the supports of the canopy.
[3] The hangings of a bed, probably the side-curtains.
[4] Americus?

plaint of intrusion against William, abbot of Nottelee co. Bucks, touching his free tenement in the parish of S[t] Mildred Bread Street.

20 April 1415 Quitclaim from Robert Thorley, esquire, senior, John Muryden, clerk, Thomas John, and John Warkworth to John Lyncoln, clerk, of all actions by reason of any entry or trespass on the manor of Fakenham Aspys co. Suffolk. Dated 8 Feb. 1415.

7 Oct. 1415 Richard Newport *alias* Spicer prays an assize of nuisance against Walter Gawtron, draper, and Joan his wife, touching his free tenement in the parish of S[t] Botolph without Aldgate.

10 June 1415 Lease from Richard Pavy, esquire, and Joan his wife to Robert Fitz Robert, junior, of London, of eight cellars in Grantham Lane in the parish of All Hallows at Hay for 3½ years at 10 marks yearly rent and one penny for the half-year, under condition that a bond of £40 from the lessor to the lessee should be of no effect if the latter enjoyed undisturbed possession, and under further condition that if the lessors paid to Laurence de Placea, merchant of Pemound[1], the sum of £40 at Michaelmas next, the lessee's interest in the premises should be annulled and the lessors be at liberty to re-enter. Dated at London 8 May.

Membr. 6
2 Sept. 1415 Memorandum that Francis Balby of Venice, merchant, came into the Chamber and complained bitterly (*querulose*) that Thomas Aleyn and John Michell, sheriffs, had arrested without reasonable cause a quantity of wool belonging to him, which was loaded in the galleys on the Thames then ready to start on their voyage, thus delaying their passage and causing loss to himself and other merchants having goods therein. He earnestly begged the mayor and aldermen to send for the sheriffs and examine them, and to make speedy delivery of the goods and do him justice.

The mayor and aldermen, regarding this petition as reasonable, sent for the sheriffs. The latter appeared and after citing

[1] Piedmont.

the charters of the king's predecessors confirmed by himself, whereby it was granted that the sheriffs should receive all forfeitures towards the payment of their farm and that no foreign merchants should buy or sell any merchandise in the city among themselves, they alleged that a bargain had been made at Bruges between a certain Simon Ramand of Lucca, merchant, and Peter Balbi, brother of the complainant, that the said Simon would deliver to Peter or his attorney in London, at the next coming of the galleys of Venice, 120 sacks of Coteswold wool, well-packed and free of all custom, of as fine quality as any in the galleys, under the supervision of Bernard Dalza who was chosen by both parties for the purpose; further the said Bernard Dalza, on behalf of the said Francis, bought 120 sacks of wool in divers places in England from divers foreign merchants, and when the vendors came to London to receive payment, the complainant sorted out the wool again, rejecting some of it, and made a fresh bargain with the vendors, which was against the custom of the city, as he was a foreigner—in proof of which the sheriffs asserted that they had the necessary witnesses, who carried out the sorting and packing; wherefore they demanded the wool as forfeit.

The complainant, being examined, admitted that he had caused the wool to be sorted out, so as to distinguish the old from the new, but he denied on oath that he had made any new price and offered to prove it by as many credible merchants as the court wished; and as it was necessary for him to go to Sandwich on urgent business and he could not tarry in London without grave loss, he begged the mayor and aldermen to examine the sheriffs and their witnesses together with Bernard Dalza and his own witnesses, and to allow him meanwhile to find sureties for accepting whatever the court should decide as the result of their examination.

Thereupon the court fixed a day on 17 Sept. for the production of witnesses. On that day both parties appeared, and since the court could not find that any new bargain had taken place between the said Francis and any other foreigner, it was considered by the mayor and aldermen that the wool should be freed from arrest and that the said Francis and his sureties should be exonerated.

Writ of *corpus cum causa* to bring John Escourt, clerk, into Chancery with the cause of his taking and detaining. Witness John, duke of Bedford, *custos* of England, at Westminster 14 Oct. 1415.

Return of the mayor and sheriffs that the said John had been taken and detained in prison in an action of trespass at the suit of Matthew Morsen, merchant. Nevertheless he would be brought into Chancery as required.

15 Oct. 1415 Bond of William Burton, grocer, to John Proffit, chamberlain, for the payment of 15 marks.

Membr. 6 *b*
5 July 1415 Alan, son of William Bridde of co. Surrey, was exonerated from his apprenticeship to Thomas Colworth, cordwainer, who had failed to teach or provide for him.

[*Latin and French*]

25 Dec. 1414 Assignment by William Park and Joan his wife to Richard Foulmere of the unexpired portion of a lease for 40 years of three messuages in the parish of S[t] Ethelburga within Bishopsgate, which had been granted to them on 31 May 1412 by Margery Buntyng, prioress of the house and convent of S[t] Helen, London, at an annual rent of £4 4s. Witnesses: Thomas Denton, William Roberd, William Wycombe, Thomas Holt and John Tebaud.

ROLL A 45

Rolls of memoranda of the time of Nicholas Wotton, mayor, from Michaelmas A° 3 Henry V to the same feast A° 4 Membr. 1

Whereas certain discords and quarrels had existed between John Hertwell and Ellen his wife on the one part and John Abbot on the other, for which no remedy had been found, though great efforts had been made to that end in the times of several previous mayors, the parties appeared in court on 15 Feb. 1416 and agreed to accept the award of Laurence Hampton, mercer, and John Fray, chosen on behalf of the said John Abbot, and of John Middelton, mercer, and William Aston, chosen on behalf of the said John and Ellen, with power to choose an umpire if necessary. Afterwards the arbitrators, being unable to decide on an umpire, begged the mayor and two aldermen to make the choice for them. The latter requested John Barton, the recorder, to act. *15 Feb. 1416*

After a careful examination of the facts, and counsel having been heard on either side, the recorder in the presence of John Abbot, John Hertwell being absent because he did not care to attend, awarded that John Hertwell had no claim against John Abbot for the sum of £400 under the will of his wife's father, Thomas Dyster, that sum having already been paid to him by John Bally, and that John Abbot, who had been unjustly troubled in the matter, be entirely exonerated and quit thereof, and further that the parties should execute quitclaims in favour of each other.

Peter Rekes, son of John Rekes, shearman, of London, was exonerated from his apprenticeship to John Parys, citizen and shearman, the latter having left the city and failed to provide for him. [*Latin and French*] Membr. 1 *b* *16 Aug. 1416*

Bond of Robert Markle, skinner, in £40 for his good behaviour towards the masters and wardens of the Skinners. *3 Sept. 1416*

Robert Thorley gave notice in Guildhall that he wished to take his writ of covenant against William Hanyngfeld, John Membr. 2 *21 Nov. 1415*

Henkele, Richard Waldegrave, kt, Robert Clerk, Thomas Lopham, John Lyncoln, clerk, James Hogge, Robert Valaunce, Thomas Hokley, clerk, and William Cavendyssh, at the suit of John Meridon, Thomas John and John Warkeworth, for the engrossing of the fine on release according to the agreement lately made. [*French*]

1 Jan. 1416 Writ to the mayor and aldermen that, whereas John Russell, woolmonger, John Estoun, joiner, and Richard Anable, pewterer, had informed the court of Exchequer of divers trespasses and contempts done against the king by Thomas Fauconer, late the king's escheator in the city[1], unjustly and under colour of his office, and had also impleaded the said Thomas by writ of the Exchequer for divers trespasses done against themselves, as was lawful to them, and whereas the mayor and aldermen for that reason were intending to deprive the said John, John and Richard of their liberties within the city and had caused their windows and doors to be closed and locked, in manifest prejudice and derogation of the king's court, therefore the king, desiring that the liberties of his court should be observed unimpaired, in order that his lieges might resort to the same to prosecute and defend as was right, orders the mayor and aldermen to cause those doors and windows to be opened, if they had been closed for no other reason, and not to molest or oppress the aforesaid John, John and Richard for the aforesaid reasons, and if they had already done to the contrary of these presents to cease from so doing, or else show cause to the treasurer and barons of the Exchequer.

Return of the mayor and aldermen that no windows or doors of John Russell and John Eston had been closed, but certain windows of the shop of Richard Anable had been closed by the mayor's orders, because of divers offences and misprisions by him against the liberty and custom of the city, in accordance with the immemorial custom of the city, which windows could not be opened without offence to the liberty of the city—which custom the mayor and aldermen were

[1] Thomas Fauconer was mayor in 1414–15 and as such was king's escheator in accordance with the first charter of Edw. III. W. de G. Birch, *Historical Charters and Constitutional Documents of London*, p. 55.

ready to record before the treasurer and barons on the morrow of St Hilary in the usual manner.

Writ of protection in favour of William Grene who was then about to cross the sea in the company of the king's uncle, Thomas, earl of Dorset, captain of the town of Hareflete, as victualler of the said town. Dated at Westminster, 1 Jan. 1416. *1 Jan. 1416*

Writ to the mayor and sheriffs that although a building on the east side of the church of St Peter Bradstret and other adjacent buildings in the churchyard belonged to Roger Sutton, parson of the church, as they had done to his predecessors, certain men of the city were intending, without cause or process, to cast these buildings down to the ground and to do other damage to the church, which the king could not tolerate, especially since law and right were open to every man, wherefore he commands the mayor and aldermen to prevent these persons from carrying out their purpose and to order them, if they had any ground of action, to sue at the common law which was denied to none. Dated at Westminster, 20 Jan. 1416. *20 Jan. 1416*

Membr. 2*b*
7 Dec. 1415

John Holand, son of Simon Holand of Walsokne co. Norfolk, brought a bill complaining that Thomas Hert, barber, to whom he had been apprenticed for eight years, was of so poor an estate that he could not feed and clothe him, nor keep him at school till he could write and read, as was covenanted in the indentures, wherefore he prayed to be discharged and committed to serve the remainder of his term with another man of the same mistery. [*French*]

As it appeared by examination of the master that he had not been able to provide for the apprentice properly, the latter was transferred to John Oston, barber, to serve for the rest of his term, and to be made free of the city if he served him well and faithfully.

Whereas John Coterell, late citizen and mercer, by his will enrolled in the Husting[1] devised to his daughter Joan, after

[1] *Cal. of Wills*, I, p. 599. Cf. John Body's will, *ibid.* II, p. 420, where he mistakenly calls his maternal grandfather "Thomas."

the death of his wife Alice, all those tenements in the parish of St Mary Magdalene Milk Street, which he and Alice jointly acquired to them and their heirs from Sir Thomas Horne, chaplain, and Thomas Coterell his brother, and whereas the said Joan married John Body, mercer, since deceased, and had a son John and a daughter Margaret successive heirs in tail to the said tenements on their mother's death, the said Joan, together with William Loveney, esquire, Sir William Genow, rector of the church of St Edmund Lumbardstrete, Sir Thomas, rector of the church of St George in Eschepe, Sir William Twichin, chaplain, Everard Flete, mercer, John Debden, Laurence David, brewer, and Richard Perewell, citizens of London, came before the mayor and aldermen and swore that the said John was the legitimate son of his father and mother, in order that he might have written evidence and that there might be no disinheriting of the said heir when his mother was dead and he came to inherit.

Membr. 3
26 Jan. 1416 Writ of error to the mayor, aldermen and sheriffs demanding that the tenor of the record and process of an action of debt brought by William Yong, haberdasher, since deceased, against John Harry, cooper, for the sum of £29 6s 8d be brought before Richard Norton, Roger Horton and William Lodyngton, justices assigned for the purpose, at the church of St Martin le Grand, and that the sheriffs warn John Walker and John Ayleward, executors of the will of the said William, to be present. Dated at Westminster, 26 Jan. 1416.

15 Feb. 1416 Reciprocal bonds of John Hertwell, mercer, and John Abbot, mercer, in £300 to abide by the award of arbitrators between them.

Membr. 3 *b*
3 April 1416 John Jurdan, tailor, and Joan his daughter came into court before the mayor and aldermen and complained that Thomas Herford, *setter*[1], and Joan his wife, purser, to whom Joan Jurdan had been apprenticed, had not enrolled her at Guildhall in accordance with the ordinance of 21 March 1415[2], which directed that all apprentices not enrolled or re-enrolled within the year next following should be enrolled within 20 days after Easter, on penalty of the apprenticeship being cancelled.

[1] See above, p. 33, n. 1. [2] *Cal. of Letter Book I*, p. 134.

As the above Thomas could not deny the complaint, which was borne out by the records, and as it appeared on examination that he and his wife had unduly castigated and governed the girl, it was considered that she be exonerated from her apprenticeship.

24 April 1416

In an action of debt for £90 by Alexander Farnell, tailor, against James Bernardyn, foreign merchant, a foreign attachment of £60 9s in the hands of John Marchaunt was delivered to the plaintiff under pledge of William Holgrave and Richard Frepurs, tailors, to answer therefor if within a year and a day etc.

27 June 1416

Writ of protection in favour of Walter Mite of St Botolph's co. Lincs, *alias* Walter Myte, *wyntner*, who was then about to cross the sea in the company of the king's brother, Humphrey, duke of Gloucester, chamberlain of England. Dated at Westminster, 27 June 1416.

Similar writ in favour of William Broke, *alias* William Brook of London, mariner, in the company of William Burgchier, knight. Dated at Westminster, 6 July 1416.

Membr. 4
28 July 1416

By virtue of a plaint levied in the Poultry Compter on 28 July 1416, John Horsle, sheriffs' serjeant, was ordered to attach John Russell, woolman, to answer Thomas Fauconer in a plea of trespass at the next Sheriffs' Court at Guildhall. The parties appeared next day when the mayor and aldermen, at Thomas Fauconer's request, removed the plaint before themselves in the Chamber of the Guildhall. Thereupon the plaintiff, by his counsel John Weston, the common counter of the city, made his declaration against the defendant, alleging that the latter had falsely and maliciously told several persons that he, the plaintiff, then being mayor and king's escheator, had been imprisoned in the Tower and fined £1000 for causing Richard Gurmyn[1], baker, to be burnt at West Smithfield, together with his letters of pardon, the said Richard having been

[1] See *Cal. of Letter Book I*, p. 180. Gurmyn's Christian name is given as "George" in the Pipe Rolls, see Tyler, *Memoirs of Henry V*, II, p. 394. He is called "Richard Baker" in Cotton Julius B II, fo. 65 b. See Kingsford's *Chronicles*, pp. 69–70, 297. Gregory, *Collections of a London Citizen* (Camd. Soc.), p. 108, gives "Rychard Turmyn," as also does Harley 565. See also *Three Fifteenth Century Chronicles* (Camd. Soc.), p. 55; Foxe, *Acts and Monuments*, III, pp. 351, 375, 531.

declared a heretic by canonical sanctions and handed over to the secular arm and having subsequently received letters of pardon from the king. Wherefore the plaintiff prayed a remedy and that the defendant be punished according to the custom of the city as a warning to other liars and detractors.

The defendant pleaded that he was a layman and did not understand the declaration, and prayed that he might have a day to answer with the advice of counsel, which day was fixed for 30 July. With the consent of the plaintiff, the defendant was handed over in bail to William Waryn, tailor, Ralph Spayne, *tapicer*, Thomas Warde, fuller, Alexander Carpenter, fuller, Richard Wellys, barber, Richard Priour, capper, Edmund Mille, scrivener, John Wellyng, *tapicer*, John Weston, capper, John atte Wode, capper, John Randolph, pewterer, and Thomas Spayne, *tapicer*, to bring him etc. on 30 July, under penalty of £100 payable to John Hill, chamberlain, and his successors.

The defendant appeared on 30 July and pleaded not guilty and put himself on the country, and the plaintiff did likewise. A jury was summoned for the last day of July and the defendant was again handed over in bail to the aforementioned persons. On that day the plaintiff again appeared, but the defendant made default, whereupon it was considered by the mayor and aldermen that they proceed to the taking of a verdict. The jury found the defendant guilty.

The same day the plaintiff, supposing that the defendant had been mainprised, prayed that he be exacted according to custom to come and save himself and his mainpernors (harmless). He was then and there exacted and did not appear. Thomas Fauconer then, on the strength of his plaint, handed in another declaration in which he alleged that the defendant on 1 June in the parish of St Bride, with other evildoers unknown, with force and arms, viz. daggers and *baslards*, lay in wait to kill John Eston and Richard Boure, the plaintiff's apprentices, and Thomas Boteler, the plaintiff's servant, and assaulted and threatened them continuously from 1 June till 27 July 1416, so that they did not dare to go about their business, to the plaintiff's damage £500.

And since it appeared plainly of record that the defendant

had not been mainprised, but had been handed over in bail, and since the plaintiff ought not to be admitted, by law and custom etc., to make a further count on one and the same plaint, it was considered by the mayor and aldermen that the second count be void and nul, and that the defendant be quit thereof. And because the mayor and aldermen were not yet sufficiently advised as to rendering judgment on the verdict, a day was given till the octave of Michaelmas[1].

Bartholomew Guyhaldy, merchant of Chomba in Lombardy, acting on behalf of Paul Remond, merchant of the same, testified that, whereas John Lawney, grocer, was bound by three writings to pay £40 to the said Paul, it was now agreed that John Lawney and his wife, Margaret, should be bound to pay that sum to Paul Remond and Gabriel Remond, merchants of Combe, in three separate portions on the Feast of All Hallows 1417, 1418 and 1419, as evidenced by three writings obligatory of even date. Membr. 4 *b* *24 Oct. 1416*

John de S[t] Cyres (*Ciryco*), dwelling in Bordeaux, brought before the mayor and aldermen letters of attorney from John de Feulias, merchant of Bordeaux, dated 27 April 1416, under the seal of the said John and the seal of the provostship of the *umbraria*[2] of Bordeaux, by virtue of which he acknowledged *26 Sept. 1416*

[1] The account of this action given in Letter Book I, fos. 194 b–195 b (*Cal. of Letter Book I*, p. 180; translated in H. T. Riley's *Memorials of London*, pp. 630–4), differs in several important particulars. The defendant is said to be mainprised, and his mainpernors were called upon to forfeit their recognisances, on his making default, but were afterwards pardoned. The court is represented as giving judgment of the pillory on the same day as the verdict.

The version of the trial in our roll, since it was set down as a precedent, is probably more correct. The distinction here drawn between bail and mainprise is noted by Blackstone, *Commentaries*, III, p. 122, n. e, "bail are only sureties that the parties be answerable for the special matter for which they stipulate; mainpernors are bound to produce him to answer all charges whatsoever." The *New English Dictionary* calls this an "alleged distinction," and legal writers either identify bail and mainprise, or say that any difference there may have been between them was soon lost sight of and the two forms of surety became confused into one. The present case, in which a man was bailed to answer a charge of slander, while a subsequent charge of intimidation was quashed, because he had not been mainprised to answer any or every charge that might be made against him, proves the correctness of Blackstone's definition.

[2] L'Ombrière. For district, castle and prévôt's jurisdiction see *Archives Municipales de Bordeaux*, i, pp. 360–4; Drouyn, *ibid.* p. 332.

receipt of 80 marks, in part payment of 105 marks, due on a bond from John Blwmel, merchant, payment having been made on the latter's behalf by Thomas Welton, mercer.

Return to a writ directed to the mayor, who reported that Thomas Kebbel had been sued separately by Edward Chestreton, John Barndusley and John Langley, senior, for detinue of a sealed box of muniments belonging to them, and in his defence he had pleaded that he had received the box from a certain William Chestreton as a pledge for the payment of 31s due to him. He had produced the box in court and was willing to surrender it to such of the plaintiffs as the court should direct, on payment of the debt. This box the mayor promised to bring before the king as the writ required.

Membr. 5 *18 March 1416* Reciprocal bonds of Philip Carpenter, William Aldewyncle, Peter Ross and William Germyn, brewers, and Thomas Mercer, haberdasher, on the one part, and John Biernes, goldsmith, on the other, in £20, to abide by the award of William Erynton, mercer, and Thomas Barwe, vintner, in disputes between the said Philip and John.

19 March 1416 Reciprocal bonds of John Cheyne, goldsmith, and John Tolington, currier, in £20, to abide by the award of Walter Cotton and Thomas Aleyn, aldermen, in disputes between them.

Membr. 5 *b* *21 March 1416* Writ of *corpus cum causa* to the mayor, aldermen and sheriffs to bring Peter Halle, esquire, into Chancery with the cause of his taking and detaining. Dated at Westminster, 21 March 1416.

Return that Peter Halle had been taken and detained at the suit of Thomas Chitterne and Margaret his wife by virtue of a plaint levied before Alan Everard, sheriff, and removed before the mayor and aldermen in the Chamber of Guildhall, which plaint was still undetermined. Nevertheless he would be brought into Chancery as required.

7 Feb. 1416 Reciprocal bonds of Robert Widyngton, grocer, and John Middilton, mercer, in £100 to abide by the award of Richard Style and William Flete, fishmongers, and John Watle and Martin Kelhome, mercers, in disputes between them.

John Welles, Thomas Knolles, Robert Chichely, William *14 Feb. 1416*
Sevenoke, William Burton and William Olyver, grocers, and John Shawe, vintner, acknowledged a debt of £764 0s 10½d payable to John Hille, chamberlain, to the use of the children of Henry Halton, late citizen and grocer.

Bond of Thomas Knolles and Robert Chichele, grocers, Membr. 6
and Thomas Beaumond and William Edward, salters, in £100 *14 May 1416*
to Robert Colbrook, ironmonger, to pay the latter or his widow the sum of £100 on condition that the said Robert, who by consent of the mayor and aldermen and of Thomas Beaumond, William Edward and other executors of the will of Richard Wodecok, salter, had married the latter's daughter Joan, an orphan of the city, should expend £100 on the purchase of an estate for the benefit of himself and his wife and their heirs, or, failing heirs between them, to his own heirs. Cancelled.

Writ of error to the mayor, aldermen and sheriffs, de- *12 April 1416*
manding that the record of an action of trespass, brought by Ralph Gresvale, ironmonger, against John Strecche, chandler, before Thomas Aleyn, sheriff, and subsequently removed before the mayor and aldermen in the Chamber of Guildhall, be produced at St Martin le Grand before William Hankeford, Robert Hill, William Ludyngton, William Cheyne and Roger Horton, the king's justices assigned for the purpose. Dated at Westminster, 12 April 1416.

Precept of the justices, dated 6 May 1416, to the same effect.

Lease from Robert Chichelegh and Thomas Aleyn, alder- Membr. 6 *b*
men, Thomas Rolf of co. Essex and Robert Fitz Robert, *10 April 1416*
junior, to Robert Mounpisson, esquire, and John Mounpisson, clerk, of lands, tenements, rents and services which they had of the grant of John Petche in the parishes of St Michael Cornhill and also of certain lands and tenements of the same in the parish of St Mary Wolnoth in the tenure of Lubricus Baker, Sampson Benet, tailor, William Coupere, Walter Hydyman, shearman, and John Ster, for a term of five years on payment of £160. Witnesses, John Whitwell, John Wyn, Simon Copschef, William Fitz Hugh, Salamon Oxneye, Philip Bernard and others. Dated 10 April 1416.

Membr. 7
5 March 1416
In an action by Paul Miliane, merchant of Lucca, against John Eton, mercer, for a debt of £158, a foreign attachment in the plaintiff's hands was delivered to him under pledge to answer therefor etc., the attachment being valued by oath of Thomas Seccheford and Roger Ameregy, mercers, and Thomas Colshill, woolpacker, in the presence of Thomas Est, one of the serjeants-at-mace of the mayor, as follows:

One cloth of velvet figured and brocaded (*figurati et brochati*) with gold on a red field, containing 21½ yds. at 30s the yd.; one cloth of satin velveted (*velvettati*) and brocaded with gold on a red field, containing 23½ yds. at 25s the yd.; one cloth of satin velveted and to a certain small extent (*aliquantulum sed minime*) brocaded with gold on a *blue* field, containing 26 yds. at 16s 8d the yd.; one cloth of satin velveted on a blue field containing 24 yds. at 13s 4d. the yd.; 30 pieces of *tartarin*[1] of divers colours at 22s each; one sarpler of *Cotesewold* wool, containing 2 sacks and a quarter, at 8½ marks the sack; sum total £145 9d.

In actions by Paul Miliany, merchant of Lucca, for a debt of £18 18s, David Galganetti of Lucca for a debt of £40 and Roger Ameregi, mercer, for a debt of 32s against Nicholas de Molino, merchant of Venice, a foreign attachment was delivered to the plaintiffs under pledge etc., being valued by oath of William Lythirpole and William Couper, goldsmiths, and Henry Lardiner and John Spencer, upholders, in the presence of John Upton, one of the serjeants-at-mace of the mayor, as follows:

One piece of silvergilt with the arms of France in the middle, weighing 2 lbs., £3; 12 spoons weighing 8⅜ oz., 20s 10½d; one gold chain with an *agnus dei*[2] hanging from it, ornamented with pearls, weighing 32½ dwt., 35s 2d; one *coler* of thread of gold with a necklace hanging from it, with 5 pearls, one *balys* and one sapphire, weighing 27 dwt., 36s; one ring with a diamond set in it, ornamented with roses in white enamel[3], 26s 8d; one other ring with a diamond, garnished

[1] *N.E.D.* "A rich stuff, apparently of silk, imported from the east, probably from China through Tartary."

[2] A representation of Jesus, the Lamb of God.

[3] *I anulus cum I diamand impresso ornatus cum rosis albis enamelitis.*

with daisies, 20s; 2 rings with 2 sapphires, to wit, one engraved as a signet and the other cut[1] (*uno sculpto in signeto et alio de entaile*), £3; 2 rings with 2 *bales* set in them, 10s each; one plain (*planus*) ring with a sapphire, 6s 8d; 3 rings, one with a sapphire and *emeraud*, another with a *baleys*, and the third with a heart carved in it as though in a box, weighing 12½ dwt., 12s 6d; 3 *filetts* containing 255 pearls, 21s 3d; one pair of beads (*precum*) of coral with a *knoppe* of pearl, *gauded* with *paternostres* silvergilt[2], 13s 4d; 2 girdles of green silk harnessed lightly with silver gilt, weighing altogether, silk and silvergilt, 12½ oz., 46s 8d; one woman's gown (*toga*) of scarlet furred with *grey fyn*[3], £5; one man's gown of scarlet furred with *grey cristey*[4] and having open sleeves furred with *fyn gray*, £5; one woman's gown of *murrey* heavily furred with *grey cristy*, 5 marks; one man's gown of scarlet furred with *calabre*[5], price 4 marks; one *pane* of scarlet for a bed furred with *grey*, 33s 4d. Sum total, £36 13s 9½d.

In an action by Bonaverus of Bologna (*Bononia Crassa*), merchant, against Peter Alfons, merchant of Portugal, for a debt of £13 10s, a foreign attachment in the hands of Gerard Danidze was delivered to the plaintiff under pledge of Arnold Guilham, vintner, to answer therefor etc., the attachment having been valued by oath of John Melcheborn and Henry Lardenere, upholders, as follows: Membr. 7 *b* *20 March 1416*

One *potelpott*, 2 quart pots, one pint pot and one half-pint pot of pewter, 2s; one image called "*pyte*"[6] of alabaster, 12d; one pair of *trussyngcofres*[7], 3s; one *tabler* with the *meigne*[8], 12d; 2 candlesticks (*candelabra*) of *laton*, 16d; one small girdle of

[1] Apparently one was a flat stone with a device sunk in it, and the other cut in facets.

[2] The rosary consisted of 165 beads, in 15 sets of 11 beads, of which 10 were small for *aves*, and the eleventh was large and ornamented, being called a "gaud," to represent *paternosters* and *glorias*.

[3] Fine grey squirrel.

[4] *Sc.* cristigrey. See above, p. 4, n. 9.

[5] The Calabrian squirrel, a much darker animal than the north European squirrel. See John Hodgkin, *Notes and Queries*, 11 S., v, March 2, 1912, p. 171; Riley's *Memorials*, p. 329.

[6] Our Lady of Pity, the Virgin with the dead body of Jesus on her lap.

[7] According to *N.E.D.* a box adapted for being trussed or packed up for travelling.

[8] A chess or backgammon board with a set of men.

purple colour, 20d; one blanket, 12d; one dagger blade, 4d; one green *crouper* for horses, 2d; 9 ells of canvas, 3s; one old *corde*, 4d; one large wallet (*mantica*), 6s 8d; 1½ ells of canvas, 6d; one *coverlyt*, one *testour*, one *cilour* and 3 curtains, and 2 *costers* of new worsted paled in red and green, whereof one *coster* contained 6 yds. and the other 11 yds., 40s; one black gown of *lire*[1] furred with *ficheux*[2], 33s 4d; 2 hoods (*capic'*) party of *sangweyn* and black, 10s; one remnant of *russet*, 12d; one old doublet (1 *vet.*? *de ploid*), 2s; one pair of black hose (*caligarum*) and two pairs of white, 4s; one sheet (*linthiamen*), 12d. Sum total, £5 13s 4d.

24 Sept. 1416 Bond of John Goodhugh, *alias* Cantyng, to John Hille, chamberlain of the city, in £40, that he would not, without the consent of the mayor and aldermen and of John Bydeford, scrivener, his co-feoffee, sell or alienate certain lands and tenements in the parish of All Hallows the Great, formerly belonging to Sir John Cosyn, clerk, deceased, in which lands he had been enfeoffed by John Syward, Walter Pope and others.

25 Oct. 1416 Whereas John Mercer, scrivener, John Piry, John Dyer and Richard Davy were bound to John Pontadour, merchant of Lucca, in £10, and the latter by a general release of 25 Oct. 1416, which was written by John Wanstall, citizen and the famous scribe and scrivener (*scribam et scriptorem*) of the city, acquitted John Mercer of the debt, and although by the law of the land such an acquittance is valid for all, although only made to one obligor, nevertheless, since all could not produce the one acquittance whenever necessary, the said John Pyry, John Dyer and Richard Davy prayed that the said John Pontadour should be summoned before the mayor and aldermen to acknowledge his release, which he did the same day[3].

[1] See above, p. 3, n. 2. [2] Polecat.
[3] Thus securing its enrolment in a court of record.

ROLL A 46

Rolls of memoranda of the time of Henry Barton, mayor, A^o 4 Henry V

Writ of *corpus cum causa* to bring Peter Rekes into Chancery Membr. 1
with the cause of his taking and detaining, and return that the *28 Oct. 1416*
said Peter Rekes, shearman, had been detained at the suit of John Parys, shearman, in a plea of trespass levied before Alan Everard, late sheriff; nevertheless the said Peter would be brought into Chancery as required.

Writ that, whereas the king by writ gave precept to the *26 Oct. 1416*
sheriffs of London that, allowing four Hustings at which John Ekelyngton, parson of the church of St Mary by Southampton, was exacted and did not appear, as reported by the sheriffs to the king's justices, they cause the said John to be further exacted at the next Husting, from Husting to Husting, until he be outlawed, according to the law and custom of the realm, if he did not appear, or if he did appear, that they take him and keep him in safe custody so that they might have his body before the king's justices at Westminster at the quindene of St Michael to answer Richard Eston, citizen and draper, in a plea of debt of £100, and the said sheriffs informed the justices on that day that, the four said Hustings having been allowed, the said Henry (*sic*) was exacted for a fifth time at the Husting of Pleas of Land on Monday the feast of St Margaret, and not appearing was outlawed, and whereas evidence was given on behalf of the plaintiff in the king's court that the defendant had been outlawed, the king requires that the record of the outlawry be brought before the king's justices at Westminster on Friday after the Feast of St Martin, that the king might proceed further in the matter. Witness R. Norton at Westminster 26 Oct. 1416.

Return of the mayor that there was no record of the outlawry of "Henry" Ekelyngton, but of a certain John Ekelyngton, which record was annexed to the writ as follows:

"On this day John Ekelyngton, by virtue of a writ concerning the allowance of four Hustings[1] and ordering that the said John be further exacted, was exacted and did not appear and was therefore outlawed."

3 Nov. 1416 William Phippe, son of Stephen Phippe, late citizen and currier, who had been apprenticed for a term of fifteen years to John Russel, formerly citizen and woolman, was exonerated from his apprenticeship, because his master had been discharged from the freedom and had left the city, without turning him over to any other master. [*Latin and French*]

Membr. 1 *b*
10 Nov. 1416 Writ to the justices of Gaol Delivery of Newgate demanding that the indictment for divers felonies, whereof William Clifford, *courtman*, son of William Broke of Clifford co. Hereford, was indicted before John Michell and Thomas Aleyn, late sheriffs, and Richard Alfeld, coroner, which indictment was delivered by them to the justices of Gaol Delivery, be sent before the king (*coram rege*) in order that it might be terminated there and that the king might proceed further in the delivery of the said William, who was detained in the Marshalsea prison. Witness W. Hankeford at Westminster, 10 Nov. 1416.

The above-mentioned indictment, as follows:—Inquest taken on Saturday after the feast of S[t] Valentine A[o] 2 Henry V (1415) before the sheriffs and coroner to inquire as to divers robberies, felonies and other misprisions against the crown and dignity of the king in the city of London by oath of John Balby, Thomas Burgh, Matthew Carter, Nicholas atte Wode, Thomas Stapulton, Luke Leyndre, John Talp, Richard Bailly, William Wykes, John Swetenham, William Mymmes and Richard Barre, good and lawful men of the city, who say on their oath that William Clifford, *courtman*, son of William Broke of Clifford co. Hereford, on Saturday 5 Jan. in the parish of S[t] Mary Magdalen in the ward of Queenhithe feloniously broke and entered the house of John Colles, clerk,

[1] On outlawry in the city of London see *Cal. of Select Pleas and Memoranda*, p. 6, n. 2; *Liber Albus* (R.S.), 1, p. 190. The writ "concerning allowance" was the writ *exigi facias de novo*, see *Registrum Omnium Brevium*, 1634, p. 61.

and then and there feloniously stole one book called "*porthas*"[1], of the value of 26s 8d, one gown of green furred with *bises*[2], of the value of 33s 4d, one *paxbrede*[3] of silver of the value of 13s 4d and other goods and chattels to the value of 10 marks of the said John Colles. In witness whereof the aforesaid jurors to this inquest have set their seals. Dated as above.

On this day came Richard Glover of Abyndon with authentic letters under the seal of the mayoralty of Oxford testifying that his apprentice William Stanes, son of John Stanes of Shryvenham, co. Oxon, had left his service without permission and gone to London, and praying the mayor and aldermen to aid in the restitution of his apprentice in such wise that they of Oxford might henceforth be bound to accede to similar requests from London. He also produced indentures of apprenticeship showing that William Stanes had been apprenticed to him for twelve years to learn the art of a glover, and begged them to send for the said William, who was now living with John Farnburgh, citizen of London, and Juliana his wife in the art of a *breuster*. *10 Sept. 1416*

John Farnburgh appeared on summons, bringing the apprentice with him, and said that the latter had been apprenticed to him for seven years, and that he himself knew nothing of any previous apprenticeship. Thereupon the court, after taking counsel, decreed that the said Richard should have his apprentice back and that the apprentice should be quit as regards John Farnburgh and his wife, notwithstanding the indentures between them.

Membr. 2
8 Jan. 1417

The mayor and aldermen were informed by William Tikhyll, saddler, and other credible persons that a certain "foreign" woman called Thomasina March, widow, of Dorneye, co. Bucks, without the knowledge or consent of the said William had apprenticed his daughter Agnes on Christmas Day 1410 to a certain William Celler, citizen and wire-drawer, for a term of fourteen years, and that afterwards

[1] *Sc. portas*, a portable breviary.

[2] The back of the squirrel in winter, of a brown or brownish grey colour. Liber Horn, fo. 249, "*gris et bis est le dos en yver desquirel.*"

[3] A tablet with a representation of the Crucifixion or other sacred subject, used as an osculatory.

William Celler had left the city, dismissing the girl with an insufficient knowledge of the trade, and that the said William had not enrolled her at Guildhall within a year and a day or at any time afterwards. He prayed that the girl, who was then in the custody of Joan, wife of William Celler, might be exonerated from her apprenticeship and given back to him.

The girl's mistress brought her to court on 11 Jan. and asked for time to answer. Next day she admitted that Thomasina March was "extraneous" to the said Agnes and that the latter was under age and had not been enrolled, but said that the girl had afterwards on Christmas day 1416 been apprenticed to her husband and herself to learn the art of a *cardemaker*[1].

Thereupon Joan and Agnes were separately examined at the request of the parties, when it was found that the indentures were made after the girl's last appearance in court and that the girl was still under age, and the girl herself declared that she had sealed the indentures under threats of a beating and that she would rather go back to her father. It was adjudged that she be exonerated from her indentures.

30 Jan. 1417 Writ of *certiorari* to Henry Barton, mayor, demanding the record and process on an indictment, whereof Edmund atte Chapell, bailiff of Fynesbury, was convicted before the mayor and his fellows, justices of Gaol Delivery of Newgate. Witness W. Hankeford at Westminster, 30 Jan. 1417.

Return of Henry Barton, mayor, as follows: Edmund atte Chapell of Fynesbury in the parish of St Giles without Cripplegate, bailiff, being taken for that he with other persons, unknown and not yet taken, on Tuesday 29 Dec. 1416 in the said parish feloniously robbed a certain John Stowe of Norwich of a white horse, price 6s 8d; 2 bolts of red worsted and 2 bolts of white worsted, price 20s; one knife harnessed with silver, price 16d; one fur of black lambswool, price 5s; and other goods and chattels to the value of 40s, and for that he is a common and notorious thief, whereof he is indicted before John Coventre and Robert Widyngton, sheriffs of London,

[1] A maker of cards for carding or teazling wool or cloth.

and Richard Alfeld, the king's coroner in the said city, now comes before the justices here, being brought by the sheriffs, and having seen the indictment, is asked how he will acquit himself of the felony aforesaid; he says that in nothing is he guilty thereof, and thereon for good and ill puts himself on the country. Therefore it is commanded to the sheriffs that they cause to come before the justices here on Saturday 30 Jan. then next etc., twenty-four as well citizens as other good and lawful men of the venue of the parish aforesaid etc., and who etc., to find etc. And meanwhile the said Edmund is remitted to prison in the custody of Robert Widyngton and John Coventre, sheriffs, etc. to be safely guarded etc. until etc. Afterwards, to wit, on Saturday 30 Jan. aforesaid before the aforesaid Henry Barton and his fellows, justices etc. assigned to deliver the aforesaid gaol etc. comes the aforesaid Edmund, being brought by the sheriff etc., and likewise come a jury of the venue aforesaid, who being chosen, tried and sworn, say upon their oath that the aforesaid Edmund is guilty of the felony aforesaid. Therefore it is considered that he be hanged. Chattels, lands and tenements of the said Edmund, none.

Quitclaim from John Kemp of Henley-on-Thames and Henry Kemp, his son, to Nicholas Wotton, woolman. *20 Feb. 1417*

Recognisance of John Botiller, mercer, Henry Rede, armourer, John Wyot, draper, and William Turnell, waxchandler, in £250 to John Hill, chamberlain. *26 Feb. 1417*

Recognisance of Eborard Flete, mercer, William Foucher, Thomas Tykhill and John Admond, mercers, in £250 to John Hill, chamberlain.

Acquittance from Thomas Chippenham, mercer, and his wife Idonea, widow of Richard Herry, mercer, to John Wellys, Richard Osbarn and Robert Large, executors of Richard Herry, for £300, that sum being received in full satisfaction of her legacy, her widow's right to a third part of all her late husband's movable goods, and a legacy of £10 to Thomas Chippenham. Membr. 2 *b* *26 Feb. 1417*

15 March 1417 Bond of John Parker, Richard Hatfeld and Thomas Ermelyn, cutlers, and Richard Snodenham, barber, to John Purchase, clerk, master or warden of the new college of minor canons of St Paul's church, and the minor canons of the same, that Nicholas Ryngwode, bladesmith, would vacate a house belonging to the minor canons in Dyser Lane[1], pay arrears of rent, and deliver to them a general release, sealed by himself and his wife Emma, which was then in the Chamber of the Guildhall as *in equa manu*.

11 March 1417 John Pelham, knight, by his attorney William Hamond, brought an original bill against Peter Mavan, esquire, and John London, clerk, executors of the will of Edward[2], duke of York, for a debt of £63 8s 6d, the balance due for services rendered to the duke, as agreed in an account made between the plaintiff and the duke on 1 Aug. 1415 in the parish of St Martin Pomers, London.

The defendants, who were attached by a gold cross, by way of foreign attachment, made four defaults, whereupon the cross was delivered to the plaintiff, who paid into the Chamber £10 9s 4d, the amount by which its value exceeded his claim, under pledge of Henry Lisurs and William Russe, drapers, to answer for the cross if the defendants appeared within a year and a day etc. The cross, which had a foot of silvergilt weighing 9 oz. 7½ dwt. troy, and was of gold, set with a ruby, 4 *baleis*, 6 pearls and a large sapphire, having on it a gold crucifix[3], the whole weighing 19 oz. troy, was valued by oath of John Palyng and Salamon Oxneye, goldsmiths, at £73 16s.

Note that the court was exonerated of the sum of £10 9s, as entered in the rolls of memoranda of William Sevenok, mayor, A° 6 Henry V.

Membr. 3 *9 Feb. 1417* John Sadiller, vintner, complained to the mayor that Henry Pountfreit had come to his house the same day with a large

[1] Otherwise called "the Rydye." See *Cal. of Select Pleas and Memoranda*, 1381–1412, pp. 79, n. 3; 311, n. 1.

[2] This was Edward, earl of Rutland, and for a period of two years duke of Aumarle, son of Edmund of Langley, fifth son of Edward III. He succeeded his father as duke of York in 1402 and was slain at Agincourt.

[3] Cross and crucifix are distinguished, the latter being the image of the crucified Christ.

crowd of armed men, while the complainant was elsewhere in the city on business, and had expelled his servants, the members of his household and his wife Alice, who was with child, so roughly and violently that her life was despaired of, and had also wasted and scattered his goods, in contempt of the king and contrary to divers statutes and to the custom of the city. The house, he informed the mayor, was held by him on an eight years' lease from John Findern, esquire, and John Lever, saddler, who had acquired it from the said Henry Pountfreit by a feoffment of 10 July 1411 and a release of 2 Dec. 1411, which were enrolled in the Husting. He himself had been in occupation for four years and had duly paid his rent and carried out the necessary repairs. He begged the mayor to afford him a remedy.

The mayor immediately sent for Henry Pountfreit and the constables, officers and more substantial people dwelling near the house, who were present when the trespass took place, and examined them. And as it was manifestly clear that Henry Pountfreit had come with a crowd and riotously entered the house, he ordered, with the consent of the said Henry, that the complainant, his wife, family and goods should be put back for the rest of the day and night and that both parties should come next day, with their counsel, before himself and the aldermen in the Chamber to do and receive what the court should adjudge[1].

The parties appeared and after the complainant's story had been recited, Henry Pountfreit was asked if he had anything to say why the complainant should not have the house in ac-

[1] The mayor could justify his action by two recent statutes, 5 Ric. II, Stat. 1, c. 7; 15 Ric. II, c. 2, the latter of which empowered a justice of the peace on complaint to go to the place and arrest the person who had made forcible entry. But city custom already gave him power to act. In those rules of the first part of the 14th century (see *Ricart's Kalendar* (Camd. Soc.), p. xx) preserved in the Liber Albus it is laid down *qe homme ne peut my entrer en nulle tenementz deinz la dite citee par force ne nulle tenement tener a force et armes ou destourbaunce de la pees. Mas si tiel entre soit fait par force adouncqes soit tiel force oustee*, *Munim. Gild. Lond.* (R.S.), I, pp. 196–7. In the common law courts the complainant might have sued a writ of *quare ejecit*, but this would only have protected him against his lessor, or later against one to whom the lessor had sold the land. If he had brought an action of *ejectio firmae*, he could only have recovered damages. Holdsworth, *Hist. Eng. Law*, III, p. 214. In the city he obtained immediate reinstatement pending the trial of the action.

cordance with his lease. The said Henry, though he had his counsel with him, had nothing to say on this point, but maintained that the house was his own[1] and asked to be reinstated and that the complainant should be at liberty to sue him if he wished. But the mayor and aldermen, seeing that he did not dispute the lease but only made a request which was contrary to justice and law, and because forcible entries of this kind would be an injustice to the public, since the portals of the law were wide open to all who needed it, adjudged that the complainant should regain possession as fully as he had it before he was expelled. As regards judgment on the contempt and trespass committed, the court wished further advice, and gave the parties a day on the quindene of Easter. Thereupon Henry Pountfreit asked permission to sue the complainant for 10 marks rent in arrears and for £80 penalty for not paying the rent, removing timber and not carrying out repairs in accordance with the terms of the lease. The complainant replied that he had always been ready to pay the rent, and he deposited the money in court, to be paid out if Henry Pountfreit would give him an acquittance. At the same time he said that the said Henry owed him 5 nobles for wine supplied and he asked that this amount should be deducted from the rent. He was willing to abide by Henry Pountfreit's oath as to whether the latter owed the 5 nobles or not. Henry Pountfreit swore that he did not owe that money, and the court gave judgment for him on that point. He was then asked if he would receive the 10 marks rent and was allowed to withdraw to one side to discuss the matter with his counsel, after which he came back and accepted the money and gave the complainant an acquittance for it, admitting that the latter had always been willing to pay it.

Afterwards on 2 April the complainant again came into court and said that Henry Pountfreit was suing him for nonpayment of the rent, in spite of the previous proceedings. Whereupon the mayor had the record and bill produced and read, and gave judgment that the said Henry take nothing by his bill, but be in mercy.

[1] By reconveyance of Findern and Lever in 1412. Hust. Roll 140 (18).

Recognisance of William Holcroft, goldsmith, to John Hill, chamberlain, in £100 to keep the peace with John Brykelesworth, apprentice of John Gedney, with similar recognisance of John Pake, Thomas Harwode, John Hille, senior, pinner, and John Vincent in £40 on behalf of the said William. Membr. 3 *b* *20 May 1417*

Memorandum that whereas Gilbert Beauchamp—who had married Katherine, daughter of Nicholas Aghton, late stockfishmonger, with the consent of the mayor and aldermen and the executors of the said Nicholas—had demanded the sum of £100, the residue of a legacy of £200 due to his wife, now deceased, the executors Robert Hurlebat and Robert Page came into the Chamber of Guildhall before the mayor and aldermen and said that they had taken the advice of persons versed in either law[1], who told them that they were not bound by law to pay the said Gilbert any portion of the £100 but that they ought to divide it among the other children of the testator, wherefore they begged the mayor and aldermen, who were guardians of orphans and minors (*pupillorum*) by reason of their office and the custom of the city, to supervise the distribution of the legacy and to save the executors harmless as against the other children of the executors. *5 March 1417*

Thereupon the mayor and aldermen, having communicated with counsel and having seen the will, took into consideration on the one hand that Gilbert ought by law to have received the £200 devised to his wife immediately on the solemnisation of the marriage with her, though he only received £100, and on the other hand, that if Gilbert had died without issue and Katherine had survived him, she would have received to herself and her right heirs certain lands and tenements of the inheritance of the said Gilbert in Horsedoun near London of the annual value of 5 marks. Accordingly they adjudicated that the executors should pay him the £100 in arrears at once or find sufficient security for payment agreeable to both parties. And upon this William Cauntbrigge, grocer, on behalf of the executors, entered into a recognisance to pay the money in four quarterly payments.

[1] *Utriusque legis periti, i.e.* civil and canon law.

Note that on 31 Dec. 1426 this recognisance was cancelled and Gilbert Beauchamp acknowledged payment.

1 April 1417 Thomas Crescy, mercer, Richard Crescy, esquire, and William Pirton, rector of Aynesbury co. Hunts, came before Henry Barton, mayor, and entered into mainprise, body for body, that they would be ready, *quo et quando*, to produce John, seigneur de Mary, John Racenet and John de Barse, who were then in the house and company of the said Thomas Crescy.

Writ of protection in favour of John Ratcliff who was then about to cross the sea with the king in the company of Thomas, duke of Clarence. Dated at Westminster, 21 May 1417.

Membr. 4
2 April 1417 Gift of goods and chattels from Thomas Senycle, goldsmith, to Thomas Harwod and Thomas Chacombe, citizens, and John Stodesbury, chaplain. Dated at London 24 June 1416.

3 April 1417 Assignment by William Wode, citizen of London, and Cristina his wife, widow of Richard Shote, cordwainer, and executrix of his will, to Nicholas Clerk, cordwainer, of all their interest in a lease made to the testator and Nicholas Clerk by the executors of Robert Forster, saddler, of premises in the parish of S[t] Michael Basinggeshawe.

26 April 1417 Reciprocal quitclaims of Thomas Fauconer, mercer, and John Russell, woolpacker.

7 May 1417 Deed of Robert Langford, son and heir of William Langford, knight, of co. Berks, confirming and ratifying a lease for 20 years of premises in Wood Street, and of a corner-house in the occupation of John Shirlok, saddler, in the parish of S[t] Sepulchre without Newgate, made by Thomas Dru, esquire, co. Berks, to Robert Fenskales, tailor, and another lease for 8 years to the same of premises in Whitecrouchestrete, all of which properties had been acquired by the above Thomas Dru from Robert Langford. The latter agreed to keep the premises in sufficient repair and to pay all quit-rents except those owed to Thomas Dru by his tenant. Witnesses, John Pake, John Teukesbury, John Archesdale, John Staunton, Richard Rowdon. Dated 27 April 1417.

Bond of Edmund Arnold of Dartmouth to John Beterenden, draper, in £70 to free from arrest a ship belonging to the latter called "*le Thomas*" of London, which had been arrested in Bordeaux at his suit. Membr. 4 *b* *8 May 1417*

Bond of the same to Walter Gautron, draper, that he would take no legal proceedings against Richard Makenham of Bordeaux, who had stood pledge for Walter to answer when the ship was arrested.

Recognisance of Thomas Penne and John Olyve, grocers, executors of the will of John Howe, grocer, who was executor of Robert Salman, mercer, of a debt of 10 marks due to William Gobyon. *Cancelled.* *28 June 1417*

Recognisance of Thomas Dane and Robert Dreys, mercers, of a debt of 20 marks due to William Gobyon. *Cancelled.*

Deed of Robert Langford, esquire, of Benefeld in the forest of Wyndesore co. Berks, confirming and ratifying a lease for 62 years of a shop in Paternosterrewe in the parish of St Michael at Corn, bounded on the east by the church, a tenement of Richard Russell on the west, a tenement of the dean and chapter of the king's chapel of St Martin le Grand on the north and Paternosterrewe on the south, from Thomas Dru, esquire, co. Berks, to Richard Hercy, draper, which shop was then in the occupation of the said Richard Hercy and had been acquired by Thomas Dru from Robert Langford. The tenant undertook to perform all repairs and to construct a cellar with masonry walls and to place good timber joists above, fixed with nails on wall-plates, in order to support the floor of the shop[1], and further to build a story on top of the dwelling house over the shop, of good and sufficient timber, so that there should be two stories over the shop under one roof, and to surrender the whole on the termination of his lease. Membr. 5 *7 May 1417*

[1] *Cum gistys sufficientibus de mearemio & tabulis eisdem clavifixis pro area eiusdem shope habenda positis et edificatis.* The "table" was a solid piece of timber laid on the stone walls to support the joists, sometimes called a "corbel-table," and both in ancient and modern days known as a "wall-plate." See Letter Book G, fo. 45 b.

Membr. 5 *b*
27 June 1417 Writ of protection in favour of Roger Wotton, merchant, who was then about to cross the sea with the king in the company of Sir Walter Hungerford, knight. Dated at Tichefeld, 27 June 1417.

26 June 1417 Similar writ in favour of William Hertwell *alias* Hertewell, goldsmith, then about to cross the sea with the king in the company of Sir John Osbaldeston, knight. Dated at Tichefeld, 26 June 1417.

28 June 1417 Similar writ in favour of John Chereseye of Brokkysborn co. Herts, *alias* John Cherteseye of Bookesbourne, *alias* John Chertesee of Brokysbourn, then about to cross to France with the king. Dated at Tichefeld, 28 June 1417.

9 May 1417 Similar writ in favour of Walter Saltmershe, then about to cross the sea with the king in the company of Sir William Hodelstone. Dated at Westminster, 9 May 1417.

Membr. 6 Richard Chipenham, tailor, and William Neubolt, dyer, having submitted their differences to Reginald Bonyng, fuller, and Thomas Orwell, tailor, the latter made the following award:—

Whereas Richard complained of a pit (*dune pewe*)[1] standing at the door of William's house, in which he put hot cloth after it had been dyed, to the great nuisance of the said Richard, it was awarded that William put no more cloth therein until it was cold. And whereas there was an oven (*fourne*) within the tenement, it was awarded that Richard take it down (*prendre jus*) and that William make a pit in its place to put his hot dyed cloth in. As regards William's gutter leading the water from the dye-house to the Thames, he ought to have the advantage of it as before.

Whereas Richard had a tenant in an apartment (*mansion*) beyond the vat in the dye-house, who left because of the nuisance of the dyeing, it was awarded that William rent it at 16s 8d yearly for as long as he held the dye-house.

And since Richard was absent in Harflu, nothing was

[1] Possibly from *puteus*, since it was something *in* which cloth could be put. An alternative is a balcony, platform, from *podium*.

awarded about the defective stair to the Thames, of which William complained, and the latter was told to do the best he could till Richard returned. [*French*]

21 July 1417

In an action for a debt of £40 by John Prestempde, grocer, against William Caden, merchant of Lincoln, ten casks of woad in the hands of William Lynne, merchant, were arrested as a foreign attachment by the mayor's serjeant, William Upton.

Membr. 6 *b*
22 July 1417

Thomas Aillesby, son of the late John Aillesby, senior, of Lincoln, lately summoned to God[1], brought a bill complaining that though he had served an apprenticeship of nine years to John Thame, draper, well and faithfully, the latter refused to make him free of the city. [*French*]

The said John Thame, on being summoned, made four defaults and was reported to have left the city, nor did his wife and family appear to show cause why the apprentice should not be made free. Thereupon the masters of the mistery of Drapers were summoned to witness whether the complainant was fit to be made free of the mistery. On 29 July Robert Whityngham, Thomas Islam and their fellows, masters of the said mistery, appeared and gave evidence that, so far as they knew, the complainant had served his master well and was sufficiently practised and instructed in the art of a draper, and that they had several times communicated with the master, but had found him obstinate and unwilling to obey their counsel. Accordingly it was considered that the complainant be admitted to the freedom.

Membr. 7
12 July 1417

Robert Domenyk and Joan his wife bring a plaint of intrusion against William Graunger and Ellen his wife and John Curteys, cutler, touching their free tenement in the parish of St Mary Magdalene in Milk Street.

6 Sept. 1417

Thomas More, dean, and the chapter of St Paul's bring a plaint of intrusion against Henry, prior of St Mary Southwark, touching their free tenement in the parish of St Dunstan in Fleet Street.

[1] *Nadgairs a dieu comaunde.*

8 Sept. 1417 William Savage, son of John Savage of the island of Garnesey, brought a bill of complaint against John Prank, tailor, alleging that the latter had left the city and failed to instruct and provide for him [breaks off]. [*French*]

16 June 1417 Lodewicus Valeres, merchant, acknowledged receipt of a debt of £126 14s and 13s 4d damages which he had recovered in court against William Randolf, goldsmith.

Membr. 7 *b*
27 Sept. 1417 Roger Sutton, rector of S[t] Peter in Bradstrete, brings a plaint of intrusion against John Piry, carpenter, John Moubray, *steynour*, John Sandoune, carpenter, Richard Ace, carpenter, and Warin Ellesworth, *corsour*, touching his free tenement in the same parish.

Henry, prior of S[t] Mary Southwark, brings a plaint of intrusion against Thomas More, dean, and the chapter of S[t] Paul's, and William Stapulford, clerk, touching his free tenement in the parish of S[t] Mary Southwark.

27 Oct. 1417 Writ of *corpus cum causa* to bring Thomas Berton into Chancery with the cause of his taking and detaining. Witness John, duke of Bedford, *custos* of England. Dated at Westminster, 27 Oct. 1417.

Return of Henry Rede and John Gedney, sheriffs, that the said Thomas Berton had been sent with certain letters from John, duke of Bedford, to Henry Barton, mayor, which he delivered, and afterwards, falsely and fraudulently plotting to deceive the king's people and defraud them of their money, he had sent agents and other persons of his covin to divers persons of the city, telling them that the duke had ordered the mayor to arrest and take all those whose names the said Thomas would deliver to him, and to send them to the duke to be imprisoned in divers prisons in England, and that he would send their names also to the mayor and accuse them of treasons and other crimes, unless they paid him certain large sums of money; and since the said Thomas thus obtained sums of money from innocent and lawful men of the city, as he himself confessed to the mayor, he was questioned as to the fraud and deception practised by him, whereupon he asserted that the duke himself would support him in what he had done, to the great scandal of that most noble prince, and accordingly he was committed to prison to await what the law and custom of the city used in like cases should adjudge to him. Although on account of the shortness of the time, the sheriffs were not able at present to certify fully as to the fraud and deception of the said Thomas, of which the mayor and aldermen had more information, they would bring him into Chancery promptly as required.

As it was reported to the mayor and aldermen that Robert Marklee, in spite of a bond[1] for his good behaviour, had refused to obey William Kent, master of the mistery of Skinners, in a matter touching the government of the mistery, and had irreverently called him "false" and "ribald", thus setting a pernicious example to others in the lower grade of the mistery, the chamberlain of the city, John Hille, prayed that the said Robert be summoned to show cause why the bond should not be executed. *18 Nov. 1418*

The said Robert, being summoned by Thomas Donyngton, one of the serjeants of the Chamber, appeared on 19 Nov. and denied the accusation. A jury of the parish of St Stephen Walbrook, consisting of William Hynt and others on the panel, said that Robert Marklee had frequently been disobedient and rebellious and had called William Kent irreverent names[2]. Accordingly it was considered that the bond be executed and that £40 be levied on his goods and chattels. On 23 Nov. the serjeant reported that he had levied £40 from moneys of the said Robert in the hands of William Kent, one of the executors of Walter Romsey, skinner, which money William Kent brought into court.

[1] See above, p. 39.

[2] *Ipsum irreverenter vocitavit.*

ROLL A 47

Membr. 1 *Rolls of memoranda of the time of William Sevenok, mayor, A° 6 Henry V*

10 Feb. 1419 Grant from John Chaumbre, knight, of Lillyngstonlovell co. Oxford to Robert Trewelove, cordwainer, of a quitrent of 40s from two shops in Friday Street, bounded on the north by an inn called "*le Fesaunt on þe hope*," on the south by a house in the occupation of William Porter, saddler, and on the west by Friday Street, which two shops were leased by the grantor and Joan, his late wife, to William Langeford, armourer. Dated at London 17 Jan. 1419.

21 Feb. 1419 Acquittance from John Chaumbre, knight, to Thomas Stone and John Stone, *hostillers*, for the sum of £117 6s 8d being the total rent payable on a lease recently made to them for eleven years of an inn in Friday Street called "*le Lyon on þe hope*," together with a little shop on the north side of the inn door and another shop late in the tenure of William Porter, saddler. Dated at London 18 Feb. 1419.

15 Feb. 1419 The lease above referred to.

25 Oct. 1418 Writ of protection in favour of Menaldus Gelagar, vintner, who was then about to cross the sea in the company of Thomas, duke of Clarence. Witness, John, duke of Bedford, *custos* of England. Dated at Westminster, 25 Oct. 1418.

Membr. 1 *b* *13(?) March 1419* John Assheton, fishmonger, and Elizabeth Wilford, widow, pray for an assize of nuisance against Edmund Lacy, bishop of Hereford, touching their free tenement in the parish of St Mary.

28 March 1419 Quitclaim from Robert Howlyn, merchant, to Robert Archbold, mercer.

Gifts of goods and chattels: 4 March 1419, Thomas Eyr, draper, to John Pellyng, skinner, and John Waltham, *brasyer*; 28 April 1419, John Salman, *malemaker*[1], to John Usk; witnesses, John Penne, alderman, John Credy, Baldewyn Tittesbury.

[1] Maker of males or trunks.

Bond of John Girdeler of Southampton to Thomas Midlyngton, burgess of Southampton, that he and his son John would enfeoff the latter with lands and tenements in Southampton or else pay to him the sum of 49 marks at several terms. *10 March 1419*

Writ of protection in favour of Thomas Forster *alias* Forester, clerk, then about to cross the sea to Normandy in the company of the king's brother, Humphrey, duke of Gloucester. Witness, John, duke of Bedford, *custos* of England, at Westminster, 10 Feb. 1420. Membr. 2 *10 Feb. 1420*

Whereas William Andrye of London had sued the abbot of Ramseye in the Guildhall and had caused the abbot's rents in the city of London to be attached, in an action of debt of £36 1s 9d, which he claimed from the abbot because he, the said William, had entered into a bond for John Overe, monk of Ramseye, and for money lent to the latter, and whereas the plaintiff and John Kirkbi, the abbot's squire, had bound themselves under a penalty of £40 to accept the award of John Gedney, alderman and draper, and Roger Hunte, as to all differences between them, the arbitrators adjudged that the abbot be quit of the claim, because it was shown by a brother-monk and the counsel of the abbot, that he had no knowledge of any such bond or loan, that he derived no benefit from the transaction, and that John Overe at the time was not an official of the house but living in London without the abbot's leave, and they further adjudged that the said William, having impleaded the abbot against all right, reason and law, present to the abbot, on his next coming to London, a gift of six *fesauntes*, and cause this award to be enrolled at the Guildhall. [*French*] *29 May 1419*

Writ of *corpus cum causa*, demanding that Richard Clerk, grocer, be brought into Chancery with the cause of his taking and detaining. Witness John, duke of Bedford, *custos* of England, at Westminster, 29 June 1419. *29 June 1419*

Return of the mayor and sheriffs that the said Richard had been arrested in an action of debt of £200 at the suit of John Botiller, draper, in the compter of John Perneys, sheriff.

12 May 1419 Quitclaim from Thomas Yonge and John Fetyplace of Abyndon, co. Berks., executors of William Chambre of Abyndon, to Richard Merlawe, merchant of London.

4 July 1419 Writ to the mayor, ordering him to send before the king at Westminster, under his seal, the mainour[1] (*manuopus*) with which Thomas Fox of Northampton, a prisoner in the Marshalsea, had been taken. Witness W. Hankeford at Westminster, 4 July 1419.

22 July 1419 Memorandum that in the church of St Dunstan in the East, in the presence of William Chichele, alderman, permission was given by the mayor to William Fromond, draper, to sue at the common law Thomas London, taverner, *alias* fishmonger, and Stephen Payn, vintner, because the latter were generally dwelling outside the city. [*French*]

Membr. 2 *b*
23 July 1419 Writ of protection in favour of Alexander Takeswell, then about to cross the sea to Normandy in the company of the king. Witness John, duke of Bedford, at Westminster, 23 July 1419.

1 March 1418 In an action for debt of £200, due on an account made at Bruges, by Betinus Dacti, merchant of Lucca, against Nicholas Sandey, merchant of Lucca, a return was made by John Combe, serjeant-at-arms of the city, that the defendant was a foreigner, having no goods within the city whereby he might be attached. Thereupon the plaintiff's attorney, William Hamond, prayed that the defendant might be attached, by way of foreign attachment, by 17 white cloths of Westroue[2] and 23 ounces of gold of Damask[3], of the value of £173 17s 6d, belonging to the defendant, in the hands of Paul Miliany, merchant of Lucca.

Membr. 3
3 July 1419 Whereas Mark Guiduichony, merchant of Lucca, late of Bruges, transmitted to a certain Paul Meliani, merchant of Lucca, the sum of £28 arising from the sale of a *crayere*[4]

[1] The stolen goods found on a thief when he is captured.
[2] West Row, co. Suffolk?
[3] Gold fringe or cloth of gold of Damascus.
[4] A small trading vessel. In medieval lists one reads of ships or galleys, cogs and crayers in descending order.

called "*le Marie de Holond*," and afterwards a certain Aldebrond Guiduichony, brother of Mark, by the said Paul Meliani, his attorney, sued Nicholas Sandey, merchant of Lucca, for a debt of £88 before the mayor and aldermen, and the said Nicholas was attached, by way of foreign attachment, by the said £28 in Paul's hands, under the supposition that this sum (though sent by Mark Guiduichony) was the property of Nicholas, there came into court on 3 July 1419 a certain Francis Baratom, merchant of Lucca, who offered to prove according to the law merchant that this sum of £28 belonged to himself and not to Nicholas Sandey. He acknowledged that a proof of this kind did not lie by the custom of the city[1], and prayed that, as he was a foreign merchant and could not conveniently spare the time to bring a suit and await the delays required by the law, the mayor and aldermen would give him a speedy and opportune remedy by the law merchant. Although he had offered sufficient and lawful proof that the money belonged to himself, he was willing, in order to move the court, to abandon all claim to it or to the *crayere*, if Paul Miliany or any other lawful merchant acting on behalf of the said Aldebrond would swear that the money or the *crayere* had at any time belonged to Nicholas Sandey.

And because the said Paul was not able to offer any evidence and neither he nor any one was willing to take an oath in the matter, and because both parties were willing to accept the order of the court, it was considered that the said Francis receive the said sum of £28 as his own property. Thereupon the said Paul willingly paid and delivered the money to him.

[1] Where a foreign attachment of goods was made in a third person's hands, under the mistaken supposition that these goods were the property of the debtor, it was open to the real owner to come into court before the fourth default or before execution was granted, to prove his ownership and to show that neither the debtor nor anyone else had property in the goods to the value of fourpence. The method of proof was by a threefold oath, himself and two compurgators. *Cal. of Early Mayor's Court Rolls*, pp. xxxvi, 17, 68; *Munim. Gild. Lond.* (R.S.), I, pp. 208–9. On the other hand proof by the law merchant was generally by examination of the parties on oath, which would not lie in a case of foreign attachment. Baratom secured his remedy by challenging the plaintiff's attorney to a peremptory oath, a form of compurgation which was occasionally used in law merchant cases. See *Cal. of Select Pleas and Memoranda*, 1381–1412, pp. xxviii–xxix.

3 July 1419 Action of debt, Thomas Bernewell, fishmonger, against Margaret Morgon, for 20 marks due on a purchase of red wine [breaks off].

Membr. 3 *b* *3 July 1419* Writ of protection in favour of Adenarius..., burgess and merchant of Bordeaux. Witness the king at his town of Mantes, 3 July 1419.

31 Aug. 1419 John de Fynton, son of William de Fynton, turner, of Bishop's Lynn co. Norfolk, was exonerated from his apprenticeship to Nicholas Stacy, leatherseller, the latter having left the city and failed to instruct and provide for him.

[*Latin and French*]

23 March 1419 Recognisance of Henry Parker, vintner, of a debt of £60 due to William Crowmere, draper, to the use of William, son of Thomas Say, vintner, deceased, with remainder to Nicholas, brother of William Say. Cancelled on satisfaction.

Membr. 4 *20 Aug. 1419* Lease from Henry Pountfreit, saddler, and William Middelton, grocer, to John Aylesham, grocer, for 16 years at an annual rent of £17, of a tenement with wharf adjacent in the parish of St Botolph Billingsgate, which property they, together with John Beaumond, chandler, deceased, had acquired from John Philip, formerly rector of St Katherine Colman and then rector of St Margaret Bridge Street, John Luton, chaplain, Thomas Exton, goldsmith, and Thomas Lyncoln, fishmonger. The lessors covenant to repair damage done to the wharf by the Thames, and to keep the tenement wind- and weather-proof.

23 Sept. 1419 Gabriel Palestrellus, merchant, being empowered to sue for and receive the goods and merchandise of the merchants of Piacenza (*Plesantinenses*), which had been loaded in the ship of John Tolk of Dansk[1] at Seville in Spain and afterwards captured at sea by Lord de Carrew[2], admiral of England, entered into a bond of £100 to the said John Tolk to abide by the arbitration of Richard Merlawe and Robert Chichele, or

[1] Danzig.

[2] Sir Thomas Carew, "baron of Carrewe" (*Cal. Pat. Rolls*, Henry V, II, p. 56), but usually called "chivaler." See *D.N.B.* and Wylie and Waugh, *Henry V*, III, pp. 45, 63, 183.

failing agreement, of William Sevenok, grocer, as to differences between them.

Similar bond of Conrad de Albertis, merchant of Florence, buyer and receiver of the goods of Flanders merchants loaded in the same ship, to John Tolk.

Similar bond of John Tolk.

Marion Petro of Bristowe brought a bill against John Tapelegh, grocer, and Alice his wife, silkwoman, to whom she had been apprenticed for eight years, complaining that they had not enrolled her at Guildhall within the first year, in accordance with the recent ordinance of the mayor, aldermen and commons of the city. [*Latin and French*] Membr. 4 *b* *24 Aug. 1419*

Richard Colyn, son of Walter Colyn of Coltesworthy co. Devon, was exonerated from his apprenticeship to Thomas Podmore, ironmonger, because the latter had not enrolled him at Guildhall and had left the city. [*Latin and French*] Membr. 5 *20 Aug. 1419*

Award of Richard Merlawe and Robert Chichele as to differences between John Tolk, master of the ship called "*le seint Esprit*" of Dansk, lately captured at sea by Lord de Carrewe, admiral of England, on the one part, and Gabriel Palestrellus, acting for the merchants of Piacenza, and Conrad de Albertys, acting for the merchants of Flanders, on the other part. The arbitrators, having examined the master's claim for freight, and the merchants' claim for damage and loss to their goods occasioned by the alleged default and indiscreet seamanship of the master, and having allowed a competent sum for damage and loss, awarded that Gabriel and Conrad pay the said John Tolk the sum of £130. Membr. 5 *b*

ROLL A 48

[*Richard Whityngton, mayor*]

Membr. 1 *10 Aug. 1419* Writ of protection in favour of John Stannerne, *talawe-chaundeller*, then about to cross to Normandy in the company of the king's brother, Thomas, duke of Clarence. Witness, John, duke of Bedford, *custos* of England at Southampton, 10 Aug. 1419.

19 Oct. 1419 In an action for debt of £42 by John Broughton, plaintiff, against Katherine, widow of Thomas Spencer, a foreign attachment in the hands of the plaintiff was delivered to him under pledge of John Spore, *ferrour*[1], and Nicholas Birchelles, tailor, to answer therefor if the defendant etc. The goods were valued by oath of John Palyng and John Patteslee, goldsmiths, as follows:—

One gold *ouche* set with a *baleis*[2], 2 diamonds and five large pearls, £20; 125 large pearls, £8; two silver candlesticks parcel-gilt, weighing 5 lbs. 6¾ oz. at 31s the lb., £8 12s 5¼d; one silver bowl (*pelvis*) weighing 2 lbs. 6½ oz. at 30s the lb., £3 16s 3d; total £40 8s 8d.

12 Nov. 1419 Writ of *corpus cum causa* to bring John Assheton, fishmonger, into Chancery with the cause of his taking and detaining, and return that he had been detained by virtue of an action of debt of £15 at the suit of William Wryght, clerk, nevertheless he would be brought into Chancery as required.

22 Oct. 1419 Writ of protection in favour of John Frelond, vintner, then about to cross to France in the company of Thomas, duke of Clarence. Witness John, duke of Bedford, *custos* of England, at Westminster, 22 Oct. 1419.

4 Oct. 1419 Acquittance from Joan, younger daughter of Sir John Daubriggecourt, deceased, to John Brynnysley, parson of the church of Hoggesthorpe co. Lincs., and Thomas Willesdon, executors of her father's will, in respect of the legacy of an annuity of 100s. Dated at London, 1 Oct. 1419.

[1] Farrier. [2] A clasp, buckle or brooch set with a balas-ruby.

Lease for 10 years from William, son of Thomas Brampton, esquire, of co. Norfolk, to Thomas Bataill, mercer, of lands and tenements, with shops and houses built above them, in Fletestrete in the parish of St Bride, bounded on the east by a tenement called "*Hell*"[1], on the west by "*le Hors on þe hoope*," on the north by Fletestrete and on the south by London Wall, the lessee being responsible for quitrents of 10s to the hospital of St Giles without Holborn Bar, 2s to the prioress and convent of the Moniales of Kilbourne, 7s to the church of St Bride and 3s 9d to the free prison of Flete[2]. Membr. 1 *b* *28 Nov. 1419*

In an action for debt of £12 by Robert Chesterford against Hugh Maundeville and John Chesterford, a foreign attachment in the hands of the plaintiff was delivered to the plaintiff under pledge of Robert Arnold, grocer, and John Martyn, cordwainer, to answer therefor if the defendant etc. The attachment was valued by oath of Thomas Daunt and John Sedbergh, painters, as follows:— *29 Feb. 1420*

A tablet (*tabula*) to stand on an altar, carved and painted with pictures (*imaginibus*) of the Passion, Resurrection and Day of Judgment, £14[3].

Afterwards 5 May 1421, John Chestreford, one of the defendants, acknowledged receipt of 40s, the amount by which the value of the tablet exceeded the debt.

John Levere, saddler, by William Hamond, his attorney, brought an action for debt of £9 against Edward White, saddler, on the ground that he had acted as a pledge for the defendant and had paid that sum to Thomas Welton, and that the defendant had promised to save him harmless. William Wode, serjeant of the Chamber, having reported that the defendant had no goods in the city whereby he might be attached, the plaintiff prayed that the defendant be attached by divers of his goods in the plaintiff's hands. The defendant Membr. 2 *18 Jan. 1420*

[1] Still called "*le Hell*" in 1520, when it was conveyed by Walter Champion, draper, to John Harys and Thomas Cole, and described as being in the parish of St Martin in Bowyer Row, Husting Roll 238 (96). At this time Ludgate Hill was known as Fleet Street.

[2] *Libera prisona*. Cf. "*Francheprison*," *Cal. of Wills*, I, p. 621. The prison for freemen of the city.

[3] This appears to have been a framed altar-picture with side-panels.

failed to appear and the goods were delivered to the plaintiff under pledge of William Anlaf, grocer, and Walter Frenyngham, saddler, to answer therefor if the defendant etc., the goods being valued by oath of Robert Large and Thomas Austyn, mercers, and John Spencer, upholder, as follows:—

21½ ells of linen cloth called "*flemmyssh white*," at 7½d the ell, 13s 5¼d; 25½ ells of *spinal*[1], at 2½d the ell, 5s 3¾d; 2¾ ells of *flemmysh* at 9d the ell, 2s ¾d; 13½ ells of *braban*, at 4d the ell, 2s ½d (4s 6d?); 16 ells of *braban* at 6d the ell, 8s; 8¼ ells of white *flemmysh* at 6½d the ell, 4s 5¾d; 39 ells of *champeyn* at 7½d the ell, 24s 4½d; 8¾ ells of *bronneswyk* at 4½d the ell, 3s 3½d; one handtowel (*manutergium*) containing 6 yds., 18d; 4½ ells of *rawflemmysh*[2], at 7d the ell, 2s 7½d; 4¼ ells of *rawflemmysh* at 6d the ell, 2s 1½d; 6 sheets (*linthiamina*), 5s; 12¼ ells of *Irissh* at 2¼d the ell, 2s ¾d; 1¼ ells of *Flemmysh*, 7d; one old *canvas* and 2 *savenapes*[3], 4d; 2¾ lbs. of white thread of *Coleyn*[4] at 8d the lb., 22d; one quarter and a half of *brounthrede*, 2d; 8½ ells of *spinal* at 2d the ell; 3 *camis*?[5] of *flemmysh*, 3s; one of *weld*[6], 12d; one of *champeyn*, 12d; 2 of *rawflemmysh*, 20d; 3 others of the same, 2s 6d; 5 of *braban*, 4s 2d; 3 others, 15d; 4 of *flemmysh*, 2s; one other of large size, 10d; 3 others, 9d; 2 others, 10d; 2 of *rawflemmysh*, 14d; 32 of small size, 5s 4d; 9 pairs of drawers (*bracce*) of *flemmysh*, 2s 3d; 17 pairs of drawers of linen cloth, 2s 10d; 4 *coyfes*[7], 3d; 3 *colerkerchefs*, 6d; 5 *mokedours*[8], 2d; 2 *volupers*[9], 3d; 8 *haperons*, 16d; certain other remnants, 3d; one gown of shot colour furred with white lambswool[10], 4s; one gown of

[1] A fabric, probably of linen, like the weaves of Flanders, Brabant, Champagne and Brunswick here mentioned. It was used among other purposes for winding-sheets.

[2] Raw signifies unfulled or unbleached.

[3] A strip of material placed over a table-cloth to prevent its being soiled.

[4] Cologne.

[5] *Sc. camises*, chemises, shirts.

[6] Evidently a linen, but origin uncertain. Possibly a linen dyed with weld, a plant producing yellow dye-stuff.

[7] A close-fitting cap. Those worn by serjeants-at-law were originally of linen.

[8] See *N.E.D. sub* muckender, a handkerchief.

[9] A woman's headdress, a kerchief.

[10] *Una toga stragulata et furrata cum albo agnello. Stragulatus* is *diverso colore variatus*, probably with warp and weft of different colours.

musterdevilers[1] furred with *ruskyns*[2], 6s 8d; one gown of *blue* colour furred with *potes*[3] of *calabre*, 2s; one old kirtle of *medle*, 8d; one hood (*capuc'*) of *blue* colour, one purse and a pair of beads (*par precum*), 12d.

In an action for debt of £100 by John Bythewater, goldsmith, against John Cheyne, esquire, of Isnampstede Cheyne[4] co. Bucks, a foreign attachment in the hands of the plaintiff was delivered to him under pledge of Peter Brendwode, goldsmith, and Richard More and John Enderby, tailors, to answer therefor if the defendant etc. The goods were valued by oath of John Mabilton, Richard Spencer, Thomas Brynklee, John Sutton, senior, William Walton and William Botoner, goldsmiths, as follows:— *5 Feb. 1420*

2 silver bowls (*pelves*), 2 silver wash-bowls (*lavacra*), 3 flat (*plani*) silver cups, 12 silver platters (*perapsides*) and one covercle (*coopertorium*) of silvergilt, weighing 34 lbs. 11 oz. troy, at 29s 8d the lb., total £51 16s 2¼d; 2 gold cups with gold covercles, weighing 3 lbs. 11½ oz. troy at £12 the lb., total £47 10s; sum total £99 6s 2¼d.

Quitclaim from Constance Pountadour, widow, of London, to Paul Melyan, merchant of Lucca. Dated 5 May. *8 May 1420*

Writ of protection in favour of John Arnold, saddler, then about to cross to France in the company of John, duke of Bedford. Witness, Humphrey, duke of Gloucester, *custos* of England, at Westminster, 27 Feb. 1420. Membr. 2 *b* *27 Feb. 1420*

Confirmation by John Hertwelle, mercer, and Ellen his wife, daughter and heiress of Joan, widow of Robert Domenyk, mercer, of a 30 years' lease made by the said Joan to William Sampson, fishmonger, and Joan his wife, dated 6 March, of a shop and solar in Bryggestrete in the parish of St Magnus, late in the tenure of John Moordon, fishmonger, bounded on the north by the shop of Robert Rikedon, fishmonger, on the south by the shop late in the tenure of John More, brewer, *15 March 1420*

[1] Originally cloth of Montivillers. See p. 88 n. 3.

[2] *Cf.* Liber Horn, fo. 249, "*Roskyn est desquirel en este*," the squirrel's reddish summer coat.

[3] Meaning uncertain, possibly the paws of fur-bearing animals.

[4] The parish of Islehampsted-Cheyneys, near Amersham.

and now of William Child, fishmonger, on the east by Bridge Street and on the west by the tenement late in the tenure of Edmund Bys, dated 9 March 1420.

27 Feb. 1420 Writ of protection in favour of William Copuldik, esquire, of Apilton co. Norfolk, *alias* Cobyldyk, *alias* Copuldyk of Hecham co. Suffolk, *alias* Copuldyk of Hecham co. Norfolk, then about to cross to France in the company of John, duke of Bedford, constable of England. Witness Humphrey, duke of Gloucester, *custos* of England, at Westminster, 27 Feb. 1420.

Membr. 3
9 Jan. 1420 Philip Best, son of John Best, late merchant of Colchester, was exonerated from his apprenticeship to John Brandon, grocer, his master having left the city and failed to provide for him. [*Latin and French*]

19 Jan. 1420
Querela levata ad sectam defendentis Precept[1] was given to John Boteler, sheriff, to bring into the king's court, to be held before the mayor and aldermen in the Chamber of Pleas of the Guildhall next day, a plaint of debt of £240 levied by Henry Martyn and William Sharp, stockfishmongers, against John Swart, merchant of Almaine. The sheriff produced the plaint with a record of proceedings showing that the defendant had been attached by 18 casks of oil in the custody of Ertmery Swart, *Esterlyng*, 20 marks in the hands of William Combe, skinner, £25 in the hands of William Stokeman, 4 barrels of *wildeware grey*[2] and other goods in the custody of Lodowicus Wydynghous, *Esterlyng*, and 12 marks in the hands of Ralph Say, grocer.

The plaintiffs appeared on 20 Jan. and prayed that the plaint and proceedings be remitted to the king's court before the sheriffs, in order that the time of the plaintiffs might be saved, as the law and custom of the city required.

[1] By ancient custom pleas pending before the sheriffs were removable by order of the mayor into the Mayor's Court, there to be terminated or remitted to the sheriffs. The document sent from the Sheriffs' Court began with the words "Querela levata" and the process became known as a "Levetur Querela." See *Munim. Gild. Lond.* (R.S.), I, p. 219; Bohun, *Privilegia Londini*, pp. 255–6.

[2] Apparently these furs are referred to below as "Smoleynwerk." *Wildeware* is the fur of wild animals, a word which covers several varieties, such as *cristigrey, bis, ermine, popel.* Here it is coupled with *grey*, i.e. grey squirrel.

At the same time came Lodowicus Wodynghous (*sic*) and prayed to be admitted, according to the custom of the city, to prove that certain of the said goods attached, as being the goods of the defendant, were his own goods. Since the plaintiffs made no objection to the proof, and the said Lodowycus took an oath on the Gospels that no one at the time of the attachment or afterwards, except himself, had any interest in those goods to the value of 4d or more, and that his proof was not made fraudulently or collusively to exclude anyone from his right of action, it was considered by the court that the aforesaid goods should be freed from arrest as follows:— *Nota bene de probacione in attachiamento forinseco*

16 casks of oil in the custody of Ertmery Swart, 1500 of *Smoleynwerk*[1] in 4 barrels, 36 *kippis*[2] of *ruskyn*[3], 2 pieces of silver, one featherbed, 2 pairs of sheets, one pair of blankets, 2 *pilwes*, one coverlet (*coopertorium*), one *selour*, one *testour*, one barrel with *spruseyeren*[4], 2 chests, 2 pewter pots, 4 pieces of *peauter vessell*, 8 brass pots, 6000 pieces of *glas*, one gown of mixed colour furred with *fucheux*[5], one green gown furred with black lambswool, one red gown lined (*duplicata*) with green cloth, one gown of mixed colour lined with black cloth, one cloak (*armilausa*) of red and green, another of red and black, 2 black hoods (*capucia*), one green hood, one *cappe* of mixed colour, one doublet (*duploid*) of red worsted, one of white worsted, one of black cloth and russet, one bolster, 2 casks of wine called "*Teynt*,"[6] half-a-pipe of *Romeney*, 2 half-casks of red wine, one pipe of wine, one pair of beads (*precum*) of silver, 2 pairs of *corall* beads, 1000 of *lettuse*[7], 6000 *bowestaves*, one napkin (*mappa*) and 3 *towailles*.

Quitclaim from John Wodecok, son of John Wodecok, mercer, to John Shadworth, mercer. Membr. 3 *b* *4 March 1418*

Testimonial letters of the burgomasters, échevins and council of Bruges, witnessing that Johan Gossubbini, merchant of Bouvines, and Guiselbert van den Pute, burgess of Bruges, *1 June 1418*

[1] *Werk* means cured furs. *Smoleyn*, of Smolensk.

[2] A kip might mean either a skin or a bundle of skins. As the other furs are in large quantities perhaps "bundles" is more probable here.

[3] The back of the squirrel in summer.

[4] Prussian iron.

[5] Polecat.

[6] *Sc. vino-tinto*, a Spanish wine of a dark red colour.

[7] *Sc.* lettice, a kind of whitish grey fur, possibly rabbit or polecat.

had appointed as their proctors the brothers Jehan Salmier and Colart Salmier, and Gilles Dabbaigne, merchants of Dynant, to recover a debt of £67 of *gros tourn monoye*[1] of Flanders due from the late Watkyn Mitton, grocer of London, for *baterie* sold and delivered in Bruges to William Ydy, factor of the said Watkyn. [*French*]

13 Dec. 1419 Acquittance from Johan Salmier, merchant of Dynant, on behalf of Johan Gossulbini and Guiselbert van den Pute, burgess of Bruges, to William Yfre, one of the executors of Watkyn Mitton, grocer, for the above-mentioned sum.

Membr. 4
29 Jan. 1420 Robert Broun, son of John Broun of Norwich, brought a bill complaining that his master, John Sutton, grocer, to whom he had been apprenticed for 10 years, kept no shop and did not exercise the art of a grocer. The latter appeared on 2 Feb. and after pleading that he kept an open house of the said mistery in the parish of St Dunstan in the East, prayed that the matter be inquired of by the oath of the masters and good men of the same mistery. On 11 Feb. came William Burton and his fellows, masters of the mistery of Grocers, and eight other good men of the same, and being charged said on their oath that the said John Sutton kept no house of the said mistery and that he had not sufficiently instructed his apprentice. Therefore it was considered that Robert Broun be exonerated from his apprenticeship. [*Latin and French*]

16 Feb. 1420 Writ of protection in favour of William Gonner of Gloucester, smith, then about to cross to France in the king's service in the company of Thomas Caule, esquire. Witness Humphrey, duke of Gloucester, *custos* of England, 16 Feb. 1420.

3 June 1420 Similar writ in favour of John Kent of London, yeoman, then about to cross to Aquitaine in the company of Sir John Typtoft, steward of the duchy of Aquitaine. Witness as above, 3 June 1420.

[1] The *gros tournois* was groats or money struck at Tours in France. Here apparently it denotes money of the same value as current in Flanders.

John Bithewater, Richard Withihale, William Boton and William Ketyll, goldsmiths, became sureties for the good behaviour of William Holcroft, goldsmith, who was reputed among his neighbours to be a nightwalker and litigious person. Membr. 4 *b* *17 Feb. 1420*

Writ of *certiorari*, returnable in Chancery, as to the same. The tenor of the mainprise sent as required. *1 June 1420*

Writ of *certiorari* demanding information as to the cause of the taking and detaining of Henry Brenge, Roger Holbeche, Peter Aleyn, Walter Vitul, Nicholas Stanour, barber, Thomas Edward, James Bromley, John Kent, William Squyer, John May, John Germyn, Nicholas Tremayn, Richard Stapilton and William Foundour, who had been committed to Newgate, of whom the first nine had been detained, while the rest were said to have been delivered by the mayor and sheriffs or rescued out of custody. Witness Humphrey, duke of Gloucester, *custos* of England, 16 June 1420. *16 June 1420*

Return of Richard Whityngton, mayor, and the sheriffs, that whereas the aldermen had been bidden to go with the constables and special collectors into their wards to collect from the men of their wards the sums at which they had been assessed towards a grant of 2000 marks made by the Common Council for the king's expedition, a disturbance had taken place on 29 April in Robert Widyngton's ward, when the above-named persons, with many other evildoers unknown, used threatening words and resisted the collection of the sums assessed, whereupon the mayor and aldermen and other good men of the city proceeded to the ward and there found these persons persevering in their attitude and justifying themselves for having rescued Nicholas Stanour from the custody of Thomas Warner, one of the serjeants-at-mace, and accordingly they committed certain of them to prison to remain there until the whole sum of 2000 marks had been collected, while certain others, who had been taken into custody only on suspicion of favouring and supporting them, were delivered under sufficient security to await what the king's justice (*lex*) and the custom of the city should require in their case.

Membr. 5 *2 May 1420* On this day came Robert Chichele, William Crowmere, Nicholas Wotton, William Sevenoke, John Whatelee and Richard Osborn and delivered an award with regard to claims made by Constance, widow of John Pontadour of Lucca, merchant, against Paul Miliany, merchant of Lucca, for certain goods which she alleged had been entrusted to him by her late husband, as follows:—

4 pieces of cloth of Arras, value £200; 6 pieces of cloth of gold called "*cremesyn velewet*," 3 being green and 3 red, £200; 3 pieces of *bastard reynes*[1], £12; a bond of James Bernardyn in £400; another bond of £14; balance due on an account, £32; a collar valued at the Exchange in Lumbardstrete at £300 marks; and £30 14s due on recognisances.

The arbitrators awarded that the said Paul be quit of all claims except for the 4 pieces of cloth of Arras, the £30 14s due on recognisances and the bond for £400. As regards the cloth, which Paul said was handed to him as security for moneys which he had paid on behalf of Bartholomew Betyn, it was awarded that it be retained by the chamberlain until the Feast of All Hallows, in case the said Bartholomew should prove that the cloth belonged to him, and if no such proof were made, it should be delivered to Constance. As regards the sum of £30 14s, which was not yet due, the said Paul was to pay the money at once, as Constance was very poor, and collect it in due course from the debtors. And further, as regards the bond of £400, which was conditional, and had been entrusted to Paul *in equa manu* as consul of the Society of the Lucchese dwelling in London, it was to be handed over to the consul for the time being, since Paul was leaving the kingdom, until the conditions had been fulfilled.

It was awarded also that Roger Armoregy be quit of all claims made against him.

4 May 1420 Afterwards the said Constance agreed that the 4 pieces of cloth should continue in court till the following Easter, as otherwise Paul was afraid that proceedings would be brought

[1] *N.E.D.* supposes *bastard* to be cloth of inferior or mixed quality or unusual make or size, and cites 1 Ric. III, c. 8, § 18, where it is applied to woollen cloth. *Reynes* is linen-cloth of Rennes in Brittany. *Bastard reynes* possibly means cloth of Reynes style manufactured elsewhere.

against him by Bartholomew Betyn, merchant of Lucca, for a quantity of lead valued at £35, which he should have received on behalf of Bartholomew, but which had been received in court by Geo Bovy.

Afterwards the said Paul asked the advice of the arbitrators as to what he could honestly do with regard to an action brought against him in the Sheriffs' Court by a certain Urban Damaske, to whom the bond had been made, for detaining it. The arbitrators, having taken advice from persons learned in the law, and understanding that if the bond legally belonged to Urban it could not be retained in custody by reason of any award made by them, to which Urban had not been a party, advised the said Paul to plead to Urban's action in the best way he could, without fraud or guile, and to take such steps as the law and custom of the city allowed to protect himself. *22 May 1421*

Thomas Wandesford, mercer, prayed leave to sue John Clerk, mercer, at common law and outside the city. He took an oath that his request was made for no other reason than that the matter and cause of his action arose outside the city and could not be tried and terminated there. The mayor gave him leave to do so. Membr. 5 *b* *26 June 1420*

Mainprised for good behaviour: Peter Aleyn, pewterer, by William Lylye, pewterer, John Copland, tailor, Gerard Gome, salter, John Body, painter, and John Frost, brewer; Henry Brenge by William White, rector of St Margaret Friday Street, Richard Alfeld, armourer, Guy Terry and Roger Lardener, bakers; Nicholas Stanour, barber, by John Boston, mercer, William Austyn, tailor, John Hethecote, armourer, and Thomas Robert, cordwainer; Walter Vitul, armourer, by John Hille, William Thurston, Laurence Blyton, Nicholas Scalton, Robert Crooke, William Chede and Thomas Robelard, armourers; Roger Holbeche, James Bromley and Thomas Edward by Robert Fenescales, Ralph Sokelache, John Killyngham, Richard Reignold and John Kyng; John Kent, *couper*, by John Dunnynge, *poyntmakere*[1], John Stone, brewer, John Wight, cordwainer, John Walkere, *steynour*, John *2 July 1420*

[1] A maker of points or laces for fastening apparel.

Lengore, tailor, and John Motte, cordwainer; William Squyre, *shether*, by William Crane, *fleccher*, Richard Catelayn, horner, Thomas Grene, brewer, and Robert Athelard, *corsour*[1]; Robert Kyng, smith, by William Dogge, John Arnold, leatherseller, Robert Brokford, brewer, John Bergone, chandler, and John Knyght, *letherdyer*; John Pynner by the same except William Dogge.

18 May 1420 Writ of *certiorari* demanding that a scrutiny of the rolls and records be made to show by what right or authority Richard Alfeld exercised the office of coroner of London and that a return be made to the justices of the Bench. Witness R. Norton at Westminster, 18 May 1420.

Return that Richard Alfeld was exercising the said office by virtue of a writ to the present mayor and sheriffs, a copy of which they were returning with the writ.[2]

Membr. 6 *18 Nov. 1419* Writ to Richard Whityngton, mayor, Richard Merlawe, Henry Barton and Thomas Knolles, aldermen, and the sheriffs, that they or any two of them, of whom the mayor should be one, inquire by the oath of good and lawful men of the city whether John Barkefold of London, wiredrawer, dwelling in the parish of St Bennet Shorhogge, had, in the presence of Henry Wryght, Richard Fox, John Dun and others, said and affirmed that taxes and tallages were falsely and unfaithfully levied from the poor and wretched people and that the king had caused liege and faithful men to be hanged and burnt and had crossed to a foreign land and there had destroyed God's people, and that neither he nor any of his race had ever done otherwise; and further that the mayor etc. return the result of their inquiry under their seals to Chancery together with this writ. Witness John, duke of Bedford, *custos* of England, at Westminster, 18 Nov. 1419.

18 May 1420 Further writ to the same commanding that the return be made before the octave of St John the Baptist to the king wherever he might be in England. Witness as above, 18 May 1420.

[1] A horse-dealer.

[2] *Cal. of Letter Book I*, p. 240. Writ to admit Richard Alfeld as deputy-coroner to Nicholas Merbury, the king's butler and *ex officio* coroner of the city, 22 Nov. 1418.

Return of Richard Whityngton etc. that they had held several inquisitions of good and lawful men of the city, and that none of the jurors were willing to present or indict the said John Barkefold as guilty of having said or affirmed the aforesaid words; moreover the jurors said and thought that he had never used words of this kind, so far as they could learn or discover by any evidence before them.

Recognisances of two debts of £20 from William Randolf, goldsmith, to Elizabeth, abbess of Burnham, co. Bucks, and to the prior of Chetwode, co. Bucks[1]. *7 Nov. 1420*

Writ of protection in favour of John Wrenche of Middlesex, yeoman, then about to cross to Aquitaine in the company of Sir John Typtoft, steward of Aquitaine. Witness Humphrey, duke of Gloucester, *custos* of England, at Westminster, 12 June 1420. Membr. 6 *b* *12 June 1420*

Writ of *supersedeatis* from Henry, king of England, heir and regent of the kingdom of France, and lord of Ireland, ordering that an action in the city by Simon Copshef, draper, against Richard Gratele, sub-escheator and attorney of Richard Bruns, escheator for the counties of Oxford and Berks, be superseded, and the plaintiff be summoned to the court of Exchequer there to prosecute his suit, in order that the king might have his prerogative of being satisfied before all other creditors. Witness W. Babyngton at Westminster, 1 July 1420. *1 July 1420*

Writ of *supersedeatis* in respect of Thomas Senycle, goldsmith, who had been taken and arrested by virtue of divers actions of debt brought against him in the city and thus prevented from keeping his day in the court of Exchequer in an action of account there between himself and John Hale, formerly rector of St John Zachary, London, William Randolf, goldsmith, and John Selman, executors of the will of Drew Barentyn, late alderman of London, contrary to the ancient custom that none should be hindered in going to the king's court to sue or defend, or in returning thence. Witness as above. *1 July 1420*

[1] Both of the order of St Augustine.

8 May 1420 Writ of *supersedeatis* in respect of Robert Midelton, late one of the sheriffs of the city of York, whom William Leventon and John Uhurst had sued in London for a debt of £12, the defendant being attached by that sum in the hands of Richard Burton, grocer. The said Richard had appeared in the court of Exchequer in obedience to a writ of the barons and had acknowledged having in his hands the sum of £15 belonging to the said Robert Midelton, which sum he paid into court to satisfy the king, in accordance with the king's prerogative of being paid before all other creditors. Witness as above. By the Red Book of the Exchequer and by the barons of the Exchequer.

Membr. 7 *1420* Writ *de minis* to the mayor and sheriffs to bind Richard Veer, woolman, under sufficient mainprise to keep the peace with Richard Lovelas, mercer, who had petitioned the king for protection. Witness Humphrey, duke of Gloucester, *custos* of England, at Westminster, 11 July 1420.

July 1420 Writ of *supersedeatis* in respect of Richard Veer, woolman, who had found sufficient security before the barons of the Exchequer to keep the peace with Richard Lovelas, mercer. Witness as above, 11 July 1420.

13 July 1420 Writ of *corpus cum causa* demanding that Richard Veer be brought into Chancery with the cause of his taking and detaining. Witness as above, 13 July 1420.

Return of Richard Whityngton, mayor, and the sheriffs, that Richard Veer had been taken and detained in prison by virtue of a writ of *supplicavit pro securitate pacis capienda*, and also by virtue of a plaint of trespass at the suit of Richard Lovelas, mercer, levied before Robert Whityngham, sheriff, on 12 July, before the writ of *supersedeatis* arrived.

Membr. 7 *b* *16 Aug. 1420* Recognisances of John Kympton and Hugh Russell, vintners, of three debts of £20, payable to Geoffrey Louther, John Darell and Richard Cliderowe of co. Kent at Easter and Michaelmas 1421 and Easter 1422.

8 May 1420 Quitclaim from Constance Pountadour, widow, to Roger Amerigy, citizen and mercer.

ROLL A 49

(*William Cauntebrigge, mayor*)

Thomas Bosdon, scrivener, and William Botreaux, esquire, who claimed to be the factor and attorney of Lady Katherine, widow of William de Beauchamp of Poywyk, knight, came into court and acknowledged an indenture as their deed to the following effect: the said William having given sufficient security before the mayor and aldermen that within one month he would bring an acquittance under the armorial seal of the said Katherine, the said Thomas had delivered to him certain muniments relating to the manors of Poywyk and Alyncestre and lands in Poywyk and Worcester, which muniments had been entrusted to M... de Wyk and had come into the hands of the said Thomas as his executor. The muniments were as follows:— Membr. 1 *12 Aug. 1420*

A letter of attorney from..., widow of John de Beauchamp, knight, to Giles Yonge and William de Beauchamp, son and heir of Sir John Beauchamp.

A feoffment in fee simple from William de Beauchamp to Henry Coterell, parson of the church of Kenemerton, and Thomas More, clerk, of lands, tenements and rents.

A letter of attorney to William Sharp and Philip Chebbesey to deliver seisin.

A deed whereby Henry Coterell and Thomas More granted the above lands etc. to William de Beauchamp and Katherine his wife, their heirs, and the heirs of the said William.

A letter of attorney to William Sharp and Philip Chebbesey to receive seisin.

A fine levied in Easter term 1394 whereby John Bray and Robert Wode conveyed to William and Katherine the aforesaid manors, lands and tenements.

William Holer prayed leave to sue Robert Hend, dyer, at common law, which was granted to him, on his taking an oath that his statements were true. *22 Oct. 1420*

Gift of goods and chattels from William Hanewell, grocer, to Robert Chicheley, grocer and alderman, William Loveney, esquire, William Doune, clerk, and John Holym. Dated at London 29 Dec. 1418.

Membr. 1 b *19 Oct. 1420* Bond of Henry Coventre and John Bungeye, skinners, and John Costantyn of London, esquire, to John Bederenden, chamberlain of the Guildhall, in £20 to find sufficient security before Easter for a legacy of £20 bequeathed to the children of Henry Roger, late skinner.

21 Oct. 1420 Recognisance of John Markby, goldsmith, of a debt of 50s payable to Alice Bedford.

21 Jan. 1421 A foreign attachment delivered to Thomas Cook, dyer, plaintiff in an action of debt of £90 against Robert Strode, mercer.

1 Oct. 1420 Thomas Broun, grocer, was mainprised by William Eryngton, mercer, and Richard Holme, woolman, on the one part, and John Hake, draper, was mainprised by Thomas Roche, vintner, and John Dommer, mercer, on the other, to abide by the arbitration of John Abbot and William Melreth, mercers, and William Lynne and William Michell, grocers, in all matters in dispute between them, with the exception of a bond of £9 in which the said John was alleged to be bound to the said Thomas.

Membr. 2 *5 Dec. 1420* John Best, son of John Best of Colchester, was exonerated from his apprenticeship to Thomas Bosse, grocer, because the latter had failed to maintain and instruct him, and had left the city. [*Latin and French*]

14 Jan. 1421 John Barwe, son of John Barwe of Framlyngham, was exonerated from his apprenticeship to John Brandon, grocer, because the latter had not enrolled him at Guildhall and had no shop in the city. [*Latin and French*]

Membr. 2 b *27 Jan. 1421* Acquittance from John Wodecok, son and heir of John Wodecok, alderman, to John Shadworth and Thomas Aleyn, mercers, and Sir Peter Gyffyn, chaplain, executors of his father's will, for the receipt of £115 11s 1¼d and the third part of a farthing, due to him after the death of his brother William, out of a legacy of 520 marks divisible between the testator's legitimate children[1].

Award of John Gedney, alderman, as umpire, and his associates, John Boteler and John Perneys, aldermen, in the presence of Robert Bambourgh, John Golyngg and John Sewarde, arbitrators, in certain disputes between John Fekenham and John Rowlande concerning a tenement called "The Glene on the hoope" in Colman Street, from which John Rowlande had been expelled by John Fekenham. They find that John Rowlande, who had leased this tenement from Richard Storm, having failed to pay the rent to John Fekenham and his wife Joan, who was executrix of Richard Storm, was in arrears 2 marks, and further that by his default he had forfeited the remaining period of his lease and incurred a penalty of £10. They award that he pay the two marks due before the feast of the Epiphany, and, moved by his entreaties, they restore to him the remaining period of the lease, remit the penalty and order that a new lease be drawn up in reasonable form. They award further that John Rowlande shall receive again a banner-staff bound with iron and other goods taken over by John Fekenham at a valuation at the time of the expulsion, if he pay the valuation, the amount to be set off against the rent due, but if he does not wish to receive them at this valuation he shall pay the rent due and give John Fekenham due notice to return them. And whereas the said John Rowlande had secured judgment in the Sheriffs' Court against Sir William Clynton, knight, for £7, and a certain Richard Westoun had been outlawed in a plea of debt of 24s, both sums being due on two tallies belonging to John Rowlande, which he alleged had been broken and destroyed by John Fekenham, the umpires award that if John Rowlande failed to secure payment owing to the breaking of the tallies, and *20 Dec. 1420*

[1] *Inter suos mulieres natos legitimos.* "Signifies the lawful issue, born in wedlock (though begotten before), preferred before an elder brother born out of wedlock," Jacob, *Law Dictionary.* "In jure Angliae, si quis concubinam post conceptum ex ea bastardum in uxorem duxerit, et ex ea filium vel filias susceperit, is filius, sive sit unus sive plures, dicitur mulier," D'Arnis, *Lexicon.*

was willing to take an oath, with five other persons[1], that the tallies had really been broken by John Fekenham, then the latter should satisfy him for the amounts due on those tallies.

11 Feb. 1421 Writ of *corpus cum causa* to bring Stephen Turnebonis, merchant, into Chancery, with the cause of his taking and detaining.

Return that the said Stephen had been summoned to answer Richard Whityngton in an action of debt of £196, and had found mainprise, and accordingly he was not in custody.

Membr. 3
21 Jan. 1421 Thomas Cook, dyer, plaintiff in an action for debt of £90 against Robert Strode, prayed that the foreign attachment, by which the latter had been attached to answer, should be delivered to him, the defendant having made four defaults. The goods were valued by the oath of Alexander Child, John Cake, William Twyere and Simon Copshef, drapers, as follows: 15 whole cloths of Ludlowe of a mixed green colour called *derkegrenemedle*, £37 10s; 8 whole cloths, of which seven were *lightgrenemedle* and one *playngrene*, £16; 4 whole cloths of a colour called *brounsoleynmedle*[2], £10; 2 whole cloths of mixed green called *Fox in þe farn*, £5; 8 whole cloths of mixed colour, of which five were of a colour called *musterdevilers*[3], two of a colour called *grenemedle* and one *redmedle*, £21 6s 8d; sum total, £89 16s 8d. The cloth was delivered to the plaintiff under security of John Lyng, John Spenser, William Marker and Roger Kelsey, drapers, to answer therefor if the defendant appeared within a year and a day etc.

21 Jan. 1421 Foreign attachment in Adam Semy, shearman, against Robert Strode, as follows:—16 whole cloths of *blewmedle*

[1] There is no sixfold oath among the different forms of compurgation used in the city. As this was an arbitration voluntarily accepted by the parties, presumably the arbitrators were free to fix any number of compurgators. For the oaths usual in the city see *Cal. of Early Mayor's Court Rolls*, pp. xxx–xxxvii; *Cal. of Select Pleas and Memoranda*, 1381–1412, pp. xxvii–xxix.

[2] *Soleyn* or *solein* denotes single, standing alone, by itself. Its meaning in this combination is not clear. Query, a medley of shades of brown?

[3] *N.E.D.* describes this cloth as a kind of mixed grey woollen cloth, but gives no instances defining the colour beyond one reference to russet.

of Ludlow, £37 6s 8d; of which four were of mixed green, one of *musterdevilers* of Winchester, one *blewmedle* mixed with red and green, and two cloths called "*deumadames*," £16; 5 pieces of canvas containing 135 ells, 39s 4½d; one piece of linen of Gildeford containing 29½ ells, 11s ¾d; 1 sarplar of canvas(?), 16d; sum total, £55 18s 5¼d. The cloth was delivered to the plaintiff under security of William Colman, *materasmaker*, William Cherwell, John Coumber, skinner, and Richard Kere, to answer therefor if etc.

Writ of protection in favour of William Rody, mercer, then about to cross to Picardy in the company of Richard de Beauchamp, earl of Warwick, captain of Calais. *26 Feb. 1421*

Acquittance from William Lumley, esquire, and Joan his wife, one of the daughters of John Wodecok, late alderman, to John Shadworth and Thomas Aleyn, mercers, and Sir Peter Gyffyn, executors of the will of the said John, for the receipt of £115 11s 1¼d and the third part of a farthing. Dated in London 19 Feb. 1421. *19 Feb. 1421*

Robert Waltham, son of John Waltham, *hurer*, was exonerated from his apprenticeship to John Ruddok, draper, who had failed to instruct him in the art of a draper and did not himself exercise that art. [*Latin and French*] Membr. 3 *b* *3 April 1421*

Writ of *certiorari* demanding the tenor of the record and process of an action[1] by Richard Whityngton, mercer, against Stephen Turnebonis, merchant, for a debt of £246. *25 April 1421*

Another writ, *sicut alias*, and note that a return was made. *3 May 1421*

John de Marcato Novo, merchant of Venice, plaintiff in an action of debt against John Cake, merchant of Dinant, prayed that the foreign attachment, by which the latter had been attached to answer, be delivered to him, the defendant having made four defaults. The goods were valued by oath of John Waltham, Thomas Pirygton, William Oxton and John Walpole, braziers, as follows:—14 large brass pans weighing 2½ cwt. 2 lbs. at 42s the cwt. and other large pans, weighing Membr. 4 *10 April 1421*

[1] This action is fully set out on membr. 5 of this Roll, see below, p. 91. See also *Cal. of Letter Book I*, p. 243.

in all 12 cwt. 3 lbs., the whole being valued at £25 5s 1½d; 92 pans of another sort (*secta*) weighing 2 cwt. 26 lbs. at 38s the cwt. and other parcels of pans of the same pattern (*de eadem secta counterfeyt*[1]), weighing in all 22 cwt. 3 qrs. 9 lbs., the whole being valued at £43 7s 6d; one large copper pan with smaller copper pans standing within it, weighing 2 cwt. 1 qr. 6 lbs. at 46s 8d the cwt., £5 7s 6d; 69 round brass basins weighing 2 cwt., at 42s the cwt., and 52 others weighing 1 cwt. 3 qrs. 6 lbs., the total weight being 3 cwt. 3 qrs. 6 lbs. and the value £7 19s 9d; 43 *cawdrons* weighing 2 cwt. 8 lbs. at 42s the cwt. and other caldrons of lesser weights, the whole weighing 13½ cwt. 16 lbs. and valued at £28 13s; 11 *scomers*[2] and 19 small basins called "*smale denaunt*" and 5 lavers called "*pendaunt lavours*[3]," weighing 3 qrs. 6 lbs. at 46s 8d the cwt., 37s 6d; 146 *papilotts*[4], weighing 3 qrs. 21 lbs. at 42s the cwt., 39s 4½d; 75 *liecuppis*[5], 25s; 2 *rede caudrons* of 9 *pame*[6] at 8s each, 16s; 4 dozen and 3 *frisours*[7] at 6s the dozen, 25s 8d; 16 *frisours*, 8s 2d; Sum total of the attachment £118 4s 7d.

16 May 1421 Foreign attachment in John Gylott, vintner, and John Baldock, waxchandler, executors of Philip Keys, clerk, against John Freland, vintner, valued by William Boton and Nicholas Bette, goldsmiths, as follows:—one old silver cup and covercle, 3 silver covercles without cups, two saltcellars of which one was covered and the other uncovered, and one silver *pouder-box*, weighing 78¾ oz. at 29d the oz., £9 10s 3¾d.

March 1421 The wardship of Thomas Cosyn, *alias* Colman, an orphan, was committed to Thomas Morested, surgeon, who entered

[1] Fashioned, made after a pattern. "Counterfeit basyns, ewers, hattes, brushes...," Stat. 3 Edw. IV, c. 4.

[2] Skimming-ladles.

[3] A laver was a washbowl. A hanging laver is defined by *N.E.D.* as a suspended basin or washbowl with a hole at the bottom so that the water could fall into another vessel.

[4] Porringers.

[5] Cups to hold lye for washing.

[6] *Pame* or *paume*, *sc.* palm, is sometimes used as a measure meaning a handbreadth of 3 or 4 inches, but a caldron of 27 to 36 inches diameter appears excessive unless the measure applies to the circumference. Judging from the prices each of these caldrons would weigh over 20 lbs. *Rede* would appear to mean red, in what sense is not clear. Copper?

[7] Frying-pans.

into a bond of £400 not to apprentice the said Thomas or give him in marriage without leave of the court. Cancelled.

Richard Michell, son of John Michell of Newport upon Uske in Wales, was exonerated from his apprenticeship to Thomas Dautre, grocer, the latter having left the city, and was turned over to John Chichele, grocer, to serve the remainder of his term. [*Latin and French*] Membr. 4 *b* *6 June 1421*

Richard Whityngton, mercer, brought an action for debt against Stephen Turnebonis, merchant, for £296. In his bill he alleged that he had bought and had in his custody a certain Hugh Coniers, a prisoner of war taken in the battle of Agincourt, and put to ransom at 1600 crowns, each crown being valued at 42d in English money, and 16 marks of silver troy weight, each mark being valued at 20s, the whole amounting to £296, and that on 10 July 1420 in the parish of St Michael de la Ryole the defendant agreed to pay that sum for the prisoner as soon as the plaintiff released to the prisoner all his right and claim in him for the ransom, and should be prepared to hand him over to the defendant and obtain for the latter authentic letters under his seal witnessing the release, and that thereupon the plaintiff released his right to the prisoner and was ready to hand him over and obtain the aforesaid letters, but the defendant had not paid the money, though often requested to do so, to the plaintiff's damage £40. Membr. 5 *25 Feb. 1421*

The defendant, being summoned by John Charleton, one of the serjeants of the court, appeared on 27 Feb. and said in protestation that the plaintiff had not released all right and claim to the prisoner and was not prepared to obtain the aforesaid letters, as he declared, and for his plea he pleaded that the plaintiff was not ready to hand over the prisoner, and therefore no debt was owed. The plaintiff prayed that the matter be inquired of by the country. The defendant, on the ground that he was an alien, prayed that one half of the jurors should be aliens, according to the form of the statute, which was granted.

On 5 March the serjeant returned the names of the jurors of the venue of the parish, viz., William Reynold, John Bacon, John Clerc, Thomas Walsyngham, John Brikles, John

Snypston, John Tetford, Thomas Sutton and Edmund Salle, denizens, and Gerard Danidze, Francis Balby, Bartholomew Valerys, Paul Miliany, John Markannovo, John Abati, Nicholas Orlandini, Philip Saty and David Galganeti, aliens. The jurors did not come and again made default on 7 March. On 8 March the jurors appeared with the exception of William Reynold, Thomas Walsyngham and John Tetford, denizens, and John Abati, Nicholas Orlandini and Philip Saty.

Thomas Sutton and Paul Miliany, being chosen by consent of the parties, were sworn on the principal issue of the plea. Of the rest Gerard Danidze and David Galganeti were challenged by the defendant, and Francis Balby, Bartholomew Valeris and John Markannovo by the plaintiff, as not having lands or rents to the annual value of 40s according to the form of the statute[1], and were removed from the jury, on being tried and found insufficient by the jurors charged upon the principal issue.

The serjeant was ordered to summon the jurors for 4 April with eight others of whom half should be aliens. He returned the names of William Essex, Nicholas Chinall, Richard Warner and Richard Skynnard, denizens, and Laurence Peravesey, Nicholas Boloyn, Francis Baratoun and Hersato Moresini, aliens. Of these and the other jurors summoned, Philip Saty and Francis Baratoun were challenged by the defendant, and John Abati, Nicholas Orlandini, Nicholas de Bologn and Hersato Moresini by the plaintiff, and were found insufficient by the two sworn jurors. Laurence Peravesey made default. The plaintiff then prayed that ten other jurors be summoned of whom half should be aliens. Accordingly the serjeant on 5 April returned the names of John Prentout, John Tendale, Stephen Bugge and Thomas Cressy, but declared that he could not find any aliens having the requisite annual value. The jury, thus being chosen, tried and sworn as follows: Thomas Sutton, Paul Miliany, John Bacon, Laurence Peravesey, John Clerc, John Brykles, John Snypston, Edmund Salle, William Essex, Nicholas Chinall, Richard Warner and Stephen Bugge, said on oath that the defendant

[1] 2 Hen. V, Stat. 2, c. 3.

owed the plaintiff £296 and assessed the damages at £10. On 10 April judgment was given that the plaintiff recover his debt and damages.

Memorandum that Mark Marcadelly, born in Italy, who had been summoned as an alien juror in the above action, declared that he was a liege of the present king, and that the late king, to whom he did liege homage, granted by his letters patent that he should, during the term of his life, be held and governed in all causes and matters as a true liege, as though he had been born within the realm of England, and that he should enjoy all customs, privileges and franchises enjoyed by the king's lieges born within the realm. He produced the letters patent as entered in Book I, fo. ccli[1]. On this ground and because he was a citizen sworn to the freedom of London, it was considered that he be separated from the aliens returned as a jury. Membr. 5 *b* *5 March 1421*

Tenor of the record in Whityngton against Turnebonis, which was exemplified by letters patent under the seal of the mayoralty on 17 Dec. 1421 at the instance of Dominic de Thomasio and Philip Saty.

John Seyntgermayn, plaintiff in an action of debt against John Frenssh, spurrier, prayed that the foreign attachment, by which the latter had been attached to answer, should be delivered to him, the defendant having made four defaults. The goods were valued by oath of John Canwyk, spurrier, William Ledbury and John Andrew, joiners, as follows:—one large *armoriall*[2], 5s; one old *pollax*, 3d; 20 pairs of whole and broken spurs called *roghe spores*, 3s 4d; one old chest without a cover, 2d; one cradle (*cunabulum*), 2d; 2 pairs of *feble bedbordes*, 6d; one iron spit, 5d; 3 old sieves, 4d; one old *pann*, 12d; *rogh rynges*, *chapes*[3] and *bokels*, 30d; 5 *bordes*, 4d; one iron candlestick called "*flour*", 1d; one old ambry (*almariolum*), 12d; 2 small, old, broken gridirons, 2d; one broken *tynpanne* and one old stool, 4d; one small *pappepanne*[4] and Membr. 6 *9 July 1421*

[1] See *Cal. of Letter Book I*, p. 243.
[2] *Sc.* armariol, a cabinet or ambry.
[3] The part of the buckle by which it is attached to a strap.
[4] A pan for making pap, soft food for infants and invalids.

one small *braspanne*, 6d; one small *verneshbarell*, 2d; one small bellows (*petit bely*), 2d; one trivet, 2d; old *trenchours* and *disshes*, 1d; 18 pairs of broken *roghespores*, ...; 3 dozen new *rowells*, 2s 6d; 6 pairs of double *bocles*, 8d; 5 pairs of rowels, 1½d; 7 pairs of double *bocles*, and one *bocle*, 10d; 24 pairs of spurs called "*hangers*," ...; ... spurs, 6s; 3 hammers, one chisel, one *thwytell*[1] and one old *shapyngknyf*, 4d; one old tankard with an old *bord*, 10d; one barell, 1d; one old iron *fyre panne*, 2s; one little *sak* with old rowels and old *harnes*, 3s 4d; one dozen of double buckles newly made, ...; 2 dozen of *roghe rynges*, 12d; one dozen and a half of *roghe hokes*, 4½d; 2 hammerheads, one pair of *sheres*, one *ponchon*[2] and one *coronall*[3], 7d; one table made for a sign (*facta pro signo*), 4d; 2 anvils and 2 broken stakes, 8d; 2 stools, one *shapyngbord* and one *blok*, 6d; one broken stool, 1d; one old dagger, 1d; one pair of tongs, 2d; 2 *musterrakkes*[4], 4d; one tripod of old iron, 4d.

The attachment was delivered to the plaintiff under security of John White, cutler, and John Fyssh, pointmaker, to answer therefor if the defendant within a year and a day etc.

19 June 1421 Foreign attachment in an action of debt by Bertram Cleyhorst and John Ryng, merchants, against Godfrey de Foy, merchant of Dinant, valued by oath of Thomas Piryton, William Oxton, Thomas Clerk and John Bammeland, braziers, as follows:—48 large pans (*patelle*)[5] weighing 5½ cwt. 4 lbs., 160 pans called "*small denaunt*," weighing 9½ cwt. 18 lbs., 160 small pans called "*denaunt*," weighing 2 cwt. 4 lbs.(?), 9 *pendaunt lavers* of latten (*auricalco*), 36 *scomers* of latten, 6 spoons of latten, ..., *cawdrons* of 8 *pawme*[6], weighing 1½ cwt. 24 lbs., at 32s 8d the cwt., 4 *cawdrons*, 4 pots of latten, and 39 bowls, weighing 1½ cwt. 17 lbs. at 28s. the cwt.[7]

[1] A knife. Chaucer, *Reeve's Tale*, 13, "A Sheffeld thwitel baar he in his hose."

[2] A pointed tool for piercing.

[3] The head of a jousting spear, ending in three or four spreading points.

[4] A pattern-rack, still used in the cutlery trade.

[5] *Patella* might signify a plate as well as a pan, but these large *patelle* seem to have weighed nearly 13 lbs each, which seems to preclude plates.

[6] See above, p. 90, n. 6.

[7] No total is given.

Foreign attachment in Peter Ayrayll against the same, valued as follows:—61 pans weighing 4 cwt. 6 lbs., 45 large pans weighing 7 cwt. 12 lbs., at 32s 8d the cwt. and 3½d the lb. Sum total, £17 10s 7d. *19 June 1421*

Writ of *certiorari* demanding that the tenor of a recognisance of Thomas Elyngham, fishmonger, for keeping the peace with William Whyte, clerk, be sent before the barons of the Exchequer. Witness W. Babyngton at Westminster, 7 Oct. 1421. Membr. 6 *b* *7 Oct. 1421*

Mainprise of the said Thomas to keep the peace with the said William, parson of the church of St Margaret Moyses, in £20, by Thomas Kyng, haberdasher, Nicholas Bury, spurrier, John Whestowe, cutler, Richard Aleyn, brewer, and John Swan, *brochemaker*[1]. *10 July 1421*

Quitclaim to Thomas Cressy, mercer, executor of William Parker, esquire, son of William Parker, mercer, from his co-executors Thomas Elys, Thomas Chapman and Thomas Nicoll, on the payment to them of £20, in part payment of 450 marks due to the said William Parker. *11 Oct. 1421*

An action of account by William Randolf and other executors of Drew Barantyn against John Presden, grocer, relating to £1051 11s 4d was respited without a day owing to a writ of protection dated 18 May 1421 in favour of the said John, who was then about to cross to France in the company of Sir Richard Stafford, knight. *27 Oct. 1421*

Quitclaim from Joan, relict of Simon Herward, mercer, to William . . ., mercer, executor of the said Simon's will, of all claims of dower or widow's portion. *6 June 1421*

Writ under the privy seal to the mayor, aldermen, sheriffs and commonalty, that they continue their diligence in suppressing usury[2]. Membr. 7 *7 March 1364*

Ordinance of the mayor, aldermen and commonalty against usurious bargains[3]. *9 March 1364*

[1] Spit-maker.

[2] For this writ see *Munim. Gild. Lond.* (R.S.), I, pp. 367–8 and Letter Book G, fo. 117.

[3] *Ibid.* pp. 368–71; Letter Book G, fo. 118 b.

12 May 1391 Ordinance describing more particularly those acts and contracts which are forbidden under the titles of usury and *chevisaunce*, the former ordinance being somewhat obscure and indefinite[1].

Membr. 7 *b*
27 May 1421 Memorandum that William Palmer, factor and apprentice of John Abbot, mercer, being examined on oath at the instance and prosecution of Rowland, Gloucester herald of arms,[2] confessed before the mayor and aldermen that on 29 Feb. 1420 in the parish of St Laurence in Old Jewry he had sold to the said Rowland, in chevisance without the knowledge of his master, white linen cloth, linen thread of Cologne and other merchandise of his master, which merchandise the said Rowland did not see, for £49 3s 5d, and that one portion of the goods the examinant sold both personally and through Thomas Austyn, broker, and the other portion he retained to the use of his master, but for the whole of the goods thus sold and retained he paid the said Rowland the sum of £40 and no more, and nevertheless he caused the said Rowland and certain other sufficient persons to be bound to his master in a simple obligation for the whole sum of £49 3s 5d, which money was not yet paid.[3]

And because John Abbot, who was present in court and was questioned on the above transaction, admitted that he had the obligation and did not deny that he would have made profit out of the bargain, although he had no knowledge of the said false contract, as appeared by the separate evidence of both parties, it was considered by the mayor and aldermen that he should exonerate the said Rowland and all his friends from the obligation and all other obligations, indentures and specialties whatever made to him concerning the said false contract. And further, in order that masters, as well as their servants and apprentices, should henceforth be afraid to tolerate and perform evil counsels, it was considered, ac-

[1] *Munim. Gild. Lond.* (R.S.), I, pp. 399–401; Letter Book H, fo. 260. For further civic measures against usurious bargains see *Cal. of Letter Book H*, pp. 157, 200, 206–7, 261–2.

[2] See Guillim's *Heraldry* (1724 ed.), Suppl. p. 39.

[3] Rowland was supposed to have bought the goods for £49 3s 5d, and Palmer pretended to have sold them on his behalf for £40, which he paid to Rowland. In effect Rowland borrowed £40 at £9 3s 5d interest.

cording to the custom of the city used in such cases, that the said John Abbot, for the said false contract made by his apprentice, should pay to the Chamber for the use of the commonalty by way of penalty £10 sterling, and nevertheless that the same William Palmer his apprentice should be committed to prison to remain there etc. until it should seem to the mayor and aldermen that he had undergone condign punishment for the said falsity.

And afterwards, because the said John Abbot received the said £40 in full court from the said Rowland and exonerated him from all obligations, indentures and specialties concerning the said contract, and of his own free will paid to the Chamber the said £10, therefore the said William Palmere, his apprentice, was delivered from prison.

The mayor, aldermen and commons being questioned before the King's Council at Westminster as to their authority for correcting usury and false chevisance within the city say that, in order to maintain the course of lawful merchandise by which every realm is sustained, there is and has been in the city from time immemorial a custom that if any merchant, by himself or by a broker, makes any bargain of horrible usury or false chevisance, to wit, sells merchandise which he does not possess, or sells merchandise which he does possess, for a great and excessive price and retains the merchandise without removing it, and then after the sale buys it back for a very small price to the loss of the buyer, and is accused or attainted thereof in lawful manner and by reasonable process, then from time immemorial such false merchants and brokers in all such cases and the like have been punished as well by imprisonment and satisfaction made to the other party for his loss, as by making a fine to the Chamber of Guildhall for the trespass, according to the discretion of the mayor and aldermen or the governors of the city for the time being and no others, which customs and usages among others, being granted and confirmed by the present king, whom God protect, and his noble predecessors in full parliament, have been peaceably used and enjoyed by the mayor and commonalty and their predecessors at all times, in approbation of which customs and usages touching this matter in particular and in order to ordain more grievous punishment upon such false bargains and chevisances than previously, the mayor, aldermen and commons in the thirty-eighth year of King Edward III, the present king's grandfather, whom God assoil, by force of divers liberties granted to them and strict letters and commandments of the king and his council, ordering them on their faith and allegiance to perform this business, made an ordinance in accordance with the said customs in the following manner: *Pur ceo* etc.[1], as appears on the other side of this roll. And inasmuch as divers persons of the city against the said good customs have made several bargains of false chevisance, whereby many innocent and sufficient people have been destroyed, of which the said persons have been lawfully convicted by due process of law in accordance with the aforesaid customs, for that reason such persons have lately been punished and chastised according to the customs, usages, liberties and ordinances aforesaid. [*French*]

Membr. 8
26 June 1421

Pleas held in the court of the king in the Chamber of Guildhall before William Cauntbrigge, mayor, Robert Chichele and William Sevenoke, aldermen, John Whatele, mercer, William Michell, grocer, John Brokle, draper, and Ralph Skynnard, skinner, commoners, assigned and appointed to hear and determine plaints touching usury and false chevisance at the prosecution of those who wished to complain in the city, Richard Whityngton, Thomas Knolles, William Waldern and William Crowmere, aldermen, also being present.

John Sadiller, vintner, was attached to answer divers prosecutors and the commonalty of the city on charges of usury and false chevisance as follows:

Bernard Gemelyan, vintner, complained that whereas it has been ordained of old that no one engage in any contract of usury and false chevisance under the penalty contained in the ordinance, and whereas in Dec. 1417 he was in a necessitous condition and by the mediation of John Lawney, broker, he prayed the defendant for a loan of £15 under sufficient

[1] The ordinance of 9 March 1364, see above, p. 95, n. 3.

security for repayment in six months, the latter refused to lend the money unless he agreed to repay £17 10s and found good security therefor, whereupon, compelled by necessity, he accepted the loan and afterwards repaid the amount agreed and thus the defendant made a damnable gain of £2 10s, of which the plaintiff prayed restitution. *50s*

Richard Trogonold, fishmonger, complained that being in lack of money he sent John Lawney, broker, to the defendant to buy from him for chevisance[1] some merchandise from the sale of which he hoped to obtain £35, and that on 20 Dec. 1417 the defendant, through the broker, sold to him among other merchandise 11 thousand[2] 7½ cwt. of Spanish iron for £28 10s, which iron never left the defendant's possession, and then, unknown to the plaintiff, the defendant repurchased the iron from the broker for £23 10s, which the plaintiff received from the broker, and nevertheless the defendant took from the plaintiff sufficient security for the payment of £28 10s, and thus the defendant made a damnable gain of £4 14s[3]. *£4 14s*

John Lawney, grocer, complained that the defendant in March 1418 sold to him a quantity of tin, then in the defendant's possession, for £12, and then immediately repurchased the tin, which had never left his possession, for £9 10s, which was paid to the plaintiff, and nevertheless the defendant received sufficient security for the payment by the plaintiff of £12, thus making a damnable gain of 50s. *50s*

The commonalty of London, prosecuting alone by John Fray, the common serjeant, complained that the defendant through a broker lent to John Bernard, clerk, the sum of £40, and then by a false covin between himself and the broker, received from the plaintiff sufficient security for the repayment of £48 in eight months, thus making a false and damnable gain of £8. *£8*

John Fray also complained that the defendant, through John Lawney, broker, sold to Ivo . . . a piece of Polish wax for £12 13s 4d, which never left his possession, and that then, by false covin and arrangement with the broker, he repurchased

[1] *Pro chevisamento.*

[2] The "thousand" probably consisted of 10 cwt., and thus amounted to 1120 lbs. avoirdupois. The amount here mentioned would be 127½ cwt.

[3] Apparently £5 less broker's fee of 6s.

the wax for £10 13s 4d, which sum was handed to the broker for the use of the said Ivo, and that nevertheless he received sufficient security for the repayment of £12, and thus the inauspicious (*infaustum*) gain of the false chevisance amounted
40s to 40s.

John Fray also complained that on 16 April 1418 the defendant sold a piece of Polish wax for £11 and in the same manner, by collusion with the broker, bought it back for £8 9d, receiving security for the payment of £11, thus making
58s 3d a damnable gain of 58s 3d.

Thus the total sum of false gain in those cases, where the commonalty prosecuted, amounted to £12 18s 3d.

The defendant said that he was not guilty and put himself on the country. Precept was given to summon twelve men not suspected of chevisance of this kind. A jury drawn from the parish of All Hallows Graschirche on 28 June found him guilty. Accordingly it was considered that he be committed to prison until he should pay to the said Bernard, Richard and
Plaintiffs £9 14s John the amounts exacted from them in usury, amounting to
Chamber £9 14s £9 14s, with a fine of a similar amount to the Chamber, and that further he should pay a fine of £25 16s 6d to the Chamber in those cases where the parties did not prosecute but the commonalty prosecuted alone, that amount being double the
Chamber £25 16s 6d usurious gain made by the defendant in those cases.

Membr. 8 *b*
8 June 1421
Pleas as to the above held before the same, there being also present John Barton, recorder, Richard Whityngton, Thomas Knolles, William Waldern, Henry Barton, John Penne, John Perneys, Robert Whityngham, John Coventre, Robert Tatersall, Nicholas James and Ralph Barton, aldermen.

John Fray, common serjeant-at-law, on behalf of the commonalty, complained that John Sadiller on 20 May 1415 sold to John Lawney, broker, for the use of the illustrious Prince Sigismund, ever august king of the Romans, then greatly in need of a loan for the saving of his honour, five casks of oil, one piece of Polish wax and half a hundredweight of pewter dishes[1] for £53 5s under sufficient security for the payment

[1] *Dimidia centena vasis electrei.*

of that sum by the prince, and then by false covin and conspiracy (*conjectura*) between himself and the broker, bought back these goods which had not been seen by the broker nor removed from the defendant's custody, for £47, without the knowledge of the prince, so that the vile and damnable gain made by this false chevisance and bargain amounted to £6 5s.

A similar sale of a bale of pepper on 3 June 1415 to the use of John Colney, goldsmith, for £24 1s was alleged, the pepper being bought back for £20 9s.

A similar sale of 9 pipes of oil on 20 Sept. 1415 to the use of the prince's treasurer for £99 was alleged, the oil being bought back for £88.

A similar sale of 11 thousand of Spanish iron on 24 Nov. 1415 to the use of Lady Elizabeth Kyngeston, widow, for £27 13s 8d was alleged, the iron being bought back for £22 4d.

On these four charges the defendant pleaded not guilty and put himself on the country.

He was also attached to answer Guy Bracy, esquire, for having on 28 March 1409 sold to the said Guy 7 casks and one pipe of Gascon wine for £50, the wine being bought back for £32 10s.

The defendant pleaded, as regards the last suit, that the plaintiff ought to have no action against him, because by a writing of 5 Oct. 1409, after the supposed chevisance, he had released to the defendant all actions real and personal etc. And as regards the suit of the king and commonalty he proffered a charter dated 1 Oct. 1415 pardoning all falsities, deceptions etc. done before 8 Dec. preceding.

The plaintiff Guy denied that the release was his deed and prayed that it be inquired of by the country, and the common serjeant said that it was apparent from the charter that the pardon was made long before the alleged false chevisance, in which case it was of no avail. He prayed judgment on the ground that the defendant did not deny the false chevisance.

A jury was summoned for 11 July, which said on oath that the defendant was guilty of the offences charged against him at the suit of the commonalty. They said further that the release was the deed of the plaintiff Guy. Therefore it was considered that as against the suit of the said Guy the defendant be acquitted, but that he be committed to prison till he satisfied the commonalty[1] for £17 10s which he did not deny having obtained from the said Guy by false chevisance, together with the sum of £53 8d, being double the amount of gain he had made from the other persons.

Membr. 9
26 June 1421

Pleas as to the above heard before the same, there being also present Richard Whityngton, Thomas Knolles, William Waldern and William Crowmere, aldermen.

Walter Chartesey, draper, was attached to answer the commonalty and John Lawney, grocer, on a contract of false chevisance, wherein the said John complained that the defendant by his servant John Ingelond lent to him on 20 May 1419 the sum of £22, on condition that the defendant should have a nine years lease of a house in Southwark, worth 8 marks per annum, that being the amount for which it had been let for certain years, and that the rent should be counted as being worth 5 marks per annum, in order that in the course of nine years the loan should be repaid, with £8 more for the accommodation, and with the further conditions that the plaintiff should keep the house in repair, and transfer his tenant John Nicholl to the defendant at a rent of 8 marks per annum. The plaintiff alleged that he had accepted this agreement because he could not borrow elsewhere and was afraid of entering the gates of penury owing to the lack of a little money. After the defendant had been in possession of the house for two years and had received 16 marks in rent, the plaintiff had offered to repay the loan of £22 and had prayed the defendant for the sake of charity to restore to him his status in the house, but the defendant, standing by his usurious covenant, had refused outright. Wherefore the plaintiff prayed a remedy according to the ordinance against false chevisance and usury.

The defendant pleaded that he had made no contract of usury and this he was prepared to verify. The plaintiff prayed that the defendant and his servant, John Ingelond, should be

[1] The plaintiff could release the defendant of the offence against himself but not of that against the community.

separately examined on the truth of the matter, and put himself peremptorily on the examination[1]. The defendant did likewise.

And since it was found on examination of the said Walter and John, and by divers sealed deeds between the parties, that the defendant had made the said contract and had received 16 marks rent, and would have gained in usury £26, if the agreement had been fulfilled, that is to say, he would have received £8 in addition to the repayment of £22, according to the supposed value of the house, but actually, according to the true value of the house, he would have received a further 40s per annum[2]—therefore it was considered that the defendant be committed to prison until he had satisfied the Chamber for £26, his gain if the bargain had stood, and until he had released the plaintiff from all obligations touching the contract as soon as the plaintiff had repaid the loan of £22, less 16 marks already received. Thereupon the plaintiff satisfied the defendant for the amount due, and the latter paid to the Chamber £26 and entirely acquitted the plaintiff of all indentures and specialties touching the contract.

Pleas as to the above heard before the same, there being *9 July 1421* also present John Barton, recorder, Richard Whitygton, William Waldern, Thomas Fauconer, Henry Barton, John Perneys, John Reinwell, Robert Tatersall and Thomas Aleyn, aldermen.

Philip Malpas, draper, was attached to answer the commonalty and John Middelton of Calais on a contract of false chevisance and usury, in which the latter complained that, being greatly in need of money, on 11 Oct. 1418 he sought from the defendant, through Nicholas Martin of Lucca, alien broker, a loan of £80 for six months, which the defendant refused to lend to him unless he agreed to secure him by a sufficient pledge, and thereupon the plaintiff being urged by necessity and anxiety, chose, as he thought, the lesser evil and

[1] He offered to abide by the result of the examination, instead of leaving the matter to a jury.

[2] Amounting in nine years to £18, and with the above mentioned sum of £8, making a total of £26.

handed over to the defendant 140 strait[1] woollen cloths and 13 other cloths as security for the payment of £115 at the end of six months, which cloth the defendant sold for £115 and converted to his own use at the end of the term.

The defendant pleaded not guilty and prayed that the matter be inquired of by the country. The plaintiff did likewise. Thereupon precept was given to summon a jury not suspected of chevisance of this kind, and the defendant was mainprised by Thomas Eyer and Robert Banborgh. On 12 July the jury found the defendant guilty. Accordingly it was considered that he be committed to prison until he restore to John Middelton his usurious gain of £35, and the like sum to the commonalty for his contempt.

Membr. 9 *b* William Burton, grocer, was summoned to answer the commonalty and John Palyng, goldsmith, on a contract of false chevisance and usury, wherein the latter complained that on 2 July 1412 he bound himself by an obligation to pay £108 to the defendant on 18 Dec. following, and on that date he paid £68 and begged the defendant to respite the payment of the remaining £40 for two months, but the latter refused to do so unless he paid £7 10s for the respite, whereupon, owing to his necessity and anxiety, he bound himself by deed to pay both the £40 and the £7 10s usury, and made the payment at the end of two months. He offered that, if the defendant wished to deny the usury, he was willing to prove it against him by the oath of two credible witnesses, viz., Thomas Grey, grocer, and Richard Holme, who arranged the respite and were cognisant of the matter.

The defendant said he was not guilty of any usury as alleged and prayed that the said Thomas and Richard be examined separately on their oath, and put himself peremptorily on their examination. But as evidence was given that Thomas Grey was abroad and not likely to return for a long time, the parties said that they would stand peremptorily on the examination of Richard Holme alone. The latter was summoned by the court, and being sworn said that it was true that the plaintiff bound himself to pay £108 on 18 Dec., and on

[1] *Strictos*, commonly called "straits" cloths of narrow width.

some subsequent day which he could not remember, the plaintiff was arrested and imprisoned at the suit of the defendant, and that the plaintiff then paid the defendant £8 in hand, and, as regards £60, handed over a certain obligation of the customs, in which Thomas Brown, grocer, and William Brekspere were bound to the king, which the defendant agreed to accept, thus leaving £40 unpaid, and that on several occasions afterwards, the examinant and Thomas Grey went to intercede with the defendant for the plaintiff's release from prison and the respite of payment of £40 for the remaining two months, but the defendant entirely refused, until the examinant together with the plaintiff should bind themselves by obligation to pay a further £7 10s for the respite, which payment was made.

Accordingly it was considered that the defendant be committed to prison until he repay John Palyng the sum of £7 10s thus damnably and usuriously exacted from him, and a like sum to the Chamber for his contempt.

William Bury, mercer, and John Chirch, his hired servant and late his apprentice, were attached to answer concerning contracts of false chevisance and usury as follows: Membr. 10

Bernard Gemelyan alleged that on 16 May 1417 he had borrowed £16 from the defendants through Nicholas Martyn, alien broker, for a term of six months, and that the defendants had sold him 11 pieces of cloth of gold for £48, immediately buying them back for £30, and then had taken from him security to repay at the end of six months the sum of £16 for the loan, £48 for the cloth, and £4 for the accommodation.

Alexander Cheyne, tailor, alleged that on 9 May 1418 he had borrowed £16 by the same broker, agreeing to repay £21 in three months and giving in pledge cloth of gold, which the defendants sold for £21 at the end of the three months.

Thomas Draper alleged that on 21 June 1418 he had borrowed £5 by the same broker for three months, giving pledges to repay £7.

William Pickeryng of Calais alleged that on 18 Aug. 1418 he had borrowed £18 by the same broker for six months, giving pledges to repay £24.

John Fray, common serjeant-at-law of the city, alleged that on 30 June 1418 Thomas Beaumound, knight, borrowed £20 by the same broker for six months, giving pledges to repay £25.

The defendants put themselves peremptorily on a sworn examination of the broker, who said that William Bury was not cognisant of or privy to the false chevisance and usury, which were committed by the apprentice with his master's goods, which he administered as his apprentice. Therefore it was considered that the said John Church be committed to prison until he repaid £31 to the plaintiffs and a like sum to the Chamber, together with £10, being double the amount of false gain he had taken from Thomas Beaumound, with regard to whom the common serjeant had sued.

Membr. 11
4 Aug. 1421 Pleas as to the above heard before the same, there being also present John Barton, recorder, Richard Whityngton, Thomas Fauconer, Henry Barton, John Michell, John Reinwell, John Gedney, John Botiller, John Wellys, Robert Tatersall, Ralph Barton and John Coventre, aldermen.

William Lylye, pewterer, was found not guilty by a jury and acquitted of a charge of usury brought against him by William, Lord de Clynton and de [Say][1], who alleged that the defendant on 20 Aug. 1412 had lent him £100 for a year, which he bound himself to repay with £27 usury, under security of Peter Thorold, goldsmith, and Thomas Bridlyngton, draper.

5 Aug. 1421 Pleas etc., there also being present John Barton, recorder, Richard Whityngton, Thomas Fauconer, Henry Barton, Robert Widyngton, John Michell, Robert Whityngham, John Botiller, John Gedney, John Perneys, John Coventre, Robert Tatersall, John Welles and Nicholas James, aldermen.

Thomas Selowe, grocer, was attached to answer Simon Marcheford, clerk, on a contract of false chevisance and usury, wherein the latter complained that on 14 Feb. 1415 the defendant, by John de Maryns, broker, sold to him a quan-

[1] William de Clynton claimed the barony of Say by right of his grandmother Idonea de Say, eldest daughter of Geoffrey, baron de Say, d. 1359. See Nicolas, *Historic Peerage*.

tity of pewter (*electrum*) and grain[1] for £120, which never left the vendor's possession, and then bought it back for £95, which was delivered to the plaintiff, who bound himself to repay £120 under security of Thomas Bridlyngton and Thomas Sutton, tailors. The defendant was found guilty by a jury and committed to prison till he repaid the plaintiff £25, and paid a like sum to the Chamber for his contempt.

Walter Rydeler, draper, was attached to answer John Russell, *wolpakker*, on a contract of false chevisance and usury, in which the latter complained that the defendant lent him £100 for three years on condition that he repaid £174 5d. The defendant was found not guilty by a jury and acquitted. Membr. 11 *b*

John Hyham, draper, was attached to answer John Pykeryng and John Middelton, citizens and merchants of Calais, on a contract of false chevisance and usury, wherein they complained that they had pledged certain cloths of gold to William Crowmere for £300 and being afraid that they might lose them through default of payment, they sent Nicholas Martyn, broker, on 28 Nov. 1419, to buy from the defendant certain merchandise from the resale of which, without any great loss, they might easily and quickly raise the said sum of £300, and that the defendant the same day sold to them woad, wax, almonds and other merchandise in his possession for £366 13s 4d, for the payment of which at the end of two months Thomas Wandeford, mercer, was bound by simple obligation, but the defendant after the sale would not allow the plaintiffs to see, have, sell or dispose of the aforesaid merchandise bought by them, but retained it in his custody so long that the plaintiffs could make no profit or advantage from it except the sum of £300 to recover the pledges given to William Crowmere, for the repayment of which sum of £300 the defendant, at the request of the plaintiffs, had made himself responsible; and thus the plaintiffs, who ought by lawful trading to have obtained a loan and to have been assisted without any great loss, if they had been allowed to sell their own merchandise freely, had actually suffered a loss of Membr. 12

[1] I.e. the Kermes or scarlet grain insect used in dyeing.

£66 13s 4d owing to the defendant's false chevisance and his retention of the merchandise aforesaid, wherefore they prayed a remedy.

The defendant, while not acknowledging any such bargain made or fulfilled, pleaded that John Middelton, one of the plaintiffs, on 28 Nov. 1419 saw and bought the aforesaid merchandise from him and John Fennell, through Thomas Draper, broker, and found security for payment as alleged, and that immediately after seeing the goods John Middelton, as he had no competent purchasers at hand, begged the defendant and John Fennell to undertake the payment of £300, which the plaintiffs owed to William Crowmere, and to retain the merchandise as security until they could make better provision for its sale, to which request the defendant and John Fennell acceded, without that they were guilty of any such unjust retention and keeping as was alleged against them. The defendant prayed the court to allow him to verify his pleading by making his law according to the ordinance.

The plaintiffs pleaded that the defendant ought not to be admitted to make his law, because, according to the immemorial custom of the city, in every case where a party before any judges of record within the city admitted any contract or matter in substance, whereof a plea was moved, then that party ought not to be admitted to make his law before such judges, and they said that on 2 Aug. in the king's court in the Chamber of Guildhall before the mayor and aldermen the defendant had admitted as of record the substance of the matter alleged in the declaration, which admission they were ready to verify, wherefore they did not consider that the court should be willing to admit the defendant to his law.

The defendant denied that there was any such record, and the plaintiffs said that there was such a record.

Afterwards on 15 Aug. John Middelton appeared on his own behalf and as attorney for John Pykeryng, his master, and the defendant likewise appeared in person. The defendant then complained piteously to the mayor and aldermen that he was being gravely and undeservedly scandalised by the suit of the plaintiffs, and in order that the truth of the matter and his own honesty might be manifested, he renounced all advantage he might have by making his law, and prayed that, counsel on both sides being removed, both parties, together with the broker, might be separately sworn and examined, and that if it were found that he had made any false chevisance or unlawful contract, he might be punished by the mayor and aldermen, on whose judgment and ordinance he put himself peremptorily by way of issue. The plaintiff did likewise.

And afterwards, as it was found by an examination of all matters, that the defendant made no usury or false chevisance, and that he retained the merchandise only at the request of the plaintiff, it was considered that the defendant be quit as against the plaintiff, and that the latter be in mercy for a false plaint.

But although the said John Hygham was acquitted as against the plaintiffs, because there was no cause or matter on which a suit could be founded to the advantage of the plaintiffs in accordance with the form of the ordinance, nevertheless, since all [unjust] and illicit acts of trading are and were punishable, according to immemorial custom, at the discretion of the mayor and aldermen for the time being, and since the said John Hygham, on an examination of the said bargain and the circumstances thereof on 2 Aug., acknowledged that by divers brokers he had sold the said merchandise for the use of the plaintiffs to divers persons, whose names he produced in court, for 100 marks less than the plaintiffs had bought the merchandise, well knowing that the plaintiffs would suffer that loss, and because such action was contrary to the good repute and ancient practice of lawful trading and would be a pernicious example to others if the defendant went unpunished, it was considered by the mayor and aldermen, in accordance with custom, that John Higham should pay to the Chamber for the use of the commonalty the sum of 100 marks by way of penalty, that sum being the loss which the said John knew would be incurred by the plaintiffs on the resale.

Memorandum that John Botiller, draper, one of the sheriffs, brought before the mayor and aldermen the record of an action before himself as follows:— Membr. 12 *b* *10 July 1421*

Plaint levied before John Botiller, sheriff, on Tuesday 20 May 1421.

Paul Miliany, merchant of Lucca, was summoned against Urban Damaske, merchant of Lucca, in a plea of detinue of a certain writing obligatory; pledges of prosecution, John Hosteller and Richard John of Marconovo.

Pleas held in the Guildhall before John Botiller...on Tuesday 27 May 1421.

Paul Miliany was summoned to answer Urban Damaske for detinue of an obligation whereby James Bernardyn, merchant of Lucca, was bound to the plaintiff in £4000. The defendant pleaded that the obligation had been delivered to him by Urban and James *in equa manu* under certain conditions, and as he did not know whether the conditions had been fulfilled, he prayed that the said James might be summoned to show cause why the obligation should not be handed over to the plaintiff.

John Carpenter, one of the Sheriff's serjeants, was ordered to summon him for 30 May and returned that he could not be found in the city and had nothing by which he could be summoned. He was ordered to summon him again for the following Thursday, on which day the serjeant again returned as above. Therefore it was considered by the court, according to the custom of the city in the like case, that the writing obligatory be delivered to the plaintiff.

ROLL A 50

(*Robert Chichele, mayor*)

Writ of error, ordering that the record and process of an action in the Husting by writ of right before the late mayor and sheriffs between Richard Quatermayn, demandant, and John Shadworth, Walter Cotton, mercer, Thomas Aleyn, mercer, Matthew Chapman, clerk, and Thomas Colrede, tenants of a messuage in the parish of St Mildred Bread Street, be produced before William Hankford, William Babyngton and William Cheyne, justices assigned to examine the said record and process at the church of St Martin le Grand, and that the parties be warned to attend. Witness, John, duke of Bedford, *custos* of England, at Westminster 21 Nov. 1421. Membr. 1 *21 Nov. 1421*

Precept of the abovenamed justices citing letters patent of 1 Nov. 1421, whereby they had been commissioned to correct the error, if any, in the record and process or in the rendering of judgment, by the law and custom of the realm and the custom of the city, and ordering the mayor and sheriffs to appear on 26 Nov. *2 Nov. 1421*

Return of Robert Chichele, mayor, Richard Gosselyn and William Weston, sheriffs, claiming the city's privilege of 40 days' respite and of presenting the tenor of the record and process *oretenus* by the recorder.

John Hudleston of Lincoln came before the mayor and aldermen complaining grievously that a certain William Forster of Lincoln had vexed and impleaded him both before John Welles, now sheriff, and on previous occasions, when he came to London to trade, on a false and forged bond of £40, and that as soon as the complainant came to the issue of denying the bond, the said William allowed his suit to drop (*cadere permittit*) and did not prosecute. Accordingly he prayed the mayor and aldermen to call the action before them in order to terminate it. Membr. 1 *b* *10 Aug. 1421*

The sheriff was ordered to bring the action and the bond on 12 Aug. and to warn the parties to attend. On that day the sheriff brought the bond, and the plea as far as it had gone, consisting of an entry that the plaint was levied on 21 July 1421 for a debt of £40, and the declaration, in which the said William Forster alleged that a bond was drawn up 10 Sept. 1419 in the parish of St Andrew Holborn, whereby the said John Hudleston bound himself to pay £40 on 2 Feb. 1420. Of this amount he alleged that £33 was in arrears, and he prayed that his action might be limited to that sum.

The parties appeared in court, and the deed and record were seen and read. And as the deed was held in suspicion for divers notable and evident causes in the writing and sealing thereof, the said William was asked, at the instance of the said John, whether he was willing to stand by the deed and avow it. The said William made no answer to this, but prayed delivery of the deed and leave to recede from his suit.

And as the said William's word was doubted in the premises, he was put on his oath, according to the custom of the city, as to whether the bond was the true deed of the said John, as alleged in his plea. He said that it was, and offered to forego all advantage from it, and to bind himself to pay £40 to the said John, if he did not bring into court before the octave of St Michael either the man who wrote the bond, or his, William's, brother John, an apprentice of the law of Lyncolnesynne, or one of his father's household servants, in whose presence the bond was made and sealed in Lincoln, or authentic letters from the town of Lincoln, or of any other place, made on the examination of the writer, the brother or the servant, testifying that the bond was the true and undoubted deed of the said John, on condition that the said John would find security to pay the amount due, with reasonable costs and expenses, on the production of such proof.

The said John having agreed, William Forster entered into a recognisance of £40 to the said John, and was mainprised by Richard Withyhale, goldsmith, and Robert Freshney, vintner, for his appearance in court on the octave of St Michael to answer the commonalty for the falsity and forgery, of which he was suspected, under penalty of £40. John

Hudleston was likewise mainprised by Henry Bradshawe and Thomas Spencer, drapers, Thomas Elyngham, baker, and John Carbonell, goldsmith, to pay the money on demand, if etc.

On which octave John Hudleston appeared, but the said William Forster did not come, nor any one on his behalf bringing authentic letters or any other proof. But a certain John Mordon, who was attorney of the said William in his plea, came and prayed leave to recede from the action, which was granted to him. This having been done, a certain foreigner brought a writ of *supersedeatis* to deliver the said bond to William on the ground that it was made in Lincoln, and that therefore the court had no jurisdiction.

By reason of this writ the bond was afterwards delivered to the said William. Thereupon John Hudleston prayed execution of the recognisance, and it was considered that he should have it and that execution be done.

Memorandum that William Multon, skinner, was sworn and admitted as a broker, being mainprised by John Goldhauk, draper, and John Comber, skinner, for the faithful exercise of his office and the observance of all the ordinances and articles concerning brokers, and that quarterly, half-yearly or yearly, at the discretion of the chamberlain, he would show the latter all the bargains in gross which he had made, in order that the court might be informed as to whether he had acted well and faithfully or not, and that he would pay the sixth penny of all his profits to the use of the commonalty, under penalty of £40 by way of recognisance. **Membr. 2** *18 Nov. 1421*

The following were similarly sworn and admitted and mainprised: Thomas Neuport, grocer, by John Godyn, grocer, and William Lilye, pewterer; Lodewicus de Portico, citizen of London, by Thomas Seccheford and Thomas Provendre, mercers; Guy Laurence, citizen of London, by John Asshwell and John Parker, grocers; Roger Harleston, citizen of London, by Sayer Acre and Simon Strete, grocers; 22 Nov. Richard Coroner, draper, by Robert Banborugh, draper, and Richard Daniel, dyer; Henry Parmenter, grocer, by John Stormorth and John Olyve, grocers; 26 Nov. Henry Otewy, grocer [breaks off].

Membr. 2 *b*
8 Dec. 1421

Writ of *certiorari*, as to the tenor of the record and process of the trial of Arnald van Harsyll of London, tailor, on the death of John Bene of London, armourer, before the mayor and other justices of gaol delivery. Witness, John, duke of Bedford, *custos* of England, at Westminster 8 Dec. 1421.

Return of William Cauntebrigge, late mayor and one of the king's justices, to the effect that Arnald van Harsill had been indicted before John Boteler and Robert Whityngham, late sheriffs, and Richard Alfeld, late the king's coroner, on view of the body, for feloniously slaying John Bene of London, armourer, on 9 June 1420 in the parish of All Hallows in Dowgate Ward, by striking him with a knife, value ½d, in the left part of the breast beneath the *canelbone*[1], the wound being two inches long, one inch wide, and in depth to the heart, of which mortal wound he died immediately. He pleaded not guilty and put himself on the country. A jury of the ward said on oath that the said Arnald and John were sitting together on a seat in a tavern called "the Moyses," when abusive words, begun by John, arose between them concerning John's concubine, and that John drew his dagger and attacked Arnald, who did his best to flee, whereupon John pursued him to a wall behind the inn door and there threw him down and fell on him, repeatedly striking at him with his dagger, and that Arnald, being in danger of death and unable to escape unless he defended himself, drew a knife and struck John in the left part of the breast, of which wound John died.

The jury, on being asked whether Arnald could in any other way have escaped death, said precisely no. Accordingly the said Arnald was remitted to prison until the next gaol delivery to await the king's grace, and precept was given to the sheriffs to inquire in the meantime as to Arnald's goods and chattels.

13 Feb. 1422

Writ of *habeas corpus* to bring Thomas Basset of Witham co. Essex, gentleman, then a prisoner in Newgate, before the king to answer John Webbe in a plea of trespass. The date of any bill or plaint levied against the said Thomas before the mayor, aldermen and sheriffs was to be returned with the writ.

[1] *Sc.* cannel-bone, apparently here meaning the collar-bone.

John, abbot of St Albans, brings a plaint of intrusion against John Aston, fishmonger, touching his free tenement in the parish of St Nicholas Coldabbey. *16 Feb. 1422*

It was considered by Robert Chichele, mayor, and the aldermen that Thomas Jolyf, armourer, and his mainpernors, whom he found here in court on 25 Feb. 1418 in the mayoralty of Richard Merlawe, on his being suspected of Lollardry, should be exonerated etc. for certain notable causes, as appears in the rolls of memoranda of the said late mayor where the whole record is more fully entered[1]. *24 Feb. 1422*

A general court[2] of Robert Chichele mayor of the city of London held in the Guildhall of the said city on Monday after the feast of the Epiphany in the ninth year of the reign of king Henry the Fifth after the Conquest. Membr. 3 *11 Jan. 1422*

ALDRICHESGATE: on this day John Reynwell, alderman, came in his proper person and proffered here the inquest taken in his wardmoot by virtue of the mandate under the mayor's seal directed to him, in order that a view having been taken thereof a remedy and correction may be made of the defaults contained therein etc., according to the custom of the

[1] The roll for Merlawe's mayoralty is missing.

[2] By ancient custom each alderman held wardmotes four times a year. For many years now past the winter wardmote has been held on St Thomas's day (21 Dec.). As will be seen, this day was chosen only by certain of the wards in 1422. The business consisted of electing common councilmen and ward officers, constables, scavengers, beadles etc. Certain articles of the Wardmote Inquest were submitted to the ward juries or inquest men, whose duty it was to present offenders, offences and nuisances, such as persons of evil character, women of ill fame, defective ovens, sales by taverners without sealed measures, etc. The traditional date for the presentment of ward returns is on Plow Monday, Monday after the feast of the Epiphany, at an assembly known as the Mayor's General Court, but subsequently called the Grand Court of Wardmote. The presentation of nuisances and offences was brought to an end in 1857 by an Act of Common Council called "Carden's Act." The wardmotes and Grand Courts are still held for receiving the results of the elections of St Thomas's Day, and the swearing in of ward beadles and other officers. For procedure at the wardmotes see *Munim. Gild. Lond.* (R.S.), I, pp. 36–9, 257–60, 277, 377–8.

The English portions of these ward returns have been printed *in extenso*, with notes and glossary, in R. W. Chambers and Marjorie Daunt, *A Book of London English*, 1384–1425, Clarendon Press, 1931.

city etc. And the officers chosen by the good men of the same ward in the said wardmoot being warned to be here, certain of them came and were sworn as appears below. And certain of them did not come. Therefore let each of them be amerced 2s, and warned as before.

Common Council: Master Richard Waltham, Adam May, Simon Sewale, John Blakden. *Constables:* William Belle, Richard Fuller, Stephen Cleant, John Mason, John Salter, John Luton, Alan Brette, 2s, Richard Hersy, 2s. *Scavageours:* John Davy, John Kene. *Beadle*, John Leyghton.

Membr. 3–4*b* [Similar lists of constables, scavengers and beadles for the other wards. The return of the ward of Cripplegate gives separate lists for the within and without divisions of the ward. Common councilmen are returned only for the wards of Lime Street, *viz.*, John Tars and Geoffrey Wymond, and Portsoken, *viz.*, John Donmer and Roger Baron. The numbers, which give some clue to the population of the wards, are as follows: *Algate*, constables, 6, scavengers, 4, beadle, William Burbache. *Bassyngeshawe*, c. 2, s. 2, beadle, Stephen Drax. *Bisshopesgate*, c. 7, s. 7, beadle, John Stokes. *Billingesgate*, c. 9, s. 3, beadle, Walter Iremonger. *Bradstrete*, c. 9, s. 7, beadle, Thomas Wanton. *Candelwykstrete*, c. 4, s. 4, beadle, Robert Sturmyn. *Bredstrete*, c. 15, s. 8. *Castelbaynard*, c. 5, s. 5, beadle, John Rowe. *Chepe*, c. 13, s. 9, beadle, Thomas Macchyng. *Cordwanerstrete*, c. 5, s. 4, beadle, Richard Boner. *Cornhill*, c. 4, s. 4, beadle, William Salle. *Douegate*, c. 8, s. 4, beadle, John Norwych. *Crepulgate* (within), c. 8, s. 7, beadle, John Ryngstede; (without), c. 4, s. 3, beadle, John Haynes. *Farndon Without*, c. 13, s. 9, beadle, Roger Olyver. *Lymstrete*, c. 4, s. 2, beadle, William Siggele. *Farndon Within*, c. 21, s. 13, beadle, William Leyghton. *Langbourn*, c. 8, s. 4, beadle, Thomas Chirche. *Bridge*, c. 17, s. 3, beadle, Richard Haywode. *Portsoken*, c. 6, s. 4, beadle, Richard Malster. *Queenhithe*, c. 10, s. 4, beadle, John Willde. *Tower*, c. 10, s. 4, beadle, John Parker. *Walbroke*, c. 6, s. 6, beadle, Richard Weston. *Vintry*, c. 8, s. 4, beadle, Elyas Boston. *Colmanstrete*, c. 4, s. 2].

COLMANSTRETE. The verdict of the inquest of the wardmote of Colmanstrete held before John Gedney, alderman, on Saturday 27 Dec. Membr. 4 *b* *27 Dec. 1421*

First they say and present that the chamberlain of the Guildhall used to pay a rakyer 26s 8d yearly to keep and cleanse the grates at London Wall and Lothbury, and because of non-payment the said grates are evilly and horribly stopped up with mud and ordure to the great nuisance of all the ward, wherein the said chamberlain is at fault.

And also the chamberlain ought to find a man to keep and cleanse the ditch there.

Also two stalls in the rent of Biterden, chamberlain of the Guildhall, in Colmanstrete are defective, being 2 ft. too high and 1 ft. too wide. Also they present that Trestremesaley used to be a common way to pass out of Colmanstrete into Bassyngeshawe and it is now stopped and forbarred and for a long time has been, because the rent, late of Richard Hamme, is set and built over that common alley, whereof they pray a remedy.

Also Margery, dwelling in the rent of William Calwer in Colmanstrete, is a common scold and by day and night throws out of her house stinking ordure, to the very great nuisance of the neighbours dwelling there.

Also John Dun, *wyrdrawer*, goes nightwalking after the time limited by the mayor, and is a maintainer and receiver of certain foreign men within his house and other places.

[*French*]

BASSYNGESHAWE. First they say that Robert Sutton and Johane his wife, being newly come from Coventry, keep their doors open on several divers nights until 11 or 12 of the clock, having divers men, who are strangers and unknown to the ward, making violent and grievous noises to the nuisance of all dwelling around.

Also they say and present that William Bracy keeps carts for hire and lets them out publicly, and on divers nights beyond the due and proper hour he causes his servants to drive out of a gate issuing from the ward, bumping and striking the sides of the gate, when going and coming with the carts, so roughly that all the neighbours dwelling round the gate are grievously disturbed and grieved of their repose and quiet at night. Further, they throw *draf wasshe*[1] and other horrible noisome things outside the gate to the great nuisance of all the neighbours dwelling there and other people passing by.

Also they say and present that all the little rents of Richard Clerk, otherwise called "the Rents of the Swan," are defective because none of them are private[2], so that all the tenants dwelling in them cast their ordure and other horrible filth and liquids before their doors to the great nuisance of Holy Church and all people passing there.

Also they say and present that a house of the prioress of Halywell is so ruinous and feeble that it is on the point of falling to the ground to the great peril of all people passing there, and the pavement before the same house is very defective and has been several times indicted and no correction has so far been made, to the great nuisance of all people passing there.

Also the paling before the house of George Gervais, standing too far on the common soil, is defective.

Also they say that the house of John Philip called "*the Bruerne*[3]" is on the point of falling to the ground and too dangerous in case of fire, to the great disquiet of all dwelling near and knowing thereof.

Also John Pymme and his wife are nightwalkers to the great fear and peril of their neighbours. [*French*]

CREPULGATE WITHOUT. First they present Alice, wife of John Morys dwelling in Goldynglane, as a common huckster; Alice the wife of Gregorie Percyvale dwelling in Whitecrouchestrete, Elene the wife of Richard Neweman, barber, in the Foreststrete[4], Elene dwelling at the corner of Grub Street in Skelton's rent, Johane the wife of Hugh Barnburgh, smith, in Grub Street, in the same rent, Isabele the wife of John Smith, currier, Isabele the wife of John Haryngey, currier, dwelling in the Morestrete, Isabele the wife of Robert Denys, cordwainer, dwelling in the Barbican, and Marione Hukster

[1] Refuse, dregs.

[2] *Sont privoes*. The remainder of the sentence suggests *ount privoes*.

[3] Brewhouse.

[4] Fore Street.

dwelling in Charleton's rent in the Barbican, as common hucksters.

Also they present and indict John Sherman, cooper, dwelling in Grub Street, for keeping *dokes* (ducks) within the franchise of the city to the great nuisance of the neighbours, and John Haukyn, skinner, in the Morestrete, Baudewyn Hoper, dwelling at the Purse by the Moor, and Robert Hulford, gardener, dwelling in Morestrete, for the same, to the great discomfort and nuisance of the neighbours.

Also they present and say that all the *hostillers* and all the brewers and hucksters are defective because they sell their ale by too scarce measure against the mayor's ordinance. [*French*]

PORTSOKEN. Inquest taken before Sir William Clerk, prior of the house of Holy Trinity the Great, then alderman of the said ward, by oath of John Dommer, Richard Lucas, John Dunche, John Norreys, Ralph Baroun, John Trewman, John Bray, William Stebrank, William Burwell, Thomas Bryght, John Stevene, John Turnour, John Edward and John Grace. Membr. 5

Who say on oath that the Master of St Katherine by the Tower has often been indicted for an earthen wall with a gate of stone and mortar inclosing the common soil opposite the Tower of London to the nuisance of the commonalty. Also they say that the same Master and his brethren have encroached upon the common soil of Pylorylane, otherwise called "Weylandeslanende," in order to widen their ditches and that they throw the *wose*[1] of the ditches beyond the limits used and accustomed of old; also that the said lane is in great part contracted and heaped up with the mud of the said ditches to the great nuisance of those passing by and of the commonalty of the city. And whereas all the inhabitants of the ward from time immemorial ought and used to have a certain common way leading to a wharf at St Katherine's in the said ward and within the liberty of the city to get water there and carry merchandise therefrom at all times necessary, which wharf lies on common soil between the watermill of the house of St Katherine on the east and the gates of Tourwharf and the king's highway leading from Algate by the Tourdiche

[1] Ooze, mud.

to the Thames on the west, the Thames on the south and the millpond on the north, the Master of St Katherine's has of late encroached on the common soil, whereby the inhabitants of the ward and the city are hindered from having their easement, to the common nuisance. Also the Master and a certain John Williamson by a new custom initiated by them have extortionately taken from Adam Copendale 12d for a boatload of chalk, from William Wodeward a covercle of silver by way of distress, because he would not pay the custom, from the church of St Botolph 12 blocks of freestone, price 6s 8d, from John Cornwaleys a *scope*[1], from the wife of John Suthwick a bottle, for washing her clothes in the river, from the wife of Robert Rampamd, labourer, ½d for a jar of water, and from the wife of William Fissh a towel by way of distress for washing her clothes outside the wharf on a staging[2] in the river. Also they take wharfage from all carts coming out of the gates of Tourwharf into the highway with loads, or even extortionately take distresses from them. Also they violently take 1d from all poor people who come on to the said common ground to beg on St Katherine's night. And thus by force and arms and with the strong hand they cease not to take such custom daily from all inhabitants of the ward and city coming to the said wharf, and hinder them of their easement in the wharf, to the great nuisance etc.

Also they say that the heirs of Henry at Hoke have and have made a ditch on the common soil to the great nuisance of passers-by, and that the wife of Thomas Wynfeld has another ditch of the same kind.

Also that a certain well (*fons*) between the Helme and the Belle in the king's highway lies uncovered and not sufficiently enclosed, to the peril of men and beasts passing. Also that the tenements late of Adam Fraunceis occupy the common soil in the king's highway to the nuisance of the whole commonalty of the city. Also that Thomas Blithe has three doors opening on the churchyard of St Botolph without leave of the parishioners, to the nuisance of the same.

Also they say that the tenements late of Thomas Clerk in divers places have stood ruinous and open on the king's high-

[1] Scoop. [2] *Scabellum.*

way for many years, and for this reason the neighbours are greatly afraid of robbery and other grave perils, to the nuisance etc.

Also they say that Cornwaleys has in his rents four posts[1], the abbot of Coggeshale one post, William Holy two posts, the tenants at the Shippe one post, John Dommer three posts, and Richard Lucas a "blok" fixed and lying in the king's highway, to the nuisance of the people of the ward and passers-by.

Also they say that the king's highway in divers places throughout the whole ward is heaped with filth to the great nuisance of the whole city.

Also they say that all the brewers, bakers and regraters of bread and ale, and all those that keep common inns throughout the whole ward, are in default against the mayor's proclamation.

BISSHOPESGATE. Inquest taken at the wardmote held before Robert Whityngham, alderman, on 1 Jan. 1422 to inquire as to disturbers of the peace and the other articles specified in the wardmotes, by oath of John Dancastre, Richard Bokyngham, John Beauchampe, John Haverell, William Calverton, Robert Broun, Simon Moysaunt, Richard Nase, William Trumpynton, Clement Yerdle, Henry Rous, Thomas Hulk and John Delavag?, good and lawful men of the ward, who say upon their oath that in the parish of All Hallows the pavements are defective (*debilia*), dangerous and a nuisance to passers-by. *1 Jan. 1422*

Parish of All Hallows

The pavements at the inn of Thomas Richer, painter, the church of All Hallows, the inn of Robert Kendale and the inns called "the Faucoun" and "the Lyon" are defective, dangerous and a nuisance to passers-by.

Parish of St Peter

A pentice at the Egle is too low so that horsemen and carts are often hindered and troubled. The pavements at the inns of John Mogoun, poulterer, Thomas Cheseman, John

[1] *Stulpes, sc.* stoops, posts.

Burton, *wexchaundeler*, Thomas Gratele, Roger Ferle and John Haverell are defective, dangerous and a nuisance to passers-by. The gutters belonging to the inns of Richard Mourdon, Hugh Neell and John Haverell, and the inn called "the Castell" are defective, noisome and putrid both in the morning and the evening.

They say also that Thomas Brid, poulterer, and David Tothedrawer on 20 Aug. and at many other times committed fornication with divers unknown women.

They say also that John Mogoun, poulterer, at Christmas and Easter and at many unknown times, against the ordinance of the city and to the prejudice of the people of the city, bought from Thomas Rowdon 10 capons for 5s before the appointed hour, which capons Richard Fardon could have had the same day for 4s.

Parish of St Martin

The pavement at the inn of Edward Tiler, the door of a cellar belonging to the inn of Agnes Fauxby and the pavement there are defective and dangerous to passers-by.

The pentices belonging to the rent of the Fraternity of Tailors, the inn of Henry Barbour, and the inn of Master Lavendre are too low so that horsemen and carts are hindered.

They say that on 20 Sept. John Cory, saddler, with other unknown companions, walked about without a light or reasonable cause after the hour limited, viz., between 11 and 1 at night, and that the said John is a common nightwalker.

They say also that Richard Shoklakhe, master of the Fraternity of Tailors, leased to the above John Cory, saddler, a messuage in the parish for a year at 20s rent, which John Cory on 20 Sept. 1420 was indicted before William Sevenok, alderman, in his wardmote in Tourstrete for divers trespasses.

Also they say that Alice, wife of John Cheyney, and Isabel Cobham on 20 Sept. and on many other occasions committed fornication with two priests and afterwards with other divers unknown men, and that they are common strumpets.

Parish of St Elena

The jurors say that the pavement before the inns of John Frenssh, Robert Coper, Henry Wycombe and the rector of the church of S[t] Ethelburga, and six chimneys of the same rent are defective, perilous and a nuisance to passers-by.

The pentice before the inn of John Draper and Richard Marshall, and the *latys* at the inns of Henry Wycombe, John Goldsmyth and Nicholas Preston are too low so that horsemen and carts are hindered and incommoded.

Parish of S[t] Ethelburga

The jurors say that the pavement before the inn of William Brownyng, and the pavement leading from the inn of John Fulmer to the gate of Bishopsgate are defective and dangerous, and that the *latys* of a solar belonging to the inn called "the Tonne," the pentice before the inn of Thomas Taillour and the *latys* before the inn of Thomas Porter are too dangerous, so that riders and carts are hindered and incommoded.

Parish of S[t] Botulph Membr. 5 *b*

The jurors say that the pentices before the inn of Grisle Taillour, the [house] of Nicholas Kyngescote and the inn of John Hogge, two *latys* belonging to the inn of J. Ladiner, the pentice before the inn of Thomas Poke, the pentice before the inn of John Burgate, the stall before the inn of Thomas Janyn, the lattices before the inns of John Ingram and John Yerdlee, the *barrez* before the inn called "the Belle" and the *barrerz* before the inn called "the Helme" are too low so that riders and carts are often hindered and incommoded.

Also they say that the ditch belonging to the rental of the Briggehous, the ditch called "the Dinnyngysmore," the gutter between Dinnyngesmore and S[t] Botulph's church, the ditch called "Turnynggate," and the gutter at the rental of Hugh Trapp are defective, noisome and putrid.

They say also that a well in front of Turnyngate and an inn called "the Aleygate," belonging to the rental of S[t] Mary Spitell, a well of the same rental, and a well at the inn of

Hugh Trapp and the pavement there are defective, perilous and a nuisance to passers-by.

They say also that William Payne, Emote Coltastatur, Margaret Poule, Margaret Clerk, Agnes Kyghley and Margaret Cambrigge on 10 Sept. committed fornication with William Payne (*sic*) and also afterwards with other divers unknown men, wherefore the same Emote, Margaret, Agnes and Margaret are common strumpets.

They say also that Maud Barbour, Joan Jolybody and Isabel Boxle are common bawds between divers unknown persons on many occasions. Also the prior of the hospital of St Maryspitell leased to Isabel Boxle a tenement in the parish for a year at 13s 4d, which Isabel was indicted before John Penne, alderman of Walbroke, at his wardmote on 20 Dec. 1420.

FARRINGDON WITHOUT. "These ben nusauncis and defautis foundin in þe warde of Farundone without, Taken in the wardemot, a fore Raulyn Barton Alderman of the same warde, the yere of the kyng aboveseyd."

They present the Master of Ludgate for throwing dung in the *canelle*[1], thus stopping the flow of water. A mud wall in the Bailly between the houses of Shelhard, haberdasher, and Hay, spurrier, is falling down *gobet-mele*[2], making the way foul. William Emery, *coser*[3], throws dung in the street. The pavements before the Chamber rent[4] in the Bailly, and before the doors of Harri Gras, barber, and Walssh, are defective. The common privy of Ludgate is defective and perilous, and the ordure rots the stone walls, which is likely to be dangerous to the walls and costly. The barriers at the end of Sholane are broken by water-carts and the pavements in divers places in the parish are defective. John Taverner is a foreigner. John Whitlock at the Bell at the end of Carter Lane and his wife are common bawds and have lately been turned out of other wards. John Swayn and his wife are forestallers, regraters and extortioners ofttimes, and lately they hired a page of the

[1] Channel, gutter. [2] Piecemeal. [3] Horse-dealer.

[4] The rents of the Chamber of the Guildhall were tenements belonging to the Corporation.

Queen's household to arrest a boatload of rushes and brought it from Queenhithe to Fleet Bridge, and took out 30 burdens of rushes and laid them in Sir Walter Bechaum's place and then paid the boatman 26d for them, whereas they ought to have paid 3d a burden, and thereof the boatman openly made much "*noysing and sclaundir.*" The taverners of St Bride's parish set their empty tuns and pipes in the high street. The barriers of Chaunselerlane and Fayturlane are all broken. [*English*]

Parish of *Seint Sepulcris*

The *Cachepolle*[1] in Smithfield is a nightwalker and throws dung on the field. Maud Hoke is a leper. John Bukstone is a common regrater. Flete, esquire, throws out dung and his pavement in Hosier Lane is defective. Halywelle throws dung on the field on both sides of *horspole*. John Tuke throws dung on the field. Stephen Rakere and Norton do the same, so that men, horses and carts cannot pass. The pavement in Secole Lane is defective and covered with dung from one end to the other. The stream of Trynmylbroke is obstructed by John Stanlake, Robert Rede, Pyers Tepertone and Philip Edmyngtone, tanners, because of their hides tied to stakes in the stream, and because of deep weirs made by them. Richard Spray is presented for *cloyng* the stream with *wylowes* set there. The jurors complain greatly of the dung about the *horspole*, which is a right grievous nuisance, and no remedy has been done, though it has been indicted and complained about for 16 years past, "wherfore we beseke yow, atte reverence of god, in salvacione of the kyngis pepul & in worshipe of the Citee that it mowe be amendid." [*English*]

Parish of St Andrew Holborn

They present that fifteen cottages in Chaunserlane which formerly belonged to William Tamworth are covered with straw, to the great danger of fire to the houses of neighbours.

Also, the common course of the water between London and Middlesex is obstructed by dwellers in the tenements of the

[1] Catchpole, a tax-gatherer or petty officer of justice, bailiff. Here it probably refers to the collector of dues at Smithfield cattle-market.

master of the hospital of S[t] Giles without the Bars of the Old Temple to the great damage of all the people passing over it.

Also, the barriers of Holburne and a small ditch belonging thereto are ruinous on both sides and broken down, to the hindrance of the guarding of the city of London, and also of the Chamber of the same, and a peril to the neighbours.

Also, the walls between the Harpe and Holbourne Bridge are ruinous and perilous, in destruction of all the people passing thereby, and to the hindrance of the guarding of the Chamber of the city.

Also, the course of the water of Trylmylle Broke is obstructed on either side by *wylowys* and mud, and by oxhides put there with stakes and by weirs, and this continues the length of the two parishes of S[t] Andrew and S[t] Sepulchre, to the great damage of all the people passing thereby.

Also a pentice at the Swan hangs two feet beyond the assize over the king's highway to the nuisance of the neighbours. Two barriers have recently been fixed at the Swan to the nuisance and great danger of the whole people. Also a paling has been erected over against (*erga*) the window of the Harpe inn, to the nuisance of the highway and the great danger of all people entering and returning to water their horses and in final destruction of the same entrance. [*Latin*]

CORDEWANERSTRETE. Presentments and indictments of the inquest of the ward of Cordewanerstrete charged before Thomas Knollys, alderman, at his wardmote the same year.

First they indict the stall of the house in which John Seward, plumber, lives on the west part of Cordwanerstrete for being too large towards the highway to the great nuisance and danger of people passing by night. Also the entrances (*huysses*) of two cellars in the rent of Robert Fitz Robert, grocer, at the east end of Aldermary Church are dangerous as being too open towards the highway and having no covers.

Also they indict the rent of Pecche because of stinking filth thrown out by the wife of Sutton, grocer. Also the gate against the well by S[t] Antelyn's church in Watlyngstrete because it is open too long at night. Also the porch of Nicholl

Tunwell in Watlyngstrete because it is too low and a great nuisance to carts passing there. Also two pentices in the rent of Squyry in Bogerowe for the same reason. Also a well lying beyond the shop of Rauf Holand, draper, in Watlyngstrete as ruinous and dangerous to passers-by. Also an entrance to a cellar in Charlton's rents, which John Tropenell holds in Watlyngstrete, opens too far towards the highroad there and has no cover. Also two pentices standing on the rent of the prioress of Derteford with a garden on the pentice[1] in Hosierlane are very defective and ruinous, to the great danger of all people passing there. [*French*]

ALDRESGATE. Indictments in the ward of Aldresgate before John Reynwell, alderman, in the feast of Christmas. Membr. 6 *25 Dec. 1421*

Parish of St Leonard

They indict in Baudesrent in Fasterlane fourteen houses and chambers with windows for casting out of ordure and urine which annoys all the people of the ward. They indict Sir John Scarle, parson of St Leonard in Fasterlane, "for a commyn putour[2] of his owne parischens alle wey duryng, and a Baratour[3], and a scolde, and a perilous Rebaude[4] of his tunge and a discurer of confessioun of the whiche women that wole not asent to his lecherie, the whiche is a gret dissese to all the parisshe. Item we endite the same parsoun, Sir John Scarle, for by cause that he presentit hym self a surgeoun & a visicioun to disseive the peopl with is false connynge, that he scheuithe unto the peopl, by the whiche craft he hathe slayn many a man." [*English*]

Parish of Saint Botulph

They indict the grate and the ditch by the Bars because the water is stopped by dung and rubbish. The way by the ditch from Aldrychesgate to Crepulgate is stopped up against the common profit. [*English*]

[1] *Ove une gardyne sur icelle pentis assise en hosierlane.*
[2] Pander.
[3] Quarrelsome person, fomenter of quarrels.
[4] Ribald.

BILLYNGESGATE.

Parish of St Marie atte Hille

John Skarburgh and his wife are in default for keeping a hostelry and being victuallers and both are foreigners.

The jurors indict all the hucksters for occupying the round land[1] at Billingsgate. Henry Mersche has a jetty in Lovelane, which is too low. The lane before the inn of the abbot of Waltham and the stables there are indicted for encumbering of dung in annoyance of the city. Nichol Busche, lodging with William Ryder, does not pay scot and lot. William, lodging with Thomas Reynewell, buys and sells and is not a freeman and does not pay scot and lot. John Pette, Pedigo[2] and White of Graveshende pay neither to loan, tallage, lot and scot, nor to watches. The cobbler dwelling before the gate of the abbot of Waltham keeps a hostelry for strangers and is a foreigner. Lamb Botham is a foreigner and retails victuals. The stair at Billingsgate is faulty and perilous. [*English*]

Parish of St Andrew

The privy in Richard Osberne's rent is indicted for the stench coming out on the highway, which is an annoyance to the people. [*English*]

Parish of St Botulph

Nichol, who lodges with John Canoun, buys and sells and is not a freeman and does not pay lot and scot. Henry Honeyman, lodging with William Child, does not pay lot and scot. [*English*]

Parish of St George

A broken house between Vannere's *hawe*[3] and the corner house, in which Drynkewater dwelt, is defective and indicted. [*English*]

[1] No doubt for *romeland*, a piece of unoccupied ground, an open space. R. R. Sharpe, *Cal. of Wills*, I, p. 222, points out that there were *romelands* adjacent to the quays of Queenhithe, Dowgate and Billingsgate. According to Wheatley there were *romelands* in front of several monasteries, St Albans, Waltham, Norwich, Bury St Edmunds and Reading. *London, Past and Present*, III, pp. 167–8.

[2] Mentioned in *Cal. Pat. Rolls*, 1416–22, p. 289 as "John" Petigo of Gravesende.

[3] A yard, close or inclosure.

FARNDON WITHIN.

Parish of St Sepulchre within[1]

They present and indict all the sheds in front of the bakehouse of the Friars Minors as a great nuisance to all the people dwelling there and passing. [*French*]

Parish of St Audoen

They present and indict the sign called "the bell on the hope" as dangerous, and likely to fall down suddenly and cause death. Isabelle Edwarde is a forestaller and regrater. [*French*]

Parish of St Michael at Corn

They present William Brooke, yeoman, dwelling before St Martyn's Gate as a foreigner keeping open shop like a freeman. A cellar door under the house of Master John Ratsee, dwelling in Paternosterrowe, is defective and dangerous to men coming and going, who are likely to be dismembered and lose their lives as well by day as by night. They indict two gutters of Madame Fraunces and one gutter of the Chamber rent. [*French*]

Parish of S^t "Martyns"

They indict William atte Wode for making a great nuisance and discomfort to his neighbours by throwing out horrible filth on to the highway, the stench of which is so odious and infectious that none of his neighbours can remain in their shops, which is a great reproof to all this honourable city, because of the lords and other gentlemen and men of the court[2] who go and pass there. Also they indict John Baddisdone and John Parker for using hucksterey at an unlawful time, keeping their doors open till 2 o'clock after midnight against the mayor's ordinance. [*French*]

ALGATE. They present that a piece of the city-wall by Bevysmark is defective and ruinous, to the great danger of

[1] At one time the parish of St Sepulchre extended within Newgate. This portion was included in the new parish of Christ Church in 1547. See Harben, *Dictionary of London*, pp. 139, 524.

[2] Probably refers to the officials of the courts at Westminster, who were generally resident within the city at this period.

the city. They say, as many times previously, that a certain common way under the city-wall towards Algate is stopped up by the prior of Crichirch so that watchmen, going on their rounds for the proper custody of the city, and carts with victuals cannot pass as they used to do for the advantage of the city. Also the prior has an earthen wall and a *paleys*[1] opposite his gate enclosing common soil as far as the garden late of William Cressewyk to the nuisance etc. Also a *getie* on the rent of the abbot of Bury is too low to the nuisance of passers-by. Also they say, as many times previously, that the highway between Pappey and Bishopesgate by the inn of the earl of Oxford is heaped with filth, and because of a certain bank continually falling on the said highway and the enclosure of the common soil under the wall, the common passage there is hindered, to the great nuisance of the whole commonalty.

Parish of St Andrew[2] Belleterlane and Crichirch

Also they say that the churchyard of St Katerine Crichirch has not been enclosed for many years in prejudice of the rites of Holy Church, but it is now illicitly and unlawfully enclosed by the prior and his tenants there, to the nuisance etc. Also they say, as many times previously, that Fridaysaley, otherwise called "Lyon Alley," which from of old ought to be a common *thurghous*[3], is stopped by the said prior, to the nuisance etc. Also a certain watercourse through the land of Lord de Roos and Blaunchapultone is stopped up beneath the tenement of John Morell because the exit is too narrow and not properly cleansed by the said John, which tenement also is situate on the common soil, to the great nuisance etc. Also they say that a certain watercourse there through the land of the Chamber, now in the tenure of William Crowmere, has often been indicted because of the stopping up of the grate through the city wall and of another grate under the foundation of Algate, whereby the highway there is often flooded and heaped with filth to the great nuisance of the whole commonalty.

[1] Paling, palisade. [2] This appears to be St Andrew Undershaft.
[3] Thoroughfare.

Also they say that all the taverners, brewers, regraters of bread and ale and the common lodging-house keepers throughout the whole ward are in default and have broken the assize, to the nuisance etc.

VINETRIE. Membr. 6 *b*

Parish of St Thomas Appostoille

Filth is thrown out of Welles's house and put under the walls of the house of Mildenhale, skinner. [*French*]

Parish of St Martin in the Vinetrie

In Spitellane there are five posts standing on the common soil. Also the gate at the end of Herberlane is set on the common soil.

Also Sir William Busshel the chaplain who sings in the church of St Martin is an apostate. [*French*]

BRADSTRETE.

Parish of St Marie Wolchirche

First the door of the cellar of Adam Smalstrete and the two windows are defective. Also one Henry Kyngeston and his wife Johanne, foreigners, keep a shop and sell victual openly against right. [*French*]

Parish of St Barthylmew the Little

Adam Semy, shearman, and Richard Kere are common colourers[1] of the goods of foreigners and are maintainers and sustainers of foreign brokers and common usurers. The rent of Norton in Legges aleye is ruinous to the great danger and nuisance of the people there. Also Guyse Pawnser and Willyman his wife are common bawds and keep a stew in their house. [*French*]

Parish of St Margaret Lothebury

A *gette*[2] there, which is too low, is defective. Two *gettes* of the rent of the abbot of Westminster are too low and defective. Two *gettes* in the rent of Rauf Stok are defective both for men and carts. [*French*]

[1] I.e. they sell the goods of foreigners under the colour of their freedom, thus evading the restrictions imposed on foreigners.

[2] An overhanging upper story.

Parish of All Hallows

Clement Taverner at the Horne carries filth and ordure into our ward. Also one *gette* there is defective. [*French*]

CANDELWYKSTRETE. First, the pavement belonging to the Chamber in Estchepe is defective. Also the door of a cellar belonging to the church of Abchirche in Candelwykstrete is defective. Also the brewers and hucksters of the ward do not sell their ale according to the proclamation, to wit, Beatrice Tye, William Crane, John at the Swan, Henry Grene, William Bailly, Katerin Fowremarke, Katerine Corsewever in St Laurence Lane, Johan Fyschewif, Alys Baker in St Nicholas Lane, Alys Edwarde, Alis Bristowe, Alys Knyghte, Alys Philpot, Johan Slipton, Katerin Walsche, Anneys Trigge, Walter Shetelmaker, William Canoun and Nicholas Yonge. John Iter, vintner, does not sell by full sealed measure according to the mayor's ordinance. Margaret, wife of Petir Swart, keeps a lodging-house for aliens to the prejudice and against the interests of the king, to wit, Otto van Doren, William Arnoldesone, Petir Hughesone and Gossoun van Lewes. Also Nicholas Yonge is a leper. Also Emmery Manaty conceals and has in his keeping the goods of orphans belonging to Thomas Stanyngburghe. [*French*]

CORNHULL. The men of the inquest have indicted the postern in Langhornesaley for the entry of strumpets there by night. The door of John York's house opens upon the churchyard of St Michael and is a great nuisance to the church and the parishioners there. [*French*]

CASTELL BAINARD. They say that the common latrine at Baynardescastell is heaped with *talgshides*[1] on either side and principally on the land of John Talworth, and thus is very ruinous, and the walls and roof of the same are broken, and divers men fix their boats and *shoutes*[2] to a post of the said latrine, and very often the post is shaken and is likely to give way, and this post is principally used by the boats and *shoutes* of Edmund Dene and William Haynesworthe.

[1] Billets, firewood. [2] A flat-bottomed river-boat. Cf. Dutch *schuit*.

CREPULGATE WITHIN. First they say that Margerie Grenelowe is a common and very noisome scold and has been indicted five or six times already for this and worse matters, and she is so maintained that no execution can be done upon her.

Also the pentice of the same corner (*sic*)[1] abuts too much on the highway. The pavement of the *estulpes*[2] outside Crepulgate as far as the *channel*[3] within the gate is defective. Also the door of the cellar of the Swan in Silverstrete and the paling there are defective. Also the tumbrel carts are greatly defective and are a great nuisance in the ward because they are not willing to have a board behind of the proper size[4].

[*French*]

DOUEGATE. First they say that the lane called Ebbegate is a common way to all people of the city to get water there and do other necessary things in the Thames, which lane is abominably stopped up with filth and privies to the great nuisance of the whole commonalty. Also they say that Brodaxlane is common to all the people of the city. Also Herteshornelane is common to all people to get water there, and there is a *swalo*[5] in it, to the great nuisance and danger of people going and coming there. Also Ermentierslane[6] is common and has now been stopped so that no one can go to the Thames water to have his easement. Also Wolseslane is common, and is stopped by a *wawt*[7] built athwart it (*pardesuys*), and also the lane is full of stinking privy filth to the great nuisance of the commonalty. Also Turinlane is stopped with filth and the pavement is defective. Also Wyndegooslane is common to all men of the city as far as the Thames to do there all things necessary, until John Norhamptone and John Slighe stopped the said lane by a house there by the width of a yard and a length of 171 feet, to the nuisance of the whole commonalty and the disinheritance of the common soil. Also

[1] No doubt the corner dominated by Margery.

[2] *Sc.* stulps, stoops, posts.

[3] Kennel or gutter.

[4] See *Cal. of Letter Book I*, p. 45. Rubbish carts had to be provided with a backboard 2½ feet high to prevent spilling the contents.

[5] A mud-pit, or deep indentation in the road.

[6] Armenters Lane, *alias* Westoneslane after a certain Weston who is recorded as having stopped it up in 1344. *Munim. Gild. Lond.* (R.S.), II, p. 448.

[7] Vault.

Cosinlane is common, and is stopped with filth and posts supporting a paling to the great nuisance of the commons, and the landing with the stairs there is defective. Also Granthamlane is common as far as the Thames. Also Carterslane is common and is stopped by filth and carts and the pavement there is defective, and there is a stone wall belonging to Lord Westmorland, which is likely to fall down and kill people passing. Also the dyers of the ward throw their *rindes*[1] into the Thames, to the destruction of the stream and the nuisance of the commonalty.

Also they say that the Esterlings and Denauntiers[2] hold tenements rented at 100 marks and more yearly, and have communities among themselves, against the ordinance and franchises of the city, for they ought to be under the same governance, as regards their communities, as the freemen of the city, and also they pay no scot or tallage to the king, whereas if Englishmen were there they would be willing to pay all manner of scots and tallages—which is a great oppression to the said ward.

Also the brewers of the ward sell ale against the mayor's *crye*[3]. Also in Grenewichelane there is a house at the *leystowe*[4] of the lane standing on the common soil, and in the same lane there is a stone wall standing too far out by one foot, to the great disturbance of the common way. Also the gable of the house of William Harveys in Granthamlane is ruinous and likely to fall *avale*[5] on the heads of people entering the lane. Also the common stairs in Heywharflane at the Thames are defective.

Also John Balynden keeps open house within the ward notwithstanding that he is a foreigner, and he is also a maintainer of bawdry and his wife is a common bawd and brawler (*contendresse*). [*French*]

LANGEBOURNE. First they present that a gutter of the *thorghous* in St Clement's Lane, in the part ownership of the abbot of Stratford and of the chaplain of the chantry in St

[1] *Sc.* rinds, bark or peel used in dyeing.
[2] Merchants of Dinant. [3] Proclamation.
[4] *Sc.* laystall, laystow, a place where dung or rubbish was deposited.
[5] Fr. *à val*, to the bottom, down.

Clement's church, is too low, so that the water cannot have its course to the highway of St Clement's Lane. Also the pavement before the rent of the said chaplain is broken and defective. Also a common privy standing by the churchyard of Fanchirche is broken and open, to the great danger of people and children at night. [*French*]

WALBROKE. The Inquisition of the faults found within the ward of Walbrook on 1 Jan. A° 9 Henry V in the time of John Penne, then alderman. Membr. 7 *1 Jan. 1422*

First, the men of the inquest of office of the said ward say that the fishmongers, butchers and hucksters occupying the Stokkes make a great nuisance and discomfort to all people passing and dwelling there because they throw entrails and offal out of the Stokkes on to the king's highway to the horribility[1] of the whole ward and city also. Further, the butchers occupy the king's highway with their stalls at the Stokkes by night, to the great danger and damage of people passing.

Also there are wanting in the ward for the common need and profit, a ladder, a hook, a *craper*[2] and ropes, to prevent danger of fire.

Also Nicholas Hay, baker, is accustomed to bake his bread with water from a horrible well in his house, to the great danger and nuisance of all men who eat of it.

Also there are several *donghepes* in Shirbournelane.

[*French*]

CHEPE. "These ben þe defautes and noisaunces founden withinne þe warde of Chepe."

John Stone, brewer, is defective because of stopping the common way through the Rose into Conyhopelane. The house called "the Angell" at Sopers Lane end is old and likely to fall down to the great peril of the people. William Edriche, brewer, throws ordure out at his door into Irmongerlane to the great nuisance of the people. All brewers and hucksters are defective because they do not keep the mayor's *crye*. All

[1] *A graund horribilite*, cf. *Romance of the Rose*, 7187, "Full many another orribilite May men in this book se."

[2] *Sc.* grapper, a grappling-hook.

taverners are defective, sell corrupt wine and do not keep the mayor's *crye*. All fruiterers and hucksters standing in Chepe with corrupt fruit are defective. All poulterers that regrate the market against the mayor's *crye* are defective. [*English*]

LYMSTRETE. Katerine Denys, a common huckster and receiver of evil covins, has been twice indicted and no remedy or execution done. John Dekun and Johane his wife, a huckster of ale, are not under frankpledge. John Sayer and his wife, a huckster of ale, not under frankpledge. John Stok and Margaret his wife are regraters and forestallers of the poultry market, and she is a common scold, who has been six times indicted, and no remedy or execution has been done. Thomas Brid and Johane his wife are forestallers and regraters of poulterers coming to the market. [*English*]

BREDSTRETE. Defaults and nuisances found in the ward.

Parish of St Nicholas Coldabbey

The jurors indict all the fishboards from Friday Street corner to Waleys' shop, and from Waleys' shop to Thomas Russell's shop on both sides. They indict all the cellar doors unclosed in Distaff Lane. The pentice of Richard Iklington's house is too low. [*English*]

Parish of St Augustine

They indict the *faux*[1] stall of John Clerk, tailor. Marion, the wife of John Thornton, is a foreigner retailing and buying as a freewoman. Maute Kelly and Isabelle Sturmyn are foreigners' wives retailing and buying as freewomen. They indict Thomas Chaucere's rent as in danger of falling, and the pavement of the same. John Austyn has stopped the common way through the Pewter Pot, which has been used from time out of mind. [*English*]

Parish of St John the Evangelist

They indict the pavement from the house where Boston dwells as far as the paling beside Hoggecote's house. They indict the cellar door at the Belle for lack of a cover. [*English*]

[1] Possibly "false," in the sense of being of illegal size or projection.

Parish of St Peter in Chepe

They indict the porter of the compter in Chepe as an extortioner and for his untrue measures. [*English*]

Parish of All Hallows Bredstret

They indict the false stalls, barrels and panniers of the salters in Bread Street for standing too far out on the king's highway. They indict the cooks of Bread Street for keeping their dung and garbage under their stalls, and for putting their spits too far out. [*English*]

Parish of St Mildred

They indict Symkyn Audele for casting out ordure at all times of the day. [*English*]

QUENHYTHE. Defaults and nuisances found by the inquest taken before Nicholas James, alderman.

They say that Dybleslane should be common as far as the Thames, and a stair should be made for the easement of the common people to wash and fetch water there, but it has been let for many years, and taken away from the common people by divers tenants named on previous occasions, and now by Thomas atte Wood the landlord.

They find that dung and water and other filth come down by Trinite Lane and Cordwanerstrete by Garlekhithe, and so by the lane between John Hatherle's shop and Richard Whitman's shop, and much of the dung goes into the Thames in destruction of the hithe and the stream, and much continually encumbers the way, which is in great need of being amended.

Also there is a common stair at the end of the lane beside the house which was formerly in the occupation of John Parker, which stair is mischievously broken and right perilous to the people that come thereto at high water or by night, as people have need to come, and this has been indicted for a long time. They understand that the Chamber ought to repair the stair. The pavement beside it is very defective. Also the pavement in the lane above on both sides is defective.

Also they say that ketches (*cacches*), which come with oysters, fish and other things, lay their ropes so high on shore, out of ill will and contempt of the people, that men, women and children fall and hurt themselves grievously, and at night-time old people are likely to fall into the Thames, which has been indicted in the wardmote before.

Also they say that all the brewers break the mayor's proclamation and sell their ale otherwise than they ought to hucksters and others, and all hucksters break the mayor's proclamation in selling of ale and have been indicted yearly for many a year.

Also Elene Steer, Katerine Lylye, the wife of Henry Racheford, Margarete Bury, Luce Clerk, Jonet Wodham, Katerine Wylde and all their fellows are regraters of fish, eggs, chickens and capons, and they keep the fish so long that it stinks, and they beguile the people therewith, and they rise in the morning and wait in the evening, when such victual or butter or cheese come, and go into the boat and buy it up privily, thus making a dearth of such victuals and hindering the common people of the city.

Membr. 7 *b* Also behind the Pye at Quenhithe is a privy place which is a good shadowing for thieves, and many evil bargains have been made there, and many strumpets and pimps have their covert there, and leisure to make their false covenants, all which the jurors think it would be good and necessary to have amended, in destruction of evil, and the place should be closed by night and opened by day at a certain hour.

There is also another thing by which men of the city and of the country and lords' caterers and chapmen and others feel themselves aggrieved, and that is this—John of Ely has taken the charge, among other charges which he has, of keeping the assay of oysters, in order that the oysters may be good, wholesome and in season for man's body and for chapmen to buy, for ofttimes men have seen ketches with oysters lying for two or three days, and not half the oysters sold, and then the ketches go out with their unsold oysters and bring the same back again with a freshening of new, which is a foul deceit; wherefore it is needful for the assayer to be true in his office; but notwithstanding this, this John of Ely lets his office to farm to women, who know not (how to do it); nor is it worship to this city that women should have such things in governance.

Also at the end of Tryggeslane there is a stair grievously broken, and the pavement thereby, which is a great nuisance to the common people and has been indicted many a year. Also in the same lane two chimneys are defective and perilous for mischief that might befall of fire. Also Ingram Couper occupies the highway with full and empty vinegar pipes and has done so for a long time throughout the year to the great nuisance of the people, and it were good to be amended. Also in Fishstrete Richard Pountfrayte, John Horle, John Knotte, James Bocher and John of Bury, fishmongers, occupy the king's highway with their boards and other things to the great nuisance of the common people. [*English*]

BRIDGE. Nuisances and defaults found in the ward of London Bridge by inquest before John Michell, alderman, in his wardmoot held on the day of St Thomas the Apostle.

First they present that there are no crooks nor iron chains nor ladder for common use in the ward in case a fire should happen, which God forbid, and this has often been presented and no remedy has been done. Also the tubs and boards of the fishmongers at the corner of St Magnus's Church, and especially in front of the shops of Deonys Broune, widow of Adam Broune, and Andrew Totyng, and also the barrels in front of the boards of the fishmongers in Bridge Street stand out on the highway beyond what is reasonable, to the great nuisance of passers-by, horses and carts.

Also they present that the brewers in the ward do not sell their ale according to the mayor's proclamation, to wit, Nicholas Aleyn, Richard Crosse at the Cokke in St Michael's Lane, Richard Aleyn, Christian Bekeswell, and John Thomas at the Egle in Graschirchestrete.

Also they present the names of the bakers in the ward, to wit, Alice Taillour and John Newcastell in Graschirchestrete.

Also they present the innkeepers in the ward for selling ale in their inns in *hanaps*[1] and not by sealed measure according to the proclamation, to wit, Robert Whaplode, senior, John

[1] Goblets or cups.

Couper, Robert Whaplode, junior, Robert Multon, Robert Scrace, Richard Vyse at the White Horse in Graschirchstrete, John Botiller, Andrew Catour and William Bateman.

Also they present the hucksters in the ward for selling ale in their houses in *hanaps*, to wit, the wife of Robert Rose, Johan Apperle, the wives of John Bartilmewe, Thomas Belamy, James Grene, William Wodeland, William Clerk, cutler, John Tanner, barber, and Ballard Emmot at the Red Latys by St Magnus, Johan Vygrus, Alys Bradwey, Alys Ade, Cristian Scot, the wife of Symond Myngeham, John Grene, cook, John Dorston, John Fouller, John Tukman, the wives of Richard Thurston, John Russell, John Elys and Hugh Brew, Alys Ulseby, Margarete Colwell, the wife of John Brokforth, and Rauf Cook at the end of London Bridge.

Also they present that in Crokedlane there is a door belonging to the cellar of Polhill, skinner, which is perilous and defective and likely to do great damage.

Also they present the orphans within the ward, to wit, four children of Adam Broun and five children of William Flete[1].

Also they present that Stepheneslane, otherwise called Chirchehawelane in Thames Street is open both by night and day towards the Thames to the great danger and mischief (of the people) if anything happens, which God forbid.

Also, Richard Taillour, clerk, is a foreigner and dwells in Thames Street against the franchise of the city, and is rebellious, in that he is unwilling to obey his alderman or come at his command.

Also, William Wodeford, Robert Cok and John Andrewe throw filth in the Oistergate of Thamisestrete to the great nuisance of the commons. [*French*]

TOWRE. Defaults and nuisances found by inquest before John Michell[2], alderman of the same ward.

They indict William Clausoun for casting out of his house *drayffe* and putting it into the Thames. Also he has standing in the street a dray which hinders the people day and night.

[1] As needing the guardianship of the Court of Aldermen.

[2] This appears to be a clerical error. William Sevenoke was alderman of Tower Ward.

Also there is a dunghill in Watergatestrete by Berelane, which is noisome to the common people, because of the casting out into this lane of the ordure of privies and other horrible sights.

Also William Brigis and his man John are extortioners of men's beasts, because they take and drive horses, swine, goats and other beasts into the Tower, and hinder the king's people, and they also bring up new customs against divers men and women, contrary to the freedom of the city, when they are fetching water, washing clothes or picking chips on the common ground, for the said William and John make them pay a certain (custom) to the Tower. They are also rebellious against the officers of the city, for whenever any officer would do his duty, they come with great cunning out of the Tower and bring the parties into the Tower against the freedom of the city.

Also in the Watergate at Wolkeye there stands a paling on the common ground, which is a hindrance to the common people. Also Allard Taillour is an alien born and keeps a hostelry, colouring many strangers, such as *Esterlinges* and other foreigners, to the great nuisance of his neighbours. Also John Kempe, carter, is a baratour and a common scold and hinders the king's people with carts standing in the street night and day. [*English*]

In an action for debt of 10 marks by Clement Yerdley against Abraham Wybbenbury, fruiterer, and Isabel his wife, widow of Simon Huntborne, *mynestrell*, the defendants made four defaults, whereupon the plaintiff prayed that the foreign attachment be delivered to him. The goods were valued by oath of Henry Clerk and John Stok, goldsmiths, and delivered to him under security of William Bolton, brewer, and William Lovekyn, pasteler, to answer therefor etc., as follows:— Membr. 8 *18 Feb. 1422*

Two pieces of silver weighing 14½ oz. at 30d the oz.; six silver spoons weighing 4¼ oz. at 30d the oz.; one pommel of a sword, consisting of a stone like the stone called "*serpentyn*," 3s 4d; one necklace (*monile*) called "*nowche*[1]" of silvergilt weighing 1¼ oz., valued at 3s 4d; one silvergilt Agnus Dei

[1] *Sc. ouche*, a clasped necklace.

weighing $\frac{3}{8}$ oz., valued at 12d; one gold ring with a precious stone called "*diamaund*" weighing 40 dwt., valued at 3s 8d; seven rings and a golden heart weighing 29$\frac{3}{4}$ dwt. at 11d the dwt.; one ring with a stone called "*amatist*," weighing 8$\frac{3}{4}$ dwt. at 11d the dwt.; one red purse of double *satyn* valued at 6d; total, £4 14s 1$\frac{1}{2}$d.

18 May 1422 Richard, abbot of St Peter's, Westminster, brings a plaint of intrusion against Thomas Dogull, rector of St Andrew's, Holborn, Richard Berneward and William Ogull, churchwardens of the same, John Snell and William Coventre, prior of the house and church of St Bartholomew Smithfield, touching his free tenement in the parish of St Andrew's Holborn.

17 Aug. 1422 Thomas, abbot of St Saviour's Bermundeseye, brings a plaint of intrusion against John White, master of St Bartholomew's Hospital in West Smithfield, and Richard Balman, cordwainer, touching his free tenement in the parish of All Hallows the Less in Temsestret.

17 Oct. 1421 John Page, ironmonger, was summoned to answer John Patteswyke for detinue of a bond in which the plaintiff was bound to Agatha, widow of John Pytman, grocer, in £50, which bond the plaintiff alleged had been delivered by him to the defendant on 1 Aug. for safe custody and return when required.

The defendant pleaded that the bond had been delivered to him by the plaintiff and the said Agatha under certain conditions, and as he did not know whether the conditions had been fulfilled, he prayed that the said Agatha be summoned to show cause why the bond should not be delivered to the plaintiff. The said Agatha was summoned by William Wode and Richard Davy, serjeants of the Chamber, to appear on 22 Nov. and did not come. Therefore it was considered that the bond be delivered to the said John Patteswyke.

27 Dec. 1421 Bond of William Maltby, mercer, executor of the will of Simon Hereward, mercer, John Olney and John Hertewelle, mercers, to John Bederenden, chamberlain, in 100 marks, to pay the sum of £66 in even portions at Easter, Michaelmas and Easter following, to the use of John and Alice, orphans of the said Simon. *Cancelled.*

14 Nov. 1421

A record of the payment of 40 marks by William Maltby, by even portions on 14 Nov. 1421, 20 Jan. 1423, 9 Feb. 1424 and 11 Feb. 1425, in accordance with a recognisance to the chamberlain, to the use of the above orphans. The moneys were delivered to John Talbot and John Admond, mercers, for the sustenance of the children.

Membr. 8 *b*
2 Sept. 1422

Mutual bonds of Stephen Elyot of co. Middlesex and John Fitz of Polangre co. Bedford, executor of the will of Thomas Wytenham, brewer, in £40, to abide by the arbitration of John Fray, William Aston and Alexander Anne, as regards a debt claimed by the above John Fitz.

...Sept. 1422

Recognisances of Thomas Stopham, prior, John Botiller, draper, and Robert Whityngham, draper, to John Bederenden, chamberlain, in £100.

27 Aug. 1421

William Aunger, renter of London Bridge, was mainprised by Robert Crulle, bowyer, and John Ergaston, stockfishmonger, for his appearance in court, under penalty of £40.

18 July 1422

Memorandum that Laurence Palavysyn came before the mayor and aldermen and being examined on oath at the instance of certain Italian merchants as to the authority under which he had caused a ship laden with goods belonging to John de Bardis and other merchants to be unloaded at Southampton, swore that he did so as proctor of a certain Antonius de Secha, who had a general commission to conduct business for John de Bardis either by himself or by his agents.

Membr. 9
5 May 1422

Arbitration of William Crowmere and Henry Barton, aldermen, William Bray, bachelor of law, and James Cole, clerk, between Sir Roger Sutton *alias* Cartelet, rector of S[t] Peter's Church in Bradstrete, on the one part and John Perye, John Mowbray, John Sandon, Henry Best and other parishioners on the other part, in disputes concerning a mansion called a "rectory" lately built next to the church in the churchyard. They award that, in view of the contiguity of the church and rectory, which will enable the rectors to administer the sacraments more promptly, the rectory shall pertain to the rector for the time being and that Sir Roger Sutton shall receive free entry and the keys thereof at Easter, and that he and his successors shall occupy and inhabit it and shall have their personal residence there, on condition that they provide two wax tapers, each weighing two lbs., to stand before the high altar in memory of the donor of the site on which the rectory was built.

17 Jan. 1422 Original bill of Robert Fitz Andrew against Ralph Hamelyn, esquire, and Agnes his wife, for the detinue of 7 marks borrowed by the said Agnes when she was "sole."

20 July 1422 Letter of attorney from John Wodecok to John Pyke, draper, and John Bryd, vintner, to receive from Walter Chertesey and Ralph Valentyn an annual rent of 12 marks 12s due from certain tenements in the parish of St Mary of Abbechirche, until they should have levied the sum of £120 from the said rent.

9 March 1422 John Trevilias, pewterer, was mainprised by John Trevilias, goldsmith, and John Elkyn, brewer, that neither he nor anyone of his covin would in future either secretly or openly engage in carrying by boat or ferrying from London to Graveshende, nor derive any profit or advantage therefrom, unless he were licensed by the court here, under penalty of £40 payable to John Bederenden, chamberlain.

Membr. 9 *b*
18 Aug. 1422 Assignment by John Bryd, vintner, and Agnes his wife to Thomas Pyk, draper, and his son John Pyk, of an annual rent of 12 marks 10s issuing from certain tenements in the parish of St Mary Abbechirche, which rent had been assigned on 30 Sept. 1421 to the said Agnes, under the name of Agnes Hampton, widow, by John Wodecok and Elizabeth his wife, John Bathe, clerk, William Randolph, goldsmith, and William Dales of co. York for repayment of a loan of £123 15s, the present assignment to continue until the balance of £115 15s had been levied.

2 Sept. 1422 Acquittance, dated 31 July in the cathedral church of St Paul, from Richard Ketford, saddler, John Seyes, saddler, Alexander Farnell, tailor, William Brid, *browederer*, John Ray, skinner, and Thomas Wryght, painter, to William, Lord de Botreaux, knight, for 48 marks 7s 1d in part payment of 468 marks 3s 4d due on eight several recognisances made in Chancery 1 Feb. 1422.

Recognisance by William Estfeld, mercer, Richard Quatermayn and Richard Esgaston, fishmongers, in £70 to John Bederenden, chamberlain. *Cancelled.* *31 Aug. 1422*

Mutual bonds of Gilbert Page, cook, and William Audely, cook, in £20 to John Bederenden, chamberlain, for their good behaviour towards each other and towards the masters and good men of the mistery of Cooks and Pastelers and for their obedience to all the good ordinances and rules ordained by the said masters and confirmed by this Court. *7 Sept. 1422*

An inquest of office taken before Robert Chichele, mayor, and the aldermen, to inquire what aliens not of the king's allegiance or other persons, not having been admitted and sworn before the mayor and aldermen, have exercised the office or occupation of broker between merchant and merchant, against the liberty of the city and the ordinance lately made for putting an end to fraud and deceit among brokers, by oath of Martin Kilham, John Somery, William Dawtre, John Furner, Robert Hulle, John Stormworth, Robert Marschal, Thomas Coke, Thomas Hardyng, Walter Frebarne, Thomas Style, Robert Herne and Laurence Parram, who say on oath that:— Membr. 10 *20 Aug. 1422*

Nicholas Orlandyn, alien, not being admitted or sworn, had exercised brokerage and was a broker, factor and intermediary between Richard Clerc and John Pyke, drapers, the sellers, and Tottus Machiavelii and Hubertyn de Bardys, merchants of Florence, the buyers, of 200 strait cloths of Essex, price £40, on 10 July 1422, long after the making of the ordinance, and that he received 16s 8d brokerage from the sellers.

Also James de Pogeo acted as a broker between Walter Chartesey, draper, seller, and Ivo Catayne, merchant of Genoa, buyer, of 11 woollen cloths of divers colours, price 20 marks, receiving 11s brokerage.

Nicholas Orlandyne, alien, acted as a broker between John Elvisch, draper, seller, and Francis Serale, merchant of Florence, buyer, of 30 woollen cloths of Ludlowe of divers colours, price £60, brokerage unknown.

James Juwe, alien, acted as a broker between Robert Whityngham, draper, seller, and Ivo Catayne, merchant of Genoa, buyer, of 10 woollen cloths of Ludlowe of divers colours, price £40, brokerage unknown.

John Hake, Englishman, and James de Pogeo, alien, acted as brokers between John Heyham, draper, seller, and Paul Miliany, merchant of Lucca, buyer, of 38 woollen cloths of Ludlowe of divers colours, price £100, each receiving 32s 8d brokerage.

David Galganete, alien, acted as broker between Peter Bernard, merchant of Lombardy, seller, and John Cherch, mercer, buyer, of 4 cloths of gold and silk, price £30, brokerage unknown, and also between Ivo Catayne, seller, and Isabel Norman, trading sole as a silkwoman, buyer, of gold of Cyprus on pipes (*in pip'*)[1], price £8, brokerage unknown.

Alexander Petit *alias* Portenale, alien, for acting as a broker between Robert Whityngham, draper, seller, and John Boteler and John Hertwell, mercers, buyers, of 7 casks of woad and a certain quantity of pepper, price £160, brokerage unknown.

Philip Saty, alien, acted as a broker between Henry Fyschere, dyer, seller, and Antony Maroffo, merchant of Genoa, buyer, of seven whole cloths (*vii integr' pann'*) of London make, price £70, brokerage unknown.

The jurors say further that the above persons are common brokers, factors, and intermediaries between merchants, both native and foreign.

4 Aug. 1422 Whereas it had been reported and proved before the mayor and aldermen that Thomas Glanton and Alice his wife, pretending to be free of the city, had taken Alice Saumple, daughter of William Saumple of Norham co. Northumberland, and Agnes Saumple, daughter of John Saumple of Newcastle-on-Tyne, as apprentices for terms of seven years to serve in

[1] A pipe was a tube or roll on which thread was wound.

the art of a *brouderer*, in which art the said Alice pretended to be practised and expert, although in fact the said Thomas Glenton (*sic*) and Alice were not free of the city, nor was the said Alice in any way practised in the art of a *brouderer*, it was considered by the mayor and aldermen that the said Alice and Agnes, thus fraudulently and deceptively taken as apprentices, should be exonerated, notwithstanding the indentures.

Memorandum that the mayor and aldermen were informed by Master Thomas Winchelse, "*sacre pagine professorem*,[1]" and his brethren, being the warden and convent of the Friars Minors within Newgate, and also by the rector and parishioners of St Nicholas Flesh Shambles that a lane called ......,[2] lying at the west end of St Nicholas' church, wherein the Friars by grant of the city from of old had free ingress and exit for the carriage of necessaries, was so heaped with dung and foul intestines from the oxen, pigs and other beasts which were herded there every week for butchering, that the Friars, the rector and others dwelling there could not have free passage, and, what was even worse, there was likely to be danger from the corrupt exhalations and other abominable and infectious smells rising all day from the filth there, unless some remedy were applied. Thereupon the mayor and aldermen, who were bound to guard against such dangers and preserve the good name of the city, with the consent and at the expense of the Friars, the rector, and the dwellers on either side of the lane, caused the pavement at the south end to be raised, so that the filth coming from the houses in the lane might the more easily run down into the kennel of the king's highway, and in order to prevent the standing of cattle there, they ordained that the rector at his own costs and expense should cause to be erected a gate 9 feet 8 inches wide across the lane from the stone wall of the rector's house on the east of the lane to the stone wall under the corner tenement on the west, and standing 33 feet this side of the gate which the Friars had for their Membr. 10 *b*

[1] Equivalent to Doctor of Divinity.

[2] This lane was called "Stinking Lane." See article by Marjorie B. Honeybourne in *London Topographical Record*, 1932. It was later known as Butcher Hall Lane and is now King Edward Street.

entrance and carriage into the lane, the width of the lane being 13 feet 7 inches between the stone walls where the Friars' gate stood, under condition that the new gate belong to the rector and his successors during the pleasure of the mayor and commonalty, and that the rector and his successors have the gate opened, when required, at all reasonable times, and permit the Friars to enjoy ingress and exit for carriage and passage.

Membr. 11
19 Sept. 1422

Reciprocal bonds of Thomas Stopeham, prior of the house of St Mary Magdalene of Tortyngton co. Surrey, John Boteler, draper, and Robert Whityngham, draper, to accept the award of John Gedney, William Weston, William Crowmere and Nicholas Wotton, drapers, in disputes between them.

Membr. 11 *b*

William Fysshewyke, son of John Fysshewyke of York, was exonerated from his apprenticeship to William Jykman, tailor, because the latter had left the city, occupied no shop there and had made no arrangements for his instruction.

ROLL A 51

(*William Walderne, mayor*)

John Wattes, son of John Wattes of Bleseworth co. Northampton, was exonerated from his apprenticeship to John Terver, grocer, because the latter had failed to enrol him in the Guildhall during the first year of his term, and had made four defaults when summoned. Pledges, Thomas North and Robert Pairs. [*French and Latin*] Membr. 1 *25 Oct. 1422*

Acquittance from Richard Ketford and John Seyes, saddlers, Alexander Farnell, tailor, William Brid, *brouderer*, John Ray, skinner, and Thomas Wright, painter, to William, Lord de Botreaux, knight, for 48 marks 7s 1d in part payment of 468 marks 3s 4d due on eight several recognisances made in Chancery 1 Feb. 1422. *28 Nov. 1422*

On the information of many neighbours of John Goman, smith, living in the parish of St Mildred Poultry, and also of the masters and good men of the mistery of Smiths, John Tepstyn, who had been apprenticed to John Godyng, deceased, and subsequently transferred by the latter's executors to John Goman, was exonerated from his apprenticeship because John Goman had not instructed or provided for him sufficiently, and the said John Tepstyn was turned over to John Toky, smith, to serve the remainder of his term. *20 Nov. 1422*

Recognisance by Brother John Neall, master of the house of St Thomas the Martyr of Canterbury called "of Acon,[1]" to repay John Barton, senior, the sum of £200 lent by him to the house. Membr. 1 *b* *10 Jan. 1423*

Reciprocal bonds of Ralph Bateman of co. Cambridge, esquire, and Nicholas Caldecot, of the same county, gentleman, in £100 to abide by the award of Henry Shelford, clerk, Robert Caundyssh, Nicholas Dixon, clerk, and Richard *6 Feb. 1423*

[1] The hospital of St Thomas of Acres, a collegiate house on the north side of Cheapside. Mercers' Hall and Chapel were erected on the site, which was purchased after the Dissolution. Harben, *Dict. of London*, p. 405; J. Watney, *Hospital of St Thomas of Acon.*

Baynard, in an assize of *novel disseisin* between them, or of an umpire, being a justice of the one Bench or the other, chosen by the said arbitrators.

10 May 1423 Richard, abbot of Westminster, brings a plaint of intrusion against Richard Gosselyn, John Weston, esquire, and Thomas Knolles, junior, grocer, touching his free tenement in the parish of St Mary at Hill.

5 July 1423 John Kyngeston and Maud his wife pray for an assize of nuisance against John Rawlyn and Robert Rawlyn, touching their free tenement in the parish of St Botolph without Aldgate.

Membr. 2
21 Dec. 1422 CASTELBAYNARD. Inquest of the Wardmote taken there before John Perneys, alderman, on the feast of St Thomas the Apostle in the first year of King Henry the Sixth by oath of twelve good men of the ward duly sworn before the alderman to inquire upon the underwritten articles:—

They present that the watergate opposite St Benet's Church is often blocked by barges and boats so that the water cannot enter and cleanse it, wherefore they pray that the barges and boats may be removed under penalty, except in time of tempest. They also present that the mud and *robous*[1], flowing from the little conduit in Westchepe and passing from the Oldechonge into Carter Lane is a great nuisance to inhabitants and passers-by; also that the steps of Poules wharf are often blocked with boats tied up there so that servants cannot draw water.

PORTSOKEN. Inquest taken before *dominus* William Clerc, prior of the church of Holy Trinity the Great, then alderman of the ward, by oath of William atte Hoke, Simon Potkyn, Peter Maundeville, John Lorys, John Dunche, Thomas Doke, Geoffrey Brid, Thomas Bryght, William Stebranke, William Haliwode, Geoffrey Cook, Richard Hardyng and William Burwell.

They present the Master of St Katherine by the Tower, the heirs of Henry atte Hoke, the well between the Belle and the

[1] Rubbish.

Helme, the tenements late of Adam Frauunceys, the grate towards Bishopsgate, and the brewers, bakers and regraters of bread and ale [in the same terms as in the preceding year][1].

QUENHITHE. The jurors, John Bate, William Key, John Beuchamp, John Thorn, William Sutton, John Arundell, John Markby, William Burton, John Berier, Richard Barr, John Yepstow and Robert Cotyng, being sworn on 26 Dec. before Nicholas James, alderman, complain of the enclosure of Dybuslane[2] [as in the preceding year]. [*English*] *26 Dec. 1422*

LYMSTRETE. Presentment and indictment made on the 10th day of January. *10 Jan. 1423*

Mawde Sheppyster keeps open shop, retails and is not a freewoman; also she is a strumpet to more than one and a bawd also. "The same" Thomas Brid is a forestaller and regrater of victuals coming to the market. John Cool is a sustainer of them in his shop. Anneys Edward, Gaas Furneys, Cateryn Sprynger and Julian Blyndale are regraters of *pollayle*[3] and wildfowl.

The wall of the garden belonging to the prior of Wenlok stands 3 feet too far on to the highway and stops the dung and water, so that no man can pass that side of the way nor on the other side either. Also the pavement belonging to the Chamber of the Yyldehalle is defective. [*English*]

BREDSTRETE. The wardmote of the ward of Bredstret held before Robert Wydyngton, alderman, on the day of St Thomas the Apostle. [*French*] *21 Dec. 1422*

They indict the porter of the Countour[4] as an extortioner of the king's people, and the outer gate for fault of closure.

[1] See above, p. 119. They no longer complain of the tenements late of Thomas Clerk, the posts on the highway and the obstruction of the highway by filth. Rampamd, labourer, is here called Rampane.

[2] See above, p. 137. Dybles, Dibles or Dybus lane was in the parish of St Michael Queenhithe. R. R. Sharpe, *Cal. of Wills*, I, p. 153.

[3] Poultry.

[4] Bread Street Compter, the office and prison of the Sheriffs' Court, was one of the two original compters, the other being in the Poultry. It was removed to Wood Street in 1555, to Giltspur Street in 1791 and closed in 1854.

Parish of St Nicholas Coldabbey

They indict as nuisances the pentice of Richard Iklyngton and the boards underneath, the fish-boards[1] from Friday Street to Waleys' shop, from thence on both sides of the road to Thomas Russel's shop, the board of Nicholas Knottisford, and the boards and barrels of William Bate and Nicholas Triplowe for standing out too far. [*English*]

21 Dec. 1422 ALDRICHESGATE. Wardmote held before John Reynwell, alderman, the day of St Thomas the Apostle. [*French*]

They present the common pavement from the Gate as far as Water Beawes' house on that side for stopping the town ditch. [*English*]

Membr. 2 *b* *25 Dec. 1422* CORDEWANERSTRETE. Indictments and presentments of office before Thomas Knolles, alderman.

Richard Bovyngton as an utterer of unlawful language and a "noyous" neighbour and Mergret his wife as a common strumpet.

John atte Watir, baker, for making bread with well water. [*English*]

21 Dec. 1422 WALBROKE. Inquest indented of the defaults found within the ward on the day of St Thomas the Apostle in the time of Robert Whityngham, alderman.

They present the fishmongers etc. and the lack of fire appliances (in the same words as in the preceding year)[2].

They say that the people of the ward suffer a great nuisance and corruption from the ordure of the privy, which comes from London Wall and runs down to the Thames through Walbrooke.

Leystowes in front of the house of William Wodemonger and the rent of Madame Fastolf[3], at the Brodeax and in Grenewichlane are stopped and forbarred to the great nuisance of all the city. [*French*]

[1] This district, now Knightrider Street, was called Old Fish Street. This passage gives evidence that the market continued to be held there long after the erection of the Stocks Market.

[2] See above, p. 135.

[3] Apparently Joan, widow of Alderman Hugh Fastolf. She had tenements in Budge Row in this ward.

BYSSHOPESGATE. Verdict of the wardmote by John Wollaxton, Thomas Richer, John Moore, William Benet, John Astell, William Edward, Richard Marchall, William Shirbourne, William Brounyng, Hugh Hakon, John Feirman, John Gildeford and Thomas Mercer, to wit:

Agnes Doget is a great scold and regrater. Roberge, the wife of William Astred, Agneys, the wife of William Savge, Margerie the wife of William Robert, and Richard Whitecastele are great regraters.

They present the ditch between the Briggehous and S[t] Mary Spetill[1] as defective because it was closed up so that the water could not have issue. For the same reason they present the ditch between Donnysmore and the bridge in front of the Briggehous, and the gutter between Donnysmore and Bisshopesgate. [*French*]

FARNDON WITHIN. They present William Emery, poulterer, for throwing goose dung, heron dung and horse dung on the highway. They indict John Stuard, a foreigner, for buying and selling capons, hens and boars and for selling brawn in his house as a freeman; John Bambiry, a foreigner, and his wife for selling oxen; John London, a foreigner, and his wife for retailing *chaffer*[2] as though they were free; the wife of Richard Bisshopp, huckster, for selling retail; Alison Herford as a common scold and a foreigner buying and selling as a freewoman; Elyn Sonde, Jonet Swainlond and her sister Alson Baldok, as hucksters; William Emery and his wife and his servants as regraters; and the wife of William Brook living against S[t] Martin's gate as a foreigner and a forestaller of divers *chaffer*. [*English*]

BASSYNGESHAWE. Henry Scarlet, John Pyteman, William Lyncoln, Robert Couper, Thomas Walter, John Stodeley, John Basile, John Richard, Thomas Shawe, William Flete, Thomas Monke and Philip Sunnynge present William Bracy for keeping carts for hire (as in the previous year). [*French*] *21 Dec. 1422*

[1] Known in early times as the New Hospital without Bishopsgate. It was a Priory of Augustinian Canons and a hospital with lay brothers and sisters to tend the sick. Tanner, *Notitia Monastica*, p. 312; *Vict. History of London*, I, pp. 530–4.

[2] Small wares.

Membr. 3 CREPULGATE WITHOUT. Presentments and indictments of the inquest of office of the ward of Cripplegate without charged before John Botiller, alderman.

They indict Gerard Clayson and his wife, occupiers of the Estewehous in Grub Street, as evildoers and receivers and maintainers of harlotry and bawdry and of an evil covin, who are of horrible life, and of strumpets and other malefactors, to the great nuisance and peril of neighbours and passers-by. They present John Sherman, cooper, of Grub Street for keeping *dokes* (ducks) to the nuisance of the neighbours. They indict the garden-wall of John Maryns in Grub Street for standing too far out on the highway. They also indict the stew-house in the ward as a nuisance and trouble to the neighbours, because it is a common house of harlotry and bawdry, and a great resort of thieves and also of priests and their concubines, to the great disgrace of the city and the danger and mischief of the neighbours and passers-by, and likewise they indict the privy of the stew-house as a nuisance because of the great corruption coming therefrom. They further indict four privies in Westyard because they stop up the common watercourse running into the ditch of the Moor, and the privies of Robert Brynkele, goldsmith, and Thomas Lucas, grocer, which stand above the common watercourse and stop the flow of water.

Also they present that three ancient watercourses, two in Fore Street and the third near the Moor, are stopped up, which is a nuisance whenever there is an abundance of water or a flood of rainwater. Also they indict the cart of John Riche of Wood Street, brewer, because the wheels have iron strakes, which destroy the pavement and make a great noise, when the cart is loaded with barrels and *draskes*[1], as often happens. [*French*]

[The remainder of this membrane contains enrolments of bonds etc., see below, p. 159.]

Membr. 4
11 Jan. 1423 CHEPE. Presentation of the defaults and nuisances by the inquest of office of the ward, 11th January.

[1] Probably a variant of draffs, brewers' grains or malt-refuse.

The house at the corner of Irmongerlane in Chepe is ruinous and about to fall down. The cellar windows in the rent at one time belonging to Adam Fraunceys in Irmongerlane stand too much on the common ground to the great harm of people passing by. [*English*]

BILLYNGESGATE. This indented inquest of the 5th January in the time of William Cambrigge then alderman of the ward testifies that these are the defaults found and indicted in the ward and presented to the alderman by the oath of Thomas Sowtham, John Folbery, Geffery Bokeler, Thomas Lyon, Nicholas Lyon, William Staunton, Robert Rase, John Sudbery, William Bakere, Robert Pawle, William Hamunde, Nicholas Hony, John Gryndere, Water Fayrestede and Hugh Scharpe:— *5 Jan. 1423*

Nicholas Busche at host with Saundir Miles pays neither lot nor scot. William Stafford at host with Thomas Reynwell buys and sells and is not a freeman and pays neither scot nor lot. John Pette, Petigo and White of Graveshende pay neither to loan, tallage, lot nor scot, nor to the watch, which should be profit or honour to the city. John Pette is a forestaller of salt and corn on the river. Lambo the boatman is a foreigner, retails victuals, is a chider and a *baratour* with his neighbours and a rebel against the king's officers. John Nelham farms a false custom, i.e., ½d for a case of herrings, and he takes quarterage of the wines, oysters, mussels and all manner of fish belonging to freemen. Robert Gerveys occupies the common ground of the *romelonde*[1], taking unlawful customs of victuals and ships both of foreigners and freemen. William Chaundeler of Grenewych is a freeman but pays neither lot nor scot. The privy in Richard Osberne's rent is indicted because of the stench of filth that comes into the king's highway. John Brymston, a foreigner, sells by retail and keeps guests. Peris Hattere, draper, dwelling outside Aldersgate, is indicted for withholding £4 due to a chantry in the church of St Margaret Patyns which was bequeathed by a will enrolled in the Guildhall in 23 Edward III[2]. [*English*]

[1] See above, p. 128, n. 1.
[2] See R. R. Sharpe, *Cal. of Wills*, I, pp. 552–3; II, pp. 367–8. By the wills of Thomas and Andrew atte Vyne.

TOWER. Verdict of an Inquest held before William Sevenoke "on seint Thomas Day of ynde,[1]" of "myslevynge men & women & other thyngis that we have charge of."

The porter of the Tower does great extortion and wrong to the city by taking barges and ferryboats and other vessels into the Tower, so that the owners must buy them, "as it were in Fraunce," by the prayers of their good neighbours and other men. [*English*]

VINETRIE. The jurors present five posts in Spitellane and the gate at the end of Herberlane as standing on the common soil. [*French*]

DOUEGATE. They say that the common lane called Ebbegate is stopped with filth, that Brodaxlane is a common lane, that Ermenterslane is common and is stopped with filth and the stair there is broken, so that no man can get water from the Thames, that Wolsilane is common and is stopped with filth and privies on either side, that Turynlane is common and is full of filth and the pavement is defective, that Gowerlane is common and that there are certain stones standing on the common soil and certain windows in the rent of All Hallows the Great which are dangerous to passers-by, that Haywharf-lane is common and is obstructed by the fullers who wash their cloths there, so that at those times when they occupy the lane no one else can draw water or make their easements there, to the great nuisance of the commonalty, and that Wyndagayngooslane is common, but is stopped up by a house projecting a yard forward for a length of 171 feet, in disinheritance of the common soil. [*French*]

BRADSTRETE. The earthen wall with a gutter under it, at one time belonging to Henry Sadeler, is a nuisance to the common people. Two dunghills on both sides of the common privy door are defective owing to the default of the Chamber. The wall of the Austin Friars in front of All Hallows Church stands on the common soil. [*English*]

[1] St Thomas is said to have been martyred on a missionary journey to India.

FARNDON WITHOUT. The common privy of Ludgate is defective and *perlous*[1] and the ordure thereof rotteth the stone walls and makes a horrible stench and a foul sight, to the great discomfort and nuisance of all folk dwelling thereabout and passing thereby, and a disgrace to all the City, that so foul a nuisance should be so nigh so common a highway, and it has often been presented and no remedy has yet been ordained.

The mud wall in the Great Bayli next to "Shellardis hous" is falling *parcelmele*[2] into the street, the timberwork of Fletebrigge is defective and perilous and the undersetting of it is insufficient, the paling on the wharf beside the bridge is broken and rubbish is thrown in there to the great hindering of the stream, and a cabin made of old boards at the shop of John Broke, waxchandler, encroaches on the common ground and is a nuisance to all folk there passing.

Also a chimney and a paling of Sir John Mapilton and a chimney of "Convers in"[3] and another chimney at the "*Newe in*"[4] are set on the common ground, and a dunghill within Temple Gate encumbers the highway.

They present and indict White the carpenter and his wife for being as common bawds as any in London and for being receivers of strumpets, and they have been twice indicted before this time and no execution has been done thereon. Membr. 4 *b*

They present Henry Grene, wheeler, as a foreigner who encumbers the field with timber, and William Emery for laying dung in the highway all through the year and for casting out horse piss that had stood under his horse a month or six weeks so that no man can pass there for *styngle*[5].

They present Grantham the goldsmith for making a *bye* door in the Spetill rent opening into Bartelmewes Lane to the great peril of the king's people and also against the will of

[1] Perilous. [2] Bit by bit.

[3] The House of Converts erected in Chancery Lane, then called New Street, by Henry III for converted Jews. The site was afterwards occupied by the Rolls Office and now by the Public Record Office. *Vict. County History of London*, I, pp. 551–4.

[4] A messuage in Chancery Lane. Husting Rolls 96 (218), 103 (44) (45) (51). The inn of court lay further west, abutting on Wych Street.

[5] Possibly means "stink" (see discussion of the word in Chambers and Daunt, *London English*, p. 256), unless it denotes a pungent, stinging smell.

the master of the hospital and all his brethren. They present John Wiltshire, cook, for a misgoverned man against his neighbours and for selling unseasonable meat. They present Roger Mannynge, porter of the Fleet, for withholding 18 marks from Roger Bonfaunt, a child under age, praying that the mayor and aldermen would send for the said Roger and receive the money from him and put it in the Chamber, because he is not sufficient. [*English*]

Also they present the course of the water of Trynmelbroke which is stopped up on either side with *wilwys* and mud, stakes and weirs, which continue the length of two parishes, to wit, St Andrew the Apostle in Holburne and St Sepulchre, to the damage of the whole people. [*Latin*]

CREPULGATE WITHIN. They present all the bakers, brewers, taverners, *hostillers* and hucksters as greatly defective. [*English*]

COLMANSTRETE. They present that the chamberlain of the Guildhall ought each year to pay 26s 8d to a rakyer to keep and cleanse the grates of London Wall and Lothbury, and because of non-payment the grates are evilly and horribly stopped up with mud and ordure to the great nuisance of the whole ward, whereof the chamberlain is in default. And also the chamberlain ought to find a man to keep and cleanse the common ditch there. Also a quitrent of 6 marks used to be paid to a pope's knight, John Chirche (*soloit estre paie a un pape dominus*[1] *Johan Chirche*), to sing in the church (from) the rent in Brambles Aley in manner of a chantry, and the money has not been paid, and for this he (the chamberlain) is in default. [*French*]

BRIDGE. They present that there are no crooks or chains nor any ladder in case of fire, which God forbid, and that the tubs and boards of the stockfishmongers at the corner of St Magnus, to wit, before the shops of John Wenman and Andrew Totyng and in front of the corner of the church-wall, project too far on the days when fish is sold, to the disturbance

[1] The phrase pope's knight is found in the 16th century in Scotland in reference to the fact that priests were called "Sir." This appears to be an early instance.

of people, horses and carts passing thereby. They present the brewers of the ward for not selling their ale according to the mayor's proclamation, namely Nicholas Aleyn, Richard Crosse, Richard Aleyn, Cristian Besilwel and John Thomas at the Egle in Graschirchstrete. Also they present the *hostillers* dwelling in the ward for selling their ale within their hostels in *hanaps*[1], and not in sealed measures according to the mayor's proclamation, namely Robert Whaplode at the Belle, John Cowper at the Sterre, Robert Whaplode at the Swan, Andrew Catour at the Tabard, John Botiller at the Sarazineshede, Robert Multon at the Whitehors, William Bateman at the Hert, Richard Bokenham at the Horne and the said Robert Multon at the Katerinwele. Also they present the hucksters for selling their ale in their houses in *hanaps*, and not by the full sealed measure, namely, the wife of William Prest, carpenter, in Puppisaley. [*French*]

Membr. 3 (*continued*) *9 Dec. 1422*

Paul Miliany, factor and general and special attorney of Mark Guideson, merchant of Lucca, as appeared by certain letters patent under the great seal *ad causas* of Bruges, which letters were produced in court, came before the mayor and aldermen and acknowledged satisfaction for the payment by Gerard Danidze of the sum of £172 6s 8d, in which Sir John Cornewaille was bound to the said Mark by an obligation under the seal of his arms, and thereupon, on behalf of himself and his master Mark, he exonerated and acquitted the said Sir John and delivered the obligation to the said Gerard by way of acquittance. [*Latin*]

Tenor of the abovementioned obligation: John, *seingner de Cornwaile*, acknowledges a debt of £172 6s 8d, payable at Michaelmas to Marc Guidichen, or to the bearer of these presents (*ou a porteur de ce presentes*)[2] or to his certain attorney. For greater security the said John has caused John Victor, merchant of Florence, to be bound by an obligation in the above sum payable fifteen days after Easter next, failing which

[1] Cups, drinking-vessels.

[2] A rare and early instance of an obligation with a pure bearer clause. See *Cal. of Select Pleas and Memoranda*, 1381–1412, p. xxxiv.

he himself will pay, as above said, at Michaelmas, in which case the said John Victor's bond shall be surrendered by the said Mark. Dated 28 Dec. 1420. [*French*]

23 Feb. 1423 John Boston, mercer, came before the mayor and aldermen in the Chamber of Guildhall and prayed to be admitted, according to the custom of the city, to prove that 15 casks and 3 hogsheads of wine—which had been attached and arrested in the custody of John Vache and John Boner, shipmen, as being the goods of Joan, widow of Roger Taunton, chapman, of Newport in the Isle of Wight, and John Thorn of the same, executors of the will of the said Roger, by virtue of a plaint of debt of £44 levied by Simon Bartelot, mercer, before Robert Tatersall, sheriff, on 1 Jan. 1423—were his own proper goods and that no one else had part in them at the time of the levying of the plaint to the value of 4d or more, and that he was not making this proof by reason of fraud, deception or collusion to bar any one from his action. And since the said John Bartelot, appearing by his attorney John Hethyngham, did not allege any matter sufficient to exclude the said John Boston from his proof, the latter was admitted and made his proof there and then. Whereupon it was considered by the court according to custom that the casks and hogsheads aforesaid be disattached and disarrested. [*Latin*]

24 Feb. 1423 Quitclaim from Robert Sewale, esqųire, of co. Essex.to Thomas Beamounde, salter.

Membr. 3 *b* *13 March 1423* Recognisance before the mayor and aldermen by Richard Holme, woolman, of a debt of £100 due to Richard Ocle, tailor.

8 May 1423 Acquittance from Thomas Elys, Thomas Chapman and Thomas Nicoll, executors of William Parker, esquire, son of the late William Parker, mercer, to William Waldern, mercer, John Whitby, rector of St Peter on Cornhill, Salamon Fresthorp and Thomas Berwyk, mercers, feoffees of the late Thomas Cressy, mercer, who was also an executor of the said William Parker, for the receipt of £20 paid in accordance with indentures between William Parker the son and Thomas Cressy. Given in the presence of the mayor and aldermen in the Chamber, 1 May 1423.

Bond of Thomas Knolles, senior, Nicholas Wotton, Richard Gosselyn and Thomas Knolles, junior, to John Darell and Geoffrey Louther, executors of the will of Richard Cliderowe, esquire, in 500 marks for the payment of that sum by the aforesaid Thomas Knolles, junior, to his, Thomas Knolles' children, Joan, Isabel, Thomas and Robert, in several portions as follows: 200 marks to Joan when she came of age or married, 100 marks to Isabel on the same terms, and 100 marks each to Thomas and Robert when they came of age, the whole sum of 500 marks having been devised to the children by the said Richard Cliderowe. It was provided that in case of death the money should be divided among the survivors and that Joan should have priority of payment. *18 Feb. 1424*

William Merfyn, clerk, one of the executors of William Kenwolmerssh late Treasurer of England, came before the mayor and aldermen and made a certain confession to the effect that he had received from Henry Barton, alderman, a silver cross parcel-gilt, otherwise called a monstrance or tabernacle (*mustrellum sive Thabernaculum*[1]) of silvergilt, with a beryl in the middle, for carrying the Lord's Body, with a cross on the top of it, valued at £45, which he was to deliver to the Treasurer during his lifetime, in order that the latter might pay Henry Barton £2000 owed to him by Henry V, as appears by the tally in Barton's possession. He had offered the cross or monstrance to the Treasurer and intimated to him the reason for the gift, but the Treasurer had answered that King Henry was so much in need of money that he could not accommodate him at that time, and he had ordered the deponent to take the cross back to Henry Barton. Accordingly on the 29 March 1419 in the hospital of St James near Westminster he had handed the cross to Henry Calcrofte, one of the Treasurer's serjeants, in order that he might take it to Henry Barton and deliver it at once to him. Having made this confession William Merfyn deposited in court a paper bill containing the confession word for word. Membr. 4 *b* (*continued*) *12 March 1423*

[1] A monstrance is defined by *N.E.D.* as "an open or transparent vessel of gold or silver in which the host is exposed," and a tabernacle as "an ornamental receptacle for the pyx containing the sacred host." Here the two words seem to be synonymous.

Membr. 5
3 Dec. 1422 Joan Poye, daughter of Thomas Poye of Oxburgh co. Norfolk, having brought a bill of complaint against Thomas Stowe, tailor, and Alice his wife, silkwoman, was exonerated from her apprenticeship to the said Alice because they had not enrolled her at Guildhall within the first year of her term. [*Latin and French*]

26 Nov. 1422 John Thornkyn, son of John Thornkyn, goldsmith, exonerated from his apprenticeship to William Markeby, goldsmith, for the same cause. [*Latin and French*]

...Jan. 1423 William Riggewyk was summoned to answer John Stikford in a plea of detinue of a silver cup with cover valued at £4 14s 4d, wherein the latter, by John Stafford his attorney, complained that on 20 Dec. 1422 his son, John Stikford, had entrusted the cup to the defendant for safe custody and for delivery, when required, to a certain John Mathy, barber, for delivery to the plaintiff, but the defendant had refused to hand over the cup. The defendant brought the cup into court and acknowledged that it had been entrusted to him as above said, but pleaded that he had always been ready to hand it over, wherefore he prayed judgment as to whether the plaintiff could maintain an action against him. And as the plaintiff did not deny that the defendant was willing to deliver the cup, it was considered that the plaintiff recover the cup, but be in mercy for a false claim.

And as John Stafford was the plaintiff's attorney only for prosecuting the suit and not for receiving the cup, it was ordered that the cup remain in court till the plaintiff or some one authorized by him should come to receive it.

Membr. 5 *b*
20 Jan. 1423 Bond of John Moleneux to Jerome Bragadini, merchant of Venice, in £100 that the latter should not be impleaded by Alice Moleneux, her parents or friends, on the pretext of any rape, trespass or injury done to her by the said Jerome or by reason of any debt, covenant or contract between them.

25 Jan. 1423 William Assh and Elizabeth his wife bring a plaint of intrusion against John Leycestre touching their free tenement in the parish of S[t] Mary Wollechirch.

William Clench of Bristol came into the king's court before the mayor and aldermen and prayed that it might be entered of record that by his wish and arrangement a certain John de Comites, his prisoner, was dwelling in the city under the custody of William Estfeld, one of the sheriffs. The said William Estfeld acknowledged the truth of the above and accordingly the matter was entered of record. *6 Feb. 1423*

Return to a writ by Robert Chichele[1], mayor, to the effect that among the immemorial customs and liberties of the city, ratified and confirmed by charters of the king's predecessors and in divers parliaments, there was a custom that if any citizen or freeman of the city using an art or mistery should rebelliously break or contravene or obstinately refuse to be justified by the good rules and ordinances ordained and used by the sworn masters and commonalty of any such art or mistery for the common good, or should wrangle with or show contempt to the masters when reproving him as an obstinate delinquent, and a complaint or report thereof should be carried by the masters of the mistery to the mayor of the city, then the mayor could and ought according to the custom aforesaid to commit such an obstinate delinquent to the king's prison there to remain until he should consent to be justified and fit amends should be made for his offence, and whereas it had been of old time provided and used by the masters and commonalty of the mistery of Goldsmiths for the common good of the people that no wrought gold or silver should be taken by any freeman or citizen of the said mistery to any fairs or markets outside the city before it had been surveyed, assayed and proved by the sworn masters of the said mistery as to whether it were good, true, fitting and perfect, a complaint and report had been made to the mayor by John Hilles, John Bernes, John Walssh and William Walton, sworn masters of the mistery of Goldsmiths, that John Teukesbury, named in the writ sewn up with this schedule, being a citizen and freeman of the city and using the art and mistery of a goldsmith, had not only rebelliously broken and contravened and obstinately refused to be justified by the ordinances

[1] Chichele was mayor the preceding year, 1421–2.

aforesaid but had also, when the masters reproved him for defaults committed in contempt of the good rule of the mistery, treated the said masters with disrespect and abuse, threatening them and calling them false in the presence of many men of the same mistery, to the probable disturbance and commotion of the mistery, whereupon—the masters having prayed a remedy in accordance with the custom of the city—the mayor, reflecting that more serious dangers might easily arise among the commonalties of other misteries by the lesser rebelling against the greater men, if heed were not taken of such complaints and malignant perversity of this kind were not checked, committed the said John Teukesbury, whom he found to be an obstinate delinquent, to the king's prison under the custody of Robert Tatersall and William Estfeld, sheriffs, according to custom, there to be kept safely until he were willing to be justified and until due amends were made for his offence according to the liberties, good rules and ordinances aforesaid.

26 Feb. 1423 Recognisance by Thomas Bosse of Colchester, merchant, to William Kyrkeby of Lincoln and Libens Botiller in £70.

Membr. 6 *22 April 1423* John Burton, son of William Burton of Charte co. Kent, was exonerated from his apprenticeship to William Fytkyn *alias* Hammes, girdler, because the latter had left the city. [*Latin and French*]

27 May 1423 Recognisance by Robert Barton, grocer, to John Bacon and Robert Marchall, grocers, in £200.

14 April 1422 Letters testimonial of the mayor and échevins of Amiens witnessing that Miquiel de Henaut, Jehan Piquet, husband and guardian[1] of Jehanne du Pont, relict of the late Hue Baptisie, being the legal representative of the said Hue[2], Christien de Hauchies, husband and guardian of Marie Galette, widow of the late Jehan le Clerc, called Murgale, Jehan Galet and Pierre

[1] *Mari & bail.* See Godefroy, *Dictionnaire de l'ancienne langue Française*: "un homme conjoint par mariage avec une femme a comme mary et bail d'icelle l'administration et gouvernement des biens et heritages de sa dite femme" (*Coust. de Lens*, 6).

[2] *Et aians cause dudit feu.* A *cause aiant* was a successor in legal rights. See Godefroy, *op. cit.*

Bertaut, as guardians of the children and property of the said Murgale, Jehan Mouret, Jehan Accard, Jehan Cosette and Robert le Maire, all burgesses and merchants of Amiens, had appointed Jehan de Berneux, senior, Pierre Clabaut, Jehan de Henaut, son of the abovementioned Miquiel, and William Ridel of London as their attorneys to negociate with Nicholas Tunwell, burgess and merchant of London, for the payment of moneys owed by the said Nicholas. Sealed with the judicial seal (*du seel aux causes*) of the town of Amiens, 14 April 1422. [*French*]

In an action for debt of 5 marks by John Blank, skinner, against Peter Vincent, esquire, and Alice his wife, the defendants made four defaults, whereupon the plaintiff prayed that the foreign attachment be delivered to him. The goods were valued by oath of Richard Balman, cordwainer, and Thomas Laurence, *upholster*, and delivered to him under security of Richard Bovyngton, skinner, and Richard Mochet, girdler, to answer therefor etc., as follows:— Membr. 6 *b* *15 July 1423*

3 brass pots weighing 11, 5 and 9 lbs. at 1¼d the lb., one brass pot weighing 7 lbs. at 1½d the lb., another of Flanders make of 3 lbs. at 1½d the lb., 5 brass pans and one *skomour* of 15 lbs. at 1½d the lb., one *halywaterstope*[1], one *sprinkyll*[2] and one bell of 3 lbs. at 2d the lb., 3 iron *rakkes* of 14 lbs. at 1d the lb., one long iron *spete* of 11 lbs., value 11d; 4 small iron spits of 14 lbs., 14d; one iron *trevet*, 3d; 4 *droppyngplates*[3], one *candelplate*, one *flesshehoke* and 3 iron knives, 8d; a woman's saddle with *paytrell*[4], *croper* and other appurtenances and one old bit, 5s; one chair of Flanders make, 12d; 2 benches of *virre*[5], 12d; total, 24s ¼d.

Acquittance from James, son of William Brampton, stockfishmonger, deceased, to Robert Malton, rector of St Magnus, Thomas Burgh, rector of St Olave Southwark, Richard Style, Robert Ottele and John Dekene, late feoffees of lands in the *16 July 1423*

[1] A holy-water stoup was a vessel for holy-water, usually set in or against the wall of a church porch.
[2] The holy-water sprinkle was a kind of brush, an *aspergillum*.
[3] A plate to catch dropping or dripping from meat.
[4] Usually a piece of armour to protect the breast of a horse, but also a breast-ornament. Here it probably means a breast-collar.
[5] Fir.

parish of St Olave, for the receipt of £53 6s 8d, that sum being a legacy to the said James and his children from his father[1], who by will devised to him a quarter of the whole amount for which the lands might be sold.

Membr. 7 *24 Aug. 1423* Thomas Botiller and Henry Martyn, stockfishmongers, John Bacoun, woolman, and Stephen Barry, stockfishmonger, came into court and acknowledged an award made by them on 4 June 1423 as regards certain disputes between Beatrice, widow of Henry Whitwell, stockfishmonger, and John Trunche, stockfishmonger, wherein they adjudged that the said John pay the said Beatrice the sum of £12 16s 3d, find security for the payment of £5 10s at the feast of St Martin, and assign to her debtors to the amount of £17 13s 9d, secured by a bond for payment of that sum in case any of the debtors refused to acknowledge that they were debtors or that they owed the sums claimed or in case any of the debts were found not to be due. [*French*]

Membr. 8 *10 March 1423* Anneys Snell, daughter of John Snell of the hundred of Hove[2], co. Kent, was exonerated from her apprenticeship to Anneys Haunsarde, widow of Thomas Haunsarde, to whom she had been apprenticed for ten years, because the said Thomas and Anneys had not enrolled her at the Guildhall within the first year of her apprenticeship. [*Latin and French*]

14 Oct. 1423 Francis Seraile, attorney of Philip de Albertis, merchant of Florence, and Dominicus de Villanis, merchant of Florence, acknowledged an acquittance, dated 17 Aug. 1423, to John Botiller, late alderman[3] and mercer, for the receipt of £64 15s 10d, paid on his behalf by the hands of William Melreth, mercer.

Membr. 8 *b* *17 Sept. 1423* Maud Pynchebek, daughter of John Pynchebek, skinner, was exonerated from her apprenticeship to Thomas Ivy, grocer, and Anneys his wife, *sylkthrowster*, to whom she had

[1] See R. R. Sharpe, *Cal. of Wills*, II, pp. 368–9. [2] Hoo.
[3] Botiller was present in the Court of Aldermen 20 July, and on 5 Oct. William Estfeld was sworn in as alderman of Cripplegate in his place. Journal 2, fos. 10, 11 b.

been apprenticed for seven years to learn the art of the said Anneys, because they had not enrolled her at Guildhall within the first year of her apprenticeship. [*Latin and French*]

Alice, prioress of the house of St John the Baptist of Kylbourne, acknowledged an acquittance dated 24 June 1423 to William Walderne, mayor, for the receipt of 26s 8d arrears of an annual quitrent of 7s issuing from a tenement in the parish of All Hallows Dowgate, called "le sterre on the hoope," the amount having been paid by the hands of Joan, widow of William Woxcombe. *14 Oct. 1423*

Membr. 9

John Roger, son of John Roger of Sandale, co. York, exonerated from his apprenticeship to Thomas Blyton, armourer, because the latter had not enrolled him within the first year of his term. [*Latin and French*] *21 Sept. 1423*

John Boston, mercer, came before the mayor in the Chamber of Guildhall and prayed leave to prosecute at common law outside the city against Adam Forster, mercer, for divers causes and matters done outside the city, affirming on oath that he made this petition for no other reason than that the said causes were foreign and could not be tried and terminated within the city. And thereupon the mayor gave him permission to sue at common law outside the city for the said foreign causes and matters. *7 Oct. 1423*

ROLL A 52

(*William Crowmere, mayor*)

Membr. 1
30 Oct. 1423 Acquittance by Richard Ketford, saddler, John Seyes, saddler, Alexander Farnell, tailor, William Bryd, *browderer*, John Ray, skinner, and Thomas Wright, painter, to William, Lord de Botreaux, knight, for the receipt of 97 marks 10d in part payment of 468 marks 3s 4d. Dated in the cathedral church of St Paul 29 Oct. 1423.

27 Nov. 1423 Writ of protection in favour of Richard Wyght, woolmonger, then about to cross to Normandy in the company of Ralph Butiller, captain of the castle of Arques in Normandy.

3 Jan. 1424 Geoffrey, master of the order of Burton St Lazarus in England, warden of the hospital of St Giles without London, brings a plaint of intrusion against Master Nicholas Mokkyng, warden of the Chapel of Corpus Christi or College of St Laurence Pulteney, touching his free tenement in the parish of St Michael Paternosterchirch.

6 Jan. 1424 Reciprocal bonds of Robert Tatersall and Robert Whityngham, drapers, in £500 [conditions not stated].

Membr. 1 *b*
20 Jan. 1424 On behalf of Sir Henry Fitzhugh, lord of Ravenswath, information was given to the mayor and aldermen that Robert Walton, who had married Ellen, widow and executrix of William Fitzhugh, goldsmith, and John Fitz Robert, goldsmith, coexecutor of the said Ellen, were slandering and troubling him, alleging that he was unjustly detaining the sum of £22 due on an obligation, £8 5s 8d due on a bill of *debentur*, and other sums owed to the late William Fitzhugh, whereas in fact he was only indebted to the testator in the sum of £15 1s 8d, which he had paid after the testator's death to John Fitz Robert, by the hands of William Holgrave, skinner, receiving a general acquittance dated 5 April 1423 from the said John, which acquittance was produced in court. The mayor and aldermen were requested to summon and examine the said Robert and John.

Robert Walton denied having slandered the complainant and brought into court the obligation and bill of *debentur* abovementioned. John Fitz Robert said that the testator on his deathbed assured him that in spite of any evidences to the contrary Sir Henry Fitzhugh only owed him £15 1s 8d, and instructed him that on payment of that sum he should give a general acquittance. Sir Henry had in fact paid the debt and he had given him the acquittance produced in court.

Thereupon Robert Walton was asked whether he had any other documents binding the said Sir Henry and he replied that he had none.

Memorandum that James Boudenson, shipman, master of the "*Jacobknyght*" of Sluys, who had been arrested and detained in prison under the custody of Nicholas James, sheriff, by reason of actions of trespass and account, touching the sum of £72 8s 2d, brought against him by Alan Everard, mercer, came into court before the mayor and aldermen. And because he took an oath that one half of the ship belonged to him and agreed to accept the award of the court according to the law merchant concerning all that the plaintiff might be able to prove against him, when the latter's servant Richard Gerard returned to England, and because he entered into a recognisance of £72 to fulfil the above conditions, the penalty to be levied on the ship and his goods in case of default, the said James, by consent of the plaintiff, was delivered from prison and allowed to go at large. *26 Nov. 1423*

Bond of Thomas Knolles, senior, Nicholas Wotton, Richard Gosselyn and Thomas Knolles, junior, to John Darell and Geoffrey Louther, executors of the will of Richard Cliderowe, esquire, deceased, in 500 marks, for the payment by Thomas Knolles, junior, of 500 marks to his children Joan, Isabel, Thomas and Robert Knowles, in accordance with the will of the said Richard Cliderowe, who devised 200 marks to Joan and 100 marks to Isabel on their marriage or coming of age and 100 marks each to Thomas and Robert on their coming of age. *18 Feb. 1424*

Membr. 2

22 Dec. 1423

Deed of bargain and sale whereby Jehan Victor, merchant of "Fleurence," dwelling in London, conveyed to Loys Joen, dwelling in Exeter, England, or in the diocese of London, and his heirs, for 3000. crowns of good and loyal weight of the coinage and alloy of France, the seigneury of Blaiville with all its appurtenances as it is bounded in length and breadth, lately acquired from Guillaume d'Estouteville, knight, seigneur of Torchy. The vendor promises to warrant the property, and desires that this deed shall have as great effect as though it had been made before two notaries of the Chastellet of Paris or other royal tabellions, and that the bearer of the deed shall receive credence on his simple oath without any further proof in case of controversy arising about this sale. The vendor also renounces[1] all fraud and chicanery, all exceptions as to deceit, local and non-local usages and customs, evil, guile, error, the breaking of agreements and circumventions, the action *en fait*, the condition without cause or with unjust and undue cause, the covenant as to place and judge, the exception "beyond the half of the just price," the exception as to not having had and received the said sum numbered and counted in these present letters, every benefit of fact and law, every written and unwritten law, canon and civil, all delays and privileges, the law saying that a general renunciation is not valid, and generally

[1] "*Je renonce expressement par ces presentes a toutes fraudes, baras, engins, cautelles, cavillacions et allegacions quelconques, a toutes excepcions de decepcion, usages & coustumes localles et non localles, de mal, de fraude, d erreur, de lesion, de circonvencion, a accion en fait, a condicion sans cause ou de non juste et indeue cause, a convencion de lieu & de juge, a la decepcion (lexcepcion ?) de oultre la moitie de juste pris, a lexcepcion de non avou eu et receu la dicte somme nombree et comptee en ces presentes lettres, a tout aide de fait et de droit, a tout droit escript et non escript canon & civil, a touces induces et previleges et au droit disant general renonciacion non valloir et generalment a tout ce qui tant de fair comme de droit len pouroit aleguer contre la teneur de ces presentes lettres.*"

Compare with this renunciatory clause those in *Cal. of Select Pleas and Memoranda*, 1381–1412, p. 312, and *Archaeologia*, XXVIII, p. 227, where the exceptions of *mal* and *fraude* appear in Latin as the *excepciones mali et doli*; the *accion en fait* is the *accio in factum appellationis*; *condicion sans cause*... is the *condicio sine causa seu ex injusta causa*; *convencion de lieu et de juge* is the *convencio judicum et locorum*; and the *excepcion de non avoir eu*... is the *excepcio non habite non recepte seu non numerate dicte pecunie*. The *droit disant general Renonciacion*... is the *jus dicens generalem renunciacionem non valere nisi quatenus precesserit speciales*. All these exceptions, conditions and covenants were not used as a direct negation of a plaintiff's story, but as a suggestion that for one reason or another he had no right of action. The vendor in this deed promises not to avail himself of any legal excuses against the fulfilment of the deed. For the *Excepcio* see Pollock and Maitland, *Hist. Eng. Law*, II, pp. 225, n. 6, 611–20.

everything both of fact and law which one could allege against the tenor of these present letters. Signed and sealed with the signet of the said Jehan's arms 12 Dec. 1423. [*French*]

Certificate of William Crowmer, mayor, that on 26 Jan. 1424 the abovenamed Loys and Jehan had appeared before him and had confirmed the above document, in witness whereof the mayor had sealed the present certificate with his seal on the day and year abovementioned. [*French*] *26 Jan. 1424*

Agreement between Nicholas Tonewell, on the one part, and Johan de Berneux, Johan de Henaut and William Rider, proctors of the following:—Michell de Hanaut, Johan Piquet, husband and guardian of Johanne du Pont, widow and legal representative of Hugh Bautisie, Christien de Hauchies, husband and guardian of Marie Gallette, widow and legal representative of Johan Leclerk *alias* Murgalle, Johan Gallet and Piere Berteut, as guardians of the children and property of the said Murgalle, Johan Mouret, Johan Acar, Johan Cossette and Robert le Maire, on the other hand, to whom the said Nicholas owed a great sum of money, whereby it was accorded that the said Nicholas pay to the other parties sums amounting to £614 13s 4d at divers terms. [*French*] *10 July 1422*

Lucia de Visconti (*Vicecomitibus*), countess of Kent and Lady of Wake, acknowledged a gift, dated 5 March 1424, of all her goods and chattels to Antonia de Arengo of Milan, Magdalena de Boisio of the same and Nicholas de Aliardis of Verona, esquire, and a quitclaim, dated 1 March 1424, of all claims upon Antonius Francisci of Vultera and his partners. *9 March 1424*

Membr. 3 *3 May 1424*

Lease from Walter Cherteseye, John Bederenden and Robert Tatersale, drapers, and John Cloos to John Boteler, draper, of a small parcel of land, measuring 7 feet less half an inch from north to south and 16½ feet from east to west, for a term of 33 years at an annual rent of 2s. The said parcel had been formerly leased by John Botiller from Richard Clyderowe, John Weston, Thomas Lytewyn and John Braghyng and lay on the north west part of a larger plot of land called "St Laurence Wowes" in the parish of St Swithin Candelwykstrete abutting on John Botiller's tenement. As the said John had built a portion of his parlour on the parcel of land the lessors agree not to obstruct his light by any buildings hereafter to be built on St Laurence Wowes. Dated at London 9 Dec. 1412.

19 June 1424 Intrusion. Robert Paunton, rector of St Edmund in Lumbardstrete, against Master Nicholas Mokkyng, warden of the chapel of Corpus Christi otherwise the college of St Laurence Pulteney, touching his free tenement in the parish of St Michael Paternosterchirche.

John Belue, grocer, and John Brigger, *lorymer*, against William Norton, draper, and Alice his wife touching their free tenement in the same parish.

John Lynne, Nicholas Overton, John Reynold, Henry Jolypas, John Essex, Richard Aleyn, chaplains, and Robert Fitz Roberd, grocer, against Andrew Bunby, vicar of St Giles without Crepulgate, and William Petville and William Groom, wardens of the fraternity or chantry of St Mary and St Giles in the said church, John Northfolk, painter, and William Toucestre, smith, touching their free tenement in the parish of St Botolph without Aldrichesgate.

Membr. 3 *b*
18 May 1424 Mutual quitclaims between William Wodecok, son of Richard Wodecok, salter, and Thomas Beaumond and William Edward, salters, executors of the said Richard's will.

17 May 1424 Award by John Fray, recorder of the city of London, and Robert Fitz Roberd, junior, who had been requested to arbitrate by the parties and by the jury in an assize of freshforce, which assize had been demanded by William de Hermondesworth, abbot of St Peter of Certesey co. Surrey, in order to recover from Master Andrew atte Kirke, perpetual vicar of St Mary and St Giles without Cripplegate, and John Northfolk, painter, and William Toucetre, masters or wardens of the fraternity in the same church, an annual quitrent of 21s 2d issuing from a tenement called "Le Hynde" belonging to the fraternity and situate in the same parish, which tenement was bounded on the west by a tenement belonging to the Chapel of Guildhall late in the tenure of Peter Fanolere, on the east by a tenement late of Simon Mody and formerly of Richard Patrike, on the south by Fore Street and on the north by a tenement of the prior of Newerk. The arbitrators awarded that the aforesaid vicar and William Grome and William Petevile, now masters and wardens of the aforesaid fraternity, pay the quitrent annually to the abbot, and also the sum of £30 arrears, and that the abbot should repay that sum to them less £5. Sealed with the seals of the arbitrators and the mayoralty seal, William Crowmere then being mayor and Thomas Wandesford and Nicholas James, sheriffs.

Quitclaim from John Abraham of Aylesbury co. Bucks. to Robert Arnold, grocer. *28 Sept. 1424*

John Buknell, son of Joan Buknell of London, exonerated from his apprenticeship (14 years) to Richard Fleccher, cordwainer, who had left the city. [*Latin and French*] Membr. 4 *28 Aug. 1424*

Grant in fee simple from William Haylle of Worcester to Henry Neudyke of Worcester and Joan his wife of all his messuages, lands, tenements and cottages with all furniture, utensils and necessaries in the county of Worcester, inherited by the grantor from his father Richard Haylle. Sealed with the seal of the grantor as well as with the seal of John Gedney, alderman of London, and the Common Seal of Worcester. Witnesses, John Whetely, William Cavendisshe and William Cantlowe, mercers of London, Walter Whasshere and Thomas White, tailors of London, William Warde and John Whytehede, citizens and burgesses of Worcester. *16 Aug. 1422*

Letter of attorney to the two last-named to deliver seisin.

Bond of Richard Coroner, draper, and Richard Danyell, dyer, to John Bederenden, chamberlain, in the sum of 100s, payable at Michaelmas following, on condition that the said Richard Coroner, who had been admitted with others as a broker according to the ordinance entered in Letter Book K[1], should occupy his office without hindrance of the mayor and Membr. 4 *b* *26 Oct. 1424*

[1] Letter Book K, fo. 22 b (p. 33 of *Cal.*), to the effect that former ordinances entered in Letter Book I (p. 264 of *Cal.*), relating to alien brokers be observed, and furthermore that at Michaelmas each year twelve citizens be sworn as brokers, giving security to the chamberlain, and that no one else meddle with brokerage.

aldermen and should receive half the fines levied from persons convicted of unlawful brokerage from the present date until Michaelmas following.

Similar bonds of Guy Laurence and John Parker, grocers, John Sutton and Robert Arnold, grocers, William Multon and John Combes, skinners, John Alcok, draper, and John Wylcokk, tailor, Thomas Austyn and Thomas Bataille, mercers, Membr. 5 Thomas Southam and William Sevenok, grocers, John Hake and Ralph Valentyne, drapers, Roger Harlton and Simon Strete, grocers, John Michell, *hostiller*, and Mark Marcadell, fishmonger, and Lodewicus de Porte and Thomas Reynwelle, citizens of London, on behalf of the first-named of each pair of obligors.

10 Sept. 1424 Award of Master Gilbert Kymer, Doctor of Medicines and Rector of medical men (*medicorum*) of London, John Sombreshete, Inceptor[1] in Medicines, and Thomas Southwell, Bachelor in Medicines, surveyors of the faculty of Physic of London, John Corby, practitioner (*practicus*) in Physic, Thomas Morstede, esquire, one of the masters of the enfranchised art of surgery in London, William Bradwardyne, esquire[2], vice-master of the same, Henry Asshborne and John Forde, surgeons enfranchised in surgery, who had been chosen arbitrators in a cause pending between William Forest, complainant, and John Harwe, free surgeon, and John Dalton and Simon Rolf, who had been admitted as barbers solely for the practise of surgery, as regards an alleged error of treatment of

[1] A candidate for the higher degrees. Cf. *Cal. of Letter Book K*, p. 11: "Maistre John Suntbreshete comensour in Medicyns."

[2] The clerk describes Morstede as "*armiger*" and Bradwardyne as "*scutifer*." It is not clear whether any distinction between the two is intended. For these surgeons see Prof. G. E. Gask, *British Journal of Surgery*, XVIII, No. 71, pp. 492–4. The "art" of surgery was "enfranchised" in the sense that it was a guild or company of freemen of the city of London. Surgeons are found giving evidence before the mayor, aldermen and sheriffs in a surgical case in 1354 and there is a record of their Masters being sworn in the Husting in 1369, Letter Book G, fos. 18, 219; *Memorials of London and London Life*, pp. 273–4, 337, 519–20, 651. Recently in 1423, the Physicians and Surgeons of the city had successfully petitioned the Court of Aldermen for permission to found a joint college for the better education and control of physicians and surgeons practising in the city. *Cal. of Letter Book K*, p. 11; South and D'Arcy Power, *Memorials of the Craft of Surgery*, pp. 53–9, 299–306 (where the regulations are printed).

a wound in the muscles of the thumb of the right hand. The arbitrators, having diligently considered and fully understood the matter, on the evidence of the parties and the sworn testimony of John Parker, a barber admitted for the practice of surgery only, and also of other trustworthy persons having knowledge of the course of the aforesaid treatment, found that the complainant William Forest on 31 Jan. last past, the moon being consumed in a bloody sign, to wit, Aquarius, under a very malevolent constellation, was seriously wounded in the said muscles and on 9 Feb., the moon being in the sign of the Gemini, a great effusion of blood took place, that Simon Rolf staunched the blood the first time and that afterwards John Harwe with the assistance of John Dalton skilfully stopped the flow, which broke out six several times in a dangerous fashion, and that on the seventh occasion, the wounded man preferring a mutilated hand rather than death, the said John Harwe, with the consent of the patient, and for lack of other remedy, finally staunched the blood by cautery, as was proper, and thus saved his life. Accordingly the arbitrators declared that the said John Harwe, John Dalton and Simon Rolf had acted in a surgically correct manner and had made no error, and that therefore they were absolved of all charges made against them by the said William. They further imposed upon the complainant perpetual silence in this matter and, so far as possible, they restored to the defendants, who were guiltless and had been maliciously and undeservedly defamed, the full measure of their good reputation, as their merits in the case required. Further they declared that any defect, mutilation or disfigurement of the hand was due either to the constellation aforesaid or some defect of the patient or the original nature of the wound. This award was made 9 June 1424 in the chapter house of the Friars Minors in London.

Bond of William Suthcote, elder son of John Suthcote, esquire, to John Brokle, draper, not to impugn the latter's title to a shop and tenement in the parish of S[t] Swithin Candelwikstret leased from the said John. Membr. 5*b* *26 Nov. 1424*

ROLL A 53

(*John Michell, mayor*)

Membr. 1 *12 July 1425* Margaret Hardelowe, daughter of William Hardelowe, tailor, exonerated from her apprenticeship to John Baron, tailor, and his wife Anneys, *braudester*[1], to whom she had been apprenticed for 8 years to learn the trade of the said Anneys, on the ground that they had not enrolled her at Guildhall within the first year of her term. [*French and Latin*]

26 Sept. 1425 Acquittance from Bernard Balby and John de Marcato Novo, merchants of Venice, to John Michell, fishmonger, and John Gedney, draper, on the receipt of £357 17s 11d.

8 Oct. 1425 John Rede, master of the hospital of St Thomas the Martyr in Suthwerk, brings a plaint of intrusion against John Feldyng, ... Lutturworth, John Hukyns of Weston Underwode co. Bucks, William Melreth, mercer, Thomas ..., grocer, John Brokour, skinner, Hugh Dyke, *setter*, and John Olney, mercer, touching his free tenement in the parish of St. Michael Hoggenlane.

Membr. 1 *b* *9 Aug. 1425* Acquittance from Richard Ketford, saddler, John Seyes, saddler, Alexander Farnell, tailor, John Ray, skinner, Alice Wright, widow of Thomas Wright, painter, and William Dogge and John Worsopp her co-executors, all of London, to William, Lord de Botreaux, on the receipt of 48 marks 7s 1d paid by the hands of his servant, John Estby, in part payment of 468 marks 3s 4d due on eight recognisances in Chancery dated 1 Feb. 1422.

18 July 1425 Reciprocal bonds of Robert Cokke, glover, on the one part, and Robert Colbrooke and William Trynmell, wardens of London Bridge, in £200 [condition omitted].

11 Aug. 1425 Bond of John Bithewater, sheriff, to keep the peace with John Andrewe.

John Russell sworn to keep the peace with the king's lieges.

[1] *Sc.* brawdster, embroiderer.

William Lichefeld, parson of All Hallows at Hay, brings a plaint of intrusion against John Wyght, Roger Mason, skinner, and Joan Palmer touching his free tenement in the same parish. Membr. 2 *11 June 1425*

John Frank, clerk, warden of the House of Converts, London, and keeper of the Rolls of Chancery, prays an assize of nuisance against William Haryngton, knight, Christopher de Morisby, William del Garth, Thomas Romondby, clerk, and Thomas Shirwode(?) touching his free tenement in the parish of St Dunstan in the West.

Reciprocal bonds of John Boys, knight, on the one part, and John Clerk, grocer, and Thomas Thirlewynd, tailor, on the other, to accept the award of John Michell, mayor, John Fray, recorder, and twelve aldermen in arbitration between the said John Boys and his wife Thomasia and the said John and Thomas as regards properties in the parishes of St Mary Wolchirch, St Michael Paternosterchirch and St John Walbrook. *24 May 1425*

Bonds to the same effect by Richard Bamme on behalf of himself and his mother Margaret Philpot, John Whaddon on behalf of himself and his wife Agnes, and Thomas Grey on behalf of Thomas Biflete and Amy his wife, John Grey, Margaret Seint Jermyn and Thomasia Seint Jermyn.

Writ of *certiorari* to the mayor demanding the cause of the arrest of 2000 Flemish crowns[1] in the hands of Matthew Conrade of London at the suit of Totto Makeavelle, which money was deposited in the king's court of the city before the mayor, as it was said. Membr. 2 *b* *29 June 1425*

[1] *Duorum millium scutorum.* The *scutum* or *écu* is said to have been originally so called because it bore on one face 3 fleur-de-lis, like a heraldic shield. There was an *écu a la couronne* of Charles VI issued in and after 1384, in which a shield was surmounted by a crown. Possibly this accounts for "crown" being the English equivalent of *écu* from the 15th century onwards. See *N.E.D.* under "crown," "écu," "scute" and "scudo." Its relation to other continental coins in the 14th century is discussed by T. F. Tout, *Administrative History*, III, p. 243 n. It appears from p. 184 below that in 1426 the value of the French gold *écu* was 3s 4d.

Return that no such arrest or deposit had taken place before the mayor in the king's court.

2 July 1425 Writ of *certiorari* as to the arrest of £200 of the goods of Bartholomew Valeres, merchant of Venice, in the hands of Matthew Conrade, merchant of Florence, at the suit of Totus Machiavell, merchant of Florence.

Return that Bartholomew Valeres had been attached, in accordance with the custom of the city, by the said sum, which had been put in defence in the hands of Matthew Conrade in a suit levied before John Bithewater, sheriff, and subsequently removed before the mayor.

6 July 1425 Further writ of *certiorari* demanding the cause of the arrest together with the above-mentioned sum of £200.

Return of John Michell, mayor, and John Bithewater and Simon Seman, sheriffs, reciting the immemorial custom of the city[1] that a person in whose hands an attachment was made might be exonerated from the attachment on his taking an oath that he owed nothing to the defendant. As the above Matthew Conrade had sworn that at the time of the attachment he owed nothing to the defendant, the attachment had been quashed, and therefore they were unable to send the above-mentioned sum of £200 to Chancery.

Membr. 3
6 Nov. 1424 Bonds of John Pake, goldsmith, William Caldewell, Richard Withiale, goldsmith, and Robert Cryngelford, goldsmith, to John Bederenden, chamberlain, in £25, to bring up Robert Leversegge before the mayor and aldermen on the octave of the Purification to answer a charge of fabricating a false bill of *debentur*.

26 Nov. 1424 Acquittance of Richard Ketford, saddler, John Seys, saddler, Alexander Farnell, tailor, William Bryd, *brouderer*, John Ray, skinner, and John Worsopp, one of the executors of Thomas Wright, painter, to William, Lord de Botreaux, knight, on the

[1] For the custom whereby a garnishee could prove with the third hand that the goods attached were his own and that the defendant had no property in them to the value of 4d, see *Lib. Alb.* I, pp. 208–9; *Cal. of Early Mayor's Court Rolls*, pp. 17–18.

receipt of 97 marks 10d in part payment of 468 marks 3s 4d due on eight recognisances in Chancery dated 1 Feb. 1422.

John Belue, grocer, and John Brigger, *lorymer*, bring a plaint of intrusion against William Norton, draper, and Alice his wife touching their free tenement in the parish of S[t] Michael Paternosterchirche. *22 Jan. 1425*

Writ of *corpus cum causa* to the mayor and sheriffs ordering them to bring Francus Vinelli, merchant of Lucca, then a prisoner in the city, into Chancery on the octave of S[t] Hilary with the cause of his taking and detaining. *13 Jan. 1425*

Return of John Michell, mayor, and Simon Seman and John Bithewater, sheriffs, that Francus Vinelli had been taken at the suit of Francis Sarraill of Florence in an action of debt of £85, and also at the suit of Philip de Albertis by virtue of a bill of debt of £77 levied and affirmed before the mayor and his associates the aldermen of London according to the law merchant.

Award of John Michell, mayor, John Fray, recorder, Robert Chichele, William Crowmere, William Sevenoke, William Cauntbrigge, John Reynewelle, John Gedeney, John Perneys, John Coventre, Robert Whityngham, Robert Tatersall, William Estfeld and Henry Frowyk, aldermen, and Simon Seman and John Bythewater, sheriffs, in arbitration between Margaret Philipot and her son Richard Bamme, John Boys, knight, and Thomasia his wife, John Whatton and Agnes his wife, Thomas Byflete, esquire, and Amy his wife, John Gray, Margaret Seint Germayn and Thomasia Seint Germayn, on the one part, and Thomas Mayned, John Clerk, John Parker, grocer, Thomas Thirlewynd, tailor, and John Bracy, chandler, on the other, whereby the arbitrators adjudge to the first-named parties all the lands and tenements in the parish of S[t] Mary Wolchirche, which were in dispute, and to the last-named parties a messuage with appurtenances in the occupation of John Clerk together with a small house annexed to it in the parishes of S[t] Michael in the Riole and S[t] John Walbrook. Membr. 3 *b*

Membr. 4
27 Jan. 1425 Laurence Smith, son of John Smith, brewer, deceased, was exonerated from his apprenticeship (8 years) to Thomas Mason, grocer, because the latter had not enrolled him at Guildhall within the first year of his term, had withdrawn to the privileged place of St Martin le Grand, had no shop of his trade of grocery, and had not committed his apprentice to any other master to learn his trade. [*Latin and French*]

19 Jan. 1425 Bonds relating to the above arbitration between Margaret Philipot and others and Thomas Mayned and others as regards messuages formerly belonging to Simon Dolsele and afterwards of Joan Fastolf.

9 March 1425 John Ruddok, draper, by John Stafford, his attorney, brought an original bill against Henry Fletewode, draper, alleging a debt of 10 marks due for meals supplied in the plaintiff's house and for the rent of a house in the parish of St Christopher. John Combe, one of the serjeants-at-arms of the mayor, having testified that the defendant had no goods in the city whereby he might be summoned, a foreign attachment was made upon 10 marks in the hands of a certain Henry Knyght which were owed to the defendant. The defendant made four defaults and the said Henry Knyght did not appear to show cause why execution should not be made upon the said 10 marks. Thereupon the court delivered the 10 marks to the plaintiff under pledge of Robert Elkyn, brewer, and William Trumpyngnton, cordwainer, to answer therefor if the defendant should appear within a year and a day.

Membr. 4 *b*
14 March 1425 John Skelton, son of William Skelton of York, exonerated from his apprenticeship to John Standsted, dyer, because the latter had not enrolled him within the first year of his term and had left the city without committing the apprentice to another master to learn his trade. [*Latin and French*]

19 Jan. 1425 Further bonds relating to the arbitration between Margaret, widow of Sir John Philpot, and others, and Thomas Mayned and others.

23 April 1425 Geoffrey, master of the order of Burton St Lazarus in England and warden of the hospital of St Giles without London, brings a plaint of intrusion against John Uske and

Joan his wife, Alice, widow of William Wodehill, *malemaker*[1], and Maud, widow of John Clerk, *netter*[2], touching his free tenement in the parish of St Mary Somerset.

John Colle and Stephen Colle, goldsmiths, Robert Fenescales, tailor, and William Shirborne, goldsmith, bring a plaint of intrusion against William White, rector of the church of St Margaret Moyses, Guy Terry, baker, and Stephen Bugge, brewer, touching their free tenement in the said parish.

Richard Scot, chaplain in the chantry founded in the church of St Martin Pomers in Irmongerlane for the soul of Henry atte Rothe, chandler, brings a plaint of intrusion against Richard Person, armourer, touching his free tenement in the parish of St Ethelburga within Bishopsgate. *14 May 1425*

Memorandum that in March 1425 Robert Moore, skinner, brought a plaint against Stephen Turnabones, merchant of Florence, in which he complained bitterly that the said Stephen had agreed to buy from him a certain quantity of woolfells for £34 13s 4d and had paid him £17 6s 8d in hand, and for the residue had delivered a certain quantity of silk which he said had been consigned to him by Matthew de Veneciis, but the said silk, though outwardly (*facietenus*) it appeared good, true and merchandisable, was inwardly false and badly packed, and though he had prayed the said Stephen to relinquish his bargain and either take back the silk or pay its equivalent, the latter had refused. Membr. 5

The said Stephen appeared and asserted that as the silk was sufficiently well packed, sound and merchandisable, the said Robert had no cause of complaint against him. Thereupon with the assent of the parties a certain John Daunde, one of the masters or wardens of the mistery of Brouderers[3], who had expert knowledge of silk and similar merchandise, was chosen and sworn to report upon the silk. He testified that the greater part of it was defective and badly packed. On this the said Stephen took back the silk and relinquished his bargain, to his great damage as he said, and gave the complainant a day for the repayment of the said £17 6s 8d.

[1] Trunk- or box-maker. [2] Net-maker.
[3] *Sc.* embroiderers. The Broderers still exist as a Livery Company.

ROLL A 54

(*John Coventre, mayor*)

Membr. 1
10 Nov. 1425 Acquittance from Henry Honyman, fishmonger, and Katherine his wife, widow of John Aylesham, grocer, to John Say, grocer, and John Faryngdon, administrators of the goods and chattels of the said John Aylesham, on the receipt of 80 marks in full satisfaction of all to which they were entitled by the common law or the custom of the city.

24 Nov. 1425 Bond of John Bocher of S[t] Ives co. Hunts, merchant, and Robert Marchall, grocer, to William Melreth, mercer, in £31, payable on 24 June next in case Walter Alleyn, factor and attorney of the said William, could prove before the said date by authentic letters under the seal *ad causas* of Bruges, that on 12 June last, on which day John Bocher received from him two letters of payment of £100 directed to the said William Melreth, he had made any condition with the said John Bocher or any claim to an obligation of Lodowicus van Culter of Tertrik of 238 nobles, which the said John had delivered to him at Calais on 13 Feb. last as security for the payment of 200 nobles; otherwise the bond to be of no effect.

Note that the said Walter produced no authentic evidences or other proof before the said date, therefore etc.

17 Dec. 1425 Quitclaim from John Trethewy and John Luky, skinners, to Lodewycus John, esquire, dated 27 Nov. 1425.

Memorandum that on 18 Dec. Thomas Yarme and Peter Malpas presented to John Coventre, mayor, certain letters directed to him by the honourable and mighty lord, John Huntyngdon[1], in these words:—

"Right dere and worshipfull sire I comaunde me to yowe

[1] John Holland (2), earl of Huntingdon, later duke of Exeter. He was captured at Baugé in 1421 and exchanged in 1425. See *Rot. Parl.* IV, p. 300; *Cal. Close Rolls*, 1422–9, pp. 270–1. His mother was Elizabeth Plantagenet, sister of Henry IV, wife of John Holland (1), earl of Huntingdon. After the latter's execution in 1400, she married Sir John Cornwall, who in 1432 became Lord Fanhope. *Great Chronicle of London*, pp. 149, 417. Louis, count of Vendôme, was taken prisoner at Agincourt, and turned over in 1417 to Sir John Cornwall by the king. Wylie, *Henry V*, II, p. 39, n. 1; *Cal. Pat. Rolls*, 1416–22, p. 89.

oft tymes w[t] all myn hert Certefiyng to yowe how my worshipfull Fadir sire Johan Cornewaill knyght for my grete ease and proffit and also for my hasty deliverance has so entretid appointid & accordit w[t] his prisoner þe Erle of Vendosme þat I sall be delivered out of þe prison of Francheman handes And as touching þe pointementz and þe paiementz for my deliverance of my fynance and Ransone to be paied howe and in qwat maner of weys it is appointed and accordet and wretin in a dede betwis my forseid Fader and me sellid w[t] my selle of armes w[t] a writ of Chancery þat is called Dedimus potestatem for þe verrey knolage þ[t] it is my dede and my fre will And for þe more knolage and conissance I confesse me and I knolage to alle maner of men and þerfore I write to yowe and to alle þe worshipfull Aldermen of London at this tyme that this his my dede and my fre will Beseching yowe and praying yowe þ[t] my forseid dede may be of Record enrolled in þe yelde halle of london for þe more knolage and seurte for all parties for this his my fre wil and my hertis desire, yefyng en garge[1] and commandement to my trusty servauntz Thomas Yarume & Piers Malpas qwych wern with me en France at makyng of this lettre, Havyng power and auctorite of me to se and ordein þ[t] my wil be fulfilled of þe enrolment of my forseid dede like as I have writen un to you at this tyme Prayng yowe tenderly thynk on this mater as ye will that I may do ony thyng that may please yowe en tyme comyng for w[t] þe grace of god it is for my hasty deliverance And I pray yowe take credence to our forseid servauntz bringers of þis lettre The hole Trinite have yowe in his holy governance Wretin at Lodon in Angewe þe xxviii dey of doctobre."

Upon this the mayor told the said Thomas and Peter to come before him and his fellows the aldermen in the king's court in the Chamber of Guildhall next day with the two writings mentioned in the letter. On which day came Walter, Lord le Fitzwater, Thomas Wenlok and Robert Shottesbroke, knights, Richard Baynard, Thomas Fox, and William Londesop, esquires, and the said Thomas and Peter as well as John Mason, clerk, John Vincent and William Bugge, being of the

[1] *Sic.* Charge?

earl's counsel. And they prayed that both writings might be read and entered as of record, which was done, and order was given to enrol them in the rolls of Memoranda of the said mayor in these words. As appears on the other part of the roll etc.

Membr. 1 *b*
29 April 1426

On 29 April 1426 John Earl of Huntyngton came before the Mayor and Aldermen and acknowledged the following writing to be his deed.

"To alle þo that these presentz lettres cometh John Erle of Huntyngdon sendith gretyng For as moche as by fortune of werre we were late take prisoner in þe parties of France and now ben prisoner in þe handes and gouvernance of þe Erle of Vendosme by wey of bying by þe seid Erle out of þe handes and gouvernance of Scottes The whiche Erle of Vendosme was and is prisoner to sire John Cornewaill knyght by deliverance of our souveraign lord þe kyng and his Conseill and oweth hym for his finance and raunceoun xlvi thousand vi hundred lxv escutz[1] of Gold, The whiche somme amounteth in al to xi thousand vi hundred lxv marks And now it is so þat we can in no wise have ne make our deliverance out of þe handes of þe seid Erle of Vendosme of lesse þan we delivere hym quite out of þe handes and daunger to þe forseid John Cornewaill Wheruppon þe same John havyng grete compassion of our long and grevouse enprisonment and effectuously willyng and desiryng our hasty deliverance, of his grete godenesse and kyndenesse hath ȝeve unto us towardes our deliverance and rebated of þe fynance of his seid prisoner ii^{m}dclxv marks And moreover for þe remenaunt of þe somme amontyng to þe somme of ix^{m} marks þat remayneth byhynde unpaide or agreed to þe seid John Cornewaill of þe fynance of his seid prisoner þe Erle of Vendosme, þe seid John Cornewaill hath to our grete ease receyveḋ and take þe lord Gaucourt and þe lord Touteville prisoners to þe value and somme of v thousand marks whiche were late oure soveraign lord þe kynges prisoners And by hym and by his Conseill delivered to þe seid John Cornewaill in helpe of our deliverance And also þe seid John Cornewaill hath agreed hym to receyve and take in helpe of our deliverance by assignement and graunte by our seid

[1] On the *écu* or crown see above, p. 177.

soveraign lord and his Conseill i thousand vii hundred and l marks to be had and resceyved of þe ferme issues and proffits of þe londes of John lord of Arundell beyng in þe kynges handes by cause of his nonnage More over þe seid John Cornewaill haþ agreed hym to þassignements I made by our souveraign lord and his Conseill of iii hundred pounds þat were to be due by our seid souveraign lord as for our wages of the Constabelerie of þe Tour of London for tyme passed, to have and to Receyve þe seid iii hundred pounds by assignement þerof made by þe Tresorer of Engeland Also þe seid John Cornewaill hath receyved by þe handes of þe Bysshopp of Duresme William Halle John Mason clerk and William Yerde Esquier our attournes generals in þe Realme of Engelond of þe issues profits and revenuz of our landes in þe same Realme v[c] Mark of money And also he hath agreed hym for our seid deliverance to be contented by diverse obligacions of our Cosins and frendes bounde un to hym in diverses severalx sommes conteyned in þe seid obligacions in þe maner as it foloweth That is to sey of Humfrey Erle of Stafford Henry Percy Erle of Northumbre and Richard Neville knyght by þeir obligacion vi hundred and l marks And also by þe obligacion of John Hals Justice and William Alyngton Esquier ii hundred marks And also by þe obligacion of William Halle Sergeant of lawe i hundred marks And by þe obligacion of William Yerde Esquier i hundred marks And by þe obligacion of John Mason parson of þe Cherche of Chidyngston and Richard Ketford citizen and sadeler of London i hundred marks, the which sommes forseid of v thousand marks for þe seid prisoners Gaucourt and Touteville as for her fynaunce þe thousand vii hundred and l marks of þe ferme of þe landes of Arundell aboveseid, þe forseid þre hundred pound for þe seid Wages of þe Toure, þe seid somme of v hundred marks in money receyved in hande, and alle þe seid sommes conteined in þe obligacions aboveseid amonteth to þe somme of viii thousand viii hundred and l marks to þe whiche sommes assignements paiements and suertees forseid þe seid John Cornewaill for þe most hasty spede of our deliverance with owte the whiche we coughde ne myghte in no wise be delivered out of prison of his grete godenesse and benivolence is agreed and contented in þe most godely wise, Wherfore we þe seid John Erle of Huntyngdon havyng consideracion to þe grete yefte frendship socour kyndenesse and godenesse þ^{t} þe seid John Cornewaill hath do and shewede to us in þis mater to his grete tarying and hyndryng of payment of Fynance of þe seid Erle of Vendosme wherof he myght and coughde rather have be agreed, we entierly thank hym as we be highly bounde þerto, And for þe more suerte of þe seid John in þis partie we wole and graunte for us our heirs and executours for evermore by þese presentz lettres þ^{t} þe seid John Cornewaill his executours and assignes have hold kepe take receyve and enjoye þe forseid prisoners Gaucourt and Touteville and all paiements assignemens suertees and obligacions aboveseid And þat it be lawfull to þe seid John Cornewaill his assignes and executours by hem here deputes and attournes to delivere the seyd prisoners for the fynance of v thousand marks forseid And also to arere and resceyve all þe assignements paiements and sommes aboveseid frely and quitly w^{t} out accion clayme pursuyte chalenge or empechement of us our heirs or executours in ony wise in tyme comyng And more over we þe forseid Erle of Huntyngdon for us our heirs and Executours relesse and quite clayme to þe forseid John Cornewaill his heirs and Executours by these presentz lettres all manere accions claymes suytes chalanges querels and demandes whiche ayenst hem or eny of hem we have or may have in eny wise be cause of þe maters and causes forseid or eny of hem in tyme comyng And more over we swere be þe trouthe of our body and on our worship and in word of trewe knyght þat we shull well and trewly hold and parfourne all þese articles and poyntes aboveseid w^{t} out eny contradiccion of us our heirs and executours or ony other in tyme to comyng. In witnesse of whiche þing we John Erle of Huntyngdon aboveseid have set here to the seal of our armes and signed with our seal manuel I writen þe vi day of Juyll In þe yere of the regne of our soveraign lord þe kyng Harry þe sixte Thridde."

Membr. 2 "Knowe alle men us John Erle of Huntyngdon have knowleched and confessed and we fully knowe and confesse be theise presentes lettres that for our grete eaise and deliverance of our person owt of our enemys hondes of our fre wylle and propre mocioun we have made and ensealed a deede wyth þe seal of our armes and also passed undir our signe manuel beryng date of the vi day of Juyll laste passed, conteynyng that we have graunted un to our welbeloved frend sire John Cornewaill knyght for to have and receyve for us and our deliverance by the hondes of þe lordes Gaucourt and Touteville v thousand mark, & xvii hundred and l mark to be receyved of þe ferme of þe londes of þe lordes of Arundell and iii hundred pound by assignement of þe Tresorer of Engelond for wages of the Tour of London and v hundred mark in moneye by þe hondes of þe bysshop of Duresme William Halle John Mason clerc and William Yerde Esquyer our attornes in Engelond and by diverses obligacions of our frendes conteyned in þe saide deede xi hundred and l mark whereoffe the somme totale amonteth in al to viii thousand viii hundred and l mark whiche deede aboveseyd we the saide Erle of Huntyngton by our fre wylle and ful agreement and assent knowlech sayen and confess for us and our heires and executours for evyr more that it ys our verray deede and by our self frely made passed and ensealed in þe fourme forseyd the whiche deede also by our welbeloved servauntes Thomas Yarme and Perys Malpas we sende un to þe forsayd sire John Cornewaill for to be delivered to hym for us and in our name as our owen deede And by our ful will and comandement in the Cite of London in presence of þe Mair of þe same Citee and other persones autentyk aftyr discrecion of þe sayd sir John Cornewaill praying the said Mair that he wole recorde the said deede to be our deede enseeled under our seal of armes and that it may be enrolled in þe yelde halle of London I wreten and enseeled and passed by oure owen hondes the secunde day of August In þe yere of þe regne of our soveraign lord kyng Henry the sixte kyng of Engelond and Fraunce the thridde."

Bond of Edmund Pinellus, Isnardus Ċatanus, Lodowicus Sigalle and Baltazar de Vivaldis, merchants of Genoa, on behalf of themselves and the society of Genoese merchants residing in London, to the Most Serene Prince, Sir Humphrey, *30 Jan. 1426* duke of Gloucester, count of Hanou, Holland, Selland and earl of Pembroke, lord of Friseland and High Chamberlain of the realm of England, in £400 to answer the king, the merchants of Florence or any one else claiming within a year a carrack and certain goods which had lately been captured in the Downes near Sandwich, and, if it were so adjudged by the king and his council, to restore the carrack and the goods, or their true value as found by an inquisition lately held in Sandwich by virtue of the king's writ under his privy seal, and in the meantime to save the duke harmless for having delivered the carrack and goods to them.

26 Jan. 1426 Reciprocal quitclaims between John Coventre, mercer, and William Chartesey, late his apprentice.

4 Feb. 1426 Acquittance from Rose, widow and executrix of William Tristour, saddler, John Croft, coppersmith, and Simon atte Welle, whitetawyer, her co-executors, to John Terell, esquire, of co. Essex, on the receipt of 50 marks in the church of St Vedast, in part payment of £100 for a term of years in a tenement in the said parish in West Cheap and Gutter Lane purchased by him from the said William Tristour and the said Rose.

4 Feb. 1426 Brother John Wakeryng, master of the hospital of St Bartholomew in Westsmethefeld, brings a plaint of intrusion against William Wodehows and Agnes his wife, Thomas Eyre and Joan his wife and Richard Nordon and Agnes his wife touching his free tenement in the parish of St Christopher London.

Geoffrey, master of the order of Burton St Lazarus of Jerusalem in England, warden of the hospital of St Giles without London, brings a plaint of intrusion against Henry Hamound, parson of St Peter Westcheap, Gilbert Pore, chaplain, and Thomas Chalyngworthe, saddler, and John Smyth, grocer, churchwardens, and Robert Smyth, brewer, touching his free tenement in the parish of St Laurence Pulteney.

20 June 1426 John Grisle, draper, obtains leave to prosecute William Randolf, goldsmith, at common law, the latter having withdrawn from the city.

William Pencrich was summoned to answer Nicholas Birchels in a plea of debt of 14 marks, wherein the said Nicholas by John Stafford his attorney alleged that the said William on 7 June 1424 agreed to pay the plaintiff the sum of 14 marks at what time the plaintiff should hand over to the defendant a certain papal bull of commission, directed to Henry, archbishop of Canterbury, for dispensing (*ad dispensandum cum*) with the said plaintiff and a certain Joan Aleyn now his wife in a matrimonial cause, which bull was dated at Rome at Santa Maria Maggiore on the 17 Kalends of July (16 July) in the sixth year of the present Pope's pontificate and was in the keeping of the archbishop on the said 7 June 1424, and though the plaintiff handed over the bull to the defendant on 1 July 1424, the latter refused to pay the 14 marks due. Membr. 2 *b* *17 Dec. 1425*

The said William admitted the agreement under the conditions mentioned in the plaintiff's count but pleaded that there was a further condition that the plaintiff should swear that the papal bull was of no validity to him so long as it was in his hands, which condition he had not fulfilled, and the defendant offered to verify his pleading as the court should adjudge and prayed a jury; and the plaintiff did likewise. A jury found for the plaintiff with 40s damages.

Margaret Philipot, Richard Bamme her son, John Boys, knight, and Thomasia his wife, John Whatton and Agnes his wife, Thomas Biflete, esquire, and Amy his wife, John Gray, Margaret Seint Jermayn and Thomasia Seint Jermayn bring a plaint of intrusion against Thomas Mayneld, John Clerk and John Parker, grocers, Thomas Thirlewynd, tailor, and John Bracy, chandler, touching their free tenements in the parishes of St Michael Paternostercherche and St John Walbroke. *4 Feb. 1426*

The latter bring a plaint of intrusion against the former touching their free tenement in the parish of St Mary Wolchirche.

At a court of the lord king held in the Chamber of the Guildhall before William Crowmere, mayor, and the aldermen. *12 March 1424*

Joan Cogenho, who together with William Sutton was indicted as having on 12 Dec. 1423 falsely, fraudulently and deceptively fabricated a certain false and fictitious writing in the similitude of a sealed obligation purporting to be from Henry Barton, skinner, to Henry Chaterton and John Tetenale in £100, pleaded not guilty and put herself for good and ill upon the country. She was found guilty by a jury of John Caleway and others. And because she was now too feeble and infirm to undergo the judgment of the pillory for her deception according to the custom of the city, it was considered by the mayor and aldermen that she should stand for an hour next to the pillory with the said obligation round her neck and that the cause of her standing there be openly published and proclaimed as an example and deterrent to others.

26 June 1425 Acquittance from Brother John Wakeryng, master or warden of the hospital of St Bartholomew, to John Coventre, alderman, John Carpenter, junior, and William Grove, executors of the will of Richard Whityngton, mercer, on the receipt of 5s due at Midsummer, being part of an annual quitrent of 20s issuing from a tenement in the Riole formerly belonging to John Stodey and lately inhabited by the said Richard Whityngton, which quitrent had belonged to the hospital from time immemorial. The master and brethren quitclaim all arrears of the quitrent. Sealed with the seals of the parties and for better evidence with the mayoralty seal and witnessed by William Babyngton, chief justice of the Common Bench, John Cokayn, justice of the same, John Barton, formerly recorder of the city, Richard Willom, John Grantham, William Pomfret, Reginald Cok and others. Dated in the chapter house of the hospital 26 June 1425.

11 March 1426 Agnes, widow of John Kent, grocer, brings a plaint of intrusion against Katherine Culpepyr, widow, John Culpepyr, knight, William Sevenoke, John de Wodechirche, Richard Rydon, Walter Segrave and John Baron, dyer, touching his free tenement in the parish of All Hallows the Less in Thamesestret.

11 Sept. 1425 Bond of John Kyng, junior, of Abyndon, to John Michell, mercer, in £7, to bring authentic evidence under the seal of the bailiff and other trustworthy persons of the town of Woxbrigge[1], testifying that a writing obligatory of £7, about which proceedings were pending between the said John and John in the Sheriffs' Court, was entered into at Woxbrigge by the said John Kyng under force and duress of imprisonment and not of his own pure and spontaneous will nor of his free disposition.

London to wit. The king's Foreign Court[2] held there according to the custom of the city aforesaid &c in the Guildhall of the same on the petition of Drew Barantyn, foreigner, before Simon Seman, one of the sheriffs of the said city. Membr. 3 *16 Dec. 1424*

Drew Barantyn, esquire, was attached to answer Henry Barton, citizen, in a plea of trespass by virtue of a plaint levied against him before the sheriff in his compter on 15 Dec. 1424, wherein the said Henry complained that the said Drew had broken and entered with force and arms and against the peace into a large house and twenty-two cottages in the parish of S[t] John Zachary to his damage £100. The defendant pleaded not guilty of coming with force and arms and whatever was against the peace and thereon put himself on the country, and touching the rest of the alleged trespass, he pleaded that as regards one fourth of the premises the plaintiff had no right of action because it belonged to the defendant and his wife Joan, and as regards the other three parts they belonged to the defendant and a certain Thomas Senykell and John Wymbysh and that in virtue of his own title and by precept of the said Thomas and John he entered, as he was entitled to do.

The plaintiff pleaded that all four parts had belonged to Drew Barantyn, late alderman, and that whereas a citizen by custom could devise lands and tenements in the city to his wife for life and to other persons in fee simple, fee tail, for life or otherwise, the said Drew devised to his wife Christiana all four parts for the term of her life and to his executors John Hale, clerk, William Randolf and William Selman the reversion of the same to be sold at the best possible price either

[1] Uxbridge, co. Middlesex.

[2] On the Sheriffs' Court for foreigners see *Cal. of Select Pleas and Memoranda*, 1381–1412, pp. viii, xii–xiv.

during or after the lifetime of Christiana at their discretion, and that the executors by a deed enrolled in the Husting of Common Pleas on 19 Oct. 1416 sold the reversion to the plaintiff in fee simple, which deed on enrolment had by city custom the same force and effect as a fine at common law outside the city, and that afterwards the said Christiana married a certain John Mannyng and they two conveyed their status to a certain Reginald Barantyn, who gave a fourth part of the house and cottages to Drew Barantyn, esquire, and Joan, daughter of the late John Drayton, knight, to hold to them and the heirs of their bodies, which Drew and Joan were afterwards married, and thereupon the plaintiff perceiving that this was an alienation which was clearly in disinheritance of himself, entered and was seised of the premises and it was subsequent to this that the said Drew broke and entered into the said fourth part, which he was prepared to verify, and as the defendant acknowledged the breaking and entering, he prayed judgment and damages. As regards the other three parts the plaintiff pleaded that he ought not to be precluded from his action by anything which the defendant had said, because the executors had sold the reversion of them with that of the fourth part to himself, while Christiana and her
Membr. 3 *b* husband John Mannyng had granted their status therein to Reginald Barantyn, who gave the three parts of the house and cottages to Drew and Joan and the heirs of their bodies, which Drew broke into and entered the three parts, as he was prepared to verify, without that the said Thomas Senycle and John Wymbissh had anything in their free tenement of the said three parts, wherefore, since the defendant had acknowledged breaking and entering into the three parts, he prayed judgment and damages.

The defendant answered that Reginald Barantyn had given to him and his wife only the status in the fourth part which he had acquired from Christiana and her husband, and that the latter were still alive, and that Reginald's grant was not such as the plaintiff alleged, and he prayed that it be inquired of by the country. The plaintiff did likewise. As regards the other three parts the defendant pleaded that John Mannyng had granted his status to the defendant, John Wymbissh, Thomas

Senycle and Reginald Barantyn, the latter of whom gave his status to the defendant and Joan, and that they continued in possession till the time of the alleged trespass, without that Reginald Barantyn had granted to them the three parts in the manner alleged, all which he was ready to verify as the court should direct.

The plaintiff said that by the law of the land he had no need to answer the defendant's pleading concerning the three parts, and the defendant said he had pleaded sufficiently in law against the plaintiff's replication, wherefore he claimed damages and that the plaintiff be precluded from his action.

As the court was not yet advised as to giving judgment on the three parts a day was given till the next court, and a jury was summoned on the issue as to the fourth part. Afterwards at a court held on 22 Dec. 1424 the jury said that the said Reginald had given the fourth part to the said Drew and Joan in the manner alleged by the plaintiff and they assessed damages for the trespass and costs at 25s and as regards the rest of the trespass alleged they assessed damages at £3 15s in case judgment should go against the defendant. But if judgment should go against the defendant in part of the rest and not the whole they assessed damages for the part at the rate of 100s for the whole trespass.

The court gave a day that they might be advised as to giving of judgment and process was continued until a court held on 7 Feb. 1425 before William Milreth, sheriff, when the plaintiff prayed judgment. Judgment was given that he recover damages of 100s both as regards the trespass on the fourth part and the other three parts. And upon this the plaintiff acknowledged that he was satisfied of the said damages.

Lease from Margaret, widow of Richard Style, fishmonger, to John Marchaunt, fishmonger, of the Kyngeshede in Briggestrete in the parish of St Magnus by London Bridge, with another tenement on the east side of it in the parish of St Margaret which the said Richard had recently acquired from John de Maryns, esquire, for a term of 20 years from Easter 1426 at an annual rent of 20 marks payable quarterly, reserving to the lessor a right of entry by the west door of the Kyngeshede and the east door of the other tenement for a space of six months in connection with the rebuilding of a bakehouse on the north, which the said Richard had also acquired from John de Maryns.

Membr. 4 *20 March 1426* Henry Wodeward, merchant, brought an original bill according to the custom of the city against Gerinus Darengos, merchant, wherein he claimed a debt of £4 10s for the freight of 4 casks and one pipe of red Gascon wine which the defendant had freighted in the plaintiff's ship the "*George of Lynn*" at Bordeaux for carriage thence to London. The defendant was attached by the said wine then being in the hands of John Neve, vintner, and made four defaults. Thereupon the said John Neve was summoned to appear on 5 April to show cause why the plaintiff should not have execution of the wine. He appeared and said that he had wooden vessels of pipes and hogsheads to the number of four casks and one pipe[1], but did not know how much the vessels contained. On the request of the plaintiff the casks and pipe of weak red wine were valued by John Ferrour, John Maillet and William de Lunes, vintners, in the presence of Thomas Botiller, the mayor's serjeant, at 4 marks 3s 4d and were delivered to the plaintiff in part satisfaction of his debt under mainprise of John Richard, salter, and Robert Enderby, tailor, to answer therefor if the said Gerinus should appear for justice according to the custom.

15 April 1426 John Wakeryng, master of the hospital of St Bartholomew in Westsmethefelde, brings a plaint of intrusion against William Babyngton, chief justice of the Common Bench, John Reynewell, Alexander Anne, Robert Brom, clerk, John Spenser, John Hervy, clerk, Adam Turvyn, John Joynour, ironmonger, and John Risley, citizens of London, Thomas Grene and Bartholomew Umfray touching his free tenement in the parish of St Martin without Ludgate.

[1] *Quod fuistas habet de pipis et capitibus porcinis ad numerum quattuor doliorum & unius pipe.* Apparently a Latin word coined from English *foist, fust*; old French, *fust*, a log, wood, barrel or cask.

John Halle, goldsmith, brings a plaint of intrusion against Laurence Dunton, parson of the church of S[t] Magnus the Martyr, Robert Cok, Walter Cok, John Serjaunt, Thomas Dufhous, John Childe and William Sharpe touching his free tenement in the said parish.

Bond of Ector Belhono, Bernard Balby and Francis Duodo of Venice, merchants, and Paul Miliani and David Galganeti, merchants of Lucca, to Dominic Thomazio, merchant of Florence, proctor and attorney of Alexander de Boromeis and Lazarus Johannis, merchants of Venice, in £240 to produce authentic evidences under the leaden seal of the dogedom of Venice before Michaelmas proving that George de Orsellis, who as factor of the said Ector had taken up by exchange (*suscepit per escambium*) at Venice from the said Alexander and Lazar the sum of 1000 ducats of gold, in connection with which the latter now have an action pending in this court against Ector for the said 1000 ducats, which amount to £178 2s 6d sterling, had come to an agreement with the said Alexander and Lazar or their factors having sufficient authority for the same with regard to the said money received in exchange. The said Dominic agrees for his part that if they fail to produce this evidence, and the sum of £240 becomes due, he will demand no more than the sum of £178 2s 6d and such reasonable damages as the mayor and aldermen may adjudge by reason of non-payment and other expenses. *22 March 1426*

"This bille endented made þe xiiii day of Novembre in þe iiii yere of þe regne of kyng henry þe sixte witnesseth þat Reynold Barentyn and Drewe Barentyn shal swere and knowleche þat þei shull make diligent serche and trewly presente and delivere now to Henry Barton citezein and Alderman of þe Cite of London before þe Feste of Candelmasse now next comyng alle þe dedes evidens & munimentes towching alle þe landes tenements and rentys þat were Drewes Barentyn late citezein and Alderman of London in þe paressh of seint John Zakarie seint Anne and seint Marie stanyng in London in your Warde now beyng at this tyme or in þe mene tyme shull be And if eny dedes and evidens touchyng þe same landes and tenementes come to your knowyng in oþer *14 Nov. 1425* mennes warde or handes beyng fro þat tyme forward ye þerof shul make full notice to þe same Henry fro tyme to tyme And do your diligens and power to bryng hem to þe handes of þe said Henry w[t] oute fraude so god you helpe and all his seintz. Also be þe othe þ[t] ye have made ye Reynold shull yeve trewe informacion of þe age of Drewe your sone."

Membr. 4 *b*
22 April 1426

John Clerk and John Parkere, grocers, Thomas Thirlewynd, tailor, and John Bracy, chandler, bring a plaint of intrusion against Margaret Philipot and her son Richard Bamme, John Boys, knight, and Thomasia his wife, John Whatton and Agnes his wife, Thomas Biflete, esquire, and Amy his wife, John Gray, Margaret Seint Jermayn and Thomasia Seint Jermayn touching their free tenement in the parish of S[t] Mary Wolchirche.

The same by Margaret Philipot and the others against John Clerk and the others touching their free tenements in the parishes of S[t] Michael Paternosterchirche and S[t] John Walbroke.

13 May 1426

John Lane, mercer, Thomas Pyke, draper, John Caundissh, *browderer*, John Wilden, *iremonger*, William Hunte, butcher, Richard Hungate of co. York, gentleman, John Stafford, clerk, Benedict Forster of co. Norfolk, and John Belue son of John Belue, grocer, bring a plaint of intrusion against John Holand, earl of Huntyngdon, John Grey of Codnore, knight, Ralph Rochefort, knight, Oliver Seynt John, knight, Richard Cassi, clerk, Thomas Gyffard, Richard Drayton, William Roos, Richard Rixton, Nicholas Rykhill, John Beverley, skinner, Thomas Rikhill, William Brygge and Thomas Aylemer, touching their free tenement in the parish of S[t] Dunstan in the East.

William, prior of the house and church of Holy Trinity, brings a plaint of intrusion against Rose, widow of William Tristour, John Croft, Simon atte Welle and Simon Sewale and Alice his wife touching his free tenement in the parish of S[t] Vedast.

Acquittance from John Wakeryng, master of the hospital of St Bartholomew by Westsmetfeld, to Richard and Agnes (Nordon)[1] for the receipt of 32s, in payment of an annual quitrent of that amount and arrears in respect of a tenement late of William Wodehous and formerly of Geoffrey de Wymburn, goldsmith, and then of Ranulph le Ferun, lying next to the church of St Christopher in Broad Street ward between the tenement of Robert de Frampton and Margaret his wife, daughter of the said William Wodehous, and formerly of Herbert de Bedeford, on the west, and the said church and churchyard on the east, as appears by deeds and evidences examined by Nicholas Conyston, chosen on behalf of Richard and Agnes, and Robert Fitz Robert, chosen on behalf of the master, which tenement Richard and Agnes hold for life by right of the said Agnes with reversion to William Wodehous. Richard and Agnes promise to pay the quitrent in future without dispute. Witnesses, John Cokayn, justice of the Common Bench, John Barton, late recorder of the city, John Grantham, William Pomfret, Richard Wellom, Reginald Cok, John Selman and others. Dated in the chapter house at the hospital the morrow of Easter, 1426. *1 April 1426*

Writ of *dedimus potestatem* to John Coventre, mayor, to admit attorneys for William Holgrave in connection with an action before the king in Chancery by writ of *scire facias* between Reginald Cokayn of Burihattele and Beatrice his wife, one of the daughters and heiresses of John Waleys and Joan his wife deceased, and the said William, by which writ the latter was called upon to show cause why certain letters patent directed to him and Robert Leventhorpe, deceased, concerning the custody of lands and tenements, formerly of the said Joan and of John her son and heir, should not be revoked and the king's hands be amoved from the manor of Wodecroft and from one croft of land lying below the garden of the Brache in the town of Luyton, with a meadow adjacent, and divers other lands called Brache, David Assheby, Brambleangre and Lalleford, and 7s annual rent issuing from a messuage next to the messuage formerly of William atte *18 May 1426*

[1] See above, p. 188.

Spetyl in the said town of Luyton, and the said Reginald and Beatrice be restored to possession of the same together with the issues and profits from the time of their expulsion. The names of the attorneys to be returned to Chancery. Witness the king at Leicester 8 May 1426.

Return of the names of Richard Selby and John Chese as attorneys.

Membr. 5
4 June 1426

Pleas held in the king's court in the Chamber of the Guildhall before John Coventre, mayor, and the aldermen 4 June 1426.

John Botiller, draper, was summoned to answer Robert Fresnoy, merchant of Amyas, administrator of the goods and chattels in London of John Fygate, merchant of Amyas, in a plea of detinue of £40, wherein the said Robert, by John Stafford his attorney, pleaded that John Botiller on 21 Aug. 1399 bound himself by a writing obligatory to pay that sum on 1 Nov. 1400 to John Fygate but had not done so and had refused to pay the plaintiff, who had been appointed administrator of the intestate's goods by David Pryce, official of London, to his damage £20.

The defendant by John Crowton his attorney produced an acquittance, dated at Dover 2 Sept. 1401, to Thomas Monmouth the defendant's co-obligor. The plaintiff's attorney pleaded that this was not John Fygate's deed, as he was ready to verify, and as Dover was of and within the Cinque Ports, where the king's writ did not run, he prayed that the issue might be tried in London where the writing obligatory was supposed to have been made, according to the form of the statute of 9 Edw. III provided for such cases[1]. A jury was summoned on the issue whether the writing was John Fygate's deed, viz., Richard Danyell, Robert Smyth, William Creke, John Boram, Richard Bridbroke, Thomas South, John Fekenham, John Fitz Robert, Stephen Colle, William Kent, hosier, William Kent, pewterer, and Thomas Ledred.

The plaintiff did not appear or prosecute his bill; therefore he and his pledges in mercy.

[1] 9 Edw. III, Stat. 1, c. 4. See *Statutes of the Realm*, I, pp. 271–2.

Bond of Robert Barry, stockfishmonger, to David Turbelvyle, vintner, John Stanle, Thomas Lyon and John Munde in 100 marks to abide by the arbitration of Stephen Forster, John Melbourne, Thomas Daunger and Edmund Custe in disputes between them. *10 Aug. 1426*

Lease from Thomas Charleton, knight, and Elizabeth his wife to David Turbilleville, vintner, of two tenements in Water Lane in the parish of All Hallows Berkyngcherche, situate between tenements of Henry Somer on the north, Thomas Turk on the south, William Vannere and Thomas Ware on the east and the lane on the west, for 30 years at an annual rent of a red rose for the first eleven years and afterwards of £4 per annum. The lessors covenant to effect external and internal repairs and to keep the pavement in order. *23 May 1425*

Membr. 5 *b*

Richard Scarlet, son of John Scarlet of Oundell co. Northampton, exonerated from his apprenticeship (11 yrs) to William Hertwell, goldsmith, because the latter had not enrolled him at Guildhall within the first year of his term. *2 Aug. 1426*

[*Latin and French*]

Edward Petyr, son of Thomas Petyr, *bladsmyth*, exonerated from his apprenticeship (10 yrs) to John Everdon, leatherseller, for the like reason. [*Latin and French*] *7 Aug. 1426*

Membr. 6

Writ of *supersedeas* that whereas persons prosecuting and defending before the justices of the Bench[1] had safe conduct thereto and therefrom, and John Boteler of London had shown that although he had been sued at Westminster by Simon Somerton in an action of trespass against the peace alleged to have been committed at Norhaston co. Oxon., nevertheless he had been attached by his goods and chattels in London at the suit of Robert Fresney, merchant of Amyas, administrator of the goods and chattels of John Fygate, merchant of Amyas, for an alleged debt of £40, in derogation of the privileges of the court of the Bench, the king orders the mayor to report to the justices at Westminster on Wednesday next the cause of the said arrest and the date of the levying of the plaint *6 July 1426*

[1] The Court of Common Pleas.

against the said John and meanwhile to supersede all further proceedings on the said plaint. Witness W. Babyngton at Westminster 6 July 1426.

Return that on 3 June the said John Boteler, having been thrice summoned according to the custom of the City, in virtue of a bill levied on 28 May, had willingly appeared before the mayor and aldermen to answer and had found security according to the custom of the city, and that he had not been attached by his goods and chattels nor arrested by his body, nor had any other plaint been levied against him, wherefore the mayor could not report the cause etc., but would supersede all proceedings as ordered.

30 Sept. 1426 Margaret Stokes, prioress of St Elena within Bisshoppesgate, brings a plaint of intrusion against Richard Thorpe, clerk, and Simon Cake, cordwainer, touching her free tenement in the parish of St Clement in Candelwykstrete.

21 Oct. 1426 Isabella Wentworth, prioress of the Blessed Mary of Clerkenwell by London, brings a plaint of intrusion against William Burton and Thomas Grey, grocers, touching her free tenement in the parishes of St Mary Colchirche and St Mildred in the Poultry.

28 Oct. 1426 Margaret Curteys, widow, prays an assize of nuisance against John Sargere, *custos* or warden of the college of the Blessed Mary Otery in co. Devon, and John Stone, touching her free tenement in the parish of All Hallows, Honey Lane.

Margaret Stokes, prioress of St Elena within Bishopesgate, brings a plaint of intrusion against William Coventre, prior of St Bartholomew of Westsmethfeld, touching her free tenement in the parish of St Bartholomew the Less.

2 July 1426 On 2 July 1426 came William Wodeward, haberdasher, and acknowledged before the mayor and aldermen that a certain obligation dated 16 Jan. 1419 in which Henry Husee, knight, lord of Hertyng co. Sussex, was bound to himself and a certain John Power, deceased, in £10 payable on 24 Jan. next after the same date, which obligation he delivered in court[1] to Martin Aleyn in satisfaction of divers debts owed to Martin by himself and John Power, was the true deed and debt of the said Henry Husee, and he granted that he would neither receive nor remit anything thereof without the consent of the said Martin, and that at the latter's expense he would be prepared either personally or by attorney to prosecute and avow all kinds of suits in whatsoever courts, moved or to be moved, whenever it should be necessary and he should be reasonably required thereto by the said Martin.

Richard Prat, son of Edmund Prat of Hogynton co. Cambs, exonerated from his apprenticeship (8 yrs) to William Porter, saddler, because the latter had not enrolled him at Guildhall within the first year of his term. [*Latin and French*]

Membr. 6 *b*
18 July 1426

John Derk was summoned according to the custom of the city to answer William Fromond in a plea of falsity and deceit, wherein the latter, by John Stafford his attorney, said that whereas on 12 May 1423 in the parish of St Martin in the Vintry he retained the defendant for a certain sum of money, viz., 6s 8d, to be of his counsel for the sale of 14 casks of red wine and to discover a merchant within the liberty of the city able and sufficient to buy the said wine and pay for it out of his own goods and chattels, the said defendant, falsely and deceptively plotting to deceive the plaintiff, brought to him on 20 May a certain Nicholas Martyn, a Lombard, whom he had caused to be clothed in good clothing, which was not his own, and whom he warranted to be a merchant, good and sufficient to pay for the wine out of his own goods and chattels, though he knew that the said Nicholas had no lands or goods within the liberties of the city or elsewhere, but lay hid and wandered within the sanctuaries of Westminster and St Martin le Grand and was insufficient to pay for the wine, and the plaintiff being quite ignorant of these facts and having faith in the defendant's warranty, then and there sold and de-

[1] On the transfer and negotiation of obligations and bonds see M. M. Postan, "Private Financial Instruments in Medieval England" in *Vierteljahrschrift für Sozial- und Wirtschaftsgeschichte*, XXIII (1), pp. 48–51; and *Cal. of Select Pleas and Memoranda*, 1381–1412, pp. xxiv–xxxvi.

livered the wine to the said Nicholas for £46 13s 4d, of which £30 was to be paid on 23 June and the remainder on 23 Aug., on which days the said Nicholas by the defendant's advice fled to the sanctuary of St Martin le Grand, where he lay hidden, so that the plaintiff entirely lost his wine, and thus the defendant falsely deceived the plaintiff to his damage of 100 marks.

The defendant by John Crowton his attorney came and defended the force and injury and, after protesting that he never gave any warranty, said as his plea that he was not guilty of falsity and deception, and on this he put himself upon the country. And the plaintiff likewise. A jury of Thomas Virley, Richard Rowe and others were chosen, tried and sworn by consent of the parties. And upon this the plaintiff, though solemnly called, did not appear or prosecute his bill. Therefore he and his pledges in mercy.

ROLL A 55

[*John Reynwell, mayor*]

John Qwyntyn, son of John Qwyntyn, late of Shorne by Gravesend co. Kent, exonerated from his apprenticeship (7 years) to Adam Smyth, brewer, because the latter had not instructed him or provided for him but had fled to the sanctuary of S[t] Martin le Grand. [*Latin and French*] Membr. 1 *15 Nov. 1426*

Memorandum that whereas Stephen Causton, mercer, John Strode, Walter Goore, John Hatter, Isabella Hynmerssh and John Parker had separately sued John Edsale, draper, for divers sums owed to them, and the defendant had been attached by goods in the hands of John Fulbourn, haberdasher, the defendant on 26 Nov. 1426 came before the mayor and aldermen and renounced all claim to the goods. On the request of the parties the goods were examined by John Higham, sheriff, who awarded that Stephen should have returned to him 70 ells of linen cloth valued at 57s 6d which he had sold to the wife of John Edsale and that John Parker should distribute the rest of the goods among the claimants. *26 Nov. 1426*

Bond of Dominic Thomazio, merchant of Florence, to Ector Belhono, merchant of Venice, in £240, that he would repay him the sum of £188 2s 5d[1], which as attorney of Alexander Boromeis and Lazarus Johani he had received from him in consideration of legal proceedings in the Mayor's Court, if the said Ector or someone on his behalf should produce in court within a year and a day authentic letters under the leaden seal of the dogedom of Venice proving that the said Alexander and Lazarus had already been satisfied of that sum; or if they had been satisfied of a portion of that sum, the said Dominic binds himself to repay that portion. *8 Nov. 1426*

Robert Coterell, son of Alan Coterell, late leatherseller, exonerated from his apprenticeship (10 years) to John Harry, cooper, because the latter had not enrolled him at Guildhall within the first year of his term. [*Latin and French*] *30 Oct. 1426*

[1] See above, Roll A 54, m. 4 (p. 195), where the sum mentioned is £178 2s 6d, the additional £10 apparently being damages given in the Mayor's Court.

Membr. 1 *b*
12 Nov. 1426 An indenture witnessing that John Cloos, one of the executors of Richard Forster, had delivered to Richard Jepe, rector of All Hallows, Honey Lane, and executor of Robert Turk, knight, late patron of the church, a deed concerning an annuity of 10 marks charged on a tenement called Blosmesynne in St Lawrence Lane, which annuity had been granted by the late Robert Turk to Laurence Pavenham, junior, and his wife Joan and their heirs and assigns. Richard Jepe, as executor, had sold Blosmesynne to Robert Braybroke, late bishop of London, who agreed that a certain subterranean gutter or receptacle of water beginning in the tenements of Thomas Knolles, senior, and Margaret Curtis, widow, and running through Blosmesynne to St Lawrence Lane, by which the water falling from their roofs and from the churchyard and the other tenements round had its passage, and also certain ancient windows and lights in the said tenements of Thomas and Margaret, should continue to be enjoyed without hindrance from the bishop, his heirs and assigns. The bishop had also agreed to have this undertaking engrossed on an indenture under seal on his next return to London, and as security the above mentioned deed of annuity had been placed in the hands of the late Richard Forster, to be delivered to the bishop if he fulfilled his agreement or otherwise to Richard Jepe. After the death of Richard Forster the deed of annuity had come into the hands of his executor John Cloos, who now delivered it to Richard Jepe as aforesaid, because the bishop in his lifetime had failed to have the promised agreement executed.

20 Jan. 1427 Isabella Wentworth, prioress of the Blessed Mary of Clerkenwell by London, brings a plaint of intrusion against John Croxton, John Reynold and John Lombe, chaplains, touching her free tenement in Bowyerrowe in the parish of St Martin within Ludgate.

3 Feb. 1427 Margaret Philipot, widow, prays an assize of nuisance against William Cantelowe, mercer, and Margaret his wife and John Caryon, brewer, touching her free tenement in the parish of St Mary Wolchirche.

Henry Barton, alderman, and Guy Fairfax pray an assize of nuisance against Richard Spicer, esquire, and William Frank *alias* Chaumberleyn, brewer, touching their free tenement in the parish of St Andrew by Crichirch, London. *26 May 1427*

Geoffrey, master of the order of Burton St Lazarus of Jerusalem in England, warden of the hospital of St Giles without London, brings a plaint of intrusion against Elizabeth Wakefeld, widow, touching his free tenement in the parish of St Edmund in Lumbardstrete. *2 June 1427*

John Wakeryng, master of the hospital of St Bartholomew in Westsmythfeld, brings a plaint of intrusion against Thomas Arlegh, abbot of the house of SS. Philip and James of Redyng co. Berks, William Wotton, John Olaund and Rumbald Hauden, labourer, touching his free tenement in the parish of St Andrew at Baynardescastell. *16 June 1427*

William Kelshill, fishmonger, prays an assize of nuisance against Alice Gayton, widow, touching his free tenement in the parish of St Nicholas Coldabbey. *18 Aug. 1427*

Membr. 2 *15 Feb. 1427*

Richard Cutmay, son of Thomas Cutmay of Toucestre co. Northampton, exonerated from his apprenticeship (9 years) to John Whyte, cutler, because the latter had no shop in London, had gone to Greenwich, which was a privileged place outside the franchise, and had not committed him to any other master to learn the trade. [*Latin and French*]

Isnardus Catan, plaintiff in an action for debt of £24, prayed that certain goods of Martin Pokelyngton, grocer, defendant, which had been attached as a foreign attachment, should be delivered to him. They were valued in the presence of John Botiller, one of the mayor's serjeants, by oath of John Care, jeweller, and William Couper, goldsmith, as follows:— one *forser*[1] of gold garnished with pearls, £23, and one gold *broche* with a *baleys*[2] and a pearl set in it, 13s 4d, and delivered to the plaintiff under security of Adam Semy, shearman, and John Parker, grocer, to answer therefor or for the price thereof if the said Martin should be willing to submit to justice within a year and a day. *12 March 1427*

[1] A box or casket. [2] A balas-ruby.

24 March 1427 John Wakefeld brings a plaint of intrusion against Edmund Chymbeham, mercer, touching his free tenement in the parishes of St Laurence Jewry and St Michael Bassyngeshawe.

23 May 1427 Acquittance from John Appelby of co. Westmorland, then staying in Enefeld co. Middlesex, to John Langham, haberdasher, on receiving by the hands of John Brainford the sum of £5 due on an obligation to the said John Appelby and Richard Bettesson of Plomtree co. Notts.

Membr. 2 *b*
7 March 1427 John Holam, son of Hugh Holam, *bokebynder*, deceased, exonerated from his apprenticeship (10 years) to Reginald Grasseford, tailor, because the latter had no shop, had taken refuge in St Martin le Grand, a privileged and enfranchised place, and had not committed him to any other person to learn the trade. [*Latin and French*]

18 July 1427 Bond of Robert Isham, son of Robert Isham, esquire, of Pightesle co. Northampton, to John Bederenden, draper, chamberlain, in 500 marks. The said Robert, having married Margaret, daughter of William Radewell, alderman, and an orphan, undertakes to cause those who had been enfeoffed in his father's lands to his use to create a firm and secure title to himself and his wife Margaret in those lands to the value of £25 yearly, the said lands to be in fee simple, not entailed or incumbered with legal proceedings or burdened by a statute staple or any other charge, except the ancient rents and services due to the chief lords of the fee, and to be held by himself and Margaret and their legitimate offspring with remainder to himself; and further he undertakes to make no alienation or demise of those lands whereby his wife's interest in them may be prejudiced.

17 July 1427 Bond[1] of John Rous, William Milreth and John Olney, mercer, to John Bithewater, Bartholomew Seman and Robert Walton, goldsmiths, in £200 that John Rous would abide by the award of William Estfeld, Henry Frowyk, Thomas Chalton and Stephen Forster, arbitrators chosen to adjudicate in disputes between himself and John Bithewater, or if they failed to agree, by the award of John Reynwell,

[1] See below, Roll A 56, m. 2 (p. 216), on the circumstances of this bond.

mayor, John Simond, recorder, and Nicholas Wotton, alderman. (Cancelled.)

Bond of John Hacche of Stoke co. Suffolk to Thomas Egle, skinner, in £15, to save the said Thomas, Thomas More and John Lenger harmless as against John Aleyn with regard to the custody of 7 bales of paper and 10 woollen cloths called "*streytes*"[1]. *22 May 1427*

At a Congregation of mayor and aldermen in the Chamber of the Guildhall 6 Nov. A° 5 Hen. VI. Membr. 3 *6 Nov. 1426*

Award of John Reynwell, mayor, and the aldermen in a dispute between Joan Grene of London, widow, and William Stephenson, goldsmith, concerning a shop, house or dwelling in the parish of St Anne by Aldrichgate, of which the said Joan claimed possession for a term of 14 years by virtue of a legacy from Thomas Hay, goldsmith, enrolled in the Husting[2] of Pleas of Land of 26 March 1408, and of which the said William claimed possession for a term of 40 years by virtue of a demise from the dean and chapter of St Martin le Grand given under their common seal in the first year of the present reign. It was judged and ordained that Joan have the house for 14 years, and that after that period or after her death, if she did not live so long, the said William should have the house according to his demise.

Quitclaim from Maud, widow of John Lane, mercer, to Richard Osbarne, Richard Riche and Thomas Shirwynd, executors of her late husband's will. *21 Aug. 1427*

Gift from Nicholas Tunwell, grocer, to John Coventre, mercer, John Welles and Thomas Seloue, grocers, of all his goods and chattels. Dated 3 Oct. 1422. *5 Sept. 1427*

Thomas Hill, son of John Hill of York, exonerated from his apprenticeship (7 yrs) to Nicholas Warderobe, tailor, because the latter had not enrolled him at the Guildhall during the first year of his term, and also because he had no shop and had left the city. [*Latin and French*] *19 Aug. 1427*

[1] *Sc.* straits, a cloth of single width as opposed to broadcloth. *N.E.D.*

[2] Cf. R. R. Sharpe, *Cal. of Wills enrolled in the Court of Husting*, II, p. 377. Thomas atte Haye left to Joan the unexpired portion of a lease from the dean and chapter.

Membr. 3 *b* *15 March 1427* Bond of John Mercatonovo and Bertusius Contaryn, merchants of Venice, Isnardus Catan and Leonardus Catan, merchants of Genoa, and Dominicus Villanis and Tottus Marchavyle, merchants of Florence, to Alexander Farrentyn in £358 that before 17 Sept. following they would put on record here in court sufficient letters under the authentic seal of Florence testifying that the order, method and custom of the Florentines, in a case where a merchant, for money paid to him, has undertaken and assumed in general terms (*per verba generalia*) the fortune and adventure of any ship[1], loaded with merchandise by another merchant, from the time of its lading in one port to its unloading or tying up in another, is such that the said merchant so assuming the fortune of the ship shall be released and acquitted from his undertaking if the same ship or merchandise in coming by sea to the port of discharge happens to be captured by enemies and is bought back[2] at first, second, third, fourth or thousandth hand by the merchant who loaded it, as is set down in a certain record made between the said Alexander and the above-mentioned obligors and entered in the mayor's rolls.

Marginal note that on 20 Sept. 1427 the above bond was cancelled, the obligors paying the money in court because they had failed to produce the record as they had undertaken to do.

1 Oct. 1427 Alice, daughter of John Harflete, saddler, and Joan his wife, exonerated from her apprenticeship (11 yrs) to William Dancastre, poulterer, and Joan his wife, *shepstere*[3], to learn the latter's trade, because the said William and Joan had not enrolled her at Guildhall within the first year of her term and had left the city.

Membr. 4 *10 March 1427* Alexander Ferrantyn came in person and demanded against John Mercatonovo, Bertusius Contaryn, Isnardus Catan, Leonardus Catan, Dominicus Villanis, Tottus Marchavile, Christoferus Stella, Baltezardus de Vivaldis, Bartholomeus Spinula, Christoferus Lomells, Radulfus de Thomazio,

[1] See below for details of this insurance by a company of merchants from three Italian cities.

[2] "*Recomperari*," a word of Italian usage.

[3] A female cutter-out, dressmaker, the word being the feminine of "shaper." See *Cal. of Letter Book I*, p. 283.

Franciscus de Pero, Laurencius Damiani, Bernardus Balbi, Ieronimus Bragadini, Dominicus de Thomazio and Zenobius Francisci Cavalari[1] the sum of £250 which he alleged they owed and unjustly detained from him, inasmuch as the plaintiff had a ship value £200 called the "*Seint Anne of London*," whereof John Starling was master, loaded with wines to the value of ..., which was overseas at the merchant town of Bordeaux, and the defendants, perceiving that he wanted to be secure as regards the wines and ship aforesaid and to commit and transfer the fortune and adventure thereof to others according to the manner and custom of merchants and especially of the Florentines, came to him on 18 Oct. 1426 in the parish of St Mary Wolnoth and for the sum of £22[2], which he paid them in hand, undertook and assumed the fortune of the ship and wines to the value of £250, counting the fortune and adventure from the time when the ship with its wines set sail from Bordeaux until it arrived safely and was anchored in the Thames, in which case there would have been the more profit to the defendants, as manifestly appears by the bill of contract signed by them and produced in court, but fortune being unfavourable the ship was captured on the high seas by enemies of the king and realm, viz., Spaniards, and taken to the port of Sluys in Flanders where it was sold; wherefore action accrued to the plaintiff by the law merchant and according to the manner, order and custom of the Florentines to demand against the defendants the said £250, which the latter refused to pay though often etc. to his damage etc. whereof he prays a remedy according to the law merchant.

Having heard the declaration and seen the bill the defendants said that the order, manner and custom of the Florentines, whereof mention was made in the bill, was as follows:—when a ship and goods, of which the adventure and fortune were assumed by others, was captured by enemies, if the

[1] This should probably be translated as Zenobius son of Franciscus Cavalare. For another form of his name, "Senobius Fraunceys," see *Cal. Close Rolls*, 1422–35, p. 93.

[2] An early instance of marine insurance by premium. Such insurance was in use in Pisa about 1400 and at Barcelona before 1435. W. Cunningham, *Growth of English Industry and Commerce*, II, pp. 489–90. For an insurance effected in England before 1509, see *Great Chronicle*, pp. 360, 454–5.

owner of the ship and merchandise or he who sold the adventure bought back by himself or by others at second, third, fourth or thousandth hand the ship and merchandise, then those who assumed and undertook the adventure were quit and absolved therefrom. They said further that the ship and wines after capture were sold to two Flemings and that the plaintiff by a certain John Waynflete bought them back from the Flemings, all of which they were prepared to verify, and they prayed judgment whether according to the law merchant in this case they ought to be charged etc.

The plaintiff said that he ought not to be precluded from his debt by anything alleged by the defendants, and further that the words concerning the order, manner and custom of the Florentines specified in the bill ought, according to the custom of the Florentines, to be construed nakedly and explicitly to the letter and to be regarded as strong arguments for the plaintiff against the defendants, and not to be construed obscurely and by implication as alleged by the defendants[1]. And this he offered to verify by letters under the seal of the city of Florence to be produced in court at a reasonable date.

The defendants said that the words as to the manner, order and custom of the Florentines in the said case of repurchase alleged by them ought to be regarded and construed by implication as tending to the exoneration and acquittance of those who undertook the risk, and this they offered to expound and verify by authentic letters etc., if the court should so consider; and this under penalty of the said £250 and £100 more, which they bound themselves to pay if they failed to bring the proof and testimony aforesaid.

Thereupon a day was given to the parties to bring their testimonies before 17th Sept. following.

14 July 1427 Writ of *corpus cum causa* to bring John Botiller, draper, into Chancery with the cause of his taking and detaining.

[1] *Sunt construenda nude & explicite ad litteram...et non obscure & implicite.* The defendants appear to have pleaded that the words about the custom of the Florentines were qualifying words, and that payment was subject to certain exceptions and conditions customary among the Florentines, but not mentioned in the contract. The plaintiff stood on the plain terms of the contract.

Return that John Botiller had been taken and detained in prison in an action for debt of £40 levied before the mayor and aldermen at the suit of Robert Fresnoy, merchant of Amyas.

Bond of Thomas Chepstede to William Hertwell, goldsmith, in 100 marks, to abide by the arbitration of Thomas Eyre, John Bracy, chandler, John Pirynton, waxchandler, William Austyn, tailor, and William Moris in causes and matters in which they were at variance. *1 Oct. 1427*

Similar bond of William Hertwell. Membr. 4*b*

The masters and good men of the mistery of Saddlers brought into court an indenture, which, at the instance of the rector and parishioners of St Vedast and by order of the mayor and aldermen, was enrolled as follows:— *12 March 1427*

Grant by William Baldewyne, saddler, to Sir William de Cranelee, rector of the church of St Vedast, and James de Thame, William Lincoln, Thomas Hassey, Thomas Renham, Hugh de Waltham, John Mapesden, Robert Champeyne, John Cappe, John Baldewyn, John Fairher, Richard Broke and John Excestre, parishioners, of a plot of ground formerly acquired from Sir Henry Cherchhelle, chaplain, which plot lay between the east end of the church and the grantor's stone wall and was 5¼ yds 1 inch wide on the south side and 5¼ yds ½ inch on the north and 20 yds long, reserving to the grantor one window and an eyelet (*oyletto*) opening on the south side of the church to give light to the buildings of his tenement and also two eyelets of his tenement giving a view into the church on the south side and also reserving two stone doorways, of which one issued from the tenement on the south of the church for giving free entrance to and exit from the church at fitting times, and the other issued from the tenement towards the east end of the church for giving free entrance to and exit from the lane of St Vedast, for a rent of a clove payable annually at the light of the Blessed Virgin Mary in the chapel of St Thomas on the north side of the church. The grantor agrees not to build on a plot of ground on the east of his stone wall, which plot extends southwards in length from the stone doorway 14 yds 9 inches, and eastwards in height (*in altitudine*) 5 ft from the stone wall. Witnessed by William de Burton, Nicholas Twyford, John Granelee, Thomas Whytcherch and William Whetelee in the presence of John Nott, then mayor, John Hiltoft and Richard de Croidon, sheriffs, and John de Chichestre, alderman of the ward, 23 Sept. 1364.

Cedula
7 Sept. 1427

An inquest of office before the mayor and aldermen by oath of Geoffrey Bokeler and others on the panel who said that Gerard Galganet, alien, on 10 July 1427 in the parish of St Margaret Patyns mixed 6 casks of old wine of La Rochelle, pale in colour and defective in taste, with new Spanish wine, and coloured, composed and sophisticated them with wine cooked and coloured to give them a pleasant appearance and delectable taste, and put the wine thus mixed into 13 butts, which had been smeared and lined with divers gums and resins (*cum diversis gummis et Rasis*. . .*unctis et linitis*) so as to give it the taste and likeness of good Romeney wine, and offered it for sale as such, in deception of the king's people and in contempt of the good ordinances of the city. And further the jurors said that the said Gerard was a common sophisticator, counterfeiter and seller of such wines.

They also presented the same Gerard for having on 20 July sophisticated 10 casks of unsound La Rochelle wine, which he placed in one butt and 20 hogsheads, and a certain Dominicus de Venire, alien, for having on 10 March at the quay of Ralph Gresvale, packer, sophisticated 8 casks of old, sour-sweet (*acredulcium*) Spanish wine, defective in taste and colour and unsound, which he placed in 16 casks and exposed for sale as good Romeney.

Membr. 5
27 Sept. 1427

An inquest of office by oath of John Bacon, woolman, and others, who said that John Lyng, draper, (*vii^o Oct. po. se*) on 10 Aug. 1427 under colour of his freedom took as a partner a certain Edgar Ducheman, alien, who was not free of the city, and with their common moneys and goods bought for their common use from a certain foreigner, whose name the jurors did not know, two packs of woollen cloth of divers colours, value £40 and more, which the said John on 10 Sept. loaded into the ship of John Parker, then lying in the port of London in the parish of All Hallows Berkyng, avowing them as his own, and paid custom and cocket (*custumavit et cokkettavit*) to the collectors of customs and subsidies, and sent them abroad to be sold for the common profit of himself and the said Edgar, thus defrauding the customs and expressly contrary to the oath which he swore when he was admitted to the freedom. Further they said that the said John was a common coverer, avower, and seller (*coopertor advocator et expositor*) of the goods of foreigners and aliens.

The jurors also say that on 10 July in the parish of St Mary Wolnoth Robert Cristemasse, draper, with the moneys of Nicholas Orlandyn and other aliens bought from Robert Whicherche and other foreigners wool to the value of £100, which he avowed and sold as his own goods to divers aliens for the profit of the said Nicholas and the others, and that the said Robert was a common avower of the goods of aliens and foreigners.

They also say that Adam Semy, shearman, on Aug. 24 1424 avowed as his own woollen cloth of divers colours belonging to a foreigner, Robert Coker of Witteham co. Essex, and sold it to divers aliens for the profit of the said Robert, thus defrauding the king of his customs, and that he was a common avower etc.

They also say that on 24 Aug. 1427 William Waryn, *jueler*, avowed a quantity of woollen cloths called "*Westerns*" of the value of £300 belonging to John Coventre "*de la Vise*," senior, a foreigner[1], and sold them to alien merchants for the profit of the said John, and that he was a common avower etc.

[1] A foreigner was a person not free of the city. Coventre is described as *forinsecus* in contradistinction to Orlandyn, who was *alienigena*. "de la Vise" was no doubt Devizes in Wilts.

ROLL A 56

(*John Gedney, mayor*)

Membr. 1
6 Feb. 1428

Memorandum that whereas John Fekenham had prosecuted a plaint against Robert Newerk and John Kyngesden before Robert Arnold, late sheriff, for breaking and entering a messuage in the parish of St Stephen in Colmanstrete and recovered 19 marks damages, and whereas Robert Newerk prosecuted a plaint of trespass against John Fekenham for breaking and entering his house in the same parish against the peace, and process was continued before John Hyham, late sheriff, until John Fekenham was found guilty by a jury, which assessed damages at 19 marks 6s 8d, and on account of divers matters in the said action judgment was respited, the said John Fekenham complained to the mayor and aldermen that he had been unjustly found guilty of trespass by a suborned jury and prayed that the actions might be examined by the mayor and aldermen in accordance with the custom of the city. The mayor and aldermen consented and on 6 Feb. 1428 in the king's court in the Chamber of the Guildhall the parties put themselves on the arbitration of the mayor and aldermen as to all matters at variance between them and as to Robert Newerk's title to the tenement aforesaid.

Thereupon the mayor and aldermen, in their examination of the parties and of the jurors, having called upon the said Robert to show his right and title, he declared that a certain John Essex, draper, by his will enrolled in the Husting on 25 Oct. 1361 left his inn in the said parish to his wife Alice for life with remainder to his son John Essex, girdler, which John took to wife a certain Maud and had a daughter Cristiana, who married a certain Philip and had issue the said Robert Newerk, and of these persons mentioned, John Essex, girdler, Maud, Cristiana and Philip died before the said Alice, on whose death Richard Wynter and John Russell entered upon the inn and enfeoffed Richard Storme and Joan, now wife of the plaintiff John Fekenham, as the plaintiff averred, but that he, the defendant, entered upon the inn by virtue of the devise of John Essex, senior, and as his heir and kinsman.

But as it was found by examination of the parties and of the jury that John Essex, girdler, was not the son of John Essex, draper, or related to him by blood, and that Robert Newerk's plaint was fictitious, false and concocted, the mayor and aldermen on 9 Feb. awarded that the said Robert take nothing by his suit, but be altogether excluded, and that he and John Kyngesden on some feast day before Whitsuntide between matins and mass go to the church of S[t] Stephen and in the presence of John Fekenham, at a time when the largest number of people were congregated, confess that his title was false and concocted, and further that, as the said Robert and John were too poor to pay the 19 marks recovered against them, the said John Fekenham should pardon and remit 9 marks, and also the said Robert and John should surrender in court all the false and concocted evidences and muniments.

John Olney, mercer, obtained leave to sue Henry Martyn, stockfishmonger, at common law, because causes and matters pending between them could not be terminated in the city and because the said Henry had fled the city. *8 May 1428*

Writ of *corpus cum causa* to bring John Jacob, brewer, into Chancery. Return that the said John had been taken and detained in an action of debt at the suit of Stephen Brown, grocer.

Robert Skerne, Robert Cotton, draper, and Robert Valaunce bring a plaint of intrusion against Symon Sely, William Dogge and Henry Playstowe touching their free tenement in the parish of S[t] Olave Silverstrete. *10 May 1428*

Proceedings in John Fekenham against John Kynggeden, John Rowland and Robert Newerk for trespass. Membr. 1 *b*

Bond of William Haukyns of Compton co. Gloucester to William Hales, mercer, in £24 [breaks off]. *11 May 1428*

Bond of Thomas Haccher, brewer, and William Knyght, butcher, to Thomas Catworth, grocer, in £40 that Walter Lowe, late of Calais, shipman, would bring before 1 May authentic letters under the seal of Bruges testifying that he had not taken charge of 6 pipes of Castell soap, value £40, *6 Feb. 1428* belonging to the said Thomas, which, it was alleged, had been loaded at Sluys into the said Walter's ship for conveyance to London.

Membr. 2
11 Nov. 1427 Thomas Pougere, son of John Pougere of St Albans co. Herts, was exonerated from his apprenticeship (15 yrs) to Richard at Gate, vintner, because the latter had withdrawn to Westminster, a privileged place outside the city, and had not committed him to any other person to learn his trade.

[*Latin and French*]

20 June 1427 Writ of error to the mayor and aldermen demanding that the record and process of a plea of trespass between Thomas Kyng, *shipwrithe*, and John Clerke, vicar of All Hallows Berkyng, be produced before William Cheyne, William Babyngton, John Cokayn and John Martyn, the king's justices, at the church of St Martin le Grand, and further ordering the mayor and aldermen, if the said John found sufficient security to pay the damages in case the judgment were affirmed, to deliver him and his mainpernors from prison.

Precept of the above justices to produce the record and process and to warn the said Thomas to appear before them on 22 Nov.

23 Dec. 1427 Cancellation of bonds entered into on 7 July[1] by John Bethewater, goldsmith, Bartholomew Seman, and Robert Walton on the one hand, and by John Rous of Lincoln, merchant, William Milreth and John Olney on the other, to abide by the award of William Estfeld, Henry Frowyk, Thomas Chalton and Stephen Forster in differences between the said John Bethewater and John Rous.

A new agreement by mediation of the mayor and other friends was made after the above cancellation, to wit, that John Rous should pay to John Bethewater the sum of £8, being part of £16 13s 4d which Michael Deard, John Stagilway and Peter van de More of Ypres were bound by an obligation in the custody of John Rous to pay to the said John

[1] See above, Roll A 55, m. 2 *b* (p. 206). There is a divergence of date, no doubt due to faulty copying.

Bethewater and his son William at the feast of Bruges called "Bruggemart" last past, and that John Rous would diligently endeavour to recover the money due and would pay anything which he recovered beyond the said £8 to John Bethewater less 7 marks for his trouble; and further it was agreed that John Rous should have with him an obligation of £13 8s 10d in which Lambsyn Fraunce and his partners were bound to the said John and William and should endeavour to recover this amount less reasonable costs with as much diligence as he would in the matter of his own debts, or else return the obligation when required, under penalty of £18.

Afterwards on 4 Aug. 1432 this recognisance was cancelled.

Bond of Clement Lyffyn, draper, and William Edulham, gentleman, to Martin Kylham, mercer, to save the said Martin harmless against the executors of Thomas Frampton, clerk, as regards a silvergilt cup weighing 39½ oz. and two silver bowls weighing 120 oz. engraved with the arms of Suffolk and Stafford impaled[1], which the said Thomas in his lifetime had delivered to the said Martin, and which Martin had now returned to Clement and William in full court to the use of the earl of Suffolk. *4 Dec. 1427*

William Curteys, son of John Curteys, *wollepakker*, exonerated from his apprenticeship (12 yrs) to John Halton, draper, because the latter had not instructed him in his trade or committed him to another master, and kept no shop. Membr. 2 *b* *12 Jan. 1428*

[*Latin and French*]

John Herry, son of John Herry, exonerated from his apprenticeship (18 yrs) to John Elwyssh, draper, for the same reason. [*Latin and French*] *22 Jan. 1428*

Nicholas James, fishmonger, Walter Grene, esquire, Richard Banastre, William Sampson, and Thomas Baybrook, fishmongers, bring a plaint of intrusion against John Pecche, abbot of St Mary of Graces by the Tower, and Richard Warbulton, ironmonger, touching their free tenement in the parish of St Botulph by Billingsgate. *26 Jan. 1428*

[1] No doubt originally belonging to Michael de la Pole, second earl of Suffolk (*c.* 1361–1415), who married Katherine Stafford, daughter of Hugh, earl of Stafford.

Membr. 3
26 Dec. 1427 Proceedings in a plaint of trespass levied in the Sheriffs' Court by Thomas Barton, gentleman, against John Denney, *furbour*, and removed on 13 Jan. at the latter's request into the Mayor's Court. The plaintiff's declaration set forth that on 20 Dec. the defendant broke and entered the plaintiff's chamber in the parish of St Martin Otewich and carried away, against the peace and to the plaintiff's damage £200, two salts with a newly-made silver covercle, value 7 marks, two dozen silver spoons, value £3 3s 4d, a pair of praying-beads of pearls with a golden gaud, value 10s, a cross with a gold chain, value 41s 8d, and 80 gold marks in coin belonging to the plaintiff, with 46s 8d in coin belonging to a certain William Cotesbroke then in the plaintiff's charge.

The defendant by John Crowton his attorney defended the force and injury etc. and put himself on the country. A jury of Alexander Hede, waxchandler, William Colman, Thomas Moisaunt, William Kent, hosier, Elias Twyer, Clement Lyffyn, Symon Eyr, John South, John Chadde, Martin Aleyn, John Sunman and Walter Adam came on 15 Jan., but the plaintiff made default. Therefore he and his pledges in mercy.

18 Nov. 1427 Writ of *habeas corpus* to bring John Kyng, chapman, of Habendon co. Berks, then in the custody of the sheriffs, before the justices at Westminster. Witness William Babyngton at Westminster 18 Nov. 1427.

Return that John Kyng was detained in prison for a debt of £7 which John Michell, mercer, recovered against him on 14 January 1427 in the Mayor's Court on a recognisance for that amount, nevertheless he would be brought before the justices as ordered.

16 Feb. 1428 Isabella Wentworth, prioress of the house and church of the Blessed Mary of Clerkenwell by London, brings a plaint of intrusion against Robert Fitz Hugh, rector of St Michael in Wood Street, and John Bagworth, William Taverner, Richard Ponchon and John Peryngton, churchwardens, touching her free tenement in the same parish.

8 March 1428 Walter Milton, William Coupere, William Serle and Edmund Warlowe, the four sworn masters of the masons and carpenters of the city, acknowledged a report which they had made at the request of John Eynesham, grocer, on the one part, and William Wright, parson, and John Hatherle and John Bartelot, churchwardens of St Michael Queenhithe, on the other, as regards certain nuisances of a tenement called the "*Glene*" in the said parish. They found that there was a stone wall[1] extending from the corner on the north to a *sconcheon*[2] on the south for 25 feet 4½ inches, that on the north part of it by the corner there was a *relese*[3] of 11½ inches from west to east and from east to west of 3¼ inches along the whole length to the *sconcheon* and for 15 feet 10 inches from the *sconcheon* southwards, and that at the southern end there were 13 inches from the said wall, and that the lengths of wall belonged entirely to the said John Eynesham. [*French*]

Writ of *corpus cum causa* to bring John Scarle, chaplain, into Chancery with the cause of his taking and detaining. *14 March 1428*

Return that the said John had been taken by reason of a plea of trespass at the suit of William Trippe, glover, levied before Henry Frowyk, sheriff, which plea was taken for certain causes before the mayor in the Chamber of Guildhall, where it had been pleaded as far as the summoning of a jury, nevertheless etc.

In an action of debt by John Pykbourn of Bordeaux, merchant, against John Saltemarsh of Hull co. York, for the sum of 4 marks due on a recognisance, a foreign attachment of 45s in the hands of the plaintiff was delivered to the latter, under pledge of John Flexmere and John Pecok, vintners, to answer therefor if the defendant should come within a year and a day and deraign etc. Membr. 3 *b* *4 March 1428*

[1] *Une mure de pier contenant en longure del coigne la en la North partie tanqe a une sconcheon envers la South xxv pees iiii pounces & demy pounce dassise Et en la North partie del West en Est par le dit Coigne nous trovons une Relese contenaunt xi pounces & demy pounce dassise & de Est en West durant la dit longure en la dit sconcheon iii pounces & une quarter dune pounce dassise et en longure del dit sconcheon en la North partie vers le South xv pees x pounces dassise et en la South partie al fin du dit longure xiii pounces dassise del dit mure.*

[2] A *sconcheon* or *scuncheon* is generally understood to be the jamb of a door. The sense here would seem to require a buttress or a projecting piece of wood or stone.

[3] *Sic.* Query, for *relefe*, a projection, or projected footing?

22 March 1428 Gift by Robert Brendwode, salter, to Alice his wife, Master William Lynwode, official of the court of Canterbury of St Mary le Bow, Henry Barton, alderman, and Thomas Rolf, serjeant-at-law, of all his goods and chattels. Witnesses, Thomas Scot, Thomas Cresy, Ralph Hoggeman, John Christofre, John Hardy and others.

5 May 1428 Award of the mayor and aldermen in a dispute between William Hertwell, goldsmith, and Thomas Chepstede of London that the latter pay the former 50 marks and that the parties execute mutual quitclaims.

Membr. 4 *12 May 1428* Richard Couper *alias* Weston, son of John Couper *alias* Weston of Weston Favell co. Northants, exonerated from his apprenticeship (9 years) to John Bithewater, goldsmith, because the latter had withdrawn to the privileged place of Westminster and had not committed him to another person to learn his trade. [*Latin and French*]

14 June 1428 Geoffrey, master of the order of Burton St Lazarus of Jerusalem in England, warden of the hospital of St Giles without London, brings a plaint of intrusion against William Andrewe, parson of the church of St Dionis Bakchirche, and Robert Akerman and John Nokes, churchwardens, touching his free tenement in the same parish.

28 June 1428 John Julyan and Joan his wife bring a plaint of intrusion against John Clerkesson of Colton co. Staffs touching their free tenement in the parish of the Blessed Mary Magdalene in Oldfisshstrete, London.

Richard, abbot of St Peter Westminster, brings a plaint of intrusion against William Caldwell, saddler, Roger Aston, knight, Robert Whityngham, alderman, Robert Rolleston, clerk, Henry Jolipas, clerk, John Bagworth, saddler, and Augustine Purden, tailor, touching his free tenement in the parish of St Alban Wood Street.

19 July 1428 Elizabeth Arundell, prioress of the house of St John the Baptist Haliwell[1], brings a plaint of intrusion against Roger

[1] A Benedictine nunnery in the street running from Bishopsgate to Shoreditch Church, called Haliwell from the supposed site of a holy well there.

Jurdan, prior of the hospital of St Mary without Bishopsgate, touching her free tenement in the parish of St Antonine London.

John, abbot of the monastery of St Albans, brings a plaint of intrusion against Thomas Parker, chaplain of the perpetual chantry at the altar of the Holy Trinity in the church of St Christopher, London, and John Newman, brewer, touching his free tenement in the parish of St Peter Bradstrete.

Richard Paris, grocer, and John Trewargh, rector of Kyngesdene co. Somerset, between whom there was a suit pending for £10 which the said Richard claimed against the said John as executor of the will of Robert Lovell, late of Rammesham co. Dorset, esquire, came before John Gedney, mayor, and John Symond, recorder, in the Chamber of Guildhall. And the said John offered that if the said Richard before the feast of All Hallows could prove before the mayor and recorder by trustworthy witnesses or other kinds of proof which should seem to the mayor and recorder, according to their discretions and consciences, consonant with truth and reason, that he, John Trewargh, had administered any goods or chattels of the testator to the value of the said £10 or less, then he would pay that sum to the said Richard without further delay. He also entered into a recognisance of £10, together with John Lacy, dyer, and John Romeyn, barber, that neither he nor any one on his behalf in the meantime or during the suit would obtain a writ or cause any other delay to the said Richard in his suit. *15 July 1428*

Reciprocal bonds of Isnardus Cataigne, Bartholomew Spinula, Christopher Stella, Leonard Cataigne and Hubert de Grimaldis, merchants of Genoa, of the one part, and Thomas Wandesford, William Flete and James Surenden, mercers, of the other, to abide by the arbitration of William Crowmere and William Estfeld, Englishmen, and Alexander Farentin and Dominicus de Villanis, aliens, in all causes and matters pending between them. Membr. 4 *b* *4 May 1428*

Recognisance of Richard Crawley and John Abbey, grocers, and John Bardolf, lighterman, to pay £80 at Michaelmas to *28 July 1428*

Denise Sudbury, Richard Fitz Nicholl of Halstede, Edmund Twyn, grocer, and John Gamelyn, executors of the will of John Sudbury, grocer.

Afterwards on 1 Dec. the said Denise and John acknowledged satisfaction.

11 June 1428 Pleas held in the court of the lord king in the Chamber of the Guildhall.

Gerard van Dale, *ducheman*, was summoned to answer William Waryn, goldsmith, in a plea of debt on demand of 11 marks by original bill remaining on the file of this year, wherein the plaintiff, by John Stafford his attorney, said that the defendant on 20 March 1428 borrowed from him 11 marks repayable on demand. The defendant having admitted the debt, judgment was given for the plaintiff with 4s damages. By request of the plaintiff and with the assent of the defendant certain goods of the latter in the hands of the former were valued by Thomas Leget, William Gotele, Thomas South, John Sergeant and Robert Hull as follows:—2 flat pieces[1] and 2 dozen silver spoons weighing 46½ oz. less half a noble and one goblet and covercle of silver gilt weighing 12 oz., were valued at 2s 2d more than the said 11 marks 4s. The goods were adjudged to the plaintiff and the balance of 2s 2d was handed to the defendant.

13 Sept. 1428 John Costantyn, esquire, prays an assize of nuisance against William Porter, knight, and Agnes his wife touching his free tenement in the parish of the Blessed Mary in Aldermanbury.

Alice, widow successively of Thomas Gylot and John Gylot, vintner, brings a plaint of intrusion against John, abbot of the monastery of the Blessed Mary of Graces[2], touching her free tenement in Estsmythfeld and on Tourhill in the parish of St Botolph without Aldgate.

[1] *Duo pec' plan'*. This appears to mean flat cups or bowls. Cf. *Cal. of Select Pleas and Memoranda*, 1381–1412, p. 127: "*quatuor pecias argenti planas unius secte cum uno cooperculo ad easdem*," and p. 211: "*tres pecie plane argenti*." *The Great Chronicle*, p. 235: "a fflat Cup with a covyr of Goold."

[2] A Cistercian house founded and endowed by Edward III in 1350 in the new graveyard of the prior and convent of the Holy Trinity by the Tower of London. *Cal. Pat. Rolls*, 1348–50, p. 484. See *Victoria History of London*, pp. 461–2.

ROLL A 57

(*Henry Barton, mayor*)

Gift by Thomas Recheford to Thomas Beaumond, salter, of all his goods and chattels. Dated 1 June 1428. Membr. 1 *3 Nov. 1428*

Writ of error demanding that the record and process of an action of debt of £14 by John Combe against William Randolf, goldsmith, be produced before the king's justices, William Cheyne, William Babyngton, John Juyn and John Martyn, at St Martin le Grand. *1 Nov. 1428*

Precept of the said justices to the same effect. *6 Nov. 1428*

Return of the mayor claiming the city's privilege of 40 days respite and the production of the record and process *oretenus* by the recorder.

Judicial writ acknowledging this claim and assigning a day, 26 Jan. 1429. Witness William Cheyne.

Gift by Walter Hunte, grocer, to John Welles, grocer and alderman, of all his goods and chattels. Dated 22 Dec. 1428. *24 Dec. 1428*

Gift by William Groos, brewer, to John Brokley, draper, Henry Trebowlance and William Ferrour, brewers, of all his goods and chattels. As the donor's seal was unknown to many he had obtained in addition the seal of the venerable Simon Seman, alderman. Dated 7 Oct. 1428. *18 Jan. 1429*

Memorandum that John de Marcato Novo, merchant of Venice, came before the mayor and aldermen in the Chamber and appointed James Bele, merchant of Venice, to acquit and absolve Alexander John as regards the sum of £100 in which he was condemned and for which he was detained in the sheriffs' compter. *28 Jan. 1429*

Reciprocal bonds of William Hales and John Admond, mercers, on the one part, and Robert Asshby, goldsmith, on the other, to abide by the arbitration of Eborard Flete, John Fauntleroy, Clement Lyffyn and Stephen Colley. Membr. 1 *b* *29 Jan. 1429*

12 Feb. 1429 Gift by Richard Sagrym to Ralph Vernon, serjeant of the Lord Mayor (*sergeant domini Maioris*), and William Hawkyn, butcher, of all his goods and chattels. Sealed for better evidence by John Michell, alderman.

11 Feb. 1429 Similar gift from Giles Warner, cutler, to John Parker, cutler, William Botillere the donor's brother, and John Stodeley, tailor. Sealed by the venerable Thomas Fauconer, alderman.

12 Feb. 1429 Recognisance of John Smyth and Robert Marchall, grocers, to Robert Sudbury, gentleman, in 100 marks payable at midsummer 1430.

13 Feb. 1429 Bond of Peter Wardelyng, barber, of Fleet Street, to John Bederenden, chamberlain, in £10 for his good behaviour, to keep the peace with Walter Chapman, constable of the ward of Farringdon Without, and to be obedient and helpful in all matters touching the king's peace and the quiet of his neighbours.

4 April 1429 Margaret Swynford, abbess of St Ethelburga of Berkyng, brings a plaint of intrusion against Thomas Rikhill and Elizabeth his wife, John Fortescu, John Armeston, vintner, Adam Someister, Robert Cristemasse and Hugh Cavendissh touching her free tenement in the parish of St Dunstan in the East.

Membr. 2 Whereas, in accordance with the liberties and customs of the city, granted by charter of the king's progenitors and confirmed by the present king, it had been ordained by the mayor, aldermen and commonalty that it should be unlawful for any citizen or free man of the city or other foreigner or alien whatsoever to be a corrector, broker or intermediary[1] in any bargain or contract between merchants or others in the city unless he had first been sworn and admitted before the mayor and aldermen for the time being, and also that it should be

[1] *Corrector, abbrocator seu medius.* Originally a corrector was an official broker of the Staple. Cf. 27 Edw. III, Stat. 2, c. 22: *Soit certein nombre des corecters sibien destranges come de privez prodes hommes sufficeantz & sachantz de tieu meistere pur loialment faire & recorder les bargaines entre les vendours et achatours come ad este usee en autres Estaples tenuz aillours.*

unlawful for any one, free or unfree, to make or practise any bargain or contract of usury or false chevisance between any persons under penalty of £20 to the use of the commonalty in case of conviction—the jurors presented that Peter Coniani of Lucca, alien broker, not having been sworn or admitted as aforesaid, acted as a broker on 8 April 1429 in the parish of St Edmund Lumbardstrete and made a bargain between Robert Bamburgh, draper, and Conrad de Passelaqua, merchant of Genoa, in divers coloured woollen cloths of Northampton and Ludlow of £40 value, which the said Robert bartered and exchanged (*barettavit & excambivit*) with the said Conrad for woad of the same value, against the liberty of the city and the ordinance aforesaid; also that the same Peter Conyan on 10 April in the parish of St Dionis Bakchirche made a bargain between Robert Spinull and James Bowier of a bale of pepper, value £30, which the said Bartholomew (*sic*) sold to the said James; also that the same Peter on 10 April in the parish of St John Walbroke made a bargain between Thomas Canynges, grocer, and John de la Tore of certain *brode clothes*, value £100, which the said Thomas bartered and exchanged with the said John for dates of the same value; and further that the said Peter was a common broker, intermediary and maker of bargains within the city and suburbs.

They also presented Franciscus de la Case, alien, for having made a bargain on 12 April 1429 in the parish of St Elena between Ralph Stoke, grocer, and Daniel de Savona of certain bales of woad, value £40, which the said Ralph exchanged with the said Daniel for woollen cloth of Essex called "*streytes*," value £60; and for having acted as a broker in the parish of St Dionis in the sale by Thomas Pyke, junior, to Isnardus Cataigne, Benedictus de Nigre and Antonius Bestaigne of woollen cloths of divers colours called "*streites*," value £130, and the sale by Bartholomew Spynull to Thomas Knolles of certain bales of *baterie*[1], value £50.

They also presented James Gentille, *Jewe*, alien, for having made a bargain on 15 April 1429 in the parish of All Hallows Honylane whereby Thomas Denton exchanged woollen cloths

[1] Hammered brass or copper ware.

called "*Westernes*," value £30, with Mathew Corade for *tarterin*[1] of the same value.

They also presented Frederick de Nawfro, alien, for having on 8 April 1429 in the parish of St Mary Wolnoth acted as a broker in an exchange by Antonius de Maffeo with Thomas Loughton, draper, of sacks of wool, value 100 marks, for woad of the same value; in the sale of a sack of saffron, value £30, by John Garro to Robert Otteley, grocer, on 15 April 1429 in the parish of St Margaret Bridge Street; in the sale of certain bales of woad, value £120, by Dary de Vivaldis to John Chesse in the parish of St Peter in the Wall, Broad Street Ward; and in the sale of woollen cloths of divers colours by Symon Eyre to the said Dary on 10 May 1429 in the parish of St Michael Cornhill.

They also presented Gerard Galganet, alien, for having on 28 April 1429 in the parish of St Margaret Bridge Street acted as a broker in an exchange of woollen cloths, value £80, by John Perneys with a Spaniard, whose name the jurors did not know, for Romeneye[2] wine of the same value.

Membr. 3
13 April 1429

Bond of John Hanmere, dwelling (*comorans*) with the countess of Arundel, Richard Honyton, skinner, and Griffith Davy, tailor, to Alexander Farentynis and John Noble, merchants of Florence, to save harmless the said Alexander, John and any other member of the society of Albertini against the heirs, executors and representatives of Peter Dyes, late of Portugal, esquire, dwelling with the same countess, as regards the sum of £4 sterling which the same Peter, when crossing to Rome, delivered to Bartholomew Dominici of Cologne to make an exchange therewith and to repay to the said Peter by way[3] etc., and which £4 the said John Noble on the day of the making of these presents here in full court repaid to the aforesaid John, Richard and Griffith who were acting on behalf of the said Peter.

7 April 1429

Reciprocal bonds of Nicholas Aleyn and Richard Aleyn of

[1] *N.E.D.* "A rich stuff, apparently of silk, imported from the East, prob. from China through Tartary."

[2] Rumney is described by *N.E.D.* as a sweet wine of Greek origin.

[3] He had bought a bill of exchange or letter of credit payable by the Albertini.

the one part and John Granesden and John Chichele of the other in 100s to abide by an award in arbitration.

Richard Hayward, son of Walter Hayward of Fulstone co. Kent, exonerated from his apprenticeship (7 yrs) to John John, mercer, who had withdrawn to St Martin le Grand. The apprentice was turned over to James Surendene, mercer, to serve the remainder of his term. [*Latin and French*] *14 April 1429*

Nicholas Walton, carpenter, brings a plaint of intrusion against John Childe, senior, and John Childe, junior, barbers, touching his free tenement in the parish of St Michael Queenhithe. *9 May 1429*

Membr. 3 *b*

Robert Barnet, son and heir of Thomas Barnet *alias* Hoddesdon, brings a plaint of intrusion against John Shenefeld, Ralph Asteley, esquire, William Rokesburgh, Richard Claymond and William Bekene, clerk, touching his free tenement in the parish of St Margaret Lothebury. *2 May 1429*

Writ of *corpus cum causa* to bring John Gladman into Chancery with the cause of his taking and detaining. *11 May 1429*

Return of the mayor and sheriffs that the said John had been taken by virtue of an original bill of debt of £7 at the suit of William Reynden of Wenlyngburgh co. Northampton levied before the mayor and aldermen on 7 May and pending undetermined. Nevertheless the said John would be brought into Chancery as required.

Recognisance of John Marchaunt, fishmonger, to Remond Cometiz, citizen and *wodemonger*, of a debt of £7 10s. *10 June 1429*

Writ of *certiorari* as to a recognisance in 100 marks made by Thomas Chepstede to William Hertwell, goldsmith, before the mayor and aldermen in the Chamber of Guildhall[1]. *11 June 1429*

Joan Payne, daughter of John Payne of Braundon co. Warwick, who had been apprenticed for eight years to John Swan, mercer, and Alice his wife, silkwoman, to learn the trade of the latter, was exonerated from her apprenticeship because she had not been enrolled at Guildhall within the first year of her term. [*Latin and French*] *27 July 1429*

[1] See above, p. 211.

Membr. 4 Memorandum that whereas on 11 March 1428 Robert Comitis, Gascon, levied a plaint of debt in the Sheriffs' Court of £17 14s 7d against Arnald Julii, executor of the will of Bernard Julian, and caused him to be attached, because he was a foreigner, by the sum of £7 which was owed to him by John Piers, sergeant, and whereas afterwards on 22 April 1428 the said Arnald by John Marchaunt his attorney sued John Piers in the Mayor's Court for the £7 owed to him, the latter on 15 May admitted the debt and offered to pay it to whomsoever the court should adjudge and asked for the return of his recognisance. The parties agreed that the money should lie in the attorney's hands, pending proof that the said Bernard in his lifetime did not owe the amount claimed by Robert. As no such proof was forthcoming, the attorney was given a day on 7 Sept. to pay the £7 to Robert.

4 July 1429 Writ of protection in favour of Robert Hoddisdon *alias* Barnett, yeoman, who was then about to cross the sea to France in the company of John Radclyff, knight.

7 July 1429 John Plumer, son of John Plumer of Halstede co. Essex, exonerated from his apprenticeship (12 years) to John Tasler, grocer, because the latter did not exercise his trade in the city, had not instructed him sufficiently and had withdrawn to Grenewych. [*Latin and French*]

Membr. 4 *b*
27 June 1429 John Stapulton, son of William Stapulton of Toryton co. Devon, prayed to be exonerated from his apprenticeship (8 years) to Thomas Brewod, grocer, on the ground that the latter had neither taught nor provided for him sufficiently. The master appeared and pleaded that he had carried out the terms of the indentures. The plaintiff prayed that the matter be inquired of by the masters and good men of the mistery of Grocers. On 9 June the defendant failed to appear, and Robert Marschal and Saier Aker, masters of the said mistery, gave evidence on oath that he had not instructed and maintained his apprentice. Thereupon the plaintiff was exonerated and turned over to John Cokkes, grocer, to serve the remainder of his term. [*Latin and French*]

John Man, son of Richard Man of Langham co. Suffolk, also exonerated from his apprenticeship to Thomas Brewod, grocer, and turned over to William Burton, grocer. *4 June 1429*

[*Latin and French*]

This day the mayor sent for Thomas Blounvyle, carpenter, and...his wife, at the instance of Reginald Lightfot, to answer a complaint by the latter that they had caused his daughter Katherine, being under 14 years of age, to be bound apprentice to them against her will and that of her father and other friends. They answered that the girl was willing and of sufficient age, to wit, 14 years and more, and offered to leave the matter to the judgment of the court after an inspection of the girl or any other reasonable form of proof. As the court was of opinion after an examination and numerous other proofs that she was still under 14 years of age, it was considered that she be exonerated from her apprenticeship. Membr. 5 *3 Aug. 1429*

John Wakeryng, master of the hospital of S[t] Bartholomew in the suburbs of London, brings a plaint of intrusion against William Gyffard, chaplain, and John Austyn touching his free tenement in the parish of S[t] Botolph without Aldersgate. *31 Jan. 1429*

Award of the mayor and aldermen in the Inner Chamber of the Guildhall in litigation between John Asshby, gentleman, Robert Asshby, goldsmith, and William Shiplake, barber, of the one part and William Hales, mercer, and John Admond, mercer, of the other. The former had sued the latter for trespass and forcible asportation of goods, value £212 19s ½d. On 29 Jan. 1429 the parties, on the ground that an issue of their litigation would be doubtful, expensive and dilatory, put themselves on the arbitration of Stephen Colley, Clement Lyffyn, Eborard Flete and John Fauntleroy, who failed to give an award, whereupon the mayor and aldermen as umpires investigated the matter. They found that the first parties claimed under a deed of 17 Jan. 1426, whereby Thomas Asshby gave to them all his goods and chattels, and the second parties claimed under another deed of gift of Edmund Draper and Thomas Asshby of 7 Jan. 1428, but that all the goods as set out in the claim had belonged to the said Edmund Draper *29 Jan. 1429* with the exception of six spoons, value 12s 8d, and three mazers, value 48s 4d, which he and Thomas Asshby held in common. Accordingly the mayor and aldermen on 15 Feb. awarded Thomas Asshby's half share of the latter articles, amounting to 30s 6d, to the first parties, and the other half share and the remainder of the goods to the second parties, and further that the deed on which the first parties had claimed should be quashed in court, while the deed of the second parties should be returned to them.

Membr. 5 *b*
14 Jan. 1429

Certificate from Davyd Pryce, licentiate in law, canon of the church of London and vicar-general of the bishop of London, that whereas John Cosyn of the parish of St Giles without Cripplegate had been reported as teaching heretical opinions repugnant to the orthodox faith, he had summoned him to answer and the said John had denied the charges, whereupon, proceeding according to the canonical sanctions in such case, he had held an inquiry in the church of St Giles as to the life, conversation and opinions of the said John by many trustworthy persons of the parish sworn and examined on the matter, and since he had found him zealous for the Catholic faith and that there was no obstacle to his purging himself, he had assigned a day for him to purge himself by the twelfth[1] hand of parishioners of good fame of the said church, which purgation the said John had lawfully performed.

7 March 1429

John Haccher, formerly apprentice of Richard Gosselyn, ironmonger, deceased, prayed the court that he might be exonerated from his apprenticeship, of which he had served nine years, and be admitted to the freedom, on the ground that Beatrice, widow of the said Richard, who by the law and custom of the city and the will of the deceased ought to have kept up his household and instructed his apprentices, had dismissed and allowed him to depart and had refused to maintain and teach him, to his manifest danger of falling into destruction and desolation. Thomas Knolles, younger brother of the said Beatrice, and other executors and neighbours gave evidence that she had sold everything belonging to the business

[1] Compurgation by the oaths of twelve persons including himself.

and had dismissed the petitioner. The court adjudged that the latter should be admitted to the freedom on payment of a reasonable fine to the chamberlain.

John Hilton, another apprentice of the said Richard, exonerated from his indentures and turned over to Richard Warbelton, ironmonger, for the remainder of his term.

21 March 1429

Acquittance from Rose, widow and executrix of William Tristour, saddler, and from John Croft, coppersmith, and Simon atte Welle, *Toloser*[1], her co-executors, to John Tirell, esquire, for the sum of £100 paid by him on the purchase of certain tenements in the parish of St Vedast.

Membr. 6
8 Aug. 1429

Recognisance of Roger Ameregi, citizen and mercer, to Walter Hungerford, lord of Heytesbury and of Homet[2], Treasurer of England, and Thomas Broun, esquire, in £1000.

Defeasance of the above on condition that the said Roger, as attorney of Paul Melyan of Lucca, or the said Paul himself, or another attorney of the same, should acknowledge before the Treasurer and Chamberlains of Receipt at Westminster that they had received from the said Walter and Thomas a sum of £1000, which had been paid to the said Thomas by the king, as appears in a certain book of the Receipt called "*le Pele*," and by him paid into the hands of Paul Melan, Lombard, to the use of John, duke of Bedford and regent of the kingdom, who had acknowledged the receipt thereof.

11 Aug. 1429

Grant by John Bederenden to Robert Cryngelford and Joan his wife of an annual rent of 60s charged on the manor of Sharrendene co. Sussex[3] for the lifetime of the said Joan, in recompense of the dowry accruing to her in the said manor as widow of John Turnour, on condition that the said Robert should make a proper acquittance for the same when received. Witnesses, Adam Ywode, John Halle, John Neylond and others. Dated 1 May 1429.

[1] Possibly an inhabitant of Toulouse; but query, toller, tollner, a toll-gatherer?

[2] Sir Walter Hungerford, first Baron Hungerford, lord of Heytesbury and of le Hommet, Manche, France.

[3] Sharnden, in the parish of Mayfield.

1 Sept. 1429 Reciprocal bonds of John Geffrey and John Horold, *wolpakker*, in £40 to abide by the award of Richard Salman, weaver, Thomas Haccher, brewer, Thomas Whityngham, tailor, and John Amour in disputes between them.

Membr. 6 *b*
14 Aug. 1429 As it appeared by examination of the parties and other evidence that William Herberd, vintner, had quitclaimed all interest in his apprentice Henry, son of John Clopton of St Albans, and that Richard Banaster, executor of John Toker, to whom the said Henry had been turned over to serve the rest of his term, had likewise quitclaimed his interest, and further, as no specialty was shown which could bind the said Henry to serve any longer as an apprentice or could secure his admittance to the freedom of the city, it was considered by the mayor and aldermen that the said Henry be exonerated from his apprenticeship.

23 Sept. 1429 Gift from Henry Flamstede, skinner, to John Coly and William Pepir, skinners, of all his goods and chattels. Sealed for better testimony by Ralph Barton, alderman, 20 Aug. 1429.

26 Sept. 1429 Gift from Robert Maylond, *foystour*[1], to John Mordon, Thomas Kyng, *loriner*, and William Bodeville of Enefeld, maltman, of all his goods and chattels. Witnesses, John Peryngton, John Nassh, William atte None and others. Dated 9 July 1429.

12 Sept. 1429 Similar gift from Margaret Sprotburgh, widow, dwelling without Cripplegate, to John Ierton, goldsmith. Dated 18 July 1429.

30 July 1429 Whereas during the episcopate of William Grey, bishop of London, Henry Barton, now mayor, had given to the cathedral church of St Paul a large thurible of good and pure silver weighing 13 lbs. 4 oz. troy to be used on the Monday, Tuesday and Wednesday in Whitweek for censing the mayor, aldermen and commonalty of the city and the people at large in their processions, it was now granted and agreed by Master Thomas Suthwell, rector of the church of St Stephen Wal-

[1] *Sc. fuster*, maker of the woodwork of saddles. *Cal. of Plea and Memoranda Rolls*, 1323–64, pp. 41, 238–40.

brook and warden of the ancient fabric of the cathedral church, on behalf of himself and his successors, that the said censer should be safely kept in the cathedral treasury among the other jewels and memorials and used for the purpose abovenamed. This indenture was sealed interchangeably by the said Henry and Thomas with the seals of their offices.

Writ of *certiorari* as to a quitclaim from Thomas Hoo and Agnes his wife to Thomas Chauser[1] of lands and tenements late belonging to William Chaumber, clerk, in the parish of St Augustine, and in the county of Middlesex. Membr. 7 *14 Oct. 1429*

Return giving the tenor of an enrolment in the Husting of Common Pleas of Monday after the feast of St Benedict Abbot (21 March), A° 4 Henry VI[2].

Reciprocal bonds of William Walton, goldsmith, (on behalf of himself, Thomas Morstede, Ralph Wemylton and Thomas Assherst) and Stephen Colney, goldsmith, in 200 marks to abide by the award of Richard Hungate, John Sutton, junior, John Pery and Nicholas Lovet in disputes between them. *20 Oct. 1429*

Gift by Francis Bandy, merchant of Florence, to Lewis John, esquire, of all his goods and chattels. Dated London 17 Oct. 1429. *25 Oct. 1429*

Reciprocal bonds of Nicholas Camulio, Isnardus Cataigne, Bartholomew Spynula, James Spynula and Loducius de Marye, of the one part, and Francis Serraelle, merchant of Florence, of the other, in £100 to abide by the award of the mayor and aldermen in disputes between them. *20 Aug. 1429*

In order to establish the truth whether Nicholas de Camulio of Genoa in Feb. 1424(5) received at the merchant town of Genoa from Francis Sirraelle, merchant of Florence, by the hands of his attorney Thomas Jacomyn, one bale containing 25 woollen cloths called "*Gildeford*," value £66 13s 8d, a second bale containing 24 woollen cloths called "*Bastardes*" Membr. 7 *b*

[1] Thomas Chaucer is described in 1406 as *consanguineus* of William Chaumbre. Husting Roll 133* (74). He was probably the son of the poet. See *Cal. of Letter Book I*, p. 21, n. 2.

[2] This is an error for Henry V. The quitclaim was dated 20 Feb. 1416 and enrolled 23 March 1416. Husting Roll 144 (4).

of the west, value £100, and a third bale containing 2064 skins called "*Middelfellis,*" value £33 6s 8d, to the use of the said Francis and to render account thereof, as the said Francis alleged in his action of account against the said Nicholas before the mayor and aldermen in the Chamber of Guildhall, or did not so receive the said bales, as Nicholas alleged in answer —it was enjoined upon the parties by the mayor and aldermen that before 1 March next they should bring into court authentic letters under the seals of the governors of Genoa in proof or disproof of the pleadings, in order that the mayor and aldermen might proceed to a decision in accordance with the agreement of the parties to submit to arbitration.

22 July 1429 James Waltham, son of Richard Waltham *alias* Ford, of London, exonerated from his apprenticeship (7 years) to William Bukston, *bocher*, because the latter did not exercise his trade. [*Latin and French*]

ROLL A 58

[*William Estfeld, mayor*]

William Biggynges, clerk, and Guy Fairfax, esquire, bring a plaint of intrusion against Margaret, widow of John Niandser, Edmund Galle, draper, John Caundissh, *brouderer*, William Loveney, Roger Spyce and John Newenham, esquires, and Richard Osbarn touching their free tenement in the parish of Holy Trinity the Less. Membr. 1 *31 Oct. 1429*

Amy, widow of Robert Tatersall and formerly wife of Richard Elton, draper, brings a plaint of intrusion against Thomas Pyrye, prior of New Place by Guildford[1], John Lacy, dyer, Richard Colton, girdler, William Rendre and Thomas Pratt, touching her free tenements in the parishes of St Peter in Westchepe, St Mary le Bow, St Mary Somerset, St Mary Abcherche, St Mary Magdalene by Oldfisshstrete, St Nicholas Coldabbey, Holy Trinity the Less, St Stephen Walbrook and St Giles without Crepulgate.

Richard Swayn of co. Essex brings a like plaint against the same parties.

Memorandum that Sir Thomas Kerdeston of co. Norfolk and Philip Possell, tailor, made an account before the mayor and aldermen of all moneys, cloth, ale and other goods received by Sir Thomas and his servants from the said Philip, from which it appeared that Sir Thomas owed 53s 2d. The money was paid forthwith, and all tallies and other evidences were cancelled. *9 Nov. 1429*

William, prior of Holy Trinity, brings a plaint of intrusion against John Costyn and Joan his wife and Robert Brampton touching his free tenement in the parish of All Hallows Stanyng. *14 Nov. 1429*

[1] Newark near Send in Surrey. It was a house of Black Canons of St Augustine. See Tanner, *Notitia Monastica*, p. 541 and note *d*.

28 Nov. 1429 Acquittance from John Fayre of co. Southampton, yeoman, and Agnes his wife, daughter of Cristine Person, to Roger Heyrun and Henry Jolypace, clerks, executors of the will of John Melborn, late servant (*domicellus*) of Master John Chitterne, and to James Surenden, executor of William Waldern, deceased, which William was the other executor of John Melborn, for the receipt of £100 devised by the said John Melborn as a marriage portion to the said Agnes.

8 Oct. 1429 Richard Ogle, son of John Ogle of Hamstalredeware co. Staffs, was exonerated from his apprenticeship (8 years) to John Multon, skinner, because the latter had withdrawn to Westminster, a privileged place. The said Richard was committed to John York, skinner, to serve the remainder of his term. [*Latin and French*]

Membr. 1 *b*
31 Oct. 1429 William Oxbrigge prays an assize of nuisance against Thomas Newton, rector of the church of S[t] Leonard in Fasterlane, and John Belle and John Stalkenden, wardens of the same, touching his free tenement in the parish of S[t] Michael at Corn.

15 Jan. 1430 Writ of *corpus cum causa* to bring William Wodeward into Chancery and return that he had been taken and detained in an action of trespass and deceipt before the mayor and aldermen at the suit of Martin Aleyn; nevertheless he would be brought in as required.

15 Nov. 1429 Memorandum that Bartholomew Contaryn, who was then visiting London, came before the mayor and aldermen and informed them that he had assigned to Stephen Forster, fishmonger, in satisfaction of certain debts, a debt of £152 10s 6d which was owed to him by Saier Acre and Nicholas Wyfold, grocers, on an obligation of 2 April 1429 payable on 14 May 1430. He undertook not to issue any acquittance to the said Saier and Nicholas without Stephen's consent, and that he would prosecute and avow, at Stephen's expense, any suits moved by Stephen in his (Bartholomew's) name for non-payment of the debt.

Bertucius Contaryn and Leonard Contaryn, merchants of Venice, similarly assigned to Robert Bamburgh, draper, a debt of £25 due to them from John Dartre, grocer, on an obligation of 21 July 1429 payable on 24 Aug. 1430. *26 Jan. 1430*

"To alle cristen peple þ[t] these lettres shull se or here Robert Large Citezein and mercer of þe Cite of London sendith gretyng in our lord Ihū Crist where as betwene Robert Cristemasse citezein and draper of þe Cite of London on þ[t] oon partie and William Chesse citezein and Skynner of þe same Citee on þ[t] oþer partie diverse contraversies discordes and debates now late were moved and hangyng not determyned nor pleynly declared wherupon as well at þe denominacion and assignement of þe Mair and Aldermen of þe Cite aboveseid as at þe special request and prayer of þe seid parties I the seid Robert Large have seen herd and diligently examyned the claymes demaundes grevaunces and alleggeances of either of þe seid parties and good deliberacion therupon had I awarde and yeve in sentence betwene the seid parties in þe fourme þ[t] sueth þ[t] is to wite—

First I awarde and yeve in sentence in caas þ[t] þe seid Robert Cristemasse fortune to take þis bille þan shall þe same Robert Cristemasse have and rejoyce the furres, and þe seid William shall paye to þe same Robert Cristemasse without tariance or delay x li. and upon such payment of x li. made shall the seid Robert Cristemasse make pleyn and quit deliverance to þe seid William of his obligacion of lix li. xi s viii d.

And on þe other partie yif it fortune þe seid William to take his bille þan shall þe same William have the furres and fynde and make to the seid Robert Cristemasse suffisaunt seurte to paye to þe same Robert Cristemasse at þe feste of Wytsontide now next comyng þe somme lix li. xi s viii d conteyned in his obligacion rebatyng and allowyng the same Robert Cristemasse to the seid William of þe seid somme of lix li. xi s viii d for his damages v li."

In an action at the suit of John Bocher, *alias* Mayken, of St Osyth co. Essex, skinner, and John Cok of the same, mariner, against Michael Wodecok of Feversham co. Kent, mariner, for a debt of £20 due on a writing obligatory, the Membr. 2 *1 Dec. 1429* defendant was attached by a ship and gear in the hands of John Skalfyn. The defendant made four defaults, whereupon the plaintiffs prayed that John Skalfyn be summoned to show cause why they should not have execution of the ship. The said John did not come.

11 Feb. 1430 Quitclaim from John Husshe, goldsmith, son of the late Thomas Husshe, to Amy Tatersall, widow of Robert Tatersall, draper, and to William Estfeld, mercer, Thomas Scot and John Boys, drapers, executors of the will of the said Robert, who was executor of the will of Cecilia Sudbury.

Gifts of goods and chattels: 22 Feb. 1430, from Roger Benyngton, barber, to Roger Crome of co. York, gentleman, Hugh Harlewyn, spurrier, Richard Gerold, mason, and William Porter, *ministrall*; witnesses, Richard Bury, Richard
Membr. 2 *b* Spray, John Hamond and others; 22 Feb. 1430, from Richard Huchons, mercer, to John Aleyn and Robert Reynham, mercers; 25 Feb. 1430, from William Posmore of Stratford atte Bowe co. Middlesex, tailor, to Richard Wellys, barber, Richard Colton, girdler, and Peter Pope, barber; 24 March 1430, from William Wydeford, tallowchandler, to Richard Selby, clerk of Chancery, William Morys, fishmonger, and John Bracy, chandler.

28 Nov. 1429 Writ of protection in favour of Walter Aleyn, senior, *trumpour*, then about to cross to France in the company of Sir John Kyghley.

15 March 1430 Recognisance from William Pepir, skinner, to Matthew Wrykhyll, of a debt of 10 marks.

Membr. 3 *9 Feb. 1430* John Thomas, son of William Thomas *alias* Poos, of the parish of St Severus co. Cornwall, who had been apprenticed for 8 years to John Davy, tailor, and on the latter's death, had been sold[1] by the executors, William Groce, brewer, and Benet Harlewyn, draper, to Henry Goof, tailor, to serve the remainder of his term, was now exonerated from his ap-

[1] *Et apres ceo les ditz executours vendirent le dit apprentys a dit Henry Goof.* On the apprentice as a chattel see *Ricart's Kalendar* (Camd. Soc. 1872), pp. xxi, 102–3; *Cal. of Plea and Memoranda Rolls*, 1364–1381, pp. xlii–xliii, 202, 294.

prenticeship, because the said Henry had withdrawn to the privileged place of Westminster. The said John was turned over to Stephen Peirce, tailor, to complete his term.

[*Latin and French*]

Recognisance of John Kyngeston, mercer, to Robert Walssh of co. Lincs, gentleman, of a debt of £8. *4 Jan. 1430*

Recognisance of William Bys, merchant, John Borham, stockfishmonger, and Robert Lord to John Notyngham and Thomas Assh of a debt of £4. Cancelled on payment. *2 March 1430*

Writ of *corpus cum causa* to bring Maud, wife of Thomas Ballyng, into Chancery, and return that she had been taken and detained by virtue of three actions of trespass, at the suits of Hugh Wyche, mercer, John Daweston and Elizabeth his wife, and Alice Everard respectively, and of one action of debt of 12s at the suit of Richard Chippenham, tailor; nevertheless she would be brought in as required. *12 March 1430*

Quitclaim from John Blaket of co. Oxon, knight, to William Holgrave, tailor. *22 March 1430*

Membr. 3 *b*

Memorandum that John Pyken, brewer, Roger Breresle, tailor, William Frank, brewer, Richard Welles, cooper, Richard Flete, *hurer*, John Rakeway, saddler, Ralph Spayne, *tapicer*, Andrew Strawton, cordwainer, and others appeared before the mayor and aldermen in the Chamber and testified that either in June, July or Aug. 1416 they were present when John Maryns *alias* Foot, esquire, son and heir of John Foot *alias* Maryns, apothecary, by his attorney John Chesham, who acted for him as he was not able to attend himself through infirmity, in accordance with a charter and letters of attorney under his seal, delivered his status and possession in all his lands and tenements in the parishes of St Dionis Bakchirch and All Hallows Stanyng to Alexander Farnell, who took seisin and possession on his own behalf and that of his co-feoffees, and all the tenants there attorned to him in legal form. *18 March 1430*

Reciprocal bonds of Stephen Colley and Walter Vytull, esquire, in £40 to abide by the arbitration of Thomas Bataill, mercer, and John Malden, grocer, in disputes between them. *19 Feb. 1430*

16 March 1430 Writ of protection in favour of John Parker, grocer, then about to cross to France with the king in the company of Sir John Cobham.

24 March 1430 Gift of goods and chattels from John Slyndon, skinner, to Thomas Davy, tailor, John Beures, haberdasher, and John Savage, vintner.

Membr. 4 *1 April 1430* Bond of Edward Russell, esquire, to John Mountgomery, knight, and Lewis John, esquire, in 1000 marks to cross the sea before Whitsuntide, if wind and breeze (*ventus & aura*) permitted or as soon after as was reasonably possible, and proceed to Pluvers in Gatenesia or elsewhere, where Thomas, brother of the said John Mountgomery, was detained in prison as pledge of the said Edward, and procure his release. Proof of his delivery was to be produced by letters under the seal of the said Thomas, or of the duke of Bedford, or of the count of Morteyn, or of Lord Willughby, or of Henry Norbury, knight, before Michaelmas.

Bond of John Kentwode in support of the above.

Quitclaim from John Stuard, knight, and Alice his wife to John Cornwaleys of London.

6 April 1430 Acquittance from Robert Wodewey, son of Henry Wodewey, skinner, to Ralph Barton, skinner, on the receipt of 115 marks, being a legacy from the said Henry. Dated 23 Jan. 1430.

Gifts of goods and chattels: 5 April 1430, John Wodehouse, goldsmith, to Peter Brendewode, goldsmith; 17 April, Thomas Cogger, butcher, to William Severn and John Hale of co. Bedford; witnesses, John Grisley, John Taillour, Ralph Lese; 20 April, John Haryngton, brewer (*braciator*), to Geoffrey Brid, *brasyer*, and William Fissh, brewer; 28 April, John Orgar, haberdasher, to William Graunger, cutler, John Orgar, tailor, and Walter Peryn, haberdasher; witnesses, Richard Blake, Walter Hersy, Peter Pilton, John Byfold, Thomas
Membr. 4 *b* Heyward; 28 April, Simon Strete, grocer, to Thomas Knolles, son of Thomas Knolles, alderman, Robert Marchall and Saier Acres, grocers, and William...; 17 May, William Huberd,

vintner, to William Child, fishmonger, and John Melton, textwriter (*scriptori texti*); 31 May, Thomas Lynne, skinner, to Richard Swetenham and Matthew Hey, gentlemen.

William Hubert, vintner, committed to prison for a debt of £19 at the suit of Thomas Dryffeld, goldsmith. *1 July 1430*

Writ of *habeas corpus* in favour of Alice Hemyngford, who had been arrested and detained in prison by the sheriffs when she was on her way to Westminster to the Court of Common Pleas to sue John Wroxhale of Dunstaple, co. Bedford, *coper*, for a debt of £8, and was thus under the king's protection. Witness W. Babyngton at Westminster. *4 July 1430*

Return that the said Alice, under the name of Alice Hemmyngford of London, widow, had been taken and detained by virtue of a plea of trespass at the suit of William Hawkyn, butcher, the plaint having been levied on 12 May in the Sheriffs' Court and afterwards taken before the mayor and aldermen in the Chamber, and that the sheriffs would bring the said Alice before the justices as ordered.

Gifts of goods and chattels: 26 June 1430, Thomas Gosse, mercer, to Robert Coventre and Hugh Wyche, mercers; 11 July, Joan Stacheden, widow, to William Rus, goldsmith, and John Stacheden, stockfishmonger; 16 June, William Austyn, tailor, to John Creek, skinner, and John Amfles, armourer; witnesses,... Turnour, shearman, Robert Reymond, draper, John Chyvaler, saddler. Membr. 5

Writ of *corpus cum causa*, witnessed by Humphrey, duke of Gloucester, *custos* of England, to bring George Luke of London, merchant, into Chancery, and return that the said Luke had been taken and detained by virtue of an original bill of account at the suit of Francis Bandy of London, merchant, levied before the mayor and aldermen in the Chamber, but that he would be brought into Chancery as ordered. *25 June 1430*

Writ of protection in favour of Thomas Cosyn of London, gentleman, who was then about to cross to France with the king in the company of John, duke of Norfolk, marshal of England. *15 May 1430*

Membr. 5 *b* 3 *Sept.* 1430 Memorandum that in the presence of the mayor and aldermen Alexander Cheyne, one of the administrators of John Evedon, merchant, late of Evedon in the diocese of Lincoln, and Katherine, widow of John Oo, apothecary, agreed to submit to the arbitration of the mayor and aldermen as regards a dispute between them pending both in the city court and at common law outside the city. The dispute concerned a claim for £74 made by the said Alexander Cheyne against the said Katherine on the ground that her late husband was the same person as John Hoo, grocer, who was bound to the late John Evedon by a writing obligatory of £74, which claim the said Katherine denied, maintaining that the persons named were not the same person. The mayor and aldermen, as well from the evidence of records as from the testimony of many ancient and trustworthy men and other kinds of proof, found that John Oo, apothecary, formerly husband of Katherine, was not a freeman of the city at the time when the obligation was made, and that he was living (*degens in humanis*) and dwelling in the parish of S[t] Benet Shorhogge in a great inn (*hospicium*) opposite the inn formerly of John Fressh, afterwards of William Waldern and now of Henry Frowik, whereas John Hoo, grocer, with whom John Evedon carried out numerous business transactions, was forced, owing to the great and excessive sums of money in which he was bound to divers persons, to flee to the sanctuary of S[t] Martin le Grand, where he spent the remainder of his life. Accordingly, in view of the trustworthy evidence of the said Katherine as against the bare and unsupported verbal suggestion of the said Alexander, it was considered and adjudged that (*cetera desunt*).

17 *July* 1430 John Pycot of Abyngton co. Cambs, merchant, William Estfeld, Henry Frowyk, William Melreth and Robert Bamburgh, draper, bring a plaint of intrusion against William Olyver, grocer, Robert Fitz Robert, Thomas atte Wode, clerk, David Knotte, chaplain, John Fitz Richard and Walter Fitz Richard touching their free tenement in the parish of S[t] Laurence in the Jewry.

13 *Dec.* 1429 Whereas a plea on a writ of right patent—which John Lincoln, son of Thomas Lincoln, goldsmith, deceased, an

orphan of the city, being under age, had pending for a long time before the mayor and sheriffs in the Husting against William Curson for divers lands and tenements belonging to the orphan by hereditary right after the decease of his grandmother Joan—had suffered and seemed likely to suffer so many delays, on account of divers persons called to warranty and other dilatory and peremptory exceptions advanced on behalf of the said William, that the orphan owing to his poverty would not be able to bear the expense of the action if it continued, and also because there were divers opinions and doubts as to the law of the case and the rights of the parties, the orphan, whose wardship belonged by custom to the mayor and aldermen, with the assent of his guardian and friends, and the said William Curson for his part, put themselves on the final award of the mayor and aldermen, who on 13 Dec. 1429 adjudged that the parties should hold the lands and tenements in common during the lifetime of the said William, all profits being divided between them after such repairs of the tenements had been made under the survey of the chamberlain as might be required by the orphan, and that after the decease of the said William the whole should fall to the orphan and his executors.

Gifts of goods and chattels: 22 July 1430, Agatha Pytman, widow of John Pytman, grocer, to Robert Stratford, fishmonger, and John Hethe, skinner; 29 July 1430, Thomas **Membr. 6** Jolyf, stockfishmonger, to Walter Milton and Thomas Whatton, stockfishmongers; 9 Aug. 1430, William Braunthwayte, stockfishmonger, to Henry Langspee, draper, and John Grafton, stockfishmonger; 1 Sept. 1430, Thomas Raweley, citizen, to William Betley of co. Warwick, gentleman, and William Latoner, tailor.

22 July 1430

In an action for debt at the suit of John Somerton, grocer, against John Colverhous, chandler, for £3 13s 4d arrears of a debt of 8 marks 8d due on a purchase of a last of white herrings, the defendant was attached to appear by John Mallom, serjeant-at-mace, and made four defaults. Thereupon the foreign attachment, which was in the hands of the plaintiff, was valued by the oath of Henry Hale, grocer, and William

Torold, tailor, as follows:—one bale of *coton* weighing 1½ cwt. 4 lbs. at 39s 6d, and a piece of woollen cloth of 21 yds. at 21s, and delivered to the plaintiff under pledge of Henry Hale, grocer, and Henry Fredyngham, saddler, to answer therefor if the defendant should come within a year and a day and deraign etc.

Membr. 6 *b*
7 Aug. 1430
Memorandum that Baptista de Nigris, merchant of Genoa, then visiting London, appeared in court and declared that he had assigned to William Crowmere, draper, in payment of certain moneys owed to him, a debt of £46 17s 6d due to him from Peter Aumener, merchant of London, and payable on 25 June 1431 by virtue of a writing obligatory of 19 Jan. 1429. He undertook not to give any acquittance therefor to the said Peter without the said William's consent, and that he would, when reasonably required, sue and avow, at the said William's expense, all suits and plaints levied and affirmed in his name against the said Peter in case of non-payment.

Similar assignments to the same of debts of £106 11s 6d due from Thomas Hardyng, draper, on three writings obligatory of 3 June 1430 providing for payment in even portions on 24 June 1431, 1432 and 1433, £60 10s 6d due from John Knotte, tailor, on three writings obligatory of 12 June 1430, providing for payment in even portions on the same dates, and £109 4s 9d due from John Whitehode and Geoffrey Chittok, drapers, on three writings obligatory of 3 June 1430, providing for payment in even portions on 1 June 1431, 1432 and 1433.

12 Aug. 1430
John Boyles, son of John Boyles, tailor, exonerated from his apprenticeship (9 yrs) to Robert Mowton, grocer, who had left the city. The said John was committed to John Somerton, grocer, to serve the remainder of his term.

[*Latin and French*]

Membr. 7
27 May 1430
In an action for debt at the suit of Richard Toky and William Forster, skinners, against John Quyntyn, girdler, for the sum of £16 due on a writing obligatory of 1 Sept. 1429, the defendant made four defaults, whereupon the plaintiffs prayed that four rings in their possession, whereby he had been attached to appear, might be valued and delivered to

them. The rings were valued by oath of Henry Clerk, John Welles and William Takele, goldsmiths, as follows, one gold ring set with a *dyamand*, 20s; another with a *rubie*, 26s 8d; and two others, each with a *saphire*, 13s 4d. They were delivered to the plaintiffs under pledge of Nicholas Dovelond, brewer, and Robert Kyng, skinner, to answer therefor if the defendant should come within a year and a day and deraign etc.

Gifts of goods and chattels: 2 Sept. 1430, Philip Jakes, saddler, to William Caldewell, John Bagworth, saddler, and John Burveyn, brewer; John Aldam, girdler, to Thomas Walys, barber, and William Lee, pewterer; Joan Burtham, widow of John Burtham, woolpacker, to Gilbert Devenysshe and John Bulle, skinners.

Bond of Bartholomew Spyngell and Ambrose Pinalus (?), Membr. 7*b*
merchants of Genoa, to John Mordok of Leicester, merchant, *26 Sept. 1430*
in £100 to abide by the award of Simon Eyre, draper, Darius de Vivaldis, merchant of Genoa, and Eborard Flete and John Olney, mercers, concerning six bales of *batery*, value £100, claimed by the said John against the said Bartholomew.

Gifts of goods and chattels: 3 Oct. 1430, Robert Holme, mercer, to John Abbot and Nicholas Drayton, mercers; 28 Oct. 1430, William Felton, armourer, to Walter Vytull, armourer, and John Body, painter; 9 Nov. 1430, John Mablean, goldsmith, to John Sutton, senior, goldsmith, and John Neve, vintner.

Elena, widow and executrix of John Joynour, ironmonger, *19 Oct. 1430*
with John Risley, John Lane and Richard Walter, her co-executors, came before the mayor and aldermen and prayed leave to sue John Vyncent, founder, at common law, and affirmed on oath that their only reason for doing so was that the dispute between them could not be terminated within the city since the said John had withdrawn therefrom.

Bond of Robert Charyngworthe to John Costyn, girdler, Membr. 8
in £50, to abide by the award of Nicholas Conyston, John *17 Aug. 1430*
Hille, pinner, Alexander Anne and Edmund Salle in disputes

between them, or in case the arbitrators could not agree, of an umpire chosen by the mayor and aldermen.

25 Oct. 1430 Bond of William Lardener, baker, to Agnes, Lucy and Isabel, daughters of Roger Lardener, in £100 to abide by the award of John Welles and Henry Frowyk, aldermen, chosen as arbitrators between the parties.

Afterwards the said arbitrators brought in an award reciting that the late Roger Lardener had taken a lease for 59 years from 10 June 1421 of a messuage in the parish of St Bride in Flete Street called "*le Popynjay*" from the abbot of the house of St Mary of Cirencester at an annual rent of 8 marks, with power to the abbot to re-enter if the rent were in arrears, and that afterwards the said Roger on 20 Jan. 1429 made his will, appointing William Lardener executor and devising to him the unexpired portion of the lease, on condition that he paid the rent and other charges and delivered any profits remaining to the testator's three daughters in equal portions. The arbitrators found that after his brother's death the said William Lardener, seeking his own profit and plotting to exclude his nieces from the benefit of the surplus, allowed the rent to fall into arrears, whereupon the lessors in accordance with the terms of the lease re-entered into possession, and that later the said lessors granted a new lease to the said William and Ellen his wife for the term of their lives at the former rent, and that all this had been confessed by the said William before the mayor, when he was sued by Alexander Anne, common serjeant-at-law of the city[1], acting on behalf of the orphans. The arbitrators now award that the said William find sufficient security in the Chamber before Christmas to pay the orphans all surplus profits from the messuage, after payment of the rent, from the date of their father's death till the end of the original term, and if he were unwilling to do so, that he should find security, according to the discretion of the mayor, aldermen and counsel of the city, to pay 100s yearly to the orphans for the same period[2].

[1] Afterwards recorder. *Cal. of K*, p. 196.

[2] The jurisdiction of the mayor and aldermen in orphanage can be traced to the thirteenth century. The common serjeant's connection with it probably arose from his duties as prosecutor for the commonalty, and in

Bond of William Gregory, John Herst, John Van and Thomas Coly to John Bederenden, chamberlain, in £200 to pay that sum into court for the use of Henry, William and Elizabeth, orphans of Ralph Skynnard, skinner, in accordance with the latter's will. Note that the money was paid on 19 July 1431 and the bond cancelled. *13 June 1430*

Gift of goods and chattels from William Porter *alias* Shipdam to Robert Colbroke, ironmonger, Ralph Stokes, grocer, and John Exham, clerk. *24 Oct. 1430*

course of time the care of orphans and their property constituted one of his most important duties. For the history of the Court of Orphans see *Cal. of Early Mayor's Court Rolls*, pp. xxii, 77; *Cal. of P. and M. Rolls, 1323–1364*, pp. 162, 205–6, 205 n. 1; *Ricart's Kalendar* (Camd. Soc.), p. 99; Strype's *Stow's Survey*, II, pp. 323–4, 372–3.

ROLL A 59

(*Nicholas Wotton, mayor*)

Membr. 1
15 Oct. 1430

In an action for debt at the suit of Thomas Chynnore against John, abbot of the monastery of the Blessed Mary of Graces, for the sum of £40 lent to the latter on 10 March 1429, the defendant was attached by divers goods in the hands of the plaintiff, and on his making four defaults, the foreign attachment was delivered to the plaintiff under pledge of Thomas Turnour and Edward Cust to answer therefor if the defendant should come within a year and a day and deraign etc., the goods being as follows:—a woman's velvet gown powdered with gold, valued by oath of Thomas Denton, mercer, and Thomas Grave, *setter*, at £15; a number of books [1] valued by oath of John Robert and William Barwe, stationers:—A psalter, 13s 4d; Luke and John glossed, 3s 4d; a book called "*Dieta Salutis*", 6s 8d; "*Stimulus Amoris*", 3s 4d; "*Speculum Religiosorum*", 2s; a volume of divers books of the Bible, 20d; "*Summa Reymundi*", the second folio beginning "*manu potest*", 2s; "*Sintillar'*", the second folio beginning "*lucet*", 8d; a book of the Gospels, 12d; and "*Ambrosius super Lucam*", 10s; and the following vessels, valued by oath of John Sutton, senior, and John Cary, goldsmiths:—a mazer bound with silvergilt, 8s; a silver goblet weighing $2\frac{3}{4}$ oz. at 30d the oz., 6s 8d; and a cup of *birell* [2] bound with silvergilt with a silvergilt covercle weighing 8 oz. at 2s 8d the oz., 23s 4d.

11 Nov. 1430

Bond of Richard Colet to Peter Ricard, vintner, in 500 marks to abide by the award of John Brokle and William Crowmere in disputes between them.

[1] *Dieta Salutis*, a treatise usually ascribed to S[t] Bonaventura (1221–74) and printed in the Mainz edition of his works, 1607, VI, pp. 272–325. The *Stimulus Amoris* was also written by him. The *Speculum Religiosorum* was printed with the *Speculum Christiani* for Jehan Petit at the sign of the Silver Lion in the Rue S[t] Jacques, Paris. The *Summa Reymundi de Pennaforti* was printed at Louvain 1480, Cologne 1498, Rome 1603 etc. *Sintillar'* was no doubt the *Liber Scintillarum*, of which MS. copies have survived in libraries.

[2] *Sc.* beryl, in the sense of fine crystal or glass.

Alexander Reve, cheesemonger, committed to prison for a debt of 5 marks 4s 6d and damages taxed by a jury at 11s 8d, which Richard atte Mille, butcher, recovered against him. *18 April 1431*

Reciprocal bonds of Thomas Galyot, waxchandler, and Alice Cays in £100 to abide by the arbitration of William Crowmere and John Michell in disputes between them. *12 Dec. 1430*

Membr. 1 *b*
17 Jan. 1431

Bond of John Mordok of Leicester, merchant, to Bartholomew Spinula, merchant of Genoa, in £200 to abide by the award of Henry Frowik and John Brokle[1] with regard to the costs incurred by the said Bartholomew, Obertus Spinula and Agapitus Grillo in sending 6 bales of *batery* from Bruges to London, and furthermore to make a sufficient letter of attorney to certain persons to be nominated by the said Bartholomew to sue John Pikwell of Leicester, John Feldyng of Lutterworth, Thomas Mayn of Beverley, and John Morton and Richard Copelond of York, for untrue and unjust packing of 86 sarplers of wool bought from the said John Mordok by the said Bartholomew, Obertus and Agapitus.

Similar bond of Bartholomew Spinula to abide by the award abovementioned and to make no claim against the said John Mordok as regards the packing of the said wool.

Gifts of goods and chattels: 12 Feb. 1431, John Collee, goldsmith, to John Kebyll, goldsmith, and Richard Kilfole, brewer; witnesses, Richard Spenser, William Walton and Reginald Welham; 23 Feb. 1431, Roger Bukbrigge, skinner, to William Thede, armourer; 6 March 1431, Richard Banbury, butcher, to Thomas Vale, butcher.

Robert Rykherst and Thomas Sumnour bring a plaint of intrusion against William Coventre, prior of St Bartholomew, West Smithfield, touching their free tenement in the parish of St Nicholas Shambles. *12 Feb. 1431*

Membr. 2

Gifts of goods and chattels: 9 Nov. 1430, Thomas Stok, stockfishmonger, to John Mablean, goldsmith, and John Blomville, carpenter; 17 Nov. 1430, Miles Standissh, grocer,

[1] The arbitrators Brokle, Crowmere, Michell and Frowik were all aldermen.

to Robert Marchall, grocer; 7 Dec. 1430, John Biernes, goldsmith, to Robert Fitz Roberd, Thomas Weston, clerk, John Sutton, junior, goldsmith, and Robert Kyngesson, vintner.

11 Nov. 1430 Reciprocal bonds of Walter Gawtron, draper, and John Snypston, vintner, in 100 marks to abide by the award of John Fray[1], Philip Malpas, William Halle, serjeant-at-law, and Thomas Gwyn, vintner, in disputes between them.

8 Jan. 1431 Geoffrey, master of the order of Burton S[t] Lazarus of Jerusalem in England, warden of the hospital of S[t] Giles without London, brings a plaint of intrusion against Henry, prior of the house and church of the Blessed Mary of Suthwerk, John, prior of the house of the Salutation of the Mother of God of the order of the Carthusians near London, Elizabeth Welford, John Fitz Andrew and John Berston and Juliana his wife touching his free tenement in the parish of S[t] Margaret Bridge Street.

Membr. 2*b* Gifts of goods and chattels: 22 Nov. 1430, William Dounyng, cooper, to Richard Gerveys and John Abbes, brewers; 9 Dec. 1430, William Cantelowe, mercer, to William Estfeld, Henry Frowyk, Robert Large and William Melreth, aldermen, John Symond, John Gargrave, Thomas Broun, esquires, John Carpenter, Thomas Gloucestre, clerks, John Olney, Thomas Bataille and John Cotford, mercers; witnesses, John Sonman, William Grymmesby, John Stodeley; 14 Dec. 1430, Robert Otewy, brewer, to Nicholas Yeo, draper, William Wemyngton, gentleman, and William Strete of High Rothing co. Essex; 18 Jan. 1431, John Pynchebek, butcher, to Richard Banbery, butcher.

8 Dec. 1430 Memorandum that Nicholas Johan of Bologna, merchant, then visiting London, appeared in court and declared that he had assigned to John Hiham, draper, in payment of certain moneys owed to him, debts of £82 13s 4d due to him from William de Lung'x[2], Richard Banastre, Hugh Dene and

[1] Formerly recorder, raised to the bench as Baron of the Exchequer in 1425.

[2] Appears as "Lunhs", *C.C.R.* 1422–9, p. 333; "Lunhx", *ibid.* 1435–41, p. 437.

Edmund Sheffeld, vintners, and payable on 14 Aug. 1431 by virtue of a writing obligatory of 14 Aug. 1430, and of £56 6s 8d due to him from William Olyver, Thomas Holm and Robert Gayton and payable on 25 March next following by virtue of a writing obligatory of 4 Sept. 1430.

Bond of Leonard Cateneus to John de Marcanovo, Francis de Molino and Thomas Contarino in £500 to abide by the award of John de la Tore, Dominicus Villani, Nicholas John of Bologna, George (son of) Nicholas Luke[1] and Laurence Damyan as regards certain disputes between the said Leonard and James Loridanus of Venice. He undertakes further not to sue Hugh Rys of Sandwich and Edmund Pynell for a debt arising out of a bond of 500 marks in any courts except those within the city of London, the said debt having become due by reason of the non-appearance of the said James in the Admiralty Court of the Cinque Ports. **Membr. 3** *20 Feb. 1431*

Similar bond of John de Marcanovo, Francis de Molino and Thomas Contarino, on behalf of James Loridanus, to Leonard Cataneus to abide by arbitration, or if the arbitrators could not agree, that the said James would find mainprise to appear in court to answer the said Leonard before the mayor or sheriffs and that the said Hugh Rys and Edmund Pynell of Genoa would do the same.

Reciprocal bonds of William Barde, brewer, and Joan Marwe, widow, in £40 to abide by the award of William Couper and John Serle, masters of the Carpenters, and of two masters of the Tilers, whom the mayor might call in, as regards the destruction and burning of a brewhouse belonging to the said Joan's messuage in the parish of St Botolph without Bishopsgate. *27 Jan. 1431*

John Marchaunt, *loriner*, and Alice his wife, sister of Simon Sely, came into court and acknowledged a deed of 23 Feb. 1431 whereby they agreed to and confirmed a lease for 20 years by the said Simon and his mother Joan to John Norman, draper, of a tavern in Milk Street called "the Horn on the Hoop", together with two small chambers on the west side built over *26 Feb. 1431*

[1] *Georgii Nicholai Luce, cf. C.C.R.* 1422–9, p. 480; 1429–35, p. 381.

a small house and latrine of the lessors, also a gate and an open piece of ground called "le Wodehawe", with a house called "le logge" on the east of it, and another house called "le coustere".

6 March 1431 Writ of *corpus cum causa* to bring Nicholas Bernard, notary, into Chancery, and return that he had been taken and detained by virtue of a plaint of detinue of a sealed box containing charters and other muniments at the suit of Geoffrey Costantyn, *leche*, levied in the Sheriffs' Court and afterwards removed into the Mayor's Court; nevertheless he would be brought into Chancery as ordered.

Membr. 3*b* *28 Feb. 1431* Assignment by William Baron, dyer, to John Bederenden, draper, Robert Holand, shearman, and John Moordon, attorney, of the unexpired portion of a thirty years lease of certain ancient tenements and a wharf called "Heywharf" situate in Heywharflane in the parish of all Hallows the Great, which he had from Richard Chambirleyn, esquire, of co. Northampton. The premises were subject to annual quitrents payable to the bishop of Winchester (26s 8d), John Brikles, draper (5 marks), and the said Richard Chambirleyn (5 marks). He further granted to the said John, Robert and John absolutely the following utensils[1] then in the custody of John Reynold, brewer, at the Heywharf:—2 leads (*plumba*) with covers, 2 leaden *taptroghes*, 2 *masshefattes*, 2 *taphosen*, 3 *messhyngshovelis*, one iron *pyke*, one iron rake, one *tyne*, one *colundre*, one horse-mill with gear, 2 *yeltonnes*, one *clensyngfat*, one *clensyng Sive*, 25 *kemelyns*, 8 *barells*, 38 *kilderkyns*, one *growtfat*, one *trey*, one *galon*, one *busshell*, one *maltshovill*, 2 *alegistes*.

16 March 1431 Recognisance of a debt of 10 marks from Conrad Rose *alias* Mayns, merchant of Almayne, to Alice, widow of John Stodeley, tailor, and Nicholas Stodeley, gentleman.

[1] A lead was a caldron or vat, originally of lead, but afterwards of other metals also. A taptrough was a trough with a tap. The mash-vat was used for mashing or mixing malt with hot water to make wort. The tap-hose was a strainer placed over the tap-hole in a mash-tub. A tyne, tine, was a tub or vat. Kemelyn, *sc.* kimnel, was also a tub. A grout-vat contained grout, which, like wort, was an infusion of malt before and during fermentation. Trey, *sc.* tray. An alegist was an ale-joist, a barrel-stand.

Recognisance of John Baladyn, dwelling in the ward of Farndon Without, to the chamberlain in £20 for his good behaviour. *27 March 1431*

Bond of Richard Colett to Peter Ricard, vintner, in 500 marks, to abide by the award of Master William Lynwode, official of the Court of Canterbury. *26 March 1431*

William Crowmere, Henry Barton, William Estfeld and John Welles, aldermen, came into court and acknowledged the following writing to be their deed:— Membr. 4 *13 April 1431*

"To alle men seyng or heryng this scripture William Crowmere Henry Barton William Estfeld & John Welles citezeins and aldermen of London arbitrous and frendly makers of pees chosen in the forme underwreten We notifie and declare that the xxii day of Januer, in the yere of oure Lord m[l]ccccxxx[ti] and in the yere of oure soverayn lord the kyng Henry the VI[te] after the conquest ix[e] In the Chirche of Seint Michell atte Corn of London be forn oure Reverent Fader in god and ryghtworthi Lord William be the grace of god Bisshop of london oure diocesan and oure honurable and worthi Mair of London Nicholas Wotton Beynge there also presentz Reverentz and honurable persones Maister Reynald Kentwode Dean of seint Paules Patron of the same Chirche of seint Michell Master Richard Moresby Archdeacon of London Walter Chertesey Shereve of london appiered personally Maister John Craas parson of þe sayd Cherche of seint Michell on the too partie and John Werk Piers Bilton occupiers of the office of Chirchwardenship and Thomas Galyot and Michell Randolf overseers of the Cherchewerk w[t] the more & sadder partie of þe parisshenes of þe same Chirch of seint Michell on the toþer partie rehersyng þe seyd parties many matiers of dissencion and discord meved be twix hem because of bildyng of þe Chauncell of the same Chirch newe to be edified and of the parsonage w[t] Inne the same Chirch with certain aisementz longyng ther to And atte last after gret altercacions be mediacion of here frendes both parties alle and eche of hem w[t] on assent & accord be licence and consent of the Reverent diocesan and Patron aforseid nameden and chosen us foure Aldermen abovenamed to be here arbitrours and frendly makeres of pees in alle matiers of dissencion aforseyd and compromitted in to us yevyng and grauntyng to us ful power auctorite and faculte special and generall to here knowe and procede in alle the matirs aforseid and to take enformacions and to arbitre ordeyne and finally determine after oure discreciouns and consciences submyttyng the same parties hem self to owre arbitrementes determinacion ordenancez and decreez of us to be maked and hadde in all þe sayd maters in hye and in lowe makyng the seid parties ful promysses and seurte to observe and kepe holliche owre seid Arbitrementz determinacion & ordenauncez and decreez and fully agree hem ther to and nought contrarie hem in onywyse The which compromises with submissioun and promises so yeven and graunted to us in þe forme aforseyd atte reverence of god specialli and atte prayer and request of oure Reverentz & honurables soveraignes diocesan and Mair aforrehersed Also for goodet of pees and essee[1] of the seid parson and his parisshenes we have admitted and take upon us the labour þerof comynyng with both seid parties eche on by hym self and with the Maistres Masons & Carpenters sworen to the Cite of London and take enformacions of hem & other persones expert in such matiers Wherfore þe xxvii day of March in the yere of oure lord m[l]ccccxxxi[ti] and in the yere of oure seid lord the kyng above wretyn in the Conseil Chaumbre atte Guyhall of London in þe presence of oure honurable & worthi Mair and Aldermen wetenes underwreten the parties aforseyd personally a fore us apperyng for to here oure Arbitrementz determinacion ordinauncez and decreez to be yeven in the matiers aforseid We William Crowmere Henry Barton William Estfeld and John Welles arbitrours and frendly makers of pees above rehersed with dewe avisement and ful deliberacion yeve oure Arbitrement determinacion ordenaunce and final decree fully concluded in maner underwreten We ben accorded þ[t] as touchyng the parsonage the parson shall make his parsonage atte his owne cost wall and tymber fro the ferst flore up & þe paresshens beneth and the parson shall have esement of Chymneys atte his owne cost and a prive w[t] a pipe of xiiii ynch wide in the wall arched beneth in the fundament vii fote beneth the grounde of the Alee and it shal be iii fote wide

[1] *Sc.* for the good of peace and ease.

and vii fote longe atte his own cost ycaved[1] And the North wall shall atte cost of þe parisshens be made forth enbatailled of o seute and þe parson shal bilde just to the wardwall as high as hym liketh As touchyng þe cost of þe pilers and arches fro þe parclos[2] of the Chauncell Estward on þe North syde it shall egally be born be twene þe parson and þe parisshens and if eny travers be betwene hem of accord in that poynt their maister mason with Croxton and Warlowe shull be their Jugges and þan þe parson shall do make the est gable and the south Coyn[3] w^t^ þe south side of the Chauncell un to þe seid parclos atte his own cost Also as touchyng the xv li. save iiiid which þe parson hath delivered to þe parisshens afore þis tyme for the seyd werk we award that he shall be recompensed of x li. and the remenaunt shall be abated in recompense of þe wall that is made ayen the parsonage on the north side overe the dore and also for his lightes to be had and for fastenyng of his tymber in the walles And as touchyng the Arche in þe west ende under his parsonage as fer as his parsonage streccheth þe parson to bere half cost þerof and þe parisshens that other half for cause of the butte of the renge[4] of þe arches and þe parson to have free entree and issue in to his parsonage be the vys[5] as he hath nowe and also þe parson shall have free esement of castyng out of his water of his parsonage with other necessary avoydauns like as he hath nowe and hath had afore þis tyme or better Also we ben accorded þ^t^ if any varyauns dowte or omyssion be founde or meved in tyme to come in this oure present awarde than we ordeigne decree reserve and referre that matir of variauns dowte or omission to the Reverentz & honurable soveraynes diocesan and mair aforseid and ther successours beyng for þe tyme they fully for to declare and finally determine all soche dowtes and omyssions betwene the forseid parties and here successours yoven tyme & place abovewretyn In presence of þe honurable Mair aforseid and John Simond Recordour Thomas Fauconer Rawlyn Barton John Broklee and Henry Frowyk Aldermen Robert Large and Walter Chertesey Shirifs of þe forseyd Cite In witnesse whereof we have sette oure seeles."

[1] Excavated. [2] Screen. [3] *Sc.* quoin, corner.

[4] The *butte of the renge* appears to mean the lower course of the vault-stones or rings of an arch. Fr. *voussoir*.

[5] *Sc.* vice, spiral staircase.

21 April 1431 Gift of goods and chattels from John Snell, clerk, to Thomas Knolles, junior, John Carpenter, junior, and John Bacon, grocer.

1 May 1431 Writ of *corpus cum causa* to bring Thomas Guyn into Chancery and return that he had been detained by the name of Thomas Gwyn, vintner, administrator of the goods and chattels of David Mountferant, late archbishop of Bordeaux, by virtue of an original bill of a plea of covenant levied against him on 15 Feb. before the mayor and aldermen at the suit of Bernard de la Mote, knight, the action still being undetermined; nevertheless he would be brought into Chancery as ordered.

9 Feb. 1431 Writ of *certiorari* demanding the tenor of the will of William Grantham, goldsmith, and note that the tenor of the enrolment[1] was returned in a schedule sewn to the writ.

24 Oct. 1430 Leave was given at his request to William Norton, draper, to sue Thomas Catworth, John Curteys and Alice his wife and Thomas Holgreve at common law outside the city.

Membr. 4*b* Recognisances of debt: 6 Nov. 1429, John Denman of Misterton and Adam Castilhill, merchants, to John Cokfeld, esquire, William Farceux, vicar of Misterton, and William Neville in £100; 8 Nov. 1429, John Denman of Misterton, John Barowe of Ludburgh co. Lincoln and Richard Norman of London, merchant, to the same in the same, payable at Easter; Thomas Thorland of Boston and John Denman to the same in the same, and John Denman and Robert Brampton, merchant, to the same in the same, payable at the feast of the Nativity of St John the Baptist.

4 June 1431 Writ of protection in favour of John Cary, pewterer, *alias* John Carre, citizen and pewterer of London, who was then about to cross to France in the company of Richard Neville, earl of Salisbury.

Membr. 5 "This is the laude[2] and award yoven be William Lyndewode clerk Nowmpere[3] chosen be þe assent of William

[1] See R. R. Sharpe, *Cal. of Wills*, II, p. 409.
[2] Decision, judgment.
[3] Nowmpere, "the original form of umpire". *N.E.D.*

Crowmere and John Brokkele Citezeins and Aldermen of þe Cite of London arbitrours chosen in a cause touching the finaunce[1] of on Alfons sumtyme Erle of Dene[2] of þe Rewme of Aragon and evidences and munymentes touching the same closed in a Chest under the kepyng of Mastre Thomas Cotyngwith whiles he lyved and after his deth under the kepyng of Alice sumtyme his wif now wedded to on Peryn Ricard meved ferst in the Shireves Court of London sithen in the Maires Court of London And after þ^t in the Constables Court of Ingelond be waye of beheste pretense broken[3] be the seid Peryn hangyng betwene Richard Colet and John Tropynell Citezein of London and þe seid Peryn in his owne name and in the name of the said Alice his wif as it appereth pleynly be the articles mynestred therupon to þe said Arbitrours and Nowmpere and the answeres yoven þ'to be þe seid Peryn and Alice his wyf."

First, the umpire with the assent of the arbitrators in the presence of Nicholas Wotton, mayor, in the church of St Thomas of Acres on 24 April 1431 awarded that the said Alice, as principal executrix and chief legatary of her first husband, ought to have the same rights as her husband, i.e. a third part of such sums of money as might accrue after the said 24th of April, on condition that she or her assigns bore the third part of the expenses, and that a chest of evidences in the keeping of Alice and her present husband and other muniments in the keeping of Richard Colet and John Tropynell should be deposited in some place to be agreed upon by the parties. Further the umpire awarded that the said Richard and John should discharge the said Peryn and Alice of all penalties arising out of suits hitherto moved by them in the Constable's Court, and that Peryn and Alice in their turn should not demand repayment of a loan of £28 13s 4d and 100 marks expenses, advanced by the late

[1] Ransom.

[2] This appears to be Alfonso, count of Denia, captured at the battle of Najara 3 April 1367, about whom there had previously been disputes. See *Great Chronicle of London*, pp. 45, 402; Galbraith, *Anonimalle Chronicle*, pp. 121–4. He was allowed to return home, leaving his son in his place. Kingsford, *Chronicles of London*, p. 291.

[3] *Sc.* by way of promise alleged to have been broken.

Thomas Cotyngwith. This award was sealed with the seals of the umpire and the arbitrators and, for better evidence, with the mayoralty seal of the city of London.

Membr. 5*b*
20 Feb. 1431

William Gray, bishop of London, came into the Chamber of the Guildhall and proffered an original bill before the mayor and aldermen whereby he claimed from John Gryffith, knight, the sum of £40 lent to him on 13 Nov. 1430 in the parish of St Stephen Walbrook. As evidence was given by John Russell, serjeant-at-mace of the mayor, that the said John Gryffith had nothing within the liberty of the city whereby he might be summoned, precept was given to attach him by certain goods of his in the custody of Robert Whityngham, alderman. The defendant having made four defaults, Robert Whityngham was summoned to show cause etc. and did not come. Thereupon at the request of John Mordon, the bishop's attorney, the goods were valued by oath of John Sutton and Matthew (?) Philip, goldsmiths, as follows:—2 *chargeours* weighing 6 lbs. at £9 6s; 6 dishes (*perapsides*) weighing 8 lbs. 11½ oz. at £13 17s 8½d; 6 plates (*disci*) weighing 6 lbs. at £9 6s and 6 *sawcers* weighing 3 lbs. at £4 13s, amounting in all to £37 2s 8½d. They were then delivered to the plaintiff under pledge of Thomas Bataill, mercer, John Thwaytes, gentleman, and John Tewkesbury, junior, to answer therefor if the said John should come within a year and a day and deraign etc.

1 Oct. 1431

Geoffrey, master of the order of Burton St Lazarus of Jerusalem in England, warden of the hospital of St Giles without London, brings a plaint of intrusion against John Werk, William Waryn, goldsmith, and Richard Hercy, draper, touching his free tenement in Goldynglane in the parish of St Giles without Cripplegate.

Membr. 6
19 July 1431

Deed of appointment of a feoffee to uses. The deed recites that John Frenssh, late citizen and goldsmith, had caused Thomas Copelond and John Elmede, chaplains, who were enfeoffed to his use with certain properties formerly belonging to Drew Barantyn in the parishes of St Sepulchre and St John Zakary, to enfeoff John Leventhorp, esquire, and Robert Dale, clerk, with the same properties to the use of himself and his wife Katherine (who had after his death married Bartholomew Seman, goldbeater) and the heirs of their bodies, with reversion to himself and his heirs or to any other person whom he might nominate. Subsequently John Frenssh had died without heirs of himself and Katherine and had declared his will in the presence of many persons to be that after the death of Katherine a chaplain should be appointed out of the issues of the property to pray for him and his two wives, and that the residue should remain to his own heirs. Accordingly his son John and his widow Katherine now require John Leventhorp to enfeoff Bartholomew Seman with the properties in fee simple with the intention that he should, by virtue of his being a citizen and freeman of London, bequeath them to the said Katherine for life with reversion to the said John Frenssh, junior, the properties being charged after her death with an annual rent of £7 payable to the rector of St John Zakary for the provision of a chaplain and the celebration of an anniversary.

William Ganty was attached to answer John Knyght of Bristol in a plea of trespass wherein the latter, by Robert Langford his attorney, said that on 12 Dec. 1430 in the parish of St James Garlikhithe the defendant by force and arms carried away 3 lasts[1] and 200 bowstaves, value £96; 8 lasts of ashes called "*wodeasshen*", value £24; 2 lasts and 4 barrels of *Osemond*, value £19; 2½ lasts of linen (*lini*), value £25; 2 rolls of *shotencloth* containing 28 hundreds, value £30 16s; and 2 packs of linen cloth called *pyghtelyng*, containing 60 hundreds, value £66, belonging to a certain David Swan and being in the plaintiff's custody, against the peace and to the plaintiff's damage £300. The defendant appeared but the plaintiff made default[1]. Membr. 6*b*

William Melreth, mercer, levied a plaint of debt of £200 before Robert Large, sheriff, in the Poultry Compter, against *26 Nov. 1430*

[1] A *last* was a burden or load, varying for different commodities. The last of bowstaves would appear to have been more than 200 bowstaves. *Wodeasshen* or woad-ashes are said in *N.E.D.* to have been the ashes of burnt wine-lees used in dyeing, but the Latin form *cineres wisde* suggests an actual connection with woad. *Osemond* or Osmund iron was a high-class Scandinavian iron used for spear- and arrow-heads. *Shotencloth* may possibly be linen sheet-cloth. *Pyghtelyng* or pickling was a coarse linen.

David Swan, merchant, and the latter being a foreigner and having nothing in the city whereby he might be summoned, except 8 lasts of ashes, 2 lasts and 4 barrels of *osmond*, 2 lasts of linen, 2 lasts of bowstaves (*baculis arcualibus*), 2 rolls or pieces of linen cloth, 2 small bales (*balettas*) of linen cloth and 2 other lasts of bowstaves, he was attached by the said goods. Afterwards the action was removed before the mayor and aldermen, when a certain William Ganty of Gascony appeared and proved that the goods belonged to himself and that no one else had any property in them to the value of fourpence. Accordingly Ralph Vernon, one of the mayor's serjeants, was ordered to disattach and disarrest the goods, which were delivered to the said William.

Membr. 7 Gifts of goods and chattels: 11 May 1431, John Hilton, *corser*[1], to Robert Cavendissh, serjeant-at-law, John Manchestre and Robert Rasyn; 1 July 1431, Richard Herman, *brasier*[2], to John Walpole, *brasier*; 22 June 1431, John Welles, goldsmith, to John Welles, alderman, Walter Chertesey, draper, John Carpenter, junior, John Selby, and John Chesham, writer of the court letter; 20 June 1431, Alan Johnsson, grocer, to John Carpenter, junior, and Laurence Picot of Dunstaple co. Beds.; 31 July 1431, John Foy of Beynton, co. Wilts, chaplain, to John Parker, brewer, and John Thorn,
Membr. 7*b* tailor; 27 July 1431, Richard Fetplace, stockfishmonger, to John Fetplace, junior, of Ardyngton co Berks, John Glynne, draper, John Bredlepe, grocer, and Margaret Fetplace; 24 Aug. 1431, John Colwell, stockfishmonger, to William Beaufitz and John Elyngham, citizens of London, and Isabel Colwell; 4 Sept. 1431, William Emery, salter, to Thomas Dounton, mercer.

Membr. 8 Assignment by Francis Spinull, merchant of Genoa, then
27 Sept. 1431 visiting London, to William Estfeld, mercer, in payment of certain moneys owed to him, of a debt of £217 10s 9d due to him from John Gedeney, draper, and payable on 14 April 1432 and 14 Oct. 1432, by virtue of a writing obligatory of 21 Aug. 1431.

[1] A horse-dealer.

[2] Possibly a brewer. Cf. *Cal. of K*, p. 284. A certain John Walpole is described as a brewer in 1446. Husting Roll 175 (34).

Assignment by Baptista de Nigris, merchant of Genoa, then visiting London, to William Estfeld, mercer, in payment of certain moneys owed to him, of a debt of £223 4s 2d due to himself and Laurence Markysano, merchant of Genoa, from Peter Jamys, burgess and merchant of Southampton, and John Wryther, citizen of Winchester, and payable on 22 May 1433 by virtue of a writing obligatory of 1 June 1430. *27 Sept. 1431*

Gift of goods and chattels, John Mylys, salter, to Thomas Beaumond, salter.

Reciprocal bonds of John Michell, *brocour*, and Nicholas Bolyn, merchant, in 10 marks to abide by the award of Alexander Farantyn of Florence, merchant. *10 Oct. 1431*

Bond of Thomas Parker, *wexchaundeler*, to Roger Wylly, waxchandler, in £20 to abide by the award of John Broke and James Coterell. *7 Sept. 1431*

John Gardyner, son of John Gardyner, of Colne co. Essex, exonerated from his apprenticeship (7 yrs) to John Stoute, *tapicer*, because the latter had not enrolled him at Guildhall within the first year of his term. [*Latin and French*] Membr. 8*b* *3 Oct. 1431*

ROLL A 60

(*John Welles, mayor*)

Membr. 1
5 Nov. 1431 Thomas Harwode, goldsmith, John Cotesmore, Robert Allerton and Roger Crome bring a plaint of intrusion against Henry Barton, skinner, touching their free tenement in the parish of St Anne.

15 Nov. 1431 Bond of Alan Bret and John Moordon, citizens of London, to John Barry, clerk, in £100 that Thomas Pofford[1], bishop of Herford, would abide by the award of John Gedney, John Brokle, John Symond and John Carpenter.

Similar bond of John Fairfeld and Anthony Astell, fishmonger, citizens of London, on behalf of John Barry to the said Thomas Pofford.

25 Nov. 1431 Writ of *habeas corpus* to bring John Tollyngton before the king[2] on 27 Nov. in order that he and William Grene might prosecute their bill against Thomas Gerard, gentleman, late dwelling at Seynt Jonestrete co. Middlesex, in a plea of trespass. Witness W. Cheyne.

Return of John Welles, mayor, and Stephen Broun and John Hatherle, sheriffs, that the said John had been detained by virtue of an original bill of debt of £3 3s 3d.

10 Feb. 1432 Leave given to William Dawtre, mercer, to prosecute at common law William Langley, weaver, on his taking an oath that the causes and matters between them could not be terminated in the city, because the said William had withdrawn therefrom.

24 March 1432 Writ of *corpus cum causa* to bring William Collyn, clerk, into Chancery.

Membr. 1 *b*
29 March 1432 Recognisance by John Sturgeon, mercer, of a debt of £20 due to William Collyn, chaplain, payable 5 marks at Easter, 5 marks at Pentecost and 20 marks at Michaelmas. On 10 May the said William acknowledged satisfaction and the recognisance was cancelled.

[1] *Sc.* Spofford.

[2] Into King's Bench.

Reciprocal bonds between William Dogge, gentleman, and Thomas Lucas, esquire, to abide by the award of Henry Barton, Thomas Bataill, John Reynwell and John Hill, pinner, in disputes between them.

Writ of *corpus cum causa* to bring Thomas Thornton, draper, into Chancery and return that he had been taken and detained by virtue of an original bill of debt of £33 3s 4d at the suit of Simon Strete, grocer; nevertheless he would be brought into Chancery as ordered. *14 April 1432*

Recognisance by Anthony Notull of Flexburgh[1] co. Lincs, gentleman, and John Broode of Mersham co. Kent to John Darell and William Darell, esquires, of a debt of 40 marks payable at Michaelmas. *10 May 1432*

Bond of Robert Shiryngton and Margery Thomasyn to Richard Banastre and Edmund Sheffeld, vintner, in £20 to abide by the award of Ralph Holand, John Assh, Simon Seman and Nicholas Metle, or failing agreement, by that of John Fray as umpire. *22 Jan. 1432*

Writ of *corpus cum causa* to bring Nicholas Frost of London, *bower*, into Chancery, and return that he had been taken and detained in an action of debt of £21 at the suit of John Motte of Bylston[2] co. Suffolk, merchant; nevertheless he would be brought into Chancery as ordered. *5 July 1432*

Membr. 2

Deed of sale by William Munde, draper, to Thomas Knolles, junior, grocer, of all his goods and merchandise in the lower shop occupied by John Malvern, haberdasher, in the parish of St Mary le Bow, and also of the rest of his goods and chattels in London. *31 Oct. 1431*

Gifts of goods and chattels: 7 Nov. 1431, Thomas Selove, grocer, to Thomas Knolles, junior, John Bacon and Ralph Say, grocers, William Olyver, mercer, and Richard Abnale, grocer; 23 Nov. 1431, Henry Wykwan, *goldbeter*, to his brother William Wykwan, William Seburgh, painter, and John Coster, goldsmith; 28 Nov. 1431, Richard Clarence, baker, to John Hatherlee, ironmonger; 3 Dec. 1431, Walter Vytull, armourer,

[1] Flixborough. [2] Bilston or Bildeston.

Membr. 2*b* to William Blyton and Nicholas Molard, merchant; 26 Nov. 1431, John Pappeworth, haberdasher, to Roger Gerebray, mercer; 14 Dec. 1431, William Barte to John Michell, alderman, William Stokes, gentleman, John Fitz Robert, goldsmith, his son Ralph Barte, and Robert Wrawton, tailor; 29 Jan. 1432, Nicholas Hill of Bristol to Edmund Broun, Walter Power and Roger Lyveden of Bristol, merchants, and Stephen Forster, merchant of London; 8 Feb. 1432, Robert Pede to John Mayster, leatherseller, and Thomas Court, saddler; 12 Feb. 1432, Richard Fyn, butcher, to William
Membr. 3 Coventre, *marbler*; William Coventre, *marbler*, to Richard Fyn, butcher, and John Osgood, ironmonger; 8 March 1432, Simon Baron, glover, to Thomas Nek, ironmonger; 15 March 1432, Richard Smythecote, merchant, to Richard Drax of London, gentleman, Richard Rawe, vintner, John Beke, grocer, and Robert Smythecote, chamberlain of Rotherfeld; 20 Feb. 1432, John Reynold, draper, to William Harri and John Pake, drapers; 26 Aug. 1432, John Wode, mercer, to William Estfeld,
Membr. 3*b* mercer, and John Picot; 18 March 1432, Richard Chamberlayn, draper, to Margery his wife and Geoffrey Chittok, draper; 29 May 1432, Richard Hille, fuller, to Hugh Wyche, mercer, and William Wetenhale, grocer; 30 July 1432, John Wattys, grocer, to Thomas Catworthe and Andrew Pulham, grocers; 31 July 1432, William Sutton of London, gentleman, to Simon Mure, barber, and John Edriche, *corsur*; 7 Aug. 1432, Philip Colyng, tailor, to John Philpot, William Ferrour, junior, and Thomas Chechele.

Membr. 4
25 July 1432

Writ of *supersedeas* in favour of William Dogge, one of the servants of John[1], bishop of Bath and Wells, the king's chancellor, who had been sued before the mayor for detinue of a will by Roger Werburgh, executor of John Standolf, goldsmith, in derogation of the privileges and customs of Chancery, by which no clerks of Chancery, their servants or households, ought to be compelled to answer before any justices or other secular judges other than the chancellor or keeper of the great seal in any pleas which did not touch the king's person, except in pleas of a free tenement, felonies and appeals. The mayor

[1] John Stafford, "Lord Chancellor" 1432, archbishop of Canterbury 1443, died 1452.

is ordered to inform the said Roger that he may sue, if he will, in Chancery.

Reciprocal bonds of John Pygot, woolman, and Thomas Knovile, citizen of London, in £300 to abide by the award of the mayor and aldermen in disputes between them. *26 Aug. 1432*

William, prior of Christchurch, Canterbury, brings a plaint of intrusion against William Babyngton, knight, John Reynwell, Alexander Anne, Robert Broom, John Spenser, John Hervy, Adam Turvyn, Richard Joynour and Richard Lucas, brewer, touching his free tenement in the parish of St Martin without Ludgate. *15 Sept. 1432*

"Be it hadde in remenbraunce how William Myldenhale in his lyf enfeoffed Rauf Barton in his tenement in Aldermarye Parisshe in the Cite of London in plegge & seurete for a certeyn somme of moneie whiche the said Rauf hadde paide for the said William And after the said feoffament the forsaid William made his testament rehersyng in these wordes Al so y bequethe half my said tenement that I have in Aldermari Parisshe to Jonet my dougther to here & here heires that is lawful gote, And yif hit be so that she dye wit oute heires of here body be gote y wolle þat halfendene þe tenement to Eleyne my dougther to here & here heires that is lawfully gote, And yif it be so that she dye wit oute heires of here body be gote I wol that halfendele the tenement turne to Jonet here suster and to here heires lawfully gothe Al so y wolle ho so levyth longer of hem to have al the hole tenement with alle the appurtenauntz therto Al so y wolle that non of hem ne non of here heires that non of hem selle ne profre to selle non of here part And yif eny of hem dothe y wol that the next heire entre in alle the hole tenement with alle the appurtenaunce ther to Al so y wol that yf thay deye and here heires y wol the same tenement be sold be myn Executours yif thay lyve or els by the parsoun of Aldermarye Parisshe that is for the tyme And by foure the best men of the same Parisshe, And the moneie that comyth ther of I wolle that v mark go to chirche werk for my Faderes soule and my moderes & myn, and alle Cristen soules And the remanaunt of the moneie be yif to pouere men and women that they seme moste nede Al so

I wolle that the parsoun of Aldirmarie chirche and iiii men have of the same moneye to have for thaire travel v mark.

And after the forsaid Jonet was weddyd to John Wotton draper in Dorchestre in the shire of dorset And the forsaid Eleyne was weddyd to William Chesse skynner of London And than the said dougthers and thaire husbondes after payment made to the said Rauf of the somme of moneye due to hym by the said William Myldenhale come to the said Rauf Barton, prayeng hym that he wolde delivere seisine of the said tenement after the entent and wille of the saide William Myldenhale, where upon the said Rauf hadde the seide dougthres wit here husbondes the vi daye of Feverer In the yer of the regne of kyng harry the sixte after the conquest the iiii^{te} yer by fore the dore of the same tenement and there dede opynly rede the said testament be fore alle peple & after that the said Rauf toke the saide Jonet & Elyne by the hondes delyvereng thaim bothe the rynge of the dore[1] & sayeng thes wordys, here y yeve & delyvere. yow bothe seisyne & possession of this tenement To have & to holde joyntly to gedyr to yow & to youre heires of yowre bodyes lawfully be goton after the wylle and affecte of the said testament In witnesse of this the said Rauf hathe put to his seal The iiii daye of Septembre in the yer of the regne of the forsaid kyng harry the sixte after the conquest the xi^{te}."

Membr. 4*b*
10 Oct. 1432 Writ of *corpus cum causa* to bring John Clerk, *brocour*, into Chancery, together with the cause of his taking and detaining.

9 Oct. 1432 Reciprocal bonds of Thomas Gwyn, vintner, John Wokkyng and William de Lunes, vintner, on behalf of the said Thomas, and Ralph Pakyngton, esquire, John Chesham, scrivener, and Thomas Aylesby, draper, on behalf of Mary Lyllyng of co. Northampton, widow, in £50 to abide by the award of Robert Large and William Melreth, aldermen, in disputes between the said Thomas Gwyn and Mary Lyllyng.

Membr. 4* Gifts of goods and chattels: 31 Aug. 1432, Richard Cok, *hostillare*, to Agnes Cok his wife, John Hergest, *hostillare*, Robert Wraton, tailor, Robert Clopton, draper, and Robert Shelle; 19 Sept. 1432, Robert Colwill, mercer, to Henry

[1] On livery of seisin *per haspam vel anulum* see Pollock and Maitland, *Hist. English Law*, II, pp. 83–4.

Frowyk, alderman, Eberard Flete, mercer, John Smyth, mercer, William Caldewell and John Baggeworth, saddlers, and William Bliton; Thomas Dounton, mercer, to John Burton, William Dounton and Walter Roger, mercers; Walter Sprakelyng, *alias* Walter Roger, mercer, to Thomas Dounton, mercer, William Dounton, mercer, John Olney, mercer, John Burton, mercer, Walter Gautron, draper, and Richard Lyndesey, scrivener; John Berdefeld, stockfishmonger, to William Holland and Simon Clay; witnesses, Thomas Noble, John Kyngeston, William Goteley, John Swepeston, Richard Pele; 24 Sept. 1432, William Charteseye of co. Essex, gentleman, to Nicholas Sibile and Richard Walssh; witnesses, John Teye, Robert Rikedon, senior, Thomas Rikedon, Robert Bury, John Stodagh, John Rouchester; 26 Sept. 1432, Thomas Richere, painter, to Henry Burghchere, earl of Ewe, John Cornwale, knight, lord of Fawnope, John Bekyngton, draper, and John Edward, tailor; 14 Oct. 1432, William Rumbald, mercer, to Hugh Wyche, mercer, Robert Rumbald, cutler, and William Bliton; 22 Oct. 1432, William Johnsson, smith, to John Clampard, smith of our lord the king within the Tower of London, Thomas South, smith, Thomas Peryn, *fynour*, and John Northwode, smith. dorse

Membr. 5 *28 Nov. 1430*

Sir Henry Merston, canon, Sir Philip Lovecok and Master William Stapulford, chaplain, executors of the will of Henry Jolypace, chaplain, came into the Chamber of Guildhall and proffered an original bill of debt against John Stormorth, grocer, for £47 owed to the testator. As it was testified by William Wode, the mayor's serjeant-at-mace, that the defendant had nothing within the city whereby he might be summoned, order was given to attach him by certain goods in the hands of the plaintiffs. On his making four defaults, the foreign attachment was valued by oath of John Pake and William Botoner, goldsmiths, and delivered to the plaintiff under pledge of John Pake, goldsmith, William West, *marbeler*, and Walter Luci, haberdasher, to answer therefor if the defendant should come within a year and a day and deraign etc., as follows:—

One piece with a covercle of silver-gilt, pounced[1] with an

[1] *Ponsonata*, embossed, chased.

eagle and roses weighing 20 oz. at 2s 9d the oz., 55s; a nut[1] with a covercle harnessed with silver gilt and with an eagle of white silver, weighing 23½ oz. at 2s 4d the oz., 54s 4d; a black nut with a covercle harnessed with silvergilt and with an eagle of silvergilt, weighing 22½ oz. at 2s 2d the oz., 44s 4d; two standing pieces of white silver with three silvergilt bands on each, and written on the middle band of the one was "*I H S autem transiens per medium eorum ibat*"[2] and on the covercle was "*I H S est amor meus*", and on the middle band of the other was "*Benedicamus patrem et filium*", etc, and on the covercle was "*Gaudeamus omnes in domino*", weighing 4 lbs. 6½ oz. at 2s 8d an oz., £7 5s 4d; another standing piece of white silver with three silvergilt bands on which was written "*Benedictus deus in donis suis*" and on the covercle "*Posui deum adjutorem meum*", with a "Michael" on the pommel (*pomellum*) of the covercle, weighing 3 lbs. ½ oz. at 2s 8d the oz., £4 17s 4d; three standing pieces of parcel-gilt with a falcon on each covercle, weighing 4 lbs. 6½ oz. at 2s 7d the oz., £7 9½d; one silver standing piece covered and chased parcel-gilt[3] with a round white pommel on the covercle, weighing 12½ oz. at 2s 7d the oz., 32s 3½d; one old covered silver *bekyr* parcel-gilt standing on three gilt lions, with "*I H S*" written on the pommel, weighing 2 lbs. ½ oz. at 2s 7d the oz., £3 3s 3½d; one low covered piece[4] of silver with a "flat" pommel weighing 12¼ oz. at 2s 7d the oz., 31s 7¾d; 6 *gobelletts* of silver chased with *bollions*[5] with a parcel-gilt covercle, weighing 22 oz. at 2s 7d the oz., 56s 10d; three salt-cellars with one parcel-gilt cover and an eagle weighing 2 lbs. 2½ oz., at 2s 7d the oz., £3 8s 5½d; one silver parcel-gilt box (*pixis*) for powder with a gilt band inscribed "*Strewe on powder y nough*", weighing 6 oz. one quarter and a half of a quarter at 2s 7d the oz., 16s 9½d[6]; fourteen silver spoons with square gilt pommels of one sort marked with leopards' heads[7] and ten silver spoons

[1] A cup made of a cokernut. [2] See Luke, ch. iv, 30.

[3] *Una pecia argenti stans cooperta et chaseata parcella deaurata.* Chased signifies ornamented in relief. [4] *Una pecia bassa cooperta.*

[5] *Bollions, sc.* bullions, bosses or knobs.

[6] There appears to be an error here; 16*s*. 9½*d*. represents 6½ oz., not 6⅜ oz.

[7] The assay mark. See letters patent of 1327 regulating the trade of goldsmiths, *Cal. of P. and M. Rolls*, 1323–64, p. 61; *Rot. Parl.* IV, p. 257 (1423).

unmarked with one square gilt pommel, weighing 2 lbs. at 2s 7d the oz., £3 2s; whereof the total amounted to £43 8s 11½d.

Writ of *corpus cum causa* to bring John Woderove of London, *pasteler*, into Chancery, and return that he had been taken and detained by virtue of a plaint of debt of £6 17s 4d at the suit of Thomas Dollay, mercer, levied before John Hatherle, late sheriff, and afterwards taken before the mayor and aldermen in the king's court in the Chamber; nevertheless he would be brought into Chancery as ordered. *18 Oct. 1432*

In an action for a debt of £4 by Sir Henry Merston, canon, Sir Philip Lovecok and Master William Stapulford, chaplain, executors of Henry Jolypace, chaplain, against Isabel Broun, widow of Thomas Broun, grocer, for a debt of £4, the following goods, attached in the hands of the plaintiffs, were delivered to them as a foreign attachment, after being valued by oath of John Pake and William Botoner, goldsmiths, viz:—One low piece of silver-gilt with a covercle engraved (*insculpta*) with a trail (*cum uno traile*) of vine-leaves round it, weighing 17¾ oz. at 2s 8d the oz., 47s 4d; another standing piece of silver with a chased and parcel-gilt covercle with an eagle on the top, weighing 2 lbs. 3 oz. at 2s 8d the oz., £3 12s; total £5 19s 4d. Membr. 5*b* *28 Nov. 1430*

The same day certain goods of Master William Pencrich were similarly valued and delivered as a foreign attachment to the same plaintiffs, viz:—one nut harnessed with a gilt covercle, standing on lions, and another nut harnessed with a gilt covercle, weighing 3 lbs. 3 oz. at 2s the oz., £3 18s; and a *canape* of blue *tartarin*[1], with a *frenge* of blue silk, 20s; total £4 18s.

Whereas there had been discords and litigation between John Pycot, woolman, and Thomas Knovile as to the title of three messuages in Cattestrete[2] in the parish of St Lawrence Jewry, about which the said Thomas had arraigned an assize of freshforce against the said John and others, and also as to the costs and expenses of the assize, the parties on 8 Aug. 1432 Membr. 6 *14 Oct. 1432*

[1] A canopy of tartarin, a rich silk material, probably imported from China through Tartary. See *N.E.D.*

[2] Cat or Cateaton Street, now Gresham Street.

bound themselves to each other in £300 to abide by the award of the mayor and aldermen. The latter on 14 Oct. 1432, inasmuch as it seemed to them that the title of John Pycot was insufficient by the laws of England and the laws and customs of the city, and that the title of the said Thomas was good and sufficient to obtain possession for himself, his heirs and assigns, awarded that the said Thomas should enter and have peaceable possession and that John Pycot, his feoffees and their assigns should execute a quitclaim of the messuages to the said Thomas, in return for which the said Thomas should pay them the sum of 20 marks and allow them to collect from the farmers and tenants-at-will such rents as were due up to Michaelmas, while John Pycot should acquit the said Thomas of all quitrents or other charges issuing or owed from the messuages from the date when he, the said John, entered into occupation until Michaelmas last.

ROLL A 61

(*John Brockley, mayor*)

Gifts of goods and chattels: 13 Feb. 1434, John Kyllyk, vintner, to John Wokkyng, William Abraham and Richard Rawe, vintners; John Shopman, cordwainer, to James Shopman, cordwainer, and Adam Semy, shearman; 25 Feb. 1434, John Waryn, goldsmith, to John Pattesle, goldsmith, Nicholas Bery, fishmonger, and John Werk, goldsmith; 10 March 1434, John Osyn, leatherseller, to William Gerveys, clerk, John Rowold, leatherseller, and William Domegode, girdler; 13 March 1434, John Lakenham, gentleman, to William Markby, John Kebyll, goldsmith, Robert Remond, hosier, and John Sire, *ferrour*; witnesses, John Newe, John Taterigge, William Marchall; 8 July 1434, Thomas Costwyk, skinner, to Thomas Goldwyn and Thomas Ulgrave, skinners; 13 Feb. 1434, John Broun, vintner, to Hugh Somervile, skinner; 12 April 1434, Thomas Benbowe, late of London, skinner, to Thomas Coburley and Thomas Brayne; 14 April 1434, Thomas Souch, smith, to John Leget, draper, and William Godeburgh, mason; 17 April 1434, Robert Coventre, grocer, to Alice his wife, Thomas Canynges, grocer, and Benedict Harlewyn, draper; 22 April 1434, Clement de London, shipman, to Robert Cristmasse, draper; 29 May 1434, Henry Plumpton, skinner, to Thomas Knolles, junior, grocer, Hugh Somervile and William Kene; witnesses, Simon Strete, William Oliver, William Chesse; 11 Nov. 1433, Nicholas Walton, carpenter, to William Colston, *plomer*, and Thomas Sexteyn, carpenter; 14 Nov. 1433, John York, junior, skinner, to Peter Powle of co. Herts, gentleman, and John Beverley, skinner; 13 Jan. 1434, John Styward, butcher, to Margaret his wife and William Rede, butcher; witnesses, John Rople, William Vale; 21 Jan. 1434, John Rothell, cooper, to Philip Malpas, draper, and Thomas South, smith; 28 Jan. 1434, Robert Cristmasse, draper, to Robert Whityngham, draper; 23 Jan. 1434, John Aleyn, vintner, to Benedict Harlewyn, draper, William Abraham and William Scarburgh, vintners; 11 Feb. 1434, Richard Payn, draper, to Hugh Wiche, mercer.

Membr. 1

Membr. 1*b*

Membr. 2

Membr. 2*b*

Membr. 3
3 Feb. 1434 Writ of *corpus cum causa* to bring Thomas Hill, bowyer, into Chancery, and return of John Brokley, mayor, and Thomas Chalton and John Lyng, sheriffs, that the said Thomas had been taken by virtue of an original bill of debt of 19 marks 6s 8d at the suit of Stephen Castwater.

13 Feb. 1434 On this day came Amphreon Spinula, factor and attorney of Bartholomew Spinula, and acknowledged in court that he had received from Almeric Mateny, draper, a copper-gilt chalice with a paten, value 6s 8d, two *mustraunces* of copper-gilt for carrying the body of Christ, value 53s 4d, and a copper girdle called "*arsgirdell*", value 13s 4d. He agreed to save harmless the said Almeric, with John Mordon and John Burgh, grocers, from all actions which the said Bartholomew might have against them by reason of two letters of payment (*pagamenti*)[1], in which the said John and John were bound to the said Bartholomew.

8 March 1434 Writ of *corpus cum causa* to bring John Kympton, gentleman, into Chancery.

22 Jan. 1434 Bond of William Bonde, draper, in £20 to William Ekton and Robert Sampton that he and his wife Constance would abide by the award of Nicholas Drayton, John Gugge, William Swan and John Rugefeld in disputes between themselves and the said William and Robert.

15 April 1434 Writ of *corpus cum causa* to bring Frederick Noffre into Chancery and return that he had been taken by virtue of an original bill of debt of £10 at the suit of William Louther.

Membr. 3*b*
24 May 1434 Geoffrey Shryggeley, master of Burton St Lazarus of Jerusalem in England, warden of the hospital of St Giles without London, brings a plaint of intrusion against Robert Clopton, draper, touching his free tenement in the parish of St Nicholas Shambles.

John Wakeryng, master or warden of the hospital of St Bartholomew by Westsmythfeld, brings a plaint of intrusion against Richard Fox, gentleman, William Flete, William Babyngton, knight, and Robert Frampton touching his free tenement in the parish of St Sepulchre without Newgate.

[1] On bills of exchange and letters of payment see *Cal. P. and M. Rolls, 1381–1412*, pp. xxxvi–xl.

Writ of *certiorari* as to the following attachments:—£10 of William Criplyng, merchant, in the hands of Thomas Bernewell, William Childe, John Welles and Thomas Weston; £39 1d of John Robynson and Thomas Wardale, merchants, in the hands of William Wyntryngham, John Seygyr, Reginald Derlyngton, Thomas Norwode, John Bromer, John Fairfeld, William Hethe, Geoffrey Wykyn, John Howard, John Stebbyng and Nicholas Drax; £38 of George Topclyf, merchant, in the hands of Thomas Emmeth, Thomas Gryme, John Weston, John Ferrour, John Poppham, Henry Jordon, John Fairfeld, William Eston and Thomas Edmond; £42 of Richard Wright, merchant, in the hands of William Childe, Thomas Bernewell, Thomas Cullyng, Thomas Downham, Robert Page, Robert Horne, Thomas Segryme, John Leget, John Sygyr, William Wyntryngham, John Welles and Reginald Derlyngton; £20 of John Danyell, merchant, in the hands of William Childe, William Laccheford, Nicholas Drax, William Notyngham and Agnes Shotton; and £30 of Richard Danyell, merchant, in the hands of John Welles, Thomas Dursley and William Downe, which attachments were made by the sheriffs and were pending before the mayor. *8 June 1434*

Return that the attachments were made in divers actions of debt at the suit of Thomas Weston, fishmonger, levied before John Lyng, sheriff.

Quitclaim from William Kyrketon, mercer, and Joan his wife, daughter of the late Martin Kylom, mercer, to John Beaver, William Holgrave and Margaret Kelom, widow of the said Martin, executors of his will. *3 July 1434*

Bond of William Warter, skinner, to John Bederenden, chamberlain of the city, in 100s for his good behaviour and obedience to the Masters and good men of the mistery of Skinners.

Gifts of goods and chattels: 31 May 1434, John Hake, draper, to John Fekenham, brewer, and Alexander Kyllyngham, tailor; 3 June 1434, Thomas Spytylman, *alias* Southam, vintner, to William Edy and William Kyrton, drapers; 11 June 1434, Robert Squyry (Squery), painter, to Agnes his wife, Master William Sprever, clerk, John Squery of co. Essex, Membr. 4

esquire, William Hook, goldsmith, and John Wyllyam, draper; 22 June 1434, Thomas Somery, mercer, to Thomas Dounton and William Dounton, mercers; 27 July 1434, John Clerk of Erdlye co. Hertford, grocer, to Anne his wife, Thomas Clerk, clerk, William Symmes, grocer, and John Tate, woolman; 6 July 1434, William Fydelewe, cordwainer, to Richard Rede and Thomas Burgate, cordwainers, and Richard Hucle,
Membr. 4*b* gentleman; 27 July 1434, Richard Fissher, shearman, to Robert Fitz Robert and John Lemman, skinner; 30 July 1434, John Robyn, *stacyoner*, to Richard atte Lee, grocer; witnesses, William Burton, Walter Hunte and Thomas Lane; 29 July 1434, John Jakes, dyer, to Richard Marchall, fuller, and John Upton, shearman; 22 Sept. 1434, John Langvile, *shethere*, to William Godyng, John Clerk, sheather, and John Richemond, sheather.

Membr. 5
28 April 1434 John Taylour of Shopelond co. Essex, came into court and being examined and sworn at the instance of William Reynold, clerk, said on oath that he had never delivered to Thomas Stambregge, Stephen Tomme, John Beauchamp, Richard Boures, Ralph Peek, John Potyn and John Samwell or any of them, any status in lands, tenements and services formerly belonging to John Reynold, uncle of the said William Reynold, who is said to be his heir, in the vills of Suthecherche and Shopelond.

23 July 1434 Letter of attorney from Elizabeth, widow of William Fitz Herry, esquire, to William Oldham, John Fastoholf and Henry Inglose, knights, John Welles and Richard Waller to receive in her name an annual quitrent of 20 marks, reserved to her for the term of her life, from lands and tenements formerly belonging to her late husband and Thomas Morestede in the parish of All Hallows the Great in the ward of Dowgate.

7 Aug. 1434 Acquittance by Robert Elmbrigge, esquire, and Joan his wife, widow of Nicholas James, ironmonger and alderman, to Thomas Badby, fishmonger, executor of the latter's will, on the receipt of 500 marks in full satisfaction of all goods due to the said Joan on the death of the said Nicholas by way of purparty[1] or legacy according to the common law or the custom of the city.

Writ of *corpus cum causa* to bring Robert Bonde, mercer, into Chancery, and return that he and a certain Robert Reynham, mercer, had been taken and detained by virtue of an action of debt of £77, levied in the Sheriffs' Court at the suit of William Alyf, mercer, and afterwards removed before the mayor, but the said Robert Bonde had been mainprised for his appearance by Elyas Davy and Hugh Wyche, mercers, wherefore the mayor and sheriffs could not obey the writ. *27 Aug. 1434*

William Wyther, clerk, brings a plaint of intrusion against Richard Gauge, tailor, and Alice his wife touching his free tenements in the parishes of St Mary Vanchurche and St Sepulchre without Newgate. *15 Feb. 1434*

Membr. 5*b*

The dean and college of the king's free chapel of St Stephen the Protomartyr within the Palace at Westminster bring a plaint of intrusion against Richard Cok and Sabina his wife, Thomas Torell, esquire, Thomas Batell, mercer, John Gobyon and Henry Bette touching their free tenement in the parish of All Hallows Stanyng. *21 June 1434*

[1] Share in an inheritance.

ROLL A 62

(*Robert Ottele, mayor*)

Membr. 1 Gifts of goods and chattels: 4 Nov. 1434, John Spenser, draper, to John Lyng, William Chervell, William Swan and John Peretre, drapers; witnesses, Clement Lyffyn, William Waryng, Robert Legge; 13 Nov. 1434, William Cullyng, mercer, to John Blomville, carpenter, and Nicholas Wolvey, mercer; witnesses, Robert Donne, John Derby, John Austyn; 29 Nov. 1434, John Machoun, butcher, to Thomas Dru, John Founteyns, John Mollesle, drover, and Richard Harryes, butcher; 10 Jan. 1435, John Roun, *cofremaker*, to Richard Collyng, clerk, and John Worsop, painter.

28 Jan. 1435 Before John Symond, recorder, in the Chamber of Guildhall John Wotton, draper, William Prest, tallowchandler, Michael Grace, tailor, William Camell, hosier, and Thomas Drayton, cook, being examined, affirmed that on St Hilary's Day in the time of Drew Barantyn, mayor, (13 Jan. 1409), in the parish of St Dunstan in the East a certain John Whyssh, son and heir of Thomas Whyssh, draper, left his mother's house.

Membr. 1*b* Gifts of goods and chattels: 13 Jan. 1435, Robert Warbyngton, tallowchandler, to Robert Clopton, draper; 5 Feb. 1435, Thomas Moreys, bottlemaker, to John Milton, cordwainer; witnesses, John Osgodby, John Stile, junior, Robert Buntyng, William Wesenham, William Brewester; 21 Jan. 1435, Thomas Basset, dyer, to Richard Benton and William Causton, tailors; Hugh Caundyssh, tailor, to Henry Brounflete, knight; 9 Aug. 1435, John Eget, haberdasher, to Walter Hercy and Thomas Heywode, haberdashers; 21 Feb. 1435,
Membr. 2 John Robert, blacksmith, to Thomas South, blacksmith, and Nicholas Rolff, cordwainer; 23 Feb. 1435, Edmund Dutton, tailor, to William Coumbes, fishmonger, and Thomas Whyte, tailor; 8 March 1435, William Goodburgh, mason, to Thomas South, blacksmith[1], and Bartholomew Stratton, mercer; 14 May 1435, Ralph Valentyn, draper, to Walter

[1] *Ferrifabro*. The smiths in the other gifts are described *Anglice* as "blaksmyth"

Chertseye and Clement Lyffyn, drapers, and Richard Claidich, clerk.

Gift of goods and chattels from William Danyell, dyer, to William Parker, draper, as follows:—four leaden vessels (*vasa*), six leaden cisterns and four great leaden *cruces*[1] belonging to the trade of a dyer and being in the donor's house. *20 May 1435*

Gifts of goods and chattels: 26 March 1435, John Aleyn, leatherseller, to Ralph Vernon and John Sonman, leathersellers; 28 April 1435, William Barton, barber, to Alice Waltham and Robert Borstall, *purcer*; witnesses, John Reyner, brewer, William Taverner, haberdasher, Richard Bisshop, *ferrour*, Robert Wollane, skinner, John Middelton, clerk; 2 June 1435, Richard Broughton, stockfishmonger, to Alexander Farnell, tailor, John Farneburgh, stockfishmonger, John Escote, innkeeper, and John Norman, goldsmith; 1 July 1435, John Swypston, sergeant, to Richard Lalford, tallow-chandler, and John Burton, girdler; 16 July 1435, John Kyng, *steynour*, to John Wetyng, gentleman, and Richard Blundell of Worcester, esquire. Membr. 2*b*

"This is the wille of me William Caldewell Citezein & Sadiller of London made the xv day of Septembre the xiii[the] ȝer of the regne of kyng harry the sixte, beside that I have devised in my testament First I wolle that Letice my wyf have all my londes tenementes rentes & services aswell in London as in all other places in Ingelond, outetake tho londes tenementes & rentes that I have in Burton up on trent, the which I woll that Richard Lokwode my Cosyn have to hym and to his eyres for ever, To have and to holde the seyd londes tenementes rentes & services with all here appurtenaunces, outake before outetake, to the seyd Letice for terme of here lyf, Doyng therefore to the chief lordes of the fee the rentes & services due & accustumed, And after here decesse I woll that the seyd londes tenementes rentes & services oute take certeyne houses underwrete where w[t] I woll have my obyt holde in manere and fourme as hit shall be declared here after Membr. 3 *15 Sept. 1434*

[1] The meaning of *crux* as a dyer's implement is uncertain. The editor has failed to find any other instance of its use in this connection.

remayne to Jonete and Margarete my doughters and to here Eyres for ever. Also I woll that the seyd Letice duryng here lyf, of the profytes & rentes comyng of the howses that Anneys Bright John of Powes cordewaner now occupien and of other iiii howses in Goldbeterslane in the parishe of Seynt Albon in Wodestrete of London, holde my ȝerely mynde in the Chirche of Seynt Fastour in London in the best manere that she kan after here gode discrecion. And after here deces I woll that the seyd howses that the seyd Anneys Bright John of Powes holden & the other iiii howses in Goldbeterslane remayne to the seyd Richard Lokwode my Cosyn terme of his lyf, he of the profites and rentes there of comyng to holde a ȝerely obit for me and Letice my wif in the best manere that he kan in the seyd Chirche of Seynt Fastour, as I trust moche on hym. And after the decesse of the seyd Richard Lokwode and of my wyf Letice I woll that the seyd howses & tenementes that the seyd Anneys Bright John of Powes now occupien & the other iiii howses in the seyd lane called Goldbeterslane remaigne & turne to the Wardeynes of my Craft of Sadillers of London and to here successours for ever, they to holde every ȝer in the seyd Chirche of Seynt Fastour my obyt otherwyse called my Anniversarie for me Letice my wyf my Children and for all Cristyn Sowles, they to yeve & paie ȝerely to the parson of the seyd Chirche or his depute xiid to every other prist of the seyd Chirche iiiid to everych of the parshe Clerkes there for here labour as well for syngyng as for the Ryngyng of the belles viiid And also to dispende among the pristes Clerkes & other comyng to the seyd obit in brede & drynke iiis iiiid. Also I woll that the seyd wardeynes of the seyd Craft and here successours for the tyme beyng ȝeve & dele among pour peple of the seyd parishe of seynt Fastour the seyd day of my Anniversarie vis viiid to pray for my sowle & the sowles of Letice my wyf our Children & all Cristyn Sowles. And also I woll that every Wardeyn of the seyd Craft comyng to the seyd obyt and offre atte the Principall masse of Requiem id, And also for to do trewly & observe my seyd wyll have for his labour every ȝere iiis iiiid, And alle the residue of the profites comyng of the seyd tenementz & howses abide in the governaunce & kepyng of the wardeynes of the seyd Craft for the tyme beyng, ther w^t they to Repair the seyd tenementz & howses and also to the helpyng of the pour men of the seyd Craft of Sadillers in London after here gode discrecion for ever. And ȝif so be that the seyd wardeynes of the Craft of Sadillers of London for the tyme beyng be necligent & do nat holde my seid obit, ne fulfille other Charges be me afore rehersed w^{t}oute lefull cause & excusacion, than I woll that the seyd tenementes & howses, that the seyd Anneys Bright John of Powes now occupien and the other iiii howses in the seyd lane called Goldbeters lane remaigne to my right eyres for ever. Also I woll that the Reversion of all the londes tenementz & rentes that Harry Caldewell my brother dwellyng now atte Stapenhill beside Burton upon Trente now holt remayne to Jonete & Margarete my doughters & to here heires. Also I woll that the seid Richard Lokwode my Cosyn have the hows that I dwelle inne in Westchepe of London terme of his lyf outetake the Chief Chambre and the drauht Chambre[1], the which I woll that Letice my wyf have duryng her lyf with free entrees and issues thereto, the seyd Richard to paye to my wyf and to my eyres xx^{ti} mark of sterlinges every ȝer atte usuell termes of London. Also I woll and I bequethe to the seyd Richard Lokwode all my Sadelles bridelles peytrall & other Stuff longyng to my Craft, And also all my Instrumentes & tooll longyng to Sadelers craft beyng now in my dwellyng place forseyd. In wyttenesse of which thyng to this my present wylle I have put my seel. Thes wyttenesseth, John Levyr Sadeler Richard Valdrian Sadeler John Stafford Clerk of the Gildehalle of London & other. The date atte London the day and yere above seyd.

"Also I William Caldewell woll that Margarete my doughter have terme of here lyf all the howses sette next my dwellyng

[1] Withdrawing-chamber, private room. The "widow's chamber" was that part of the tenement which she had occupied with her husband and which, by the custom of London, she was allowed to occupy for life. Though this will does not mention more than the chief chamber and the draught chamber, the "widow's chamber" or "free bench" also included the hall and cellar, and use of the oven, stable, privy and yard. See *Munim. Gild. Lond.* (Rolls Series), I, p. 393; R. R. Sharpe, *Cal. of Wills*, I, pp. xli–xlii, 448, 516; Calthrop, *Ancient Customs* (1655), p. 165. For the manorial custom see Jacob's *Law Dictionary* under "Free Bench".

place in Westchepe in London on the Est syde joynyng to the ho[s] that Cole sadeler holt w[t] all the appurtenaunces up right longyng to the seyd howses, outake the Shoppe that Richard Lee draper holt, The which shoppe I woll that Letice my wif have terme of here lyf, To have and to holde the seyd houses w[t] the appurtenaunces, oute take before oute take, to the seid Margarete for here oune dwellyng place frely no thyng paying ther fore, and after here decesse to remaigne to my eyres than beyng levyng, this wyttenesses Richard Lokwode Sadeler & William Ocle Sadeler citezeins of London and other."

30 July 1435 Quitclaim from Benedict Spinula, merchant of Genoa, to Henry Hale, grocer.

Membr. 3*b*
9 Nov. 1434 William Skydmore, son of John Skydmore of Edrop co. Bucks, gentleman, who had been apprenticed for 14 years to Thomas Fawconer, mercer, was released from his indentures on the ground that Philippa, widow and executrix of the said Thomas, had not taught or provided for him after her husband's death. [*Latin and French*]

Membr. 4
1 Dec. 1434 David Brownyng, brewer, brought an original bill against John Pye, clerk, for failure to repay a loan of £8 13s 4d. The latter was attached by certain goods in the hands of the plaintiff and, on his making four defaults, the foreign attachment was valued by oath of William White and Godard Sot, goldsmiths, and delivered to the plaintiff under pledge of the said William and Guy Lyncoln, painter, to answer therefor if the defendant should appear within a year and a day and deraign etc., as follows:—three broken chalices weighing 3 lbs. 9¼ oz. at 32s the lb., one spiceplate with images of Saints Mary, Katherine and Margaret, weighing 14 oz. at 2s 6d the oz., one foot of a silver-gilt mazer, weighing 4¾ oz. at 2s 8d the oz., total, £8 8s 4d.

6 Dec. 1434 John Horne, son of Roger Horn of Kyrketon in Lyndesay co. Lincs, exonerated from his apprenticeship (7 yrs) to Robert Young, grocer, on the ground that the latter no longer exercised the art and had left the city. [*Latin and French*]

17 Aug. 1435 Reciprocal bonds of Henry Merssh, citizen of London, on the one part, and Bertram Questenburgh and Hermann van Wesyll, merchants of Almaine, on the other, in £200 to abide by the award of John Bedham, William Rider or Clement Lyffyn, John Brickles and John Bederenden in disputes between them.

Acquittance from William Dogge of London to Thomas, abbot of the monastery of the Blessed Mary of Rewley[1] near Oxford, for the receipt of 73s 4d. Membr. 4*b* *26 Feb. 1435*

Writ of privilege[2] ordering that no molestation be offered to John Ludlowe, one of the messengers of the Exchequer, whose continuous residence was required there, or to his servants, inasmuch as it was a matter of the king's dignity as well as of ancient custom that the resident barons of the Exchequer, clerks and all other ministers there ministering, (whether) they were of the clergy or the king's court, who sit there by command, should not be summoned to attend any other causes under any judges from the day on which they assembled until the general cessation[3], and if by chance they were summoned they should be excused by reason of their public authority[4], but if those who were sitting were plaintiffs and not defendents and had other law suits, it should be at their choice either to make trial by a proctor or to defer the day without prejudice to their right, (and) they should be free and quit of all common assizes, as well of their demesnes as of their fees...[5] and also of *murdrum*, scutages, danegelds and all payments whatsoever by name of custom on household *26 June 1433*

[1] The Cistercian abbey of Rewley, *de Regali Loco*, in North Osney.

[2] See T. F. Tout, *Chapters in Medieval Administrative History*, II, p. 97; III, p. 208 as to "residence" of the barons and clerks of the Exchequer. This writ is based on c. viii of the *Dialogus de Scaccario*. Texts are printed by Madox, *History of the Exchequer* (1711), Appendix; Stubbs, *Select Charters*, pp. 168–248, from Madox; and a definitive edition by A. Hughes, C. G. Crump and C. Johnson, Clarendon Press, 1902. A translation was published by John Rayner in 1758.

[3] *Secessionem*. So also Hughes, Crump and Johnson. Madox reads *sessionem*. Rayner correctly translates "cessation".

[4] This is also the reading of Madox and of Hughes, Crump and Johnson. But note that the writ given in the margin of the *Dialogus* in the *Red Book of the Exchequer* (Rolls Series), III, p. 823 has *racione regie potestatis* (*et*) *publice utilitatis*.

[5] This passage is untranslatable. The words of our writ "*de quibuscumque communibus assisis que de fundis suis cognita summa per hidas distribuntur* (sic) *tam de dominiis suis quam de feodis suis*" appear to be an attempt to summarize the passage in the *Dialogus* (Madox, p. 23) which runs "*assise...que ideo dicuntur communes quia cognita summa que de comitatu requiritur communiter ab his qui in comitatu fundos habent per hydas distribuitur...*", etc.

victuals bought in cities, castles and maritime places, and of all assarts of their lords and of suits of counties, hundreds, wapentakes, ridings and other courts whatsoever, and that they should not be impleaded elsewhere than in the Exchequer, as appears by inspection of the Red Book of our Exchequer under the title, "*que sunt jura & dignitates residencium ad Scaccarium racione cessionis*[1] *sue*", and that if our ministers or those of any of our lieges compel payment thereof[2], provided that there is present his servant who is willing to prove on oath that these things were bought for his use, the whole money exacted shall be restored to the baron and the unjust exactor shall pay a money-penalty according to the nature of the person and the offence. Witness J Juyn at Westminster 26 June A° 11, by the aforesaid Red Book, folio 36, and by the barons.

13 March 1435 Writ of *habeas corpus* to the mayor and aldermen, witnessed at Dogmersfeld, to bring John Forthey, gentleman, before the king (into King's Bench), and return that John Forthey had appeared before the mayor and aldermen to answer a plea of debt of £5 1s 5d at the suit of Robert Cavyndissh, brother of William Cavendissh, mercer, William Flete and William Bernewey, mercers, executors of the said William Cavendissh, and had found mainprise; further that the mayor and aldermen were not in charge of any prison of the king in the city, and that the said John was not in prison for any other cause and that therefore they were unable to bring his body with the cause of his taking and detaining.

17 May 1435 Bond of Francus Vanell of Lucca and John Cok, draper, in £50 to Philip de Albertis, merchant of Florence, that the said Francus would abide by the award of Amphrion Spinula and Victor Capell, in an action of debt of £39 brought by the said Philip against the said Francus in the Sheriffs' Court.

Membr. 5 *23 March 1435* Bond of Thomas Hawkyn, grocer, to Henry Merssh, tallowchandler, in £11, that he would save him harmless in

[1] *Sc. sessionis*, as in Madox.

[2] The *Dialogus* reads "*quod si minister vectigalium de hiis quicquam solvere compulerit*".

case eleven weys of Bay salt[1], acquired from him by the said Henry, should be proved not to have been customed, in fraud of the king and his custom.

Gifts of goods and chattels: 22 July 1435, William Kemp, mercer, to James Kelom and Richard Sturgeon; John Brigge, mercer, to the same; 11 Oct. 1435, William Hoker, dyer, to William Stranxhill, skinner, Thomas White, tailor, and Peter Aumener, gentleman; 11 April 1435, John Michell, stockfishmonger, to Henry Barton, alderman, Thomas Morestede, esquire, John Carpenter, William Sidney, William Berkyng, John Maynard and John Beford. Membr. 6

Award of John Michell, John Reynwell, Robert Large and Robert Clopton, aldermen, who were chosen arbitrators in the Mayor's Court between Thomas Badby, executor of Nicholas James, alderman, plaintiff, and Thomas Bernewell, Thomas Donham and Robert Pele, executors of John Perneys, alderman, defendants, as regards a claim of £386 7s 7d made by the said Thomas Badby. The arbitrators awarded to the latter the sum of £186, of which £160 should be paid at Christmas and Michaelmas following and £26 remain at the discretion of the mayor and aldermen. As regards a claim of £10 by the executors of John Perneys on account of a legacy from Nicholas James, the arbitrators found that John Perneys had in his lifetime received certain *furrures* and other goods exceeding the aforesaid sum of £10, and accordingly they acquitted Thomas Badby thereof. [*English*] Membr. 6*b*

Writ to the mayor, setting forth that complaints had been received from merchants of the Hanse dwelling in England that a cog of Prucia called the "*George*", of which Court Stole was master, laden with divers goods and merchandise of merchants of the Hanse for a voyage to Flanders, had been driven by contrary winds into the Downs, where it had been captured by a ship of Newcastle-on-Tyne called the "*Gost*" and another ship of Orewell, of which Thomas Andrew was owner, and had been taken into the Thames, and thereupon the king in consideration of the friendship existing between Membr. 7 *20 Aug. 1435*

[1] Salt from the Bay of Bourgneuf near La Rochelle. See Power and Postan, *English Trade in the Fifteenth Century*, pp. 127–31.

his subjects and those of Almaine, and desiring further information, had sent a writ ordering that the ship and its cargo be put in arrest until the king's council gave other commands, and subsequently he had been credibly informed on behalf of certain merchants of London that the cog had been captured by certain pirates and robbers and had remained in their possession for eight days until it had been rescued by the abovementioned ships, after which it was taken into the Thames and there sold with its cargo to the said merchants, by whom it had been fitted out for a voyage to Bordeaux, wherefore now the king, desiring that justice should be done, orders the mayor to have the ship and gear valued by the oath of persons expert in such matters, and if the merchants who had brought her would find sufficient security before the mayor to answer to the merchants of the Hanse for the ship and goods or their true value, in case it should be proved before the king's council that they ought to belong to the said merchants of the Hanse, then the mayor should disarrest the ship and deliver her to the purchasers, nothwithstanding the former writ, and report the security to Chancery.

Return of the Mayor that on 23 Sept. the ship had been valued by twelve good and lawful men of the city, experts in the art of duty on ships (*navigii*), at £60, and that whereas John Atherle, John Hornmede, William Colston, John Knotte, William Marwe, Richard Banastre and Richard Cullyng, merchants of London, had undertaken to answer the merchants of the Hanse, in case it were proved that the ship and cargo ought to belong to them, he had delivered the ship to them as commanded.

10 Oct. 1435 Thomas Aleyn, Eborard Flete, William Trynmell, mercers, Richard Lyndesay, chaplain, and Richard Hungate bring a plaint of intrusion against Geoffrey Feldyng, mercer, touching their free tenement in the parish of St Laurence in Old Jewry.

Membr. 7*b*
7 July 1435 Henry Bertyn of Stone co. Kent, esquire, who intended in a short time, as he said, to cross to France on the king's service and was uncertain whether he would ever return alive and unharmed, came into court before the mayor and alder-

men and appointed his brother Robert Bertyn, draper, Richard Alred of co. Suffolk, esquire, and William Fyge of London, tailor, his true, certain, lawful and undoubted proctors, agents, factors, performers and managers of his wishes and business, general and special, to take charge of and supervise all his possessions etc., concerning all of which matters he prayed the court that public letters might be made and delivered to the said proctors whenever they required them.

Laurence Drayton, girdler, was attached to answer the king and the commonalty of the city that, whereas on 25 Jan. 1364 it was ordained[1] by John Notte, then mayor, the aldermen and commonalty of the city, as well by virtue of divers letters from the king to the mayor and commonalty as of divers liberties granted to the mayor and citizens by the king and his progenitors and approved in divers parliaments, that no one of the city or other henceforth make any false bargain or chevisance or meddle therein under penalty of imprisonment without mainprise or bail, as often as he be convicted by indictment or other due manner, until he satisfy the injured party of all his loss and exonerate him from all obligations and other specialties touching the said false bargain and chevisance, if the said party sues for the same within forty days, and pay a fine to the Chamber of Guildhall of the same amount as the injured party would have lost if the bargain had remained in force, and that in case the injured party does not wish to sue, then any person who will sue for the king and commonalty shall be heard, and if any one be convicted by indictment he shall pay the same fine to the Chamber and further as much as he would have paid to the injured party, if the latter had sued, and that whereas such false bargains and chevisance rarely happen without false brokers, it was ordained on 8 Oct. 1424[2] by William Crowmere, then mayor, the aldermen and commonalty that no one should make any bargain or contract through any broker who had not been admitted and sworn by the mayor and aldermen and had not

[1] This ordinance is set out in *Liber Albus* (Rolls Series, 12), pp. 368–71, from Letter Book G, fo. 118b.

[2] See *Cal. of K*, p. 33.

found sufficient security for the faithful discharge of his office—the said Laurence on 10 April 1431, by the aid of John Hake and Robert Wynchecombe, acting as brokers without having been admitted, fraudulently under colour of a lawful bargain bought from Richard Botele, tailor, then in serious need, a fictitious deed in the form of an obligation setting forth that an unknown person was bound to the said Richard in £24 payable on 31 Oct., which was not the case, paying for this deed the sum of £19, on the understanding that the said Richard should retain the deed and bind himself to pay Robert the said sum of £24 on the above-mentioned date, which he subsequently did pay, and thus the same Laurence, without any risk or adventure or contract of merchandise, falsely and for base gain received from the said Richard the sum of £5 more than his due, and further that the said Laurence made other false bargains, with Richard Asshby, goldsmith, on 26 April 1434, and with William Prentys, mercer, and Robert Gerebray, and that he was a common usurer and maker of false bargains, whereof he was indicted before Robert Otteley, late mayor, and the aldermen.

The defendant having appeared, and the presentments having been read, the defendant was asked at the instance of Alexander Anne, common serjeant, who sued for the king and the commonalty, in what manner he would acquit himself. He pleaded not guilty and put himself on the country. On 2 Aug. came a jury of twelve good and lawful men who, after hearing the evidences, prayed leave to go apart into the inner chamber of the court to consult together as to their verdict, which was granted to them. And when the jury came to the bar prepared to give their verdict, before they could do so the defendant confessed the false bargains and chevisances, alleging that at the time he made them he thought he had done well and that the bargains were quite lawful and proper, whereas they were not, as he now perceived. He put himself on the favour of the court and prayed that the jury might be exonerated from giving a verdict. This was done, in accordance with immemorial custom, and a day was given on the 5 Aug. that the court might consult as to their judgment. On which day, as it appeared from the acknowledgment of the defendant, the confession of the brokers and the report of Robert Large and Robert Clopton, aldermen, and certain commoners charged to investigate such false bargains, as well as from many other kinds of proof, that the defendant was guilty, it was considered that he pay to the Chamber £5, as regards the £5 profit which he had made, and which he would have paid to Richard Botle, if the latter had prosecuted, and also that he pay another £5 to the Chamber for his contempt.

A "close writ" to Robert Ottele, mayor, and Thomas Bernewell and Simon Eyr, sheriffs, reciting the Acts of 15 Ric. II c. 2 and 8 Hen. VI c. 9 against Forcible Entries, and bidding them go to certain houses of Joan Marshall in Bread Street into which Almaric Matany of London, draper, and John Hunt were alleged to have entered forcibly, and if they found that such was the case, they were to arrest the malefactors and cause them to be put in the prison of Newgate, and to reinstate the said Joan, and to carry out the other provisions of the statute. Dated at Westminster 15 Feb. 1435. **Membr. 8**

In accordance with this writ the mayor and sheriffs went to the premises but found no one in forcible occupation. A jury was summoned, as laid down in the acts, of persons having lands and tenements of the annual net value of 40s, viz, Thomas Beamond, Robert Marcheford, Ralph Marke, Walter Ledbury, John Riche, William Newenham, William Rede, John Bartelot, Ralph Hogman, John Bay, Saier Acre and William Chesse, who said on oath that neither the persons mentioned nor any one else on their behalf had made any forcible entry.

ROLL A 63

(*Henry Frowyk, mayor*)

Nov. 1435 Quitclaim from Thomas Pyke, junior, son and heir of Thomas Pyke, senior, draper, to Nicholas Yoo, draper, John Chesham, scrivener, and Thomas Merye, executors of his father's testament.

Thomas Recheford of London brought before the mayor and aldermen a letter of attorney made to him by Ralph Humberston of Leicester, *brasyer*, for the purpose of receiving from Robert Reynham of London, mercer, the sum of 40 marks, which the said Robert had been condemned to pay to him. The letter was dated at Leicester 17 Oct. 1435 and sealed, for better evidence, by Adam Racy, mayor of Leicester, with the mayoralty seal of that town.

14 Jan. 1436 Gift of goods and chattels from Henry Feriby, brewer, to William Petyvile, brewer, John Haselton, tailor, and John Broun, cooper.

26 Nov. 1435 Writ of protection in favour of Luke de Puteo, *alias* de Pocha, *alias* de Pozo, of Venice, merchant, who was then about to cross to France on the king's service in the company of Richard Wastenes, esquire.

13 Jan. 1436 Gift of goods and chattels from William Preest, chandler, to Roger Honyngton, gentleman, Nicholas Preest, grocer, Stephen Tychemerssh, mercer, and William Isham, chandler.

Membr. 1 *b*
6 Feb. 1436 William[1], prior of Holy Trinity, London, brings a plaint of intrusion against John Perneys, John Fray, Thomas Dursle and Thomas Badby touching his free tenement in the parish of St Margaret Bridge Street.

Gifts of goods and chattels: 5 Dec. 1435, Walter Frebarn, draper, to Joan his wife and John Whitehode and Benedict Redyng, drapers; 9 Feb. 1436, John Bargon, chandler, to Peter Bargon his son and Thomas Ostrich, haberdasher;

[1] Clark.

23 Jan. 1436, Thomas Blythe, goldsmith, to John Walssh and John Sturdys, goldsmiths; 13 Dec. 1435, John Hebbe, grocer, to Thomas Yong of Bristol, gentleman, Richard Chokke of Staunton Drewe co. Somerset, gentleman, and John Billyngton, grocer; 18 Feb. 1436, John Swanne, mercer, to Sir Robert Mowter, clerk, Robert Cristendom, draper, and Thomas Bernard, gentleman; 5 Nov. 1435, Robert Clifton, baker, to John Sturdys, goldsmith; witnesses, John Pake, John West, Thomas Blithe; 20 Nov. 1435, John Austyn, tailor, to John Cantlowe and Robert Langeley, mercers; witnesses, John Norman, John Notebroun, John Sturgeon; 7 Dec. 1435, Laurence Knyght, armourer, to Richard Pynchebek, *upholdster*; 13 Jan. 1436, John Werk, goldsmith, to John Sutton, junior, and John Waryn, goldsmiths; 9 Jan. 1436, John Orgor, haberdasher, to William Aston, Walter Peryn, haberdasher, and John Orgor, tailor; witnesses, Walter Hersy, John Walker, Peter Bilton, Robert Freman, Richard Blake; 18 Feb. 1436, John Clerk, cutler, to Richard Harpele, cutler, and John Aleyn, clerk; 29 Feb. 1436, John Bysle, tailor, to William Chapman, tailor, and Richard Rouge, *marbler*; 3 March 1436, William Style, *corsour*, to John Bovile, esquire, Thomas Style, Thomas Namby and John Namby; 15 March 1436, John Middelton, vintner, to John Stapull, vintner; 17 March 1436, William Doegge to Joan his wife, John Stafford, bishop of Bath and Wells, and Robert Cowton of co. Lincs, gentleman.

Membr. 2 · Membr. 2 *b*

Gifts of goods and chattels: 12 March 1436, Alice, wife of Robert Coventre, grocer, Thomas Canynges, grocer, and Benedict Harlewyn, draper, to Robert Coventre, grocer, of such goods as were previously given to them by the latter[1]; Robert Coventre, grocer, to Richard Hill and Richard Bartfeld, founders, with power of attorney; 29 April 1436, Thomas Coote, ironmonger, to Sir Roger Helwys, clerk, and John Petersfeld and John Lane, ironmongers; 7 May 1436, Richard Everley, mercer, to William Savage, clerk, and William Olyver, mercer; 23 May 1436, Andrew Colson, woolpacker, to William Cantelowe, mercer, Alan Johnson, grocer, John Broke, brewer, and William Blyton; 10 July

Membr. 3 · Membr. 3 *b*

[1] See above Roll A 61, m. 1 *b* (p. 271).

1436, John Norman, goldsmith, to Richard Broughton, stockfishmonger, Robert Comytis, vintner, and John Langley, goldsmith; 24 July 1436, Richard Heryot, cordwainer, to Robert Peny, Isabel the donor's wife, Richard Nasing *alias* Gilkyn, *ferrour*, and Simon Burnham, cordwainer; 19 July 1436, John South, *setter*, to John Golenge, cooper, and John Berston; 11 May 1436, Robert Pellykan, stockfishmonger, to John Paddesle, alderman, John Carpenter, clerk of the commonalty of the city of London, William Baron[1] of the Exchequer, and Thomas Fulbourne and John Grene, stockfishmongers, and all his lands and tenements etc. in the city; witnesses, John Michell, Thomas Dufhous, Thomas Leget, Alexander Farnell, John Elyngham; 9 July 1436, Henry Tewayn, tailor, to Alice his wife, William Bolton, tailor, and
Membr. 4 John Kebell, goldsmith; 2 June 1436, Bernard Barbo of Venice to Master Thomas Frank, Doctor in Medicine, and William Toby, clerk, with the exception of his wearing apparel; 21 July 1436, William Fouller, *pasteler*, to William Downe, chandler, and Richard Appulton, vintner; 27 July 1436, Geoffrey Savage, draper, to Thomas Walsyngham, vintner, and Andrew Tye, *upholder*; 24 March 1436, John Lacy, fishmonger, to John Norman, draper, and John Leget, fishmonger; 20 July 1436, Alan Johnson, grocer, to Laurence Pygot of Dunstaple, John Carpenter, junior, and Robert
Membr. 4 *b* Langford; 10 Aug. 1436, Richard Edmond, brewer, to John Verney, clerk, dean of Lichfield, and John Norman, draper; 1 Oct. 1436, Richard Harper, mercer, to Robert Gladman and William Leche, mercers; witnesses, John Rokeby, Robert Brandesby, William Cory; 9 Oct. 1436, Thomas Enmeth, fishmonger, to Thomas Drury and William Gerveys, clerks; witnesses, William Waleys, Thomas Edmund, Thomas Hamme, Thomas Gryme, John Lynne.

Membr. 5
13 July 1436

Writ of protection in favour of William Haukyn, butcher, who was then about to cross to Picardy in the company of Humphrey, duke of Gloucester, earl of Pembroke and captain of Calais.

[1] Apparently a surname, as he appears later in the same deed as "William Baroun".

On this day came John Tatersall, gentleman, son and heir of the late Robert Tatersall, draper and alderman, and acknowledged a deed signed by John Chesham, public notary. *7 April 1436*

The deed recites that the said Robert, his wife Amie, William Estfeld, alderman, and William Aston were seised of the manor of Wansted co. Essex and of the advowson of the church there to themselves and the heirs of the said Robert by a fine "rerid and lyfte" between themselves as plaintiffs and William Rous, esquire, deforceant, and that afterwards the said Amie, William and William granted their estate in the manor and the advowson to the said John Tatersall, and that the said Robert towards the end of his life had felt great remorse in his conscience for purchasing the manor because he knew that it was "*tayled*" to William Rous and the heirs of his body lawfully begotten, and he had instructed Amie, William, William and John to restore the manor, "after the deth of Margarete late the wyfe of John Hundrecombe squyer and the seid William Rous", to the heirs of William Rous. Accordingly John Tatersall, in the presence of William Estfeld and John Brokley, aldermen, Alisaundre Anne, recorder of the city, the said Amie, William Aston and John Chesham, scrivener and notary, had sworn and promised to fulfil his father's request or to satisfy the heirs of William Rous as faith and conscience required. Dated at London 9 March 1436. [*English*]

Certificate of John Chesham, public imperial notary, that he had placed his signature and mark to the above document.

Acquittance from John Tatersall, gentleman, to Amie Tatersall, widow and principal executrix of Robert Tatersall his father, William Estfeld, mercer, and Thomas Scot, draper, her co-executors, for the receipt of £1528 14s 11d in part payment of goods assigned to him, by virtue of a legacy from his father. Dated at London 5 April 1436.

Writ of *corpus cum causa* to bring Belisardus de Barde, merchant, into Chancery, and return of the mayor and sheriffs that the said Belisardus had been taken and detained in prison by virtue of a plaint of detinue of two writings obligatory at the suit of Roger Talbot and Philip Malpas, *11 Oct. 1436* drapers, levied in the Sheriffs' Court and removed into the Mayor's Court, and also by virtue of an original bill of detinue of two writings obligatory at the suit of Christopher Stella, merchant of Genoa, and Simon Eyr, draper, affirmed before the mayor and aldermen in the Chamber, which plaint and bill were pending undetermined; nevertheless the said Belisardus would be brought into Chancery as required.

Membr. 5 *b* 20 *Sept.* 1435 Bond of Thomas Ivy and Thomas Grene, skinners, executors of the will of John Lemman, one of the executors of John Penne, skinner, to William Aston, the other executor of John Penne, in 500 marks, to abide by the award of the mayor and aldermen in disputes between them.

Membr. 6 12 *Dec.* 1435 Recognisance by John Hebbe, grocer, of a debt of £125 10s 10d due to Stephen Forster, merchant.

18 *Dec.* 1435 Writ of *corpus cum causa* to bring Richard Monk, chaplain, into Chancery.

20 *Jan.* 1436 Similar writs relating to Nicholas Toller, skinner, and William Bysmer of Thorley co. Hertford, gentleman.

23 *Jan.* 1436 Writ of *habeas corpus* to bring William Bysmere before the king's justices at Westminster, it having been shown to the king that the said William when on his way to the king's court had been taken and detained in prison by the sheriffs on pretext of a plea of debt affirmed against him before the mayor in the king's court in the Chamber of Guildhall. Witness W. Babyngton at Westminster.

Return that the said William had been summoned to answer Thomas Peretre, draper, in a plea of debt of 24 marks 6s 8d by virtue of a bill levied and affirmed before the mayor and aldermen, but that it was not true that the said William had been taken and detained in prison.

Membr. 6 *b* 25 *Jan.* 1436 Further writ reciting that plaintiffs and defendants attending before the justices of the Bench were under the king's protection against arrest of their bodies or goods by any inferior court, and that the king had learnt that when William Bysmere was in London to consult with his counsel as regards an action of trespass before the justices of the Bench, in which he was plaintiff against John Drakelowe of Stortford, smith, a certain Thomas Peretre had caused him to be summoned before the mayor and aldermen in an action of debt and to find mainprise, in derogation of the liberty and privilege of the king's court of the Bench, wherefore the king orders the mayor to bring before the justices the cause, terms and date of the said mainprise. Witness W. Babyngton at Westminster.

Letter of attorney from Alan Johanessone, grocer, John *12 Jan. 1436* Carpenter, clerk of the commonalty of the city, Laurence Pygot of Dunstaple, John Pygot of Hicchen and Robert Langford, clerk, to John Parke and Richard Rouhede to receive seisin of certain lands and tenements in the parish of St Nicholas at Calais, which lands had been conveyed to the said Alan and the others by feoffment from Ralph Barton, skinner, brother and heir of Henry Barton, alderman of London, who had received them by feoffment from Elianora, widow of Peter Mildenale, esquire.

Geoffrey Shriggeley, master of Burton St Lazarus of Membr. 7 Jerusalem in England, warden of the hospital of St Giles *13 Feb. 1436* without London, brings plaints of intrusion against John Waleys, prior of the new hospital of St Mary without Bishopsgate, touching his free tenement in the parish of St Andrew, Holborn, and David Pris, rector of St Magnus, touching his free tenement in the parish of St Margaret Bridge Street.

Henry Werkworth, prior of St Mary Southwark, brings *5 March 1436* plaints of intrusion against Thomas Dufhous, fishmonger, touching his free tenement in the parish of St Magnus, and John Perneys, John Fray, Thomas Dursle and Thomas Badby touching his free tenement in the parish of St Margaret Bridge Street.

Writ of protection in favour of Robert Barton, skinner, who *13 Feb. 1436* was then about to cross to France in the company of Edmund Beaufford, earl of Moritoun.[1]

[1] Edmund Beaufort, count of Mortain and Harcourt, afterwards created earl and marquis of Dorset and duke of Somerset, slain at the battle of St Albans 1455.

14 March 1436 Writ of *corpus cum causa* to bring Richard Haddelsey of London, notary, into Chancery.

23 March 1436 Similar writ relating to Angel Nany.

Membr. 7 *b*

29 March 1436 On this day John Holland, factor of the wool of the lord cardinal of England[1] in Harflete, and John Halstede, servant of John White of Salisbury, who was executor of the will of John Arlyngham, came into court and delivered two acquittances, the one under the seal of the lord cardinal and the other under the seal of arms of the earl of Morton, as follows:—

Acquittance, dated 20 Oct. 1433, from Henry, cardinal of England and bishop of Winchester, to John Hayne and John White, executors of the will of John Arlyngham late of Tymby in Wales, merchant, for the receipt of £100 paid by them on behalf of the said John Arlyngham in the name of John Holland, the cardinal's factor in Harflete, for the cardinal's wool demised to the said John Holland, whereof the cardinal acquits the executors and John Holland.

Acquittance, dated 11 March 1433, from Edmund Beaufort, earl of Morton, on behalf of Henry, cardinal of England and bishop of Winchester, to John Arlyngham, merchant, for the receipt of £100, which John Holland delivered to John Arlyngham for payment to the cardinal.

The two acquittances were to be kept in court as evidence of the exoneration of the parties from the abovementioned debt, and to be lent to either of the parties requiring them under security for their safe return.

[1] Henry Beaufort, bishop of Winchester.

ROLL A 64

(*John Michell, mayor*)

Recognisance of Philip Malpas, draper, to the king in 300 marks that he would not cause or procure any bodily harm to Christopher Stella, merchant of Genoa. Membr. 1 *10 April 1437*

Recognisance of the same to John Chichele, chamberlain, in 200 marks that he would not cause or procure any bodily harm during the next six years to any Genoese dwelling in or visiting the city.

Writ of *certiorari* to the mayor and his fellow-justices assigned to deliver the gaol of Newgate, demanding that the tenor of the appeal of Richard Yate, lately adjudged to death and then in custody, be sent to the office of the Privy Seal by some person for whom they were willing to answer. *4 May 1437*

Indenture of covenant between John Lematon and John Yedele, gentleman, son of John Yedele of the parish of Assh and Redle co. Kent, recites that Lematon had bought from Yedele for the sum of 90 marks a "manoire meece and a tenement" called "Yedele," at the request of the said John Yedele, which manor the latter had acquired by feoffment from John Martin, one of the king's justices, John Chymbeham, John Swayn, clerk, and John Fulsham, clerk. In virtue of this sale Yedele had conveyed the property by feoffment of 27 Oct. 1433 to Lematon, Robert Staunton, Roger Legh and John Phelipp, and had quitclaimed it, under the description of a meese, 5 acres of land, 6 acres of wood and 2s rent, to Lematon and his heirs by a fine of 9 Feb. 1434, which purchase, and deeds, with other expenses of assuring the title, had cost the latter the sum of 130 marks. Membr. 2 *8 Aug. 1437*

It was now agreed that Yedele should by a further deed quitclaim all his right and title and that any person deriving any title from Yedele or his father should do the same. Lematon on his part agreed that if Sir Thomas Kyrkeby, knight, and Yedele repaid him his expenses of 130 marks at midsummer next and such a further sum as Richard Dann and John Knottesford, squires dwelling with Lord Huntingdon[1], should award in the presence of the mayor of London, then he and his co-feoffees would re-enfeoff Yedele and Sir Thomas Kyrkeby to them and their heirs and deliver to them all evidences relating to the property; otherwise Lematon should retain the property without interruption. The deed closes with the above-mentioned quitclaim from Yedele and mutual bonds in £20 to keep the covenants of the agreement. [*English*]

Membr. 2 *b*
21 Oct. 1437

Writ of *habeas corpus* to the mayor and sheriffs, reciting the privilege of plaintiffs and defendants attending the Bench, and ordering them to bring before the justices Henry Lynster, who complained that he had been arrested in the city, when he and his wife were lodging there in order to prosecute in an action of waste against William Dogge in the king's court of the Bench, the action having been begun by writ returned to the court by the sheriff of Surrey.

Membr. 3

Gifts of goods and chattels: 20 Nov. 1436, Richard Bunne, mercer, to William Kerver, mercer; 7 Jan. 1437, John Ronn, *cofrerer*, to John Worshopp, painter; witnesses, Richard Collyng, clerk, Henry Bovyngton, John Polhill, Robert Colyn, John Upton, shearman; 20 May 1437, Thomas Danby, chandler, to Adam Turvey, brewer, and John Layner, bladesmith; witnesses, William Bocley, John Kyng, John Robert, Nicholas Rolf, Thomas Skotte; 1 June 1437, Edmund Sheffeld, vintner, to Thomas Knolles, grocer, and William Chedworth; 18 July 1437, Amy, widow of John Bokenell, grocer, to Isabel Arnold, widow of Robert Arnold, grocer, and Alan Johanessone,
Membr. 3 *b* grocer; 3 June 1437, William Burdon, girdler, to John Russell of London, *sergeaunt*[2], Thomas Reynold, vintner, Richard Sygryme, *sergeaunt*, John Brenyng, grocer, and Richard Botley, tailor; witnesses, Hugh Glene, John Lane, Richard Shepton; 19 July 1437, James Caton, tailor, to Sir William Sheffeld, clerk, and Edmund Sheffeld, vintner; 23 July 1437, William Bacon, butcher, to William Hotyng, butcher, John Mordon, attorney, John Leche, *pulter*, and John Lynke,

[1] John Holland, later duke of Exeter.
[2] One of the serjeants-at-mace of the city. *Cal. of K*, 312.

tallowchandler; witnesses, Henry Roppeley, Thomas Mollesley, John Toucestre, Thomas Bakster, Robert Tewe; 25 Feb. 1437, Thomas Whyte, tailor, to Robert Large, alderman, William Flete, mercer, Peter Aumener and William Hoker, dyer.

John Estby, shearman, and Margaret his wife and John Broun, cooper, came into court and, being singly and separately examined according to custom, acknowledged as their deed an indenture witnessing that the latter had leased from the former for a term of twenty years at an annual rent of 26s 8d a tenement in the parish of St Botolph without Aldrichegate, late in the tenure of Henry Edward, lying between a tenement in the occupation of Robert Cawode on the east and a tenement held by Stephen Ungle from the abbot of Kyrkestede on the west, on condition that the said John Broun execute inside and outside repairs, maintain as much of the pavement by the king's highway as pertained to the tenement, cause the latrines to be emptied and cleansed whenever necessary at his own expense and hand over the premises at the end of the lease in good and sufficient repair, excepting damage caused by fires started by others, sudden tempest and the ageing of timber. It is provided that if both parties faithfully perform their undertakings reciprocal bonds in £20 shall be cancelled. Membr. 4 *9 May 1437*

Writ of *corpus cum causa* to bring John Kyngesden of London, goldsmith, into Chancery. *15 May 1437*

Writ of *procedendo* to continue with the action between John Martyn, goldsmith, and the said John Kyngesden, notwithstanding the previous writ. *20 May 1437*

Writ of attachment to bring John Judde of London, merchant, before the king in Chancery to answer concerning those things which shall then and there be objected against him and further to do and receive what the court shall have considered in this part. *15 May 1437*

Writ of protection in favour of Robert Mewe, butcher, then about to cross to Normandy in the company of Sir Thomas Kyryell, captain of the castle and town of Gourney. Membr. 4 *b* *15 May 1437*

14 May 1437 Writ of *corpus cum causa* to bring William Dogge into Chancery and return that the said William had been summoned to answer Gerard Hesyll, clerk, and Richard atte Lee, grocer, in an action of debt of £21 13s 4d, levied before William Gregory, sheriff, and subsequently removed to the Mayor's Court, and that he had been mainprised, wherefore the mayor and sheriffs could not bring the body of the said William with the cause of his taking and detaining into Chancery.

22 June 1437 Writ of *certiorari* reciting that it had been shown that William Dogge had been attached by his goods in the city when he and his wife Joan, executrix of the will of John Benton of Slape in the parish of S[t] Peter in S[t] Albans, were awaiting the verdict of a jury in an action of trespass brought by them in the Bench against Robert Colyn of Tudenangre co. Herts—which attachment was contrary to the liberties of that court, and in answer to a writ of *certiorari* the mayor and sheriffs had returned that the said William had not been attached but that a sequestration had been put upon his dwelling-house in the parish of S[t] Olave, Silver Street, in connection with an action of covenant affirmed before the mayor and aldermen at the suit of John Wydehall. As several other similar sequestrations had been put on the said William's houses since the date of the return to the writ, the mayor and sheriffs are ordered to inform the justices of the Bench as to the number and causes of the same.

1 July 1437 Recognisance by Thomas Badby, fishmonger, and William Wetenhale, grocer, of a debt of 250 marks due to William Estfeld and Robert Large, mercers, John Bacon, grocer, and John Levyng, fishmonger.

Membr. 5
19 Jan. 1437 Certificate of John Tatersall, son and heir of Robert Tatersall, draper and alderman, that in the presence of William Estfeld and John Brokley, aldermen, Alexander Anne, recorder, Amye, late the wife of Robert Tatersall, William Aston and John Scrivener he had sworn to restore the manor of Wansted to the next heirs in tail of Thomas Huntercombe and Maude his wife or to satisfy them for the same. The manor and advowson had been the subject of a fine raised in

the court of King Edward, son of King Edward, in the eighth year of his reign whereby it had been conveyed by Geoffrey, parson of the church of Bekenesfeld, Gerard of Halsted, priest, and Richard Cakeston, as deforceants, to Thomas Huntercombe and Maude his wife, plaintiffs, and the heirs of their bodies in tail. The late Robert Tatersall had subsequently acquired the manor by fine in the king's court at Westminster, raised on 12 Nov. 1427 and granted and recorded on 20 Jan. 1428, to himself, his wife Amye, William Estfeld and William Aston, as plaintiffs, from William Rous, esquire, as deforceant, and in his last days, knowing that the manor had been entailed, he had charged and required the said Amye, William, William and his son to restore the manor, after the death of Margaret, widow of John Huntercombe, and the death of William Rous, to the next heirs in tail of Thomas Huntercombe and Maude his wife.[1] [*English*]

7 Feb. 1437 Recognisance by John Kyngesden, goldsmith, John Amour, mercer, Richard Gisburgh, tailor, and James Tregustok, goldsmith, of a debt of £200 due to John Chichele, chamberlain, at Easter.

3 July 1437 Robert Helder, son of John Helder of Essex, exonerated from his apprenticeship (7 yrs.) to Thomas Welles, mercer, because the latter had failed to teach or provide for him. [*Latin and French*]

Membr. 5 *b* Condition of the above recognisance:—that John Kyngesden should bring into court all deeds relating to John Lincoln, William Lyncoln (*sic*), Roger Lincoln and Alice Lincoln, children of the late John Lincoln, goldsmith, and orphans of the city, who had been entrusted to him as guardian, and that he should render an account of their property when required before auditors assigned by the court of mayor, aldermen and chamberlain according to the law and custom of the city.

27 July 1437 Original bill of John Dykon, son of William Dykon of Eltylsey co. Cambridge, praying to be exonerated from his

[1] See above Roll A 63, m. 5 (p. 291) for the certificate of which the present appears to be a correction.

apprenticeship (7 yrs) to William Kerver, grocer, because the latter had not enrolled him at Guildhall during the first year of his term. [*Latin and French*]

19 Sept. 1437 Writ of *corpus cum causa* to bring John Rosencranns, *Esterlinge*, into Chancery, witness the king at Dogmersfeld, and return of the mayor and sheriffs that John Wipperford *alias* Rosencrans was detained in prison by virtue of two plaints of trespass levied in the Sheriffs' Court on 14 Aug. 1437 at the suits of Andrew Canturbury, prior of the Carmelite Friars of London, and John Fastolf, knight, which plaints had afterwards been removed before the mayor and aldermen; nevertheless he would be brought into Chancery as ordered.

Membr. 6
17 Dec. 1436 Covenant between Philip Caxton of Little Writtyng (*sic*) co. Suffolk, gentleman, and John Cristemasse, draper, whereby the former sells to the latter the manor of Wrattyng co. Suffolk with the advowsons of the churches of Wrattyng and Berneston late belonging to Philip Caxton, father of the said Philip, and sometime to Sir Thomas Hamgrave, knight, and agrees to cause those feoffees, to whom his father had conveyed the manor and advowsons in trust, to make him an estate in fee simple with open livery of seisin before next Candlemas, and afterwards give him a release in the same, and that within fourteen days thereof he would by the advice of counsel give a sufficient estate to the said John in the manor and advowsons with livery of seisin and release, and also obtain from Thomas West of Sudbury and Deonyse his wife, being mother of the grantor, a quitclaim to be acknowledged before a justice, in return for which the said John agrees to pay the sum of 100 marks on the making of this covenant, of which sum the said Philip acknowledges receipt, and a further sum of 100 marks on receiving a full estate in the manor, and furthermore the said Philip for his part binds himself in £200 to perform the terms of this covenant.

Certificate from John Michell, mayor, Robert Large and Thomas Cateworthe, aldermen, that the said Philip had acknowledged himself to be of the full age of twenty-four years and that at his special request the mayor had set the mayoralty seal and the aldermen their own seals to the part of this indenture remaining with John Cristemasse.

[*English*]

Whereas William Aston, executor of the testament of John Penne, had sued divers actions of debt, account and detinue against Thomas Ive and Thomas Grene, executors of John Lemman, who was co-executor with William Aston, and by mediation of Thomas Otteley and Thomas Whityngham the parties had agreed on 20 Sept. 1435 to submit to the award of the mayor and aldermen, the latter on 10 Sept. 1436 adjudicated as follows:— Membr. 6 *b* *10 Sept. 1436*

The mayor and aldermen take into account a schedule in the handwriting of Thomas Grene showing the receipts and disbursements of John Penne's goods and chattels subsequent to the death of John Colchestre, another of the co-executors, in these words: "Charges of money reseived, ccccxv li xv d, Item reseived of alle maner rent—xvii li x d, Item reseived of sale of the Inventarie—xi li ix s, Summa totalis of alle manere charges of money reseived—iiii^{c}xliii li x s vii ob; alle manere descharges of þe saide summe that is to wit in parcelles of distribucion—iii^{c}xxiiii li xvi s x d ob. So þere shulde remayn in hande—cxviii li xiiii s x d ob."[1] Further, they take into account that John Lemman owed John Penne the sum of £20 lent to him. Accordingly they award that Thomas Ive and Thomas Grene pay William Aston these sums from the goods of the testator already in their hands, or which shall next come into their hands, and that as executors they shall sue at William Aston's expense for the payment of all obligations made to John Lemman for the use of John Penne, and deliver whatever is received to William Aston.

[1] The schedule appears to have been incorrectly copied, as the figures do not add correctly.

End of Rolls A 43—A 64

A LIST OF LESS USUAL WORDS IN THE TEXT

acredulcis, sour-sweet, 212
alegist, 4, 252 n. 1
almariolum, ambry, cabinet, 93
almerye, 4 n. 1
ambassiata, embassy, 1
armoriall, 93 n. 2
arsgirdell, 272
aunderns, 3 n. 9
auricalcum, latten, 94
avale, 134 n. 5

bail, 164 n. 1
baletta, small bale, 260
balys, *baleis*, *baleys*, 48, 49, 56, 72 n. 2, 205
banker, a covering for a bench or chair, 3
baratour, 127 n. 3, 155
barettavit, bartered, 225
bastard reynes, 80 n. 1
bastardes, 233, *see* above
baterie, *batery*, 78, 225 n. 1, 245, 249
bathingfat, 4 n. 5
beheste, 257 n. 3
bely, bellows, 94
birell, 248 n. 2
bis, *bises*, 53 n. 2, 76
bollions, 268 n. 5
bordclothes, 4 n. 2
botiller, bottle-maker, 24
bower, *bowyer*, 263
braciator, brewer, 240
braudester, 176 n. 1
brochatus, brocaded, 48
brochemaker, 95 n. 1
broderer, *brouderer*, *browderer*, embroiderer, 144, 147, 149, 178, 196, 235
brounsoleynmedle, 88 n. 2
bruerne, 118 n. 3

cachepolle, 125 n. 1
calabre, 45 n. 5, 75
caligae, hose, 50
calperell', 5 n. 1
camise, 74 n. 5
canelbone, 114 n. 1
canelle, 124 n. 1
capa, mantle, 33
capicium, *capucium*, hood, 50, 77
cardemaker, 54 n. 1
cartel, 11 n. 3
chaffer, 153 n. 2
champeyn, linen of Champagne, 74
channel, 133 n. 3
chapes, 93 n. 3
chauffour, chafer, pan, 4
chaux, 3 n. 6
chevisamentum, *chevisance*, bargain, 99
cilour, 35 n. 1, 50
cofrerer, coffer-maker, 296
cokkettavit, paid cocket, 213
colerkerchefs, neckerchiefs, 74
conjectura, conspiracy, 101
coopertor, a person avowing the goods of an alien or foreigner as his own in order to escape custom, 213
coopertorium, covercle, cover, 75; coverlet, 77
coronall, 94 n. 3
corrector, 224 n. 1
corser, *corsour*, *corsur*, *coser*, 64, 82 n. 1, 124, 260, 264
coster, 35 n. 3, 50
counter, common, 15, 15 n. 1
counterfeyt, 90 n. 1
countour, 3 n. 8
courtman, 52
coyfes, 74 n. 7
coyn, 255 n. 3
craper, 135 n. 2
crayere, 68 n. 4, 69
cristigrey, 4 n. 9, 76
custumavit, paid custom, 213

denaunt, brassware of Dinant, 90, 94
de ploid, *duploid*, doublet, 50 77
deumadames, cloth called, 89
domicellus, servant, 236
draf wasshe, 118 n. 1
draskes, 154 n. 1
drayffe, 140
droppyngpannes, 4
droppyngplates, 165 n. 3

electreum, 100 n. 1
engreine, 3 n. 3
entaile, 49 n. 1
escutz, 184 n. 1
esterlyng, *esterlinge*, inhabitant of North Germany, 76, 141, 300
estulpes, 133 n. 2

INDEX OF SUBJECTS

INDEX OF NAMES AND PLACES

For EU product safety concerns, contact us at Calle de José Abascal, 56–1°, 28003 Madrid, Spain or eugpsr@cambridge.org.

www.ingramcontent.com/pod-product-compliance
Lightning Source LLC
LaVergne TN
LVHW080012210926
848481LV00011B/2999

* 9 7 8 1 1 0 7 4 6 4 0 2 5 *